The Red Army in Austria

The Harvard Cold War Studies Book Series
Series Editor: Mark Kramer, Harvard University

Recent Titles in the Series

Mao and the Sino-Soviet Partnership, 1945–1959: A New History
  Zhihua Shen and Yafeng Xia
The Soviet Union and the Horn of Africa during the Cold War: Between Ideology and Pragmatism
  Radoslav A. Yordanov
Dynamic Détente: The United States and Europe, 1964–1975
  Stephan Kieninger
The Tito–Stalin Split and Yugoslavia's Military Opening toward the West, 1950–1954: In NATO's Backyard
  Ivan Laković and Dmitar Tasić
Bridging the Baltic Sea: Networks of Resistance and Opposition during the Cold War Era
  Lars Fredrik Stöcker
US–Spanish Relations after Franco, 1975–1989: The Will of the Weak
  Morten Heiberg
Stalin's Legacy in Romania: The Hungarian Autonomous Region, 1952–1960
  Stefano Bottoni
Mao and the Sino-Soviet Split, 1959–1973: A New History
  Danhui Li and Yafeng Xia
A Cold War over Austria: The Struggle for the State Treaty, Neutrality, and the End of East-West Occupation, 1945–1955
  Gerald Stourzh and Wolfgang Mueller
The Soviet Invasion of Czechoslovakia in 1968: The Russian Perspective
  Edited by Josef Pazderka
Stalin's Double-Edged Game: Soviet Bureaucracy and the Raoul Wallenberg Case, 1945–1952
  Johan Matz
The Red Army in Austria: The Soviet Occupation, 1945–1955
  Edited by Stefan Karner and Barbara Stelzl-Marx

The Red Army in Austria

The Soviet Occupation, 1945–1955

Edited by Stefan Karner
and Barbara Stelzl-Marx

Translated by Alex J. Kay

LEXINGTON BOOKS
Lanham • Boulder • New York • London

Published by Lexington Books
An imprint of The Rowman & Littlefield Publishing Group, Inc.
4501 Forbes Boulevard, Suite 200, Lanham, Maryland 20706
www.rowman.com

6 Tinworth Street, London SE11 5AL, United Kingdom

Copyright © 2020 by The Rowman & Littlefield Publishing Group, Inc.

All rights reserved. No part of this book may be reproduced in any form or by any electronic or mechanical means, including information storage and retrieval systems, without written permission from the publisher, except by a reviewer who may quote passages in a review.

British Library Cataloguing in Publication Information Available

Library of Congress Cataloging-in-Publication Data

Library of Congress Control Number: 2020942744

ISBN: 978-1-7936-2660-8 (cloth)
ISBN: 978-1-7936-2659-2 (electronic)

Contents

Acknowledgments vii

Introduction ix

Abbreviations xvii

PART I AUSTRIA IN GLOBAL POLICY

1 The Policies of Presidents Roosevelt, Truman, and
   Eisenhower toward Austria, 1943–1955   3
   Günter Bischof

PART II SOVIET DIPLOMACY TOWARD AUSTRIA

2 Soviet Plans for Rebuilding Austria from 1941 to 1945   25
   Aleksei Filitov

3 Under Soviet Control: The Establishment of the Austrian
   Government in 1945   37
   Stefan Karner and Peter Ruggenthaler

4 Soviet Policy toward Austria from 1945 to 1955   75
   Peter Ruggenthaler

5 The Development of Soviet Policy toward Austria
   after Stalin's Death from 1953 to 1955   95
   Mikhail Prozumenshchikov

PART III ASPECTS OF OCCUPATION

6 Occupation and Exploitation: Soviet Economy Policy
  toward Austria from 1945 to 1955/63   123
  Walter M. Iber

7 Intelligence in Occupied Austria 1945 to 1955: The Soviet Side   149
  Dieter Bacher

8 Stalin's Judiciary in Austria: Arrests and Convictions during
  the Occupation   165
  Harald Knoll and Barbara Stelzl-Marx

9 Ivan's Children: The Consequences of Sexual Relations
  between Red Army Soldiers and Austrian Women   193
  Barbara Stelzl-Marx

Archival Sources   215

Bibliography   221

Index   253

About the Contributors   265

Acknowledgments

For the realization of this volume, it is necessary to thank several people: first of all, Professor Mark Kramer, Harvard University, who promptly took up our suggestion of an English-language volume on the Red Army in Austria and enabled the inclusion of this book in the Harvard Cold War Book Series. Particular thanks are due to Dr. Alex J. Kay for the accomplished translation of the German-language essays into English, the editing of the contributions and the compilation of the appendices. Thanks are likewise due to Professor Peter Ruggenthaler, Ludwig Boltzmann Institute for Research on Consequences of War, who was from the outset a driving force behind the genesis and completion of the volume, as well as to Dieter Bacher and Kornel Trojan for their support in creating the registers. We are very grateful to all authors for the submission and reworking of their contributions, as well as the archives, institutions, and private individuals for allowing us to reproduce images from their collections. Thanks are also due to the Ludwig Boltzmann Gesellschaft, Vienna, for financial assistance with the translation costs and the University of Graz as well as the City of Graz that became partners of BIK in 2018.

Introduction

Stefan Karner and Barbara Stelzl-Marx

On Holy Thursday, March 29, 1945, units of the 3rd Ukrainian Front under Marshal Fyodor Tolbukhin crossed the old Austrian border at Klostermarienberg in Burgenland. Thus began the Allied military occupation of Austria. Parallel to this in the course of the advance of the Red Army and later the troops of the Western Allies, the Nazi system collapsed.[1] Austria was liberated externally from Nazi rule. Resistance on the part of Austrians had admittedly grown and was large in places, but it could not yet decisively contribute to the overthrow of Nazi rule.[2] At least 26,000 Red Army soldiers lost their lives on Austrian territory in the final weeks of the Second World War.[3]

Hundreds of thousands of soldiers and officers, their wives and children, as well as the civilian occupation personnel, often came to Austria for years. At the end of the war, about 400,000 Red Army soldiers were in Austria. The majority of them were withdrawn again in 1945/1946. At the end of the occupation in 1955, around 40,000 members of the army together with 7,600 relatives of officers were stationed in Austria. By means of their blanket presence they belonged during the post-war period to everyday life in the Soviet occupation zone. Compared to the quantitatively fewer American, French, and British occupation troops, the Soviet occupation soldiers in eastern Austria thus constituted "strangers" per se. "The Russians," as they were, and still are, generally called in popular parlance shaped the first post-war decade in Austria particularly strongly. Old propaganda patterns from the nineteenth century and the Nazi era often continued to have an effect here.

The Soviet occupation of eastern Austria from 1945 to 1955 constituted until a few years ago one of the most significant research gaps in Austrian contemporary history.[4] While the zones of Austria occupied by the Western Allies had already been the subject of numerous academic studies, research into the Soviet occupation lagged drastically behind. The reason for this lay first and foremost in a major, decade-long imbalance in the source situation. As a result of the partial opening of relevant sources in Russian archives, several research projects could dedicate themselves to Austrian-Soviet relations at a bilateral level, questions relating to Soviet influence on Austrian policy as well as plans vis-à-vis Austria or everyday life in the Soviet occupation zone from the Austrian perspective.

As a result of a three-year, bilateral research project[5] (with preparatory work lasting several years), in April 2005, a two-volume publication appeared under the title *Die Rote Armee in Österreich. Sowjetische Besatzung 1945–1955*, in which for the first time the ten-year Soviet occupation of Austria was comprehensively analysed on the basis of documents from many Russian and Austrian archives.[6] In Russia this concerned in particular repositories of the Central Archives of the Ministry of Defence (TsAMO) in Podol'sk, for the declassification of which a special commission was set up; the Central Archives of the FSB;[7] the Archives of the Foreign Ministry; the Russian State Archives for Contemporary History (former archives of the Central Committee of the CPSU, RGANI); the Russian State Archives for Social and Political History ("Party Archives" until 1952, now RGASPI); the Russian State Archives for Military History (formerly "Special Archives" of the Ministerial Council of the USSR, now RGVA); and the State Archives of the Russian Federation (GARF). In the framework of the bilateral, joint treatment, almost all of the named archives opened many collections on Austria for the first time. This affected, among others, records of the "Stavka," the administrations of the 2nd and 3rd Ukrainian Front, which operated in Austria, their political sections, as well as the NKVD units operating behind the front on Austrian soil; the Politburo for the period after 1945, among them the resolutions passed in particular secrecy from the collection "special folder" ("osobaya papka"); and likewise from the collections of Vyacheslav Molotov, the Foreign Policy Commission of the Central Committee and the Soviet Component of the Allied Commission for Austria.

The Ludwig Boltzmann Institute for Research on Consequences of War (BIK) continued with this project its long-term research in close cooperation with Russian archives and research institutions. From 1990/1991, Stefan Karner carried out research on Austrian-Soviet relations after 1945 and on the topic of prisoners of war,[8] before founding the BIK in 1993. Under his leadership, research on POWs in captivity and forced labor in the Soviet Union and in the "Third Reich" were continued.[9] Research focus was also placed on aspects of the Cold War.[10] In 2008, a research project on the "Prague Spring" was successfully completed. A two-volume publication with almost 3000 pages appeared in international cooperation.[11] A 500-page edition appeared in the Harvard Cold War Studies Book Series under the title *The Prague Spring and the Warsaw Pact Invasion of Czechoslovakia in 1968*.[12] In 2011, several joint publications on the Vienna Summit of 1961 between John F. Kennedy and Nikita S. Khrushchev were released.[13] A study on 104 Austrian victims of Stalin who were sentenced to death and shot in Moscow between 1950 and 1953,[14] the postdoctoral thesis[15] of Barbara Stelzl-Marx, which appeared as a book in 2011 under the title *Stalins Soldaten in Österreich*,[16] and publications on children of occupation are furthermore devoted to the Soviet occupation in Austria and its consequences.[17]

Current research is carried out moreover in the framework of the Austria-Russian Historical Commission (chairpersons: Stefan Karner and Alexander Chubar'ian; secretaries: Barbara Stelzl-Marx and Viktor Ishchenko). The aim of the commission, which was founded in 2008, is the joint treatment of Austrian-Russian/Soviet relations in the nineteenth and twentieth centuries. Thanks is due in this context to the Austrian Federal Ministry for European and International Matters for the financial assistance provided to the projects of the ÖRHK.

The current volume constitutes a selection of in part revised contributions from the German-language publication *Die Rote Armee in Österreich. Sowjetische Besatzung 1945–1955* as well as other research carried out at the Ludwig Boltzmann Institute for Research on Consequences of War in collaboration with Graz University and the City of Graz. The research was primarily supported by Ludwig Boltzmann Gesellschaft, the Governments of Styria and Lower Austria as well as the Austrian Federal Ministry of Education, Science and Research, Vienna. Professor Günter Bischof, University of New Orleans, a proven expert in the field of Cold War studies, was furthermore recruited for an introductory chapter.

The aim of the current volume is to provide an account of central aspects of the Soviet occupation in Austria from 1945 to 1955 and to embed them in the context of the early Cold War. Against this backdrop, Günter Bischof provides in his introduction an insight into "The Policies of Presidents Roosevelt, Truman, and Eisenhower toward Austria, 1943–1955." With his publication *Austria in the First Cold War*, Bischof presented as early as the 1990s the theory that in 1945 in Austria the Anglo-Soviet Cold War had already set in, from which an Anglo-American-Soviet Cold War developed in 1946. In doing so, he contradicted from the supranational point of view the long-advocated theory that there had never been a cold war in Austria ("KeinKalter Krieg in Kakanien" or "No Cold War in the Dual Monarchy").[18] Advocates of the latter theory viewed this above all from the perspective of an Allied cooperation in Vienna that always functioned, even in hot phases of the early Cold War (joint patrols, etc.).

Bischof emphasizes Marshall Plan aid as a particularly important element, which Austria—as the only country under Soviet occupation—received from 1948 till 1952. In the per head distribution of the Marshall Plan funds, the Austrians were at the forefront. Austria turned out to be one of the principal recipients of Marshall Funds on a per capita basis. This European Recovery Program served not only as a counterweight to the economic exploitation by the Soviets but also as a political means to contain Communist influence in Austria and to promote the Western orientation of the country and Austrian society.

In the context of European policy, it was for a long time not clear to Washington that a commitment to Austria would be so extensive. Initial disinterest in Austria during the Second World War gradually gave way to the increasingly identified strategic importance of Austria in Central Europe for the entire "old continent." In the early Cold War Austria was a gateway between East and West and in this way a direct setting for disputes between the systems. Following the founding of NATO in 1949, the Alpine region took on a varied importance in the strategic defense plans of the alliance. After initial neglect of Austria in the defense concepts, this changed above all as a result of French pressure. For Paris it was first and foremost a question of being able to commence with military defense as far as possible from French territory in the event of an attack from the east, in order to prevent a repeat of the trauma of the Second World War. In the years after 1948, NATO's defense line moved year for year further forward—initially from the Pyrenees and the Atlantic coast to the Rhine and then the East German border. Following the so-called putsch attempt in October 1950 in Austria, the strategic importance of the Austrian Alpine region for the defense of NATO territory also became clear for the American military in Austria and the Pentagon planning. Bischof traces the significance of Austria in these strategic considerations and in American policy and thus embeds Austrian post-war history in the East-West confrontations of the early Cold War.

In the second part of the book, the contributions from Aleksei Filitov, Stefan Karner, and Peter Ruggenthaler provide an overview of Soviet planning on Austria during the Second World War and 1945. The main aim here was the reestablishment of Austria as an independent but "smaller and weaker" state in its pre-war borders, which was designed above all to bring about a weakening of Germany. The Soviet Union refused to be a party to plans to unite states in a confederation (with Vienna as a potential capital city), as propagated above all by Winston Churchill, in order not to create any significant power factor in the Balkans or Central Europe, who, like centuries before, could become a direct rival of Moscow. With the reestablishment of Austria as an independent (small) state, the Soviet leadership pursued above all the aim of a sustained weakening of Germany. The establishment of the provisional state government under Karl Renner on April 27, 1945, confronted the Western Allies with a fait accompli, as Stalin had acted in this matter independently and against the agreements reached in the European Advisory Commission. They suspected—correctly—an attempt to set up a people's front government, like previously in the central and eastern European states, and believed that Renner ran the risk of degenerating into a Soviet puppet.

In his essay, Peter Ruggenthaler reconstructs Stalin's Austria policy from the "Anschluss" in 1938 to his death in 1953. On the basis of documents mostly made available for the first time in the framework of the project on the "Red Army in Austria," a clear picture emerges. From the beginning, the Soviet occupation of eastern Austria was for Moscow of strategic importance for its policy on Eastern Europe, guaranteeing as it did the maintenance of troops in Romania and Hungary. For this reason, the Austrian State Treaty was not signed in 1949, in spite of supposed preparations for a troop withdrawal. Stalin allowed negotiations to be broken off. The human factor also played a role here. The Soviet dictator was not prepared to render Tito a service. A withdrawal of Soviet troops from the vicinity of Tito's Yugoslavia could have been celebrated by the Western powers as a great victory. In light of Soviet files, the benefit of the Soviet occupation is clearly shown, the maintenance of which was importance to the Kremlin as long as it remained advantageous. Thus, Stalin's death should not necessarily be regarded as a break in Soviet policy on Austria.

Michail Prozumenshchikov addresses the closing phase of Soviet Austrian policy up to the signing of the Austrian State Treaty on May 15, 1955, in Vienna's Belvedere; the withdrawal of occupation troops until October 25, 1955, and the neutrality decided on by the Austrian national council the following day. He emphasizes the economic importance of the Soviet occupation, which failed to yield any gains after 1953, however, and traces the discussion within the Soviet leadership, according to which Khrushchev was strongly supported by Foreign Trade Minister Mikoyan against Foreign Minister Molotov, who had long blocked a solution to the Austrian question.

In the third part of the book, several central aspects of the ten-year period of Soviet occupation in Austria are illuminated. Walter M. Iber first of all addresses Soviet economic policy toward Austria, which was governed by the pursuit of "booty" and by exploitation. This policy was initially characterized following the war by dismantling operations, from autumn 1945 by the establishment of exterritorial Soviet economic bodies (the Administration for Soviet Property in Austria, USIA, and the Soviet Mineral Oil Administration, SMV), which administered the "German property" confiscated by the occupying power in accordance with the Potsdam Agreements. Of particular importance was the SMV, as it administered in Lower Austria the third largest oil field in Europe (after the USSR and Romania). As a result of the Moscow Memorandum of April 1955 and the completion of the State Treaty on May 15, 1955, the Soviet economic administrations were ultimately transferred—for extensive release payments—to the Republic of Austria.

Harald Knoll and Barbara Stelzl-Marx examine in their contribution the fate of the around 2,400 Austrian civilians who were arrested by Soviet organs in eastern Austria. More than half of them were subsequently sentenced by military tribunals to generally long prison terms and taken to the USSR; more than 150 were executed. They were accused of illegal weapons possessions, war crimes, crimes against the Soviet occupying power, membership of "Werewolf" units at the end of the war, and especially espionage. Against the backdrop of the Cold War, the fourfold-occupied Austria, and above all Vienna, developed into a hub of espionage activity; here East clashed with West. A large proportion of those civilians convicted were rehabilitated by the Main Military Public Prosecutor of the Russian Federation in the 1990s, among them the vast majority of those Austrian victims of Stalin who were shot.

Barbara Stelzl-Marx addresses a topic that remains to this day taboo: after the Second World War, so-called "children of occupation" were born all over Austria and Germany as a result of voluntary sexual encounters between local women and foreign occupation troops, but also as a consequence of rape. They were often regarded as "children of the enemy" and—together with their mothers—frequently discriminated against. In accordance with Stalin's policy, weddings between Soviet soldiers and Austrian women were practically impossible. Most soldiers or officers were even sent back to the USSR when their liaisons with local women became known. For several decades hardly any contact was feasible. Thus, the majority of "Ivan's children" in Austria grew up as a fatherless generation. Many of them have been in search of their biological fathers for several decades, regardless of the difficulty of obtaining any reliable information. This is linked with the desire to explore one's own identity and look for one's personal roots.

NOTES

1. Manfried Rauchensteiner, *Der Krieg in Österreich 1945* (Vienna: Donauland, 1985), p. 126.

2. On this see, among others, Stefan Karner and Karl Duffek, eds., *Widerstand in Österreich, 1938–1945. Die Beiträge der Parlaments-Enquete 2005*, Vol. 7 of Veröffentlichungen des Ludwig Boltzmann-Instituts für Kriegsfolgen-Forschung series (Graz/Vienna/Klagenfurt: Verein zur Förderung der Forschung von Folgen nach Konflikten und Kriegen, 2007).

3. Peter Sixl, *Sowjetische Kriegsgräber in Österreich. SovetskiemogilyVtoroimirovoivoiny v Avstrii*, Special Vol. 6 of Veröffentlichungen des Ludwig Boltzmann-Instituts für Kriegsfolgen-Forschung series (Graz/Vienna/Klagenfurt: Verein zur Förderung der Forschung von Folgen nach Konflikten und Kriegen, 2005); Peter Sixl, *Sowjetische Tote des Zweiten Weltkrieges in Österreich. Namens- und Grablagenverzeichnis. Ein Gedenkbuch*, Special Vol. 11 of Veröffentlichungen des Ludwig Boltzmann-Instituts für Kriegsfolgen-Forschung series (Graz/Vienna/Klagenfurt: Verein zur Förderung der Forschung von Folgen nach Konflikten und Kriegen, 2010).

4. On this see also: Günter Bischof, "Eine historiographische Einführung: Die Ära des Kalten Krieges und Österreich," in Erwin A. Schmidl, ed., *Österreich im frühen Kalten Krieg 1945–1958. Spione, Partisanen, Kriegspläne* (Vienna/Cologne/Weimar: Böhlau, 2000), pp. 19–53.

5. The bilateral research project "Die Rote Armee in Österreich 1945–1955" was provided with financial assistance from July 2002 to December 2005 from the Austrian Federal Ministry of Education, Science and Culture, Vienna. Project leader: Stefan Karner; project coordination: Barbara Stelzl-Marx.

6. Stefan Karner and Barbara Stelzl-Marx, eds., *Die Rote Armee in Österreich. Sowjetische Besatzung 1945–1955. Beiträge*, Special Vol. 4 of Veröffentlichungen des Ludwig Boltzmann-Instituts für Kriegsfolgen-Forschung series (Graz/Vienna/Munich: Oldenbourg, 2005); Stefan Karner, Barbara Stelzl-Marx and Alexander Tschubarjan, eds., *Die Rote Armee in Österreich: Sowjetische Besatzung 1945–1955. Dokumente. Krasnaya Armiya v Avstrii: Sovetskaya okkupatsiya 1945–1955. Dokumenty*, Special Vol. 5 of Veröffentlichungen des Ludwig Boltzmann-Instituts für Kriegsfolgen-Forschung series (Graz/Vienna/Munich: Oldenbourg, 2005).

7. Stefan Karner and Barbara Stelzl-Marx, eds., *Stalins letzte Opfer. Verschleppte und erschossene Österreicher in Moskau 1950–1953*, Vol. 5 of Wissenschaftliche Veröffentlichungen des Ludwig Boltzmann Instituts für Kriegsfolgen-Forschung series (Vienna/Munich: Böhlau/Oldenbourg, 2009).

8. Stefan Karner, *Im Archipel GUPVI: Kriegsgefangenschaft und Internierung in der Sowjetunion 1941–1956*, Vol. 1 of Wissenschaftliche Veröffentlichungen des Ludwig Boltzmann Instituts für Kriegsfolgen-Forschung series (Vienna/Munich: Oldenbourg, 1995).

9. Stefan Karner and Peter Ruggenthaler, with assistance from Harald Knoll, Peter Pirnath, Arno Wonisch, Wolfram Dornik, Jens Gassmann, Gerald Hafner, Herbert Killian, Reinhard Möstl, Nikita Petrov, Edith Petschnigg and Barbara Stelzl-Marx, *Zwangsarbeit in der Land- und Forstwirtschaft auf dem Gebiet der Republik Österreich 1939–1945*, Vol. 26/2 of Veröffentlichungen der Österreichischen Historikerkommission. Zwangsarbeit auf dem Gebiet der Republik Österreich series (Vienna/Munich: Oldenbourg, 2004).

10. Stefan Karner, Erich Reiter and Gerald Schöpfer, *Kalter Krieg: Beiträge zur Ost–West-Konfrontation 1945 bis 1990*, Vol. 5 of Unserer Zeit Geschichte series (Graz: Leykam, 2002).

11. Stefan Karner, Natalja Tomilina, Alexander Tschubarjan, Viktor Iščenko, Michail Prozumenščikov, Peter Ruggenthaler, Oldřich Tůma and Manfred Wilke, eds., *Prager Frühling. Das internationale Krisenjahr 1968. Beiträge*, Vol. 9/1 of Ver-

öffentlichungen des Ludwig Boltzmann-Instituts für Kriegsfolgen-Forschung series (Cologne/Vienna/Weimar: Böhlau, 2008); Stefan Karner, Natalja Tomilina, Alexander Tschubarjan, Viktor Iščenko, Michail Prozumenščikov, Peter Ruggenthaler, Oldřich Tůma and Manfred Wilke, eds., with assistance from Irina Kazarina, Silke Stern, Günter Bischof, Aleksej Filitov and Harald Knoll, *Prager Frühling. Das internationale Krisenjahr 1968. Dokumente. Pražskajavesna. Meždunarodnyjkrizisnyj 1968g. 2. Dokumenty*, Vol. 9/2 of Veröffentlichungen des Ludwig Boltzmann-Instituts für Kriegsfolgen-Forschung series (Cologne/Vienna/Weimar: Böhlau, 2008).

12. Günter Bischof, Stefan Karner, and Peter Ruggenthaler, eds., *The Prague Spring and the Warsaw Pact Invasion of Czechoslovakia in 1968*, Harvard Cold War Studies Book Series (Lanham, MD: Lexington, 2010).

13. Stefan Karner, Barbara Stelzl-Marx, Natalja Tomilina, Alexander Tschubarjan, Günter Bischof, Viktor Iščenko, Michail Prozumenščikov, Peter Ruggenthaler, Gerhard Wettig and Manfred Wilke, eds., *Der Wiener Gipfel 1961. Kennedy—Chruschtschow* (Innsbruck/Vienna/Bozen: Studienverlag, 2011); Stefan Karner, Natal'ia Tomilina, Aleksandr Chubar'ian and Barbara Stelzl-Marx, eds., *"Venskiival's" cholodnoivoiny (vokrugvstrechi N. S. Chrushcheva i Dzh. F. Kennedi v 1961 godu v Vene)* (Moscow: Rospen, 2011); Gerhard Wettig, with assistance from Stefan Karner, Horst Möller, Michail Prosumenschtschikow, Peter Ruggenthaler, Barbara Stelzl-Marx, Natalja Tomilina, Aleksandr Tschubarjan, Matthias Uhl and Hermann Wentker, eds., *Dokumentation Chruschtschows Westpolitik 1955–1964. Gespräche, Aufzeichnungen und Stellungnahmen, Band 3: Kulmination der Berlin-Krise (Herbst 1960 bis Herbst 1962)* (Munich: Oldenbourg, 2011).

14. Stefan Karner and Barbara Stelzl-Marx, eds., *Stalins letzte Opfer. Verschleppte und erschossene Österreicher in Moskau 1950–1953*, with assistance from Daniela Almer, Dieter Bacher and Harald Knoll (Vienna/Munich: Oldenbourg/Böhlau, 2009).

15. Barbara Stelzl-Marx, "Die Innensicht der sowjetischen Besatzung in Österreich 1945–1955. Erfahrung, Wahrnehmung, Erinnerung," post-doctoral thesis, University of Graz, 2009.

16. Barbara Stelzl-Marx, *Stalins Soldaten in Österreich. Die Innensicht der sowjetischen Besatzung 1945–1955* (Vienna/Munich: Oldenbourg/Böhlau, 2011).

17. Barbara Stelzl-Marx and Silke Satjukow, eds., *Besatzungskinder. Die Nachkommen alliierter Soldaten in Österreich und Deutschland* (Vienna/Cologne/Weimar: Böhlau Verlag, 2015).

18. Manfried Rauchensteiner, *Der Sonderfall. Die Besatzungszeit in Österreich 1945 bis 1955*, new edition (Graz/Vienna/Cologne: Styria, 1995), p. 248.

Abbreviations

ABÖK	Antifaschistisches Büro österreichischer Kriegsgefangener (Anti-Fascist Office of Austrian Prisoners of War)
AdBIK	Archiv des Ludwig Boltzmann Instituts für Kriegsfolgen-Forschung (Archives of the Ludwig Boltzmann Institute for Research on Consequences of War)
AEL	Arbeitserziehungslager (Work Education Camp)
AP RF	Arkhiv Prezidenta Rossiiskoi Federatsii (Archives of the President of the Russian Federation)
AVP RF	Arkhiv Vneshnei Politiki Rossiiskoi Federatsii (Foreign Policy Archives of the Russian Federation)
BMI	Bundesministerium des Inneren (Austrian Federal Ministry of the Interior)
BTA	British Troops Austria
Comecon	Council for Mutual Economic Assistance
CPSU	Communist Party of the Soviet Union
CWIHP	Cold War International History Project
DDSG	Donaudampfschifffahrtsgesellschaft (Danube Steam Navigation Company)
EAC	European Advisory Commission
EDC	European Defence Community
ERP	European Recovery Programme
FRG	Federal Republic of Germany
FRUS	Foreign Relations of the United States
GARF	Gosudarstvennyi Arkhiv Rossiiskoi Federatsii (State Archives of the Russian Federation)
GBLÖ	Gesetzblatt für das Land Österreich (Law Gazette for the Country of Austria)

GDR	German Democratic Republic
GOKO	Gosudarstvennyi Komitet Oborony (State Defence Committee)
GULag	Glavnoe Upravlenie Lagerei (Main Administration of Camps)
GUPVI	Glavnoe Upravlenie Po Delam Voennoplennykh i Internirovannykh (Main Administration for Affairs of Prisoners of War and Internees)
GUSIMZ	Gosudarstvennoe Upravlenie Sovetskim Imushchestvom Zagranitsei (Main Administration of Soviet Property Abroad)
GVP	Glavnaya Voennaya Prokuratura (Main Military Public Prosecution Office of the Russian Federation)
ITL	Ispravitelno-Trudovoi Lager (Corrective Labor Camp)
KPD	Kommunistische Partei Deutschlands (Communist Party of Germany)
KPÖ	Kommunistische Partei Österreichs (Communist Party of Austria)
MGB	Ministerstvo Gosudarstvennoi Bezopasnosti (Soviet Ministry for State Security)
MID	Ministerstvo Inostrannykh Del (Ministry for Foreign Affairs)
MVD	Ministerstvo Vnutrennikh Del (Ministry for Internal Affairs)
NARA	National Archives and Records Administration
NKGB	Narodnyi Komissariat Gosudarstvennoi Bezopasnosti (People's Commissariat for State Security)
NKID	Narodnyi Komissariat Inostrannykh Del (People's Commissariat for Foreign Affairs)
NKVD	Narodnyi Komissariat Vnutrennikh Del (People's Commissariat for Internal Affairs)
NÖLA	Niederösterreichisches Landesarchiv (Regional Archives of Lower Austria)
ÖBM	Österreichische Botschaft Moskau (Austrian Embassy in Moscow)
OHI	Oral History Interview
ÖROP	Österreichisch-Russische Ölprodukte (Austrian-Russian Oil Products)
ÖSK	Österreichisches Schwarzes Kreuz (Austrian Black Cross)
OSO	Osoboe Soveshchanie MGB (MGB Special Commission)
ÖStA/AdR	Österreichisches Staatsarchiv/Archiv der Republik (Austrian State Archives/Archives of the Republic)
ÖVP	Österreichische Volkspartei (Austrian People's Party)

PCF	Parti communiste français (Communist Party of France)
PCI	Partito Comunista Italiano (Communist Party of Italy)
POEN	Provisorisches Österreichisches Nationalkomitee (Provisional Austrian National Committee)
RAVAG	Radio-Verkehrs-Aktiengesellschaft (Radio Communication Company)
RGAE	Rossiiskii Gosudarstvennyi Arkhiv Ekonomiki (Russian State Archives for Economics)
RGAKFD	Rossiiskii Gosudarstvennyi Arkhiv Kinofotodokumentov (Russian State Archives of Film and Photo Documents)
RGANI	Rossiiskii Gosudarstvennyi Arkhiv Noveishei Istorii (Russian State Archives for Contemporary History)
RGASPI	Rossiiskii Gosudarstvennyi Arkhiv Sotsial'no-Politicheskoi Istorii (Russian State Archives of Socio-Political History)
RGVA	Rossiiskii Gosudarstvennyi Voennyi Arkhiv (Russian State Military Archives)
RGW	Rat für Gegenseitige Wirtschaftshilfe (Council for Mutual Economic Assistance, Comecon)
RSFSR	Rossiskaya Sovetskaya Federativnaya Sotsialisticheskaya Respublika (Russian Soviet Federative Socialist Republic)
SAG	Sowjetische Aktiengesellschaft (Soviet Joint Stock Company)
SBZ	Sowjetische Besatzungszone (Soviet Occupation Zone)
SChSK	Sovetskaya Chast' Soyuznicheskoi Komissii po Avstrii (Soviet Element of the Allied Commission for Austria)
SDAG	Sowjet-Deutsche Aktiengesellschaft (Soviet-German Joint Stock Company)
SHAEF	Supreme Headquarters Allied Expeditionary Force
SMERSH	Smert' shpionam ("Death to Spies," Soviet Military Counterintelligence)
SMV	Sowjetische Mineralölverwaltung (Soviet Mineral Oil Administration)
SPÖ	Sozialistische Partei Österreichs (Socialist Party of Austria)
StLA	Steiermärkisches Landesarchiv (Federal Archives of Styria)
TsA FSB RF	Tsentral'nyi Arkhiv Federal'noi Sluzhby Bezopasnosti (Central Archives of the Federal Security Service of the Russian Federation)
TsAMO	Tsentral'nyi Arkhiv Ministerstva Oborony Rossiiskoi Federatsii (Central Archives of the Ministry of Defence of the Russian Federation)
TsGV	Tsentral'naya Gruppa Voisk (Central Group of Forces)

USIA	Upravlenie Sovetskim Imushchestvom v Avstrii (Administration of Soviet Assets in Austria)
USIF	Upravlenie Sovetskim Imushchestvom v Finlyandii (Administration of Soviet Assets in Finland)
VDK	Volksbund Deutscher Kriegsgräberfürsorge (German War Graves Commission)
VdU	Verband der Unabhängigen (Federation of Independents)
VKP(b)	All-Union Communist Party (Bolsheviks)
VOKS	Vsesoyuznoe Obshchestvo Kul'turnykh Svyazei s zagranitsei (Society for Cultural Relations with Foreign Countries)
VSRF	Verkhovnyi Sud Rossiiskoi Federatsii (Supreme Court of the Russian Federation)
WStLB	Wiener Stadt- und Landesbibliothek (Vienna City and Regional Library)

Part I

AUSTRIA IN GLOBAL POLICY

Chapter One

The Policies of Presidents Roosevelt, Truman, and Eisenhower toward Austria, 1943–1955

Günter Bischof

The historiography of the Austrian occupation after the Second World War has come in fits and starts. An initial wave of works published in the 1960s by contemporaries who experienced the occupation personally[1] was followed by standard works defining the scholarly discourse in the 1970s.[2] The high point of scholarship came in the 1980s and 1990s, when a cohort of scholars worked with newly opened archival sources to write doctoral dissertations.[3] In the past fifteen years some notable publications have appeared, but there was no longer a strong cohort of scholars working on the occupation decade and motivating each other's research—it is rather "lone wolves" who do research disconnected from a larger community of scholars.[4] Basic monographs covered the American political, cultural, and security policies vis-à-vis Austria.[5] Kurt Tweraser's prodigious research on American policies in its occupation zone in Upper Austria is unrivaled in research on occupation zones.[6] The conference volume of a big scholarly meeting on the occupation decade organized by the Austrian Academy of Science in the "memorial year" 2005 presented a *"summa"* of sorts of Austrian occupation studies to date.[7] The fifth edition of Gerald Stourzh's classic history of the Austrian State Treaty negotiations was also republished in the "memorial year" 2005, as was Rolf Steininger's short history of the Austrian State Treaty.[8] Stourzh's definitive work on the political arena was matched by Hans Seidel's history of the Austrian economy in the occupation decade, which became an instant "classic."[9] A similar massive and long overdue volume of essays has recently been published on Austrian defense and security policies during the Cold War within the context of the rival block systems in Europe.[10] The most dramatic recent advances in the study of the post-war Allied occupation of Austria have been made on the Russian zone as a result of the opening of the Soviet archives after the end of the Cold War and the collapse of the Soviet Union, whereby the Ludwig Boltzmann Institute for Research on War Consequences in Graz and the Austrian Academy of Sciences have led the way (also in the publication of weighty documentary volumes);[11] the essays in this volume are testimony to this most recent progress in occupation studies.

PRESIDENT ROOSEVELT'S AUSTRIAN POLICY

American planning for the post-war world started early, long before the Second World War came to an end. The elite Council on Foreign Relations of the State Department in New York initiated the planning work before the United States entered the war. After the Pearl Harbor attack the State Department took over the entire post-war planning effort in 1942 and systematically and very deeply explored all options for the restructuring of the post-war world ("Notter Committee," named after the secretary of this planning committee). The "Austrian Question" was discussed in various contexts. It was part of the debates about German dismemberment (e.g., a breakup of the "Third Reich" into smaller units); the (re)creation of a Danubian entity (e.g., federation, confederation, customs union), particularly pushed by the principal US ally Winston Churchill; and finally the option of reestablishing an independent Austria in the form or shape of pre-Anschluss Austria.[12]

Starting in 1943, the ideas contemplated separately in American, British, and Soviet planning councils (later the "Free French" too) culminated in the discussions of the Moscow Foreign Ministers Conference in late October 1943. Here the Allied powers decided to reestablish an independent Austria in the pre-Anschluss borders. The Allied "Moscow Declaration" on Austria of November 1943 would become the principal foundational document of the Second Austrian Republic; its contents were selectively adapted and proclaimed by the Provisional Government of Karl Renner on April 27, 1945.[13]

The Moscow Declaration was a highly ambiguous document. It proclaimed Austria as "Hitler's first victim" and promised to reestablish the country; Austrians were reminded that the Allies expected a contribution from them toward their own liberation; at Soviet insistence the Allied declaration reminded Austria(ns) that they also bore responsibility for Hitlerite war crimes. The Moscow Declaration was in part an Allied propaganda document that aimed at encouraging domestic Austrian resistance against the Hitler regime. The Moscow Declaration was followed up by the determination of Austrian occupation zones by the "European Advisory Commission" established by the Allied foreign ministers in Moscow. The United States, Great Britain, France, and the Soviet Union would occupy Austria jointly like they planned to do in Germany. But Austria would be treated differently after the war as a "liberated country" from Germany—a "defeated country." Austria would be governed by a four-power Allied Commission, not a Control Commission. The Austrian "peace treaty" would be a "state treaty."[14] By the end of the war at the latest, however, the importance of Austria had been clearly recognized in Washington: "Austria is a strategic center for which there is bound to be a political struggle, the outcome of which will affect the economic well-being and stability of Southeastern Europe, an area of tension out of which WWI and II arose and where the dangers of future conflict could arise."[15]

TRUMAN'S AUSTRIAN POLICY

The new administration of Harry S. Truman,[16] successor to the deceased President Roosevelt, had been in office for barely three weeks when the Provisional Government of Karl Renner under the aegis of the Soviet occupation power proclaimed Austria's independence on April 27, 1945. The British government was very upset over this unilateral act against all wartime agreements. Churchill and his advisors in the Foreign Office considered the Renner government a Soviet puppet regime—like the ones established in Poland, Romania, and Bulgaria in the previous months. Whitehall did not recognize the Renner regime. The United States and its representative in Austria, General Mark Clark, acted more pragmatically and mediated throughout the summer of 1945 in what looked like an emerging Soviet-British "cold war" over the future of Austria.[17]

Four-power Allied control of Austria slowly emerged in the summer and fall of 1945. In July, the four occupation powers moved or retreated into their zones agreed upon in the European Advisory Commission. The powers began to implement the first Control Agreement in early July. In August, the Western powers moved into their assigned sectors in Vienna. In early September, the Allied Council began to meet in Vienna. In late October 1945, the Western powers finally recognized the provisional Renner Government. In late November, free elections were held out of which there emerged a conservative-socialist coalition government; in spite of the very disappointing vote count for the Communists (5 instead of the expected 25 percent of the vote), one Communist minister was included in the Cabinet too. Leopold Figl from the People's Party (ÖVP) was the first elected post-war Austrian chancellor.[18]

The Soviets acted piqued and began to put serious economic pressure on the new Austrian government. They seized most of the important industrial assets in their zone ("German assets") in the winter/spring of 1946 and thereby sparked the outbreak of the Cold War in Austria. The US government started to pour considerable economic aid into Austria (including the

Soviet zone) to counter Soviet economic pressure and ensure the survival of Austria. Initially, much of the aid was foodstuffs, as Austrians experienced serious food shortages and famine. Eventually during later 1946 and 1947 this became financial aid to balance the trade deficits and revive industrial production and rebuild the infrastructure after the massive destruction the war had left, particularly in the cities.[19]

While the United States concentrated on economic recovery and the spiritual and mental renewal of the post-Second World War nation ("denazification") during this initial phase of the Austrian occupation, the Americans increased in 1946 efforts to write an Austrian treaty ("peace treaty," "state treaty") to end the occupation and release the country into full independence. The chances of writing an Austrian treaty were discussed on the periphery of the Foreign Minister negotiations in Paris in the summer of 1946 when the treaties were written with Hitler's five satellites. Austrian treaty negotiations seriously took off during the initial round of negotiations by the Deputies of the Foreign Ministers for an Austrian treaty in London (January/February 1947).[20] The Foreign Ministers met in Moscow (March–April 1947) to negotiate Austrian and German "peace" treaties. In the Austrian treaty talks the most difficult issues were the "German assets" questions. The Soviets wanted the Austrians to pay for the "German assets" they seized in 1945/1946 as part of their "reparations" settlement with the Western Allies at the Potsdam conference. The other unbridgeable issue in 1947 was Yugoslav border demands in Carinthia/Styria.[21] In the 1948 Deputy negotiations in London, progress was made on both these issues. After the Tito-Stalin split, Moscow no longer supported Yugoslav territorial demands against Austria. In Austrian treaty negotiations, the Truman administration and the American negotiators strongly supported Austrian positions against maximum Soviet demands intended to weaken Austria economically.[22]

The United States played a key role both in defending Austria against Soviet economic depredations and in continuing to pour extensive economic aid into Austria and Europe. During the spring of 1947 the Truman administration reacted to Communist pressure on Greece, the Communist coup in Hungary, and the ongoing negative trading balance of Western European nations (including Austria) by announcing a major initiative toward economic recovery of the continent—the European Recovery Program. Better known under the name of Truman's new Secretary of State George C. Marshall, the "Marshall Plan" began to pour twelve billion dollars into Western Europe in 1948; the program lasted until 1952. Austria turned out to be one of the principal recipients of Marshall Funds on a per capita basis. Without the American pre-Marshall Plan and ERP economic aid, Austria would not have recovered as quickly from its wartime destruction.[23]

The arrival of the Marshall Plan gave the Soviets convenient cover to consolidate their bloc in Central Europe. With the formation of the military bloc came the militarization and nuclearization of the Cold War.[24] As a result of the Communist coups in Hungary (1947) and Prague (1948), along with the Berlin crisis (1948–49), Western European governments felt threatened and launched a military organization—the Brussels Pact (1948). In 1949, the United States and Canada joined Western European defense efforts and initiated the North Atlantic Treaty Pact (1949). After the detonation of the first Soviet atomic device in late August 1949 and the victory of the Communists in the Chinese civil war in October 1949, the United States responded with a reassessment of its entire national security strategy, culminating in the document NSC 68. The United States quadrupled its defense spending after the outbreak of the Korean War in June 1950 and built an awesome nuclear arsenal alongside an increase in the conventional forces.[25]

The militarization of American Cold War policies and strategies also proliferated into the Austrian occupation. American fears of Communist *subversion* in Austria gravely increased after the Czech coup ("Prague is west of Vienna") in the American occupation element in Austria.[26] There were recurrent fears of a Communist putsch attempt among Austria's political elite and these were duly reported to the American High Commission. In October 1950, the Communists tried to launch a general strike that the Austrian government considered a "putsch attempt." The "Korean scenario" of a direct Communist attack in Austria was deemed less likely.[27] US High Commissioner Geoffrey Keyes began planning for building the "core" of a future Austrian Army as early as 1948. In the basic National Security Council document for Austria NSC 38/5 military security considerations became prevalent, like in the case of NSC 68.[28]

It was the "October 1950 general strike" attempt, however, that allowed General Keyes to move forward with the "militarization" of Austria too. In 1951, the Austrian government with the help of the United States launched the "B-Gendarmerie." Police officers were trained to become the "core" of a future Austrian Army once the State Treaty had been signed and the occupation powers withdrawn. The CIA also placed almost 100 secret arms caches in the Austrian Alps. These were designed to be activated by Austrian "guerilla forces" in the event of a Communist attack on Austria. Western military planning included a withdrawal of Western occupation forces in Austria from the Alpine region into Northern Italy in case of a Soviet attack. By the time the Austrian State Treaty was concluded in 1955, some 9,000 Austrian policemen had been trained in the "B-Gendarmerie" to constitute the core of the Austrian Army launched in 1956. Austria had become a "secret ally" of the West.[29] Even though through the American occupation element the Austrians came to liaise closely with NATO and NATO planning for Central Europe, the Austrian leaders never seriously considered joining NATO since the Soviets would never have evacuated their Austrian zone had Austria become a NATO member. NATO defense planning moved from a peripheral strategy on the European continent (withdrawal behind the Pyrenees and to England) in the early phase toward an eventual forward defense on the Rhine and then on the GDR border. Austrian defense planners seemed to have operated with the tacit assumption that in the event of nuclear war NATO would cover Austria too in case of a Soviet attack.[30]

As a result of both unreasonable Soviet demands in State Treaty negotiations in 1950 (the unrelated Trieste issue and the Austrian "dried peas" debt from 1945) and an ice age in East-West relations as a result of the Korean War, Austrian State Treaty negotiations likewise entered an "ice age" of no progress. The Austrian political elites and public opinion were extremely frustrated over this lack of treaty progress and demanded an end to the occupation ("to be liberated from the liberators").[31] The US State Department launched the "abbreviated treaty" initiative in the winter of 1952 in order to signal to the Austrians that they had not been forgotten. In early March 1952 the "short treaty" draft was presented in a diplomatic note in Moscow. The Americans hoped that with a much shorter and simplified treaty draft the Soviets could be persuaded to sign. But given that the "short treaty" contained no provisions any more to compensate the Soviets for the "German assets" (including the vast oil industry assets) they had seized in 1945/1946, this treaty initiative was stillborn. The Soviets simply ignored the Western abbreviated treaty proposal, and the Eisenhower administration elected to office in the fall of 1952 quietly withdrew the short treaty draft in 1953 to jump-start Austrian treaty negotiations again.[32] The presentation of the Austrian short treaty draft was also overshadowed by Stalin's German initiative in March 1952 ("Stalin notes") that promised to unify and neutralize Germany. The Austrian question was still linked willy-nilly to the resolution of the larger post-war German issues.[33]

In the summer and fall of 1952 the United States experienced a very contentious presidential campaign. The Republican Party made a desperate effort to regain the White House after twenty years of presidents from the Democratic Party. The Republicans crowned the moderate Dwight D. Eisenhower as their standard bearer. Eisenhower had just returned from Europe, where he had served as NATO commander, turning NATO into an effective military alliance during his two-year tenure in Europe. In order to pacify the Republican stalwarts and anti-Communist hardliners, Eisenhower picked Richard Nixon as his running mate and John Foster Dulles as his foreign policy adviser and prospective Secretary of State. Nixon was supposed to act as the go-between with Senator Joseph McCarthy and get his anti-Communist crusade under control; McCarthy and his supporters in Congress were looking for communists inside the US government. Dulles also had a reputation as a tough ideological hardliner. During the 1952 campaign he announced a campaign to "roll back" communism and promised the "liberation of the captive peoples" in Eastern Europe. Eisenhower promised to end the war in Korea. Eisenhower was elected president in November 1952 and assumed control of the White House on January 20, 1953.[34]

EISENHOWER AND AUSTRIA

Eisenhower's assumption of the presidency almost coincided with the surprising death of Iosif Stalin in early March 1953. Early on in office he had to deal with the new Soviet leader, Georgii Malenkov, who announced the new Soviet foreign policy initiative of "peaceful coexistence." Was it typical Kremlin propaganda, or was it a serious policy departure to improve relations with the West? Eisenhower's staff was divided. Secretary of State J. F. Dulles strongly advocated not negotiating with the new Kremlin leaders. Eisenhower responded in mid-April with one of the most important speeches of his career before the Society of American Newspaper Editors. Eisenhower told the Kremlin that he expected "deeds not words." The Kremlin could prove its seriousness for better relations by signing the German and the Austrian peace treaties, by entering into an armistice and ending the Korean War, and by initiating nuclear disarmament. This was a tall order. Meanwhile, British Prime Minister Winston Churchill strongly advocated that the American President negotiate with Moscow. Churchill wanted to meet Malenkov and the new Kremlin leaders in a summit meeting to personally test their intentions toward "peaceful coexistence." Both the American leadership and the British Foreign Office opposed Churchill's plans for summitry since the Kremlin leaders first needed to demonstrate their will to ease tensions with the West.[35] On June 17, the Red Army intervened against an uprising of workers in the German Democratic Republic and squashed it with tanks. The Soviet wolves shed their sheep's clothing.

Domestically, Eisenhower also faced a tall order to meet the onslaught of the stalwarts in his own party. In spite of a Republican in the White House, Wisconsin Senator McCarthy continued his attacks against "communists in governmental institutions." The anti-communist crusader McCarthy suspected communists in the State Department, the CIA, and the Army. For weeks he held up in the Senate Foreign Relations Committee the confirmation of the distinguished Soviet expert Charles Bohlen as ambassador to the

Soviet Union (precisely during the weeks when an experienced hand would have been needed in Moscow to help the Eisenhower administration make sense of the Kremlin's "peaceful coexistence" initiative). McCarthy also opposed the confirmation of former Harvard President James B. Conant as Control Commissioner to Germany. In a gesture to the Republican hardliners, the Eisenhower administration continued with its rhetorical crusade of "rolling back" communism in the Soviet bloc and "liberating the captive peoples" of Eastern Europe. Dulles called for full independence for Eastern European nations no fewer than three times, charging that: "under the cloud of threatening war, it is humanity hanging from a cross of iron."[36]

Yet at the same time the Eisenhower administration was reviewing basic US national security strategy and its nuclear posture. In the summer of 1953, Eisenhower gathered the top national security experts to reconsider the basic American approach to dealing with the Soviet Union in the so-called "Solarium exercises." Should Truman's containment policy written down in the iconic document NSC 68 be continued, or should the United States embark on a more aggressive policy of rolling back communism? The experts pleaded for a continuation of containment and an end to all the dangerous talk about "rollback." "Rollback" threatened to provoke nuclear war. Yet the Joint Chiefs of Staff with their truculent chairman Admiral Arthur Radford kept pushing for "aggressive actions involving force against Soviet bloc territory." But Eisenhower personally ruled out any and all "preventive war" options. As two of the foremost experts on Eisenhower's national security strategy put it: "for Eisenhower preventive war of aggressive rollback would be a reckless and self-defeating gamble."[37]

The massive review process of basic national security strategy in the Eisenhower White House resulted in what would become known as his "new look" strategy, formalized in the basic National Security Council directive NSC 162/2. For one, to save on defense spending, Eisenhower wanted to reduce the conventional force structure and increase the nuclear arsenal. Nuclear weapons were cheaper than divisions in the field. Eisenhower wanted "more bang for the buck," and John Foster Dulles threatened "massive retaliation" in case of a Soviet attack. Eisenhower put it all down in the formula "in the event of hostilities, the United States will consider nuclear weapons to be available for use as other munitions." Such statements seemed to indicate that the threshold to using nuclear weapons had been reduced dramatically. In the Third World, where the Cold War was beginning to move after the massive wave of decolonization, the Eisenhower administration now put a premium on all forms of psychological warfare and cover operations. CIA covert operations pacified Iran (1953) and Guatemala (1954) after considerable turmoil in those countries sparked by leftish regimes.[38]

In October 1953, NSC 162/2 replaced NSC 68 as the basic American national security strategy. NSC 162/2 reflected the "Solarium exercises" by rejecting "rollback" of communism as a realistic strategy, now arguing "the detachment of any major satellite from the Soviet bloc does not now appear feasible except by Soviet acquiescence or by war."[39] In the fall of 1953 Eisenhower's basic policy toward Eastern Europe was refined in NSC 174. It ended Eisenhower's active "liberation" policy. The Eisenhower administration continued psychological warfare in order to undermine Soviet control of the Eastern European satellite regimes in the long run. It promised to "support the spirit of resistance" via ongoing propaganda initiatives. But, very significantly, it wanted to avoid the "incitement of premature revolts" in the Soviet bloc. Undermining the satellite regimes in the long run would promote "conditions favorable to eventual liberation."[40] While the Eisenhower administration's "new look" strategy was very cautious, his "rhetorical diplomacy" was very aggressive.[41]

While the Eisenhower administration was reinventing its basic national security strategy, it also conducted a basic review of its Austrian policy. First, it needed to shelf the unproductive "short treaty" draft, which had been a very unproductive "propaganda" instrument and had basically arrested the negotiations of the Deputies of the Foreign Ministers, which had been the most productive arena of Austrian treaty talks. Secondly, it needed to respond to Austrian initiatives that tried to restart treaty negotiations on new terms. The new government of Julius Raab had reacted positively to the Kremlin's "peaceful coexistence" initiative, which had produced an easing of the Soviet occupation regime in its Austrian zone. Long-time Austrian Foreign Minister Karl Gruber had begun to test the option of a neutral Austria via Indian intermediaries directly with the Kremlin. Soviet Foreign Minister Molotov was not (yet) ready to consider a neutralization of Austria in the summer of 1953. Washington and London viewed Gruber's unilateral moves not coordinated with the Western powers with great suspicion ("Gruberisms"). The new Austrian government threatening to embark on its own diplomacy to end the interminable four-power occupation of the country, sparked a review of American policies vis-à-vis Austria in the summer/fall of 1953.[42]

This review of Austrian polices culminated in NSC 164/4, adopted in October 1953; it paralleled the larger review of basic US national security policy NSC 162/2. NSC 162/2 stated: "there is no evidence that the Soviet leadership is prepared to modify its basic attitudes and accept any permanent settlement with the United States, although it may be prepared for a *modus vivendi on certain issues*" [my emphasis].[43] Might the Austrian question be such an issue? The debate in the National Security Council on adopting NSC 164/4 was vigorous. Admiral Radford, the uncompromising JCS chairman, opposed a neutralization of Austria; he feared severe repercussions on Germany and demanded that the United States "vigorously resist the neutralization of Austria as contrary to U.S. interests." Secretary of State J. F. Dulles, who was known to be a vigorous opponent of fence-sitting neutrality in the Cold War, turned out to be remarkably sensitive to the Austrian issue and noted "while we should of course oppose the neutralization of Austria just as far as possible in any negotiation, *the decision in the long run would depend on the Austrians themselves*" [emphasis mine]. He added "an embittered Austria would never prove a reliable ally of the U.S." And then Harold Stassen, Eisenhower's Special Assistant for Disarmament issues, added a brilliant insight that would produce an opening in the future: "to his mind the status of neutralization did not necessarily imply disarmament."[44] Was this an indication that he was thinking of the Swiss model of armed neutrality? We can only surmise, though we will never know.

The formula that the American national security managers found in the final document NSC 162/2 was a compromise. Along the lines of Radford's cautious remarks, Washington would "vigorously resist the neutralization of Austria as contrary to U.S. interests." However, along the lines of Dulles' thoughts, "should the Austrians, British, and French press strongly for accepting some degree of neutralization, the United States may be required to make some concession to avoid the onus of unilaterally blocking a Treaty."[45]

In the fall of 1953, the Deputies' talks on the Austrian treaty were not resumed even though the State Department officially withdrew the still-born short treaty draft. Representatives from the great powers' foreign offices, however, were working on an agenda for a future meeting of the Foreign Ministers. Churchill, who had been out of action all summer due to a stroke in June, kept pleading for a summit meeting. His Western allies agreed only to a Western Summit meeting in Bermuda late in 1953. Little progress was made in unmooring the deadlock of entering negotiations with the new leaders in the Kremlin on crucial issues such as Germany, Indochina, and nuclear disarmament. However, it was agreed that the Foreign Ministers' meetings would resume in Berlin in February 1954 with the German and Austrian treaties back at the forefront of the international agenda.[46]

While the Foreign Ministers made no progress on the German question, the neutralization of Austria was prominently discussed in Berlin, in the end without leading to a decisive breakthrough. Agreeing with Governor Stassen's observation in the National Security Council's debate over NSC 162/2, State Department position papers had stressed since October 1953: "that neutralization of a nation did not necessarily mean its disarmament." This view seems to have percolated over to the White House as well. Before the Secretary of State departed Washington for the Berlin Council of Foreign

Ministers, Eisenhower and Dulles discussed the Austrian question in a breakfast conference on January 20, 1954. The President was in agreement with the earlier State Department position on possible Austrian neutrality: "He [Eisenhower] could see *no objection to the neutralization of Austria if this did not carry with it the demilitarization*. If Austria could achieve a status somewhat *comparable to Switzerland*, this would be quite satisfactory from a military standpoint" [emphasis added].[47]

The Council of Foreign Ministers met in Berlin in early February 1954. Molotov remained non-concessionary on the German issues. A high-level government delegation led by Foreign Minister Figl was officially admitted to present the Austrian point of view. They strongly pleaded for a neutral solution to end the interminable Austrian occupation. Dulles agreed with the Austrian position and made a strong statement on February 13, 1954, on behalf of Austrian armed neutrality along the lines of the Swiss model:

> A neutral status is an honorable status if it is voluntarily chosen by a nation. Switzerland has chosen to be neutral, and as a neutral she has achieved an honorable place in the family of nations. *Under the Austrian State Treaty as heretofore drafted, Austria would be free to choose for itself to be a neutral state like Switzerland.* Certainly the United States would fully respect its choice in this respect, as it fully respects the comparable choice of the Swiss nation. However, it is one thing for a nation to choose to be neutral. It is another thing to have neutrality forcible imposed on it by the other nations as a perpetual servitude [emphasis added].[48]

Molotov, however, was not prepared to make a major concession on Austria and end the Austrian occupation. He continued to link the solution of the Austrian question with the conclusion of a German peace treaty. Dulles and the Austrian delegation left Berlin highly disappointed about another breakdown of Austrian treaty negotiations.[49]

For the rest of 1954 nothing happened to bring about an agreement on the Austrian question. The Western powers, however, moved decisively on the German question. After the French parliament rejected the ratification of the European Defense Community, British Foreign Minister Anthony Eden quickly organized a meeting in London to find another solution to West German rearmament. The "London Agreements" of October 1954 admitted the Federal Republic into the NATO alliance. West Germany's Adenauer government pledged not to build any ABC weapons. West German rearmament and integration into NATO constituted a major failure of Molotov's intransigent Stalinist foreign policy.

This decisive breakthrough of West German integration into the North Atlantic defense framework sparked dramatic changes in the Kremlin leadership. By early 1955, Malenkov had been demoted because he had not "distanced himself from Beriia,"[50] Molotov lost his almost iron grip on formulating Soviet foreign policy and executing Stalin's putative legacy, and Nikita Khrushchev emerged as the *primus inter pares* among Kremlin leaders. It was Khrushchev who ordered Molotov to break the linkage between the Austrian and German questions and show the Western powers goodwill to come to a resolution of the Austrian issues. After Molotov publically announced in late February that the Austrian question was no longer linked to the conclusion of a German peace treaty, dramatic movement on the Austrian treaty occurred in the next few weeks. In informal bilateral meetings in Vienna, Austrian officials heard from Soviet diplomats that armed neutrality along the lines of the Swiss model offered a viable solution to the Austrian question. Moscow invited an Austrian delegation to come to Moscow for a round of bilateral negotiations.[51]

Chancellor Raab led such a high-level Austrian delegation to Moscow in mid-April and returned with decisive Soviet concessions. The longstanding economic issues that had been unresolved since the fall of 1949, when the Austrian treaty had come close to an agreement in the New York Deputies' talks, were now resolved *bilaterally*. The Austrian government agreed to pay the Soviet Union directly the 150 million US dollars demanded by Moscow for the return of the "German assets" (including the valuable oil assets in the Soviet zone). The Austrian government would pay in kind (not in cash) over a number of years. The Soviet leaders also agreed with the Austrian delegation that Austria would declare its armed neutrality along the lines of the Swiss model after the withdrawal of occupation forces three months after the ratification of the Austrian treaty.[52]

During the spring of 1955, the Western powers were relegated to the sidelines to watch in utter amazement the quick progress of the bilateral Austrian–Soviet negotiations. The British Foreign Office was gravely worried about the bilateral diplomacy with Moscow. Geoffrey Harrison, the experienced Soviet expert who was in charge of Austrian affairs in London, observed with a biblical allusion: "the Austrians are rushing across the precipice like the Gadarene swine." Foreign Minister Eden, sensing Austrian eagerness to move ahead after Molotov unlinked the Austrian and the German question, expressed his worry: "I hope I won't wake up one morning and see Raab in Moscow." The State Department in Washington was more collected and demanded to be fully briefed by the Austrian government about Austria's bilateral negotiations with Moscow. As Dulles had observed earlier, the Austrians could not be stopped if they wanted a treaty for the price of neutrality. CIA Director Allen Dulles observed in the National Security Council discussions after the breakthrough in Moscow that the Soviet concessions on

Austria after all these years constituted "the most significant action since the end of World War II."⁵³

After the return of the Raab delegation from Moscow, diplomacy moved at breakneck speed to finish the Austrian State Treaty. The ambassadors of the four powers met in Austria with Foreign Minister Figl to put the final touches to the Austrian treaty draft. Among many other fine points negotiated by the ambassadors, the United States demanded in a secret agreement from the Austrian government that the Western oil corporations be compensated for the loss of their assets as a result of the Soviet return of the oil assets to the Austrian Government ("Vienna Memorandum"). The final details of the extensive Austrian State Treaty draft were agreed on only two days before the foreign ministers met in Vienna to sign the Austrian State Treaty on May 15, 1955. The conclusion of the Austrian State Treaty came amid dramatic changes in the international framework in Europe. A few days before the signatures were attached to the Austrian State Treaty, Dulles had visited Paris for the official ceremony incorporating the FRG into NATO. Molotov had signed the Warsaw Pact Treaty in the Polish capital a day before the conclusion of the Austrian treaty in Vienna. The tighter military integration of its sphere of influence in Eastern Europe, culminating in the conclusion of the Warsaw Pact, was Moscow's answer to West German rearmament. On the other hand, Moscow's concessionary mood could also be gathered from its withdrawal from a naval base in Finland and a marked improvement of relations with Tito's Yugoslavia. The final conclusion of the Austrian State Treaty thus needs to be seen against a larger backdrop of dramatic changes in Soviet domestic politics and its turn toward "peaceful coexistence" as well as both the further consolidation of military blocs in Europe and the fateful steps toward the post-war division of Germany.⁵⁴

As soon as the signatures of the foreign ministers dried on the Austrian State Treaty on May 15, the Austrian Foreign Office began its whirlwind of diplomacy to get the treaty ratified by the great powers and the rest of the world. Once the ratification process was complete on July 26, the three-month clock began to tick toward the withdrawal of occupation forces. Once the occupation powers had withdrawn their troops, the Austrian parliament passed a constitutional law proclaiming Austria's permanent neutrality to the world on October 26, 1955. Austria thus consummated its agreement with Moscow to enter a state of neutrality in accordance with the Swiss model once the Austrian treaty was concluded and the occupation powers evacuated the country. The neutralization of Austria was also the Soviet "deed" that finally broke a diplomatic logjam of sorts in East-West relations. After two years of procrastination, the Western leaders final met the Kremlin bosses to test their seriousness over promoting "peaceful coexistence" in a summit meeting in Geneva in July 1955.⁵⁵

CONCLUSION

The United States, however, was a crucial midwife in the final rounds of Austrian treaty negotiations. Presidents Truman and Eisenhower and their representatives in Austria had played a decisive role in putting Austria on a trajectory of economic recovery and growth with their massive pre-Marshall Plan and ERP economic aid. Austria's incipient "economic miracle" by 1955 gave the Raab government the wherewithal to enter bilateral agreements with the Soviet Union to pay for the return of the "German assets." In addition, US support for Austria's secret rearmament since 1951 and the transfer of American military hardware after 1955 allowed Austria to quickly start its army in 1956. The "core" of the future Austrian Army built with American support before the conclusion of the State Treaty in 1955 pacified the Pentagon sufficiently for it to reluctantly agree to an Austrian treaty. This "core" allowed the Austrians to quickly build a credible armed force to follow the Swiss model of armed neutrality.

NOTES

1. William Lloyd Stearman, *The Soviet Union and the Occupation of Austria: An Analysis of Soviet Policy in Austria, 1945–1955* (Vienna: Siegler, 1962); William B. Bader's Stanford Ph.D. Diss., "Austria between East and West, 1945–1955," Stanford, 1966, was published in Austria almost forty years later in a German translation but without updating the theses and literature, see, *Österreich im Spannungsfeld zwischen Ost und West 1945 bis 1955* (Vienna: Braumüller, 2002).

2. Gerald Stourzh's "kleine Staatsvertragsgeschichte" was first published in 1975 and is now in its fifth edition, much expanded; see *Um Einheit und Freiheit. Staatsvertrag, Neutralität und das Ende der Ost-West-Besetzung Österreichs 1945–1955* (Vienna: Böhlau, 1998 and 2005 [with a new bibliographic essay]); see also the "Historiography Roundtable" on it in Günter Bischof, Anton Pelinka and Ruth Wodak, eds., *Neutrality in Austria*, Vol. 9 of Contemporary Austrian Studies (New Brunswick/London: Transaction Publications, 2001), pp. 236–292; and Manfried Rauchensteiner, *Der Sonderfall. Die Besatzungszeit in Österreich* (Graz/Vienna: Verlag Styria, 1979), reprinted in 1995 and republished in 2005 with only minor revisions and barely any engagement of the literature written in the previous thirty years as *Stalinplatz 4. Österreich unter Alliierter Besatzung*.

3. Oliver Rathkolb, "Politische Propaganda der amerikanischen Besatzungsmacht in Österreich 1945 bis 1950. Ein Beitrag zur Geschichte des Kalten Krieges in der Presse-, Kultur- und Rundfunkpolitik," Ph.D. Diss., Vienna, 1981; Josef Leidenfrost, "Die amerikanische Besatzungsmacht und der Wiederbeginn des Politischen Lebens in Österreich, 1944–1947," Ph.D. Diss., Vienna, 1984; Alfons Schilcher, "Die Politik der Provisorischen Regierung und der Alliierten Grossmächte bei der Wiedererich-

tung der Republik Österreich," Ph.D. Diss., Vienna, 1985; Günter Bischof, "Between Responsibility and Rehabilitation Austria in International Politics 1940–1950," Ph.D. Diss., Harvard, 1989; Ralph W. Brown, III, "A Cold War Army of Occupation? The U.S. Army in Vienna, 1945–1948," Ph.D. Diss., Tennessee, 1995. This cohort is maybe best represented by Günter Bischof and Josef Leidenfrost, eds., *Die Bevormundete Nation. Östereich und die Alliierten*, Vol. 4 of Innsbrucker Forschungen zur Zeitgeschichte (Innsbruck: Haymon-Verlag, 1988).

4. Much valuable research appeared in conference volumes and collections of essays, see Anton Pelinka and Rolf Steininger, eds., *Österreich und die Sieger* (Vienna: Braumüller, 1986); Wolfgang Kos and Georg Rigele, eds., *Inventur 45/55. Österreich im ersten Jahrzehnt der Zweiten Republik* (Vienna: Sonderzahl, 1996); Alfred Ableitinger, Siegfried Beer and Eduard G. Staudinger, eds., *Österreich unter alliierter Besatzung 1945–1955*, Vol. 63 of Studien zu Politik und Verwaltung (Vienna: Böhlau, 1998); Erwin A. Schmidl, ed., *Östereich im frühen Kalten Krieg 1945–1958. Spione, Partisanen, Kriegspläne* (Vienna: Böhlau, 2000); Stefan Karner, Erich Reiter and Gerald Schöpfer, eds., *Kalter Krieg. Beiträge zur Ost-West-Konfrontation 1945 bis 1990* (Graz: Leykam, 2002); Robert A. Bauer, ed., *The Austrian Solution: International Conflict and Cooperation* (Charlottesville: University Press of Virginia, 1982).

5. Reinhold Wagnleitner, *Coca-Colonisation und Kalter Krieg. Die Kulturmission der USA in Österreich nach dem Zweiten Weltkrieg* (Vienna: Verlag für Gesellschaftskritik, 1991); Audrey Kurth Cronin, *Great Power Politics and the Struggle over Austria, 1945–1955* (Ithaca/London: Cornell University Press, 1986); Oliver Rathkolb, *Washington ruft Wien. US-Großmachtpolitik und Österreich 1953–1963* (Vienna/Cologne/Weimar: Böhlau, 1997); Günter Bischof, *Austria in the First Cold War, 1945–1955: The Leverage of the Weak*, Cold War History Series (Houndmills/New York: Macmillan, 1999); James Jay Carafano, *Waltzing into the Cold War: The Struggle for Occupied Austria* (College Station: Texas A & M University Press, 2002); Jill Lewis, *Workers and Politics in Occupied Austria, 1945–1955* (Manchester: Manchester University Press, 2007).

6. Kurt Tweraser, *US-Militärregierung Oberösterreich, Vol. 1: Sicherheitspolitische Aspekte der amerikanischen Besatzung in Oberösterreich-Süd 1945–1950* (Linz: Oberösterreichisches Landesarchiv, 1995); idem, *US-Militärregierung Oberösterreich 1945–1950, Vol. 2: Amerikanische Industriepolitk in Oberösterreich am Beispiel VOEST und Steyr-Daimler-Puch* (Linz: Oberösterreichisches Landesarchiv, 2008). Siegried Beer noticed years ago that a similar study is still extant for the American zone in Salzburg: see "Die US-Besatzungspolitik in Österreich bis Herbst 1945," in Manfried Rauchensteiner and Wolfgang Etschmann, eds., *Österreich 1945. Ein Ende und viele Anfänge*, Vol. 4 of Forschungen zur Militärgeschichte (Graz/Vienna/Cologne: Styria, 1997), pp. 207–228, here p. 208.

7. Arnold Suppan, Gerald Stourzh and Wolfgang Mueller, eds., *Der Östereichische Staatsvertrag. Internationale Strategie, rechtliche Relevanz, nationale Identität*, Vol. 140 of Archiv für österreichische Geschichte (Vienna: Böhlau, 2005).

8. Rolf Steininger, *Der Staatvertrag: Österreich im Schatten von deutscher Frage und Kaltem Krieg 1938–1955* (Innsbruck: Studienverlag, 2005), now translated into English but with a much broader title that is misleading; see *Austria, Germany,*

and the Cold War: From the Anschluss to the State Treaty 1938–1955 (New York: Berghahn, 2008).

9. Hans Seidel, *Österreichs Wirtschaft und Wirtschaftspolitik nach dem Zweiten Weltkrieg* (Vienna: Manz'sche Verlags- und Universitätsbuchhandlung, 2005).

10. Manfried Rauchensteiner, ed., *Zwischen den Blöcken: NATO und Warschauer Pakt und Österreich* (Vienna: Böhlau, 2010).

11. Stefan Karner and Barbara Stelzl-Marx, eds., *Die Rote Armee in Österreich*, 2 vols (Graz/Vienna/Munich: Oldenbourg, 2005); Wolfgang Mueller, *Die sowjetische Besatzung in Österreich 1945–1955 und ihre politische Mission* (Vienna: Böhlau, 2005); Stefan Karner and Othmar Pickl, eds., with assistance from Walter M. Iber, Harald Knoll, Hermine Prügger, Peter Ruggenthaler, Arno Wonisch and Silke Stern, *Die Rote Armee in der Steiermark: Sowjetische Besatzung 1945* (Graz: Leykan, 2008); Wolfgang Mueller, Arnold Suppan, Norman M. Naimark and Gennadij Bordjugov, eds., *Sowjetische Politik in Österreich 1945–1955. Dokumente aus russischen Archiven*, Vol. 93 of Fontes Rerum Austriacarum. Zweite Abt. Diplomararia et Acta (Vienna: Verlag der Österreichischen Akademie der Wissenschaften, 2005).

12. Basic works on American post-war planning are Gerhard L. Weinberg, "Franklin D. Roosevelt," in idem, *Visions of Victory: The Hopes of Eight World War II Leaders* (Cambridge: Cambridge University Press, 2005), pp. 175–210, and Patrick J. Hearden, *Architects of Globalism: Building a New World Order during World War II* (Fayetteville, AR: University of Arkansas Press, 2002); basic works on American planning for post-war Austria are Robert H. Keyserlingk, *Austria in World War II: An Anglo-American Dilemma* (Kingston/Montreal: McGill-Queen's University Press, 1988); see also Leidenfrost, "Amerikanische Besatzungsmacht," pp. 1–147; Bischof, "Responsibility and Rehabilitation," pp. 14–25; idem, "Anglo-amerikanische Planungen und Überlegungen der österreichischen Emigration während des Zweiten Weltkrieges für Nachkriegs-Österreich," in Rauchensteiner, ed., *Österreich 1945*, pp. 15–29.

13. Günter Bischof, "'Opfer' Österreich?: Zur moralischen Ökonomie des österreichischen historischen Gedächtnisses," in Dieter Stiefel, ed., *Die Politische Ökonomie des Holocaust: Zur wirtschaftlichen Logik von Verfolgung und 'Wiedergutmachung'* (Vienna: Verlag für Geschichte und Politik, 2001), pp. 305–335.

14. Keyserlingk, *Austria in World War II*, pp. 123–157 and 205–208; Stourzh, *Einheit und Freiheit*, pp. 11–28; Günter Bischof, "Die Instrumentalisierung der Moskauer Deklaration nach dem Zweiten Weltkrieg," in *Zeitgeschichte*, Vol. 20 (1993), pp. 345–366; Stefan Karner and Alexander O. Tschubarijan, eds., *Die Moskauer Deklaration 1943: "Österreich wieder herstellen."* Vienna: Böhlau, 2015.

15. Cited in Bischof, *Austria in the First Cold War*, p. 46.

16. On Truman see Arnold A. Offner, *Another Such Victory: President Truman and the Cold War 1945–1953* (Stanford, CA: Stanford University Press, 2002); Wilson D. Miscamble, *From Roosevelt to Truman: Potsdam, Hiroshima, and the Cold War* (Cambridge: Cambridge University Press, 2002).

17. Bischof, *Austria in the First Cold War*, pp. 43–51; Leidenfrost, "Amerikanische Besatzungsmacht," pp. 148–203.

18. Bischof, "Responsibility and Rehabilitation," pp. 149–291.

19. Bischof, "Responsibility and Rehabilitation," pp. 292–360; Leidenfrost, "Amerikanische Besatzungsmacht," pp. 563–720; Cronin, *Great Power Politics*, pp. 50–52.

20. Bischof, "Responsibility and Rehabilitation," pp. 536–588; Stourzh, *Einheit und Freiheit*, pp. 34–66.

21. Stourzh, *Einheit und Freiheit*, pp. 67–103; Bischof, "Responsibility and Rehabilitation," pp. 589–622.

22. Stourzh, *Einheit und Freiheit*, pp. 113–121.

23. Seidel, *Österreichs Wirtschaft*, pp. 281–342; Günter Bischof, Anton Pelinka and Dieter Stiefel, eds., *The Marshall Plan in Austria*, Vol. 8 of Contemporary Austrian Studies (New Brunswick, NJ: Transaction Publications, 2000); Günter Bischof and Hans Petschar, *The Marshall Plan—Since 1947: Saving Europe—Rebuilding Austria*. Vienna: Brandstätter 2017; Günter Bischof and Dieter Stiefel, eds., and Hannes Richter, digital ed., *Images of the Marshall Plan: Film, Photographs, Exhibits, Posters* (Innsbruck: Studienverlag, 2009); Manfried Rauchensteiner, *Die Zwei. Die Große Koalition in Österreich 1945–1966* (Vienna: Österreichischer Bundesverlag, 1987), pp. 68–88; Franz Nemschak, *Zehn Jahre österreichische Wirtschaft 1945–1955* (Vienna: Österreichisches Institut für Wirtschaftsforschung, 1955); for Germany see also Charles S. Maier with Günter Bischof, eds., *The Marshall Plan and Germany: West German Development within the Framework of the European Recovery Program* (Oxford: Berg, 1991).

24. Vojtech Mastny, "Stalin and the Militarization of the Cold War," in *International Security*, Vol. 9 (1984–85), pp. 109–129; Thomas J. McCormick, *America's Half Century: United States Foreign Policy in the Cold War* (Baltimore: The Johns Hopkins University Press, 1989), pp. 92–108.

25. Ernest R. May, ed., *American Cold War Strategy: Interpreting NSC 68* (Boston, MA: St. Martin's Press, 1993); Bruno Thoss, "Österreich in der Entstehungs—und Konsolidierungsphase des westlichen Bündnissystems (1947–1967)," in Rauchensteiner, ed., *Zwischen den Blöcken*, pp. 19–88, here p. 50.

26. Günter Bischof, "'Prag liegt westlich von Wien'. Internationale Krisen im Jahre 1948 und ihr Einfluss auf Österreich," in Bischof and Leidenfrost, eds., *Bevormundete Nation*, pp. 315–346; Stourzh, *Einheit und Freiheit*, pp. 121–143.

27. Audrey Kurth Cronin avers a *"second attempted Communist Putsch,"* following the old "traditionalist" line of Stearman and Bader, see her *Great Power Politics*, pp. 108–111; see also Thomas St. John Arnold, *Austria and the United States Forces* (Manhattan, KS: Sunflower University Press, 2001), pp. 85–90. Revisionist historiography, based on a much broader source base than seen by the "traditionalists" speaks of a "strike," see Michael Ludwig, Klaus Dieter Mulley and Robert Streibel, *Der Oktoberstreik 1950. Ein Wendepunkt der Zweiten Republik* (Vienna: Picus, 1991); see also Günter Bischof, "Austria looks to the West. Kommunistische Putschgefahr, geheime Wiederbewaffnung und Westorientierung am Anfang der fünfziger Jahre," in Thomas Albrich, Klaus Eisterer, Michael Gehler and Rolf Steininger eds., *Österreich in den Fünfzigern*. Vol. 11 of Innsbrucker Forschungen zur Zeitgeschichte (Innsbruck: Studienverlag 1995), pp. 183–196.

28. Günter Bischof, "Österreich – ein 'geheimer Verbündeter' des Westens?," in Michael Gehler and Rolf Steininger eds., *Österreich und die europäische Integration 1945–1993* (Vienna: Böhlau, 1993), pp. 425–450, here pp. 441–442.

29. On the "secret ally" thesis, see Gerald Stourzh, "The Origins of Austrian Neutrality," in Alan T. Leonhard, ed., *Neutrality. Changing Concepts and Practises* (Lanham: University Press of America, 1988), pp. 35–57, here pp. 39–40; idem, *Einheit und Freiheit*, pp. 192–220. Austria's "secret rearmament" in the early 1950s has garnered considerable attention in the 1990s, see Christian Stifter, *Die Wiederaufrüstung Österreichs. Die geheime Remilitarisierung der westlichen Besatzungszonen 1945–1955* (Innsbruck/Vienna: Studienverlag, 1997); Bischof, "Austria looks to the West"; idem, "Österreich – ein 'geheimer Verbündeter' des Westens?"; idem, *Austria in the First Cold War*, pp. 111–122; Rathkolb, *Washington ruft Wien*, pp. 144–152; this secret remilitarization of Western Austria is well covered in Carafano, *Waltzing*, pp. 134–192; Bruno W. Koppensteiner, "Béthouarts Alpenfestung. Militärische Planungen und Verteidigungsvorbereitungen der französischen Besatzungsmacht in Tirol und Vorarlberg," in Schmidl, ed., *Österreich im Frühen Kalten Krieg*, pp. 193–238; Walter Blasi, *Die B-Gendarmerie 1952–1955* (Vienna: Bundesministeruim für Landesverteidigung: Landesverteidigungsakademie Wien, 2002); now also in a number of essays in Rauchensteiner, ed., *Zwischen den Blöcken*.

30. Thoss in Rauchensteiner, ed., *Zwischen den Blöcken*, pp. 41–73.

31. Stourzh, *Einheit und Freiheit*, pp. 173–184.

32. Günter Bischof, "'Recapturing the Initiative' and 'Negotiating from Strength': The Hidden Agenda of the Short Treaty Episode," in Suppan et al., eds., *Staatsvertrag*, pp. 217–248.

33. Peter Ruggenthaler, *Stalin's grosser Bluff: Die Geschichte der Stalin-Note in Dokumenten dersowjetischen Führung* (Munich: Oldenbourg, 2007); the linkage of the Austrian and the German questions is also stressed by Steininger, *Austria, Germany, and the Cold War*, pp. 95–109; for a broader comparison of the Austrian and German occupations, see Günter Bischof and Hans Jürgen Schröder, "'Nation Building' in vergleichender Perspektive: Die USA als Besatzungsmacht in Österreich und Westdeutschland 1945–1955," in Michael Gehler and Ingrid Böhler, eds., *Verschiedene europäische Wege im Vergleich. Österreich und die Bundesrepublik Deutschland 1945/49 bis zur Gegenwart. Festschrift für Rolf Steininger zum 65. Geburtstag* (Innsbruck: Studienverlag, 2007), pp. 155–176.

34. Günter Bischof, "The Politics of Anti-Communism in the Executive Branch during the Early Cold War: Truman, Eisenhower and McCarthy(ism)," in André Kaenel, ed., *Anti-Communism and McCarthyism in the United States, 1945–1954: Essays in the Culture and Politics of the Cold War* (Paris: Editions Messene, 1995), pp. 53–77.

35. Günter Bischof, "Eisenhower, the Summit, and the Austrian Treaty, 1953–1955," in Günter Bischof and Stephen E. Ambrose, eds., *Eisenhower. A Centenary Assessment* (Baton Rouge: Louisiana State University Press, 1995), pp. 131–161; idem, "Österreichische Neutralität, die deutsche Frage und europäische Sicherheit 1953–1955," in Günter Bischof, Rolf Steininger et al., eds., *Die doppelte Eindämmung. Europäische Sicherheit und Deutsche Frage in den Fünfzigern* (Munich: v.

Hase & Koehler, 1993), pp. 133–176, idem, "The Robust Assertion of Austrianism: Peaceful Coexistence in Austria after Stalin's Death," in Klaus Larres and Kenneth Osgood, eds., *The Cold War after Stalin's Death: A Missed Opportunity for Peace?*, The Harvard Cold War Studies Book Series, ed. Mark Kramer (Lanham: Harvard University Press, 2006), pp. 233–256; on global diplomacy after Stalin's death see the exhaustive Klaus Larres, *Churchill's Cold War: The Politics of Personal Diplomacy* (New Haven/London: Yale University Press, 2002), pp. 189–317; see also Saki Dockrill, *Eisenhower's New Look National Security Policy, 1953–61* (Basingstoke: Macmillan, 1996).

36. László Borhi, *Hungary in the Cold War 1945–1956: Between the United States and the Soviet Union 1945–1956* (Budapest/New York: Central European University Press, 2004), pp. 269–324; idem, "Containment, Rollback, Liberation or Inaction? The United States and Hungary in the 1950s," *Journal of Cold War Studies*, Vol. 1 (1999), No. 3, pp. 67–108, as well as Günter Bischof, "Eindämmung und Koexistenz oder "Rollback" und Befreiung? Die Vereinigten Staaten, das Sowjetimperium und die Ungarnkrise im Kalten Krieg, 1948–1956," in Erwin A. Schmidl, ed., *Die Ungarnkrise 1956 und Österreich* (Vienna/Cologne/Weimar: Böhlau, 2003), pp. 101–146; Bernd Stöver, *Die Befreiung vom Kommunismus. Amerikanische Liberation Policy im Kalten Kriegs 1947–1991* (Cologne/Weimar/Vienna: Böhlau, 2002).

37. Robert Bowie and Richard Immerman, *Waging Peace: How Eisenhower Shaped an Enduring Cold War Strategy* (New York: Oxford University Press, 1998), p. 165.

38. Ibid.; see also John Lewis Gaddis, *Strategies of Containment: A Critical Appraisal of American National Security Policy* (New York: Oxford University Press, 1982), pp. 150–162.

39. Christian Ostermann, "Das Ende der 'Rollback'-Politik: Eisenhower, die amerikanische Osteuropapolitik und der Ungarn-Aufstand von 1956," in Winfried Heinemann and Norbert Wiggershaus, eds., *Das Internationale Krisenjahr 1956: Polen, Ungarn, Suez*, Vol. 48 of Beiträge zur Militärgeschichte (Munich: Oldenbourg, 1999), pp. 515–532, here p. 520; see also Gaddis, *Strategies of Containment*, pp. 155–156.

40. NSC 174 is reprinted in Czaba Békés, Malcolm Byrne and János M. Rainer, eds., *The 1956 Hungarian Revolution: A History in Documents*, National Security Archives Cold War Readers (Budapest: Central European University Press, 2002), pp. 34–53.

41. Chris Tudda, *The Truth Is Our Weapon: The Rhetorical Diplomacy of Dwight D. Eisenhower and John Foster Dulles* (Baton Rouge: Louisiana State University Press, 2006).

42. Stourzh, *Einheit und Freiheit*, pp. 220–283; Bischof, *Austria in the First Cold War*, pp. 133–135; see also idem, "A Soviet 'New Look' on the Danube and the Emacipation of Austrian Foreign Policy in 1953. Peaceful Coexistence in Austria after Stalin's Death," in Siegfried Beer et al., eds., *Focus Austria. Vom Vielvölkerreich zum EU-Staat. Festschrift für Alfred Ableitinger* (Graz: Selbstverlag des Instituts für Geschichte der Karl-Franzens-Universität Graz, 2003), pp. 441–466.

43. NSC 162/2. "Basic National Security Policy," October 10, 1953, in *Foreign Relations of the United States* [hereafter *FRUS*], *1952–1954, Vol. II/1* (Washington, DC: United States Government Printing Office, 1984), pp. 577–596, here p. 593; see also Bowie and Immerman, *Waging Peace*.

44. NSC 164/4, "U.S. Objectives with Respect to Austria," October 14, 1953, and 166th NSC Meeting, October 13, 1953, in *FRUS, 1952–1954, II/2* (Washington, DC: United States Government Printing Office, 1986), pp. 1909–1922, here pp. 1912 and 1918; see also Günter Bischof, "Der Nationale Sicherheitsrat und die amerikanische Österreichpolitik im frühen Kalten Krieg," in Ableitinger, Beer, and Staudinger, eds., *Östereich unter allierter Besatzung*, pp. 106–111; Rathkolb, *Washington Ruft Wien*, pp. 23–30.

45. *FRUS, 1952–1954, II/2*, pp. 1919–1920; Bischof, *Austria in the First Cold War*, pp. 137–139.

46. Bischof, *Austria in the First Cold War*, pp. 137–139.

47. Memorandum of Breakfast Conference with the President, January 20, 1954, folder "Meetings with the President 1954 (2)," box 1, Memoranda Series, John Foster Dulles Papers, Seely G. Mudd Library, Princeton University.

48. Dulles statements on February 12 and 13, 1954, *FRUS, 1952–1954, VII/1*, pp. 1061–1065 and 1088–1089.

49. Stourzh, *Einheit und Freiheit*, pp. 301–334; Bischof, *Austria in the First Cold War*, pp. 138–139; Larres, *Churchill's Cold War*, pp. 341–355.

50. See the contribution by Mikhail Prozumenshchikov in this volume.

51. Stourzh, *Einheit und Freiheit*, pp. 335–400; Bischof, *Austria in the First Cold War*, pp. 142–147; Rolf Steininger, "1955. The Austrian Treaty and the German Question," in *Diplomacy & Statecraft*, Vol. 3 (1992), pp. 211–225; idem, *Austria, Germany and the Cold War*, pp. 197 and 110–120.

52. Stourzh, *Einheit und Freiheit*, pp. 400–485; Steininger, *Austria, Germany, and the Cold War*, pp. 126–129; on the eventual costs of the treaty, see Seidel, *Österreichs Wirtschaft*, pp. 458–479.

53. Seidel, *Österreichs Wirtschaft*, pp. 120–125; Bischof, *Austria in the First Cold War*, pp. 144–146; Allen Dulles in 245th NSC-Session, Box 6, NSC-Series, Ann Whitman Files, Dwight D. Eisenhower Library, Abilene, Kansas.

54. Seidel, *Österreichs Wirtschaft*, pp. 130–135.

55. Günter Bischof, "The Making of the Austrian Treaty and the Road to Geneva," in idem, and Saki Dockrill, *Cold War Respite: The Geneva Summit of 195?* (Baton Rouge, LA: Louisiana State University Press, 2000), pp. 117–154.

Part II

SOVIET DIPLOMACY TOWARD AUSTRIA

Chapter Two

Soviet Plans for Rebuilding Austria from 1941 to 1945

Aleksei Filitov

The attitude of the Soviet leadership to the post-war status of Austria was already defined and even written out in full at the earliest stage of the Second World War, at the climax of the Battle for Moscow. As a concrete date, November 21, 1941, can be named. It should be made clear, however, that it was not an official declaration but a top-secret telegram which the People's Commissar for Foreign Affairs, Vyacheslav Molotov, sent on this day to the delegated Soviet representative in London, Ivan Maiskii. In all likelihood, Maiskii was somewhat bemused as to the choice of words used by Iosif Stalin in a speech on November 6, 1941, for Stalin expressed the following: "As long as the Hitler people were busy with collecting German lands and the reunification of the Rhineland, Austria, etc., one could characterise them with a certain justification as nationalists."[1] With reference to a request made by the British communists, the USSR's political delegate in London sent a telegram on November 14 with a request to People's Commissar Molotov for an elaboration of Stalin's statement, which had indeed raised a number of questions.

The occupation of the left bank of the Rhine by Entente troops, in accordance with the Versailles Treaty, drew to a close at the time of the Weimar Republic and the operation carried out in 1936 by Hitler did not constitute a "reunification" but a remilitarization of the Rhineland—two terms which can in no way be equated with one another. Just as difficult to interpret was the attempt by Stalin to equate the Rhineland with Austria, which had at no point in history prior to the Anschluss been part of Germany. From the formulation selected by Stalin, one could thus deduce a renunciation of the early assessment of the Anschluss as a manifestation of the aggressive and predatory policies of National Socialist Germany.

Molotov's telegram response of November 21, mentioned above, ran as follows:

In relation to your enquiry, I can inform you that the passage in question in Stalin's speech on Austria was commented on by Comrade Stalin in the following manner: The annexation to Germany of an Austria inhabited by a majority of Germans can be viewed in the framework of German nationalism, but this in no way means that Comrade Stalin is trying to justify this annexation, for Comrade Stalin does not regard German nationalism as a justifiable and acceptable concept. At this point, Stalin wanted to say that even from the point of view of German nationalism, the current policy of expansion on the part of the Nazi leadership [literally: "Hitler people"] is to be regarded as disastrous for Germany and that the NSDAP is a coarse [and] imperialist and not a nationalist party. Stalin wanted thereby to cause confusion in the ranks of the Nazi leadership and drive a wedge between Hitler's government and the nationalist strata of the German nation. Regarding the attitude of Comrade Stalin toward Austria, the Rhineland etc., Stalin is of the opinion that Austria is to be separated from Germany in the form of an independent state and that Germany itself, including Prussia, must be broken up into a series of more or less autonomous states in order to be able to safeguard a peaceful future existence for the states of Europe.[2]

How can one assess this dialogue between the People's Commissar and the Ambassador, in which the "Soviet leader" indirectly participated in the form of a third person or a higher authority? Just saying that a statement made by Stalin was not entirely clear and necessitated an explanation required under the conditions prevailing at that time a considerable measure of fearlessness and moral courage on the part of the person voicing the request—in official form at that—for an explanation. Every statement made by the "Soviet leader" was to be regarded as a truth from the highest authority, and any scepticism as to the wisdom and perfection of the statement, regardless of how it was expressed, could have the most serious consequences. It is correct that Maiskii did not raise the question of his own accord but rather at the request of the British Communist Party, but in this form his telegram could be construed as a manifestation of independent thought, which at that time was not approved of in any form whatsoever.

No less unusual were the reactions of Molotov and Stalin himself, whom the People's Commissar for Foreign Affairs had approached with the request for explanation, as emerges from the text of the telegram from November 24. This was not followed by a brusque rebuke but by an attempt to provide a detailed and to-the-point response to a question that was in no way straightforward. Molotov's (or rather Molotov's and Stalin's) answer testifies to a certain discrepancy between pragmatic and propagandistic components in Soviet policy. Dogmatic teachings and the objectives actually pursued by Soviet policies constituted in the eyes of the Soviet leadership completely different categories, which did not necessitate any conformity or adjustment. It was evidently believed that such a correlation between these two components could ensure a political flexibility and efficiency. The accuracy of such an approach is more than questionable. In the concrete case at hand, one could argue that the reference to German nationalism at the time of the Second World War did not have any noticeable results. If the aim was "confusion," then this was at most caused among the opponents of National Socialism.

But now for the most decisive factor in the context of the issue being addressed: The aforementioned telegram from Molotov to Maiskii undeniably demonstrates that the separate treatment of the "German" and the "Austrian" questions and the particular emphasis placed on an Austrian identity (as defined at the beginning of the operation of the radio station "Freies Österreich" on November 19, 1941)[3] was not merely hollow propagandistic rhetoric designed to weaken the enemy but that the reestablishment of the Austrian state, its independent existence in the post-war world, constituted a declared aim of the Soviet leadership from the earliest phase of the Second World War, despite propagandistic shifts.

This factor deserves all the more attention if one keeps in mind that within the leadership circles of the other states in the anti-Hitler coalition and among Austrian émigrés for a long time no such clear concept for the future of Austria had existed. During a discussion with Maiskii on November 27, 1941, the British Prime Minister, Winston Churchill, made no differentiation between the status of Bavaria, Austria, and Wurttemberg when determining the future framework of peace, according to Maiskii.[4] Against the backdrop of the Anglo-American talks in March 1943, the Soviet Ambassador in the United States, Maksim Litvinov, submitted a report to Moscow on the different ideas on the future of Austria proposed during these negotiations. The ideas ranged from the reestablishment of Austrian statehood via "unification with Czechoslovakia"[5] to a restoration of the Habsburg monarchy. Litvinov painted a particularly ambivalent picture of the position of the United States. If, according to the words of the British Foreign Minister, Anthony Eden, "the President ([Franklin D.] Roosevelt) and [Cordell] Hull (US Secretary of State) [. . .] [had] shown no interest in a resurrection of the Habsburg monarchy," the Soviet Ambassador had received entirely contradictory information from his Italian dialogue partner, Carlo Graf Sforza: "The flirting of the USA with Otto Habsburg has its origins in the White House, and [. . .] the President is under the influence of different monarchist circles residing in the USA and in Italy."[6]

A letter written by Litvinov, who had just returned from the United States, on the eve of the Moscow Conference of Foreign Ministers of the three victorious powers, contained a similar analysis of the plans for Austria with balanced arguments for the resurrection of an independent Austria. Litvinov stated that plans were circulating in the West for the establishment of various federations—an Austrian-Hungarian federation (a variation which, according to Litvinov, was brought into play by Eden), a southern German one, a central European one, and an eastern European one. Among Austrian émigrés, there were "persons who are prepared to leave Austria in a democratic Germany," while alongside them also advocates of a "federal solution" (in this context, the "former Austrian envoy to London, Kunz" was named). As Litvinov pointed out, "the opponents of an independent Austrian state [would] invoke above all the inability of such a state to survive. But at least Austria existed for 20 years as an independent state and its population hardly lived under worse conditions or greater hardship than the populations of Austria's neighbours, the Balkan states."

Litvinov brings an additional argument against the Austro-sceptics into play: in the war years, the economic potential of Austria grew sharply; oil production reached 0.5 million tons and steel production was doubled following the launch of the "Hermann Göring Works."

In concluding the Austria-related part of his letter, Litvinov even suggests that the possibility of an expansion of the territory of a future Austrian state be considered: "Austria can make a justifiable claim for the incorporation of a small part of German territory, the districts of Passau and Berchtesgaden. One might also return South Tyrol, which was taken by Italy, to Austria, though that is connected with the question of the treatment of Italy."[7]

The last named idea was admittedly not implemented, but Litvinov's remarks otherwise reflected the basic stance of the three powers and the resurrection of an independent Austria was defined as one of the aims of the anti-Hitler coalition in the "Declaration on Austria" agreed on November 1, 1943, at the Moscow Conference. This aim was ultimately realized.

The question of fixing the occupation zones in Austria deserves particular attention. This was discussed in the "European Advisory Commission" (EAC), whereby the position of the Soviet Union in this three-power organ had been formulated within the People's Commissariat for Foreign Affairs of the USSR on the basis of the recommendation of the "Commission for Cease-fire Matters," established in accordance with the resolution of the Politburo of the Central Committee of the Communist Party from September 4, 1943. Marshal Kliment Voroshilov was appointed head of the Commission, for which reason it was for the most part dubbed the "Voroshilov Commission."

In a first variation of a draft of the summary "Conditions of Surrender for Germany" from February 4, 1944, the demarcation line "between the armed forces of the USSR on the one hand and the armed forces of the United Kingdom and the USA on the other hand" was fixed as follows (Article 16):

> From Heiligenhafen (not Soviet) along the western coast of the Bay of Mecklenburg to the city of Lübeck (not Soviet), further along the western border

of Mecklenburg as far as the River Elbe and further upstream as far as the administrative border of the Prussian province of the Altmark, then further to the western border of Anhalt, further along the western administrative border of the Prussian province of Saxony and Thuringia as far as the intersection of their border with the Bavarian [border] and further in an easterly direction along the northern border of Bavaria as far as the Czechoslovakian border at the village of Hof, further along the western, south-western and southern border of Czechoslovakia as far as the city of Bratislava and then from this city the course of the Danube downstream to the city of Silistra and further eastwards along the Romanian-Bulgarian border as far as the Black Sea coast.

The "disarming of the German troops, the troops of other Axis powers and of the so-called 'volunteers'" in the territories east of this line would be incumbent on the armed forces of the USSR, in the territories west of this line the troops of the Western powers.[8] A glance at the map is sufficient to come to the conclusion that this planned line excluded a military presence on the part of the USSR not only in Austria but also in the western part of Hungary.

In a second variation of this draft (from February 8, 1944), the term "occupation zones" (Article 15) appears for the first time, whose borders were only fixed, however, as far as the intersection of the Bavarian and Czechoslovakian borders. Their further course across the borders of Germany remained open.[9]

Only in a third variation of the draft, which Molotov sent to Stalin on February 12, 1944, to be signed, was Austria addressed, for which the same status was envisaged as for Berlin—the status of a "common zone."[10] In this context, Article 15 was supplemented with point "d," according to which the "territory of Austria is to be occupied jointly by the troops of the USSR, the United Kingdom and the USA." Stalin signalled his agreement to this variation in his resolution "To Molotov. Stalin."

In his telegram of February 12, 1944, to the Soviet delegate in the EAC, Fedor Gusev, Molotov mentioned that the proposed status for Berlin and Austria was to be regarded as an "exception" to the rule because "each zone will only be occupied by troops of that particular one of the three powers [. . .] to whom the respective zone is allocated."[11] It is understandable why so much importance was attached to this rule on the Soviet side and why the British draft, according to which in each zone the presence of troops from the other Allied countries was also allowed, was regarded as unacceptable: the variation of a "mixed occupation" carried with it the danger of an uncontrolled growth in contact between members of the armed forces of "East" and "West" and, accordingly, would potentially have paved the way for that which was designated "ideological diversion" in Soviet jargon. It is more difficult to understand why an exception to this rule was considered permissible in the cases of Berlin and Austria.

Incidentally, both in Berlin and in Austria, the principle of territorial demarcation was soon being spread between the occupation contingents. In the case of Berlin, it was a matter of two sectors; with regard to Austria, of two zones. In the following, the relevant article (Article 2) of the draft of the "Voroshilov Commission" from April 17, 1944, is quoted in full:

> For the occupation of Austria, the following zones will be established:
> a) The territory of Austria east of the line starting at the border city of Retz in a south-westerly direction as far as the city of Horn and further south in the direction of the city of Krems, from where it runs in an easterly direction along the right shore of the Danube as far as the city of Tulln and further in a southerly direction via the cities of Hainfeld, Mürzsteg, Turnau, Bruck, Leoben and further along the Rivers Mur and Lavant as far as the southern border of Austria, will be occupied by troops from the USSR with the exception of the special occupation arrangement noted under point "d";
> b) the territory west of the line named in point "a" with western boundary via the line starting from the Austrian-Bavarian border along the right shore of the Danube as far as the confluence of the Enns and further along the aforementioned river in a southerly direction as far as the city of Eisenerz and from there to the south-east along the stipulated line to the city of Leoben, will be occupied by troops from the United Kingdom;
> c) the entire remaining territory of western Austria will be occupied by troops from the USA;
> d) the city of Vienna will be occupied by troops from the USSR, the United Kingdom and the USA with the following allocation of zones: troops from the USSR occupy the eastern part of the city located between Danube and Danube Canal; troops from the United Kingdom and troops from the USA the remaining territory of the city, whereby the demarcation line between the troops from the United Kingdom and the troops from the USA will be established by an agreement between the command of the United Kingdom and that of the USA.[12]

During the course of the session of the "Voroshilov Commission" on the issue of occupation zones in Austria, held the following day, April 18, 1944, Admiral Ivan Isakov and Maiskii spoke their mind. Isakov referred to the borders of the Soviet zone having to allow for a direct rail and shipping connection on the Danube, and Maiskii stressed "that the Soviet zone should if at all possible border both Yugoslavia and Czechoslovakia." Furthermore, Maiskii noted that "the location of the industrial plants in this country and the population figures for the individual federal regions of Austria must be taken into account. All three zones must possess approximately the same population."

In another of his remarks, Maiskii underlined his vision, according to which "the borders between the zones must be drawn by and large in accordance with the administrative borders between the federal regions or between individual districts (municipalities)."

On this, the Commission's minutes of the session note that "Comrade Bazarov was given the task of obtaining a map of Austria with the borders of federal regions marked on it, in order to be able to discuss at the next session of the Commission the issue of the allocation of occupation zones among the three Allied powers on the basis of the administrative structure of Austria."[13]

In its session on April 30, the Commission again returned to the question of the drawing of borders between the occupation zones. The suggestions submitted for review were found "by and large" to be good. As noted in the minutes, the "Soviet occupation zone was allocated the following federal regions: Burgenland, half of Lower Austria and of Styria; the zone of the United Kingdom—half of Lower Austria and of Styria as well as half of Carinthia; the zone of the USA—Upper Austria, Salzburg, Tyrol and half of Carinthia. The population in each of the zones amounts to around 1.5 millions." With regard to Vienna, the decision reached earlier regarding the zones was confirmed.[14]

The final results of the preparatory work of the "Voroshilov Commission" on Austria were summarized in a résumé by its chairman to Stalin, Molotov, Vyshinskii, and Dekanozov, dated June 12. It read:

> In Austria, the Soviet occupation zone has an area of 21,066 square kilometres with a total population of 1,407,000 people. The remaining part covers an area of 62,587 square kilometres with 2,738,000 inhabitants. The city of Vienna, with its population of 1,929,000 people is to be treated separately as an independent unit with a joint occupation by troops of the three powers.
>
> The Commission is of the opinion that the demarcation line between the British and the American zone in Austria and in the city of Vienna must be fixed by the English and the Americans themselves.
>
> The territorial components do not underlie the allocation of zones in Austria, but rather the population figures and the distribution of industry.
>
> A large proportion of the industrial plants are located in the Soviet zone (whose population makes up a third of the population of Austria), and the Soviet zone is furthermore connected directly with Yugoslavia, Czechoslovakia and Hungary via railway routes.[15]

The history of the debate on the Austrian question within the EAC constitutes one of the hitherto least handled topics in the literature. This can already be seen in the differing reading of dates: thus, for example, according to one author, the Soviet proposal regarding the zones was put forward on June 29, 1944;[16] according to another, this happened only on July 1.[17] Considerably more important, however, is the question as to how the delegates of the Western powers in the EAC responded to this proposal and how and when an agreement was reached that was acceptable to all parties.

If one is to believe the brief comments in Aleksei Roshchin's book (himself a member of the European Advisory Commission and author of the only work on this institution in the Soviet and Russian historiography), the proposal for the Soviet zone made by the British side on August 22, 1944, actually foresaw a larger territory than the Soviet side had envisaged. This was connected with the circumstance that the American side had initially not wanted to participate in the occupation of Austria and only declared itself willing to send merely "symbolic contingents" (France's position was similar). For this reason, the British plan was based on merely on a Soviet-British occupation of Austria. The territory of Upper and Lower Austria (excluding Vienna) was intended for the Soviet side—the remaining part of the country was to be occupied by British troops. Vienna was elected as a zone of common occupation in which the aforementioned "symbolic" contingent of the United States would have been stationed.

The stance of the United States and France later underwent a change, upon which the British side submitted a new proposal in the EAC on January 30, 1945, according to which the USSR would only receive the territory of Lower Austria (without Vienna) for its occupation zone. Styria and Carinthia were foreseen for Great Britain; Salzburg and Upper Austria would be allocated to the United States, and Tyrol along with Vorarlberg to France. The Soviet side responded to this by proposing an enlarged Soviet zone: the territory of Upper Austria situated on the left (northern) bank of the Danube and Burgenland should belong to this. Ultimately, this proposal met with approval and constituted the basis for the Allied agreement regarding the occupation zones for Austria, signed on July 9, 1945 (five days earlier, on July 4, 1945, the agreement on the control machinery had been signed).[18]

It should be noted that there existed with regard to the zone boundaries a considerable difference between the situation in Austria and that in Germany. Whereas the zone agreement for Germany had already been signed on September 12, 1944, at that point in time—as demonstrated by the correspondence of Churchill and Stalin from May 17 and 18, 1945—there had been no contracted decision for Austria regarding the establishment of zones in that country.[19] Against this backdrop, it makes sense to correct a portrayal of the diplomatic history of the final phase of the war in Europe by Valentin Falin:

> In April 1945, Soviet troops in Austria pressed forward westwards in pursuit of the enemy across the demarcation line agreed by the three powers. In the framework of a consultation with Stalin, the head of the 3rd European (German) Section of the People's Commissariat for Foreign Affairs, Andrei Smirnov, expressed the opinion that the Soviet Union cling to the line reached and, if need be, bring about a fresh examination of the Allied agreement. Stalin's reaction to this was as follows: "Wrong and harmful." On his order, a telegram had already

been prepared for Eisenhower with the following substance: "The military situation has made it necessary for the troops of the Red Army to cross the line agreed on by the Allies. It goes without saying that these troops will be pulled back into the territory foreseen for the USSR upon the cessation of hostilities (communication to the author by Vladimir Semenov, who was present at the aforementioned consultation)."[20]

It is evident that Semenov's memory had let him down and that Falin borrowed from the memories of his oral history source too uncritically. Just to repeat: until July 9, 1945, there were no "agreed demarcation lines." Nevertheless, there is no reason to assume that the quoted passage entirely lacks a certain authenticity. It is most probable that certain Soviet circles contemplated for a period of time the option of using the most advanced Soviet formations on Austrian territory in order to force through the Soviet proposal for the zone boundaries, which the Western powers were initially not prepared to accept. It is most probable that numbering among the advocates of this tactical option was the aforementioned Smirnov, whose proposal was rejected by Stalin, although this—and even this possibility cannot be excluded—did not necessarily happen immediately.

Indirectly, the fact that different contemplated approaches toward the Allies existed within Soviet politics as well as the chosen variant of non-confrontation is also reflected in Western historiography, for example, in the monograph of the American researcher Audrey Kurth Cronin. Together with the information that "an arrival in Vienna on the part of the leaders of the Western missions was only allowed on 3 June—almost two months after the entry of Soviet troops into the city—and the Western garrisons did not arrive until the end of August," Cronin cites a notification in the *Times* from June 22, 1945, according to which "the Russian requests for a most rapid arrival of the Allies in Vienna were fulfilled." According to Cronin, a "change" in the Soviet position had come about, which she explains in that "the Soviet commanders on the ground had recognized that they were not in a position to feed the civilian population," which is why they were subsequently interested in being able to share the responsibility for this with the Western powers. Such a change in position cannot, incidentally, be discerned for Stalin, which is demonstrated by the fact that it was suggested to the leaders of the Western missions following a one-week stay to leave the capital again.[21]

There is much in this portrayal of events and their interpretation that arouses well-founded doubts. In this context, it is above all the differing positions of Stalin and the Soviet representatives "on the ground" that seem to be exceedingly unlikely. If one of these had allowed himself even to the slightest extent to think independently and, furthermore, in relation to such an important political issue as relations with the Allies, one would in no way have wished to be in his shoes. The reason given by Cronin for the change in the Soviet stance is also not very convincing. She bases it on the preconceived and in no way provable theory of the "plundering" of the Soviet-occupied territories of Austria by Soviet troops. It should be pointed out here that even following on from this point of departure, which indicates that large-scale confiscations were carried out on the Soviet side, it should at all costs be kept in mind that the confiscated goods were, firstly, industrial installations and, secondly, items whose value for the provisioning of the population with food can be described as minimal. On the other hand, statistics exist for the delivery of foodstuffs to Austria during 1945, which show that the Soviet contribution to these deliveries was the largest.[22] Is this a case of distorted statistics, which give a false picture? If not, then the cause and effect relationship established by the American academic is to be characterized in essence as incorrect.

In my opinion, the Soviet side pursued a specific tactic with the aim of forcing through a settlement for the zone allocation that was most favorable for them. How efficient this tactic actually was can be questioned in view of the fact noted by Cronin that the Western Allies (at least the Americans) were not initially interested in a rapid deployment of their troops on Austrian territory and that the inflexible approach of the Soviets only gave them an excuse to conceal their "wait and see" policy. Ultimately, both sides moved away from their policy of irrational tactical manoeuvres, which eventually led to the signing of the aforementioned jointly drafted documents, which established both the zone borders and the fundamental principles of the occupation regime. The territory of the Soviet zone covered a larger area than had been foreseen in the aforementioned paper of the "Voroshilov Commission" from June 12, 1944 (it comprised a territory of 26,273 square kilometres with a population of 1,843,000 people, whereas the letter of the "Voroshilov Commission" had talked merely of 21,066 square kilometres with 1,407,000 inhabitants), but was nevertheless considerably smaller than the territory that had been liberated by the Soviet armed forces and was under their control at the end of the war (36,551 square kilometres with a population of 4,532,000 people).[23]

NOTES

1. *Vneshnyaya politika Sovetskogo Soyuza v period Otechestvennoi voiny. Dokumenty i materialy*, Vol. 1 (Moscow: Ob"edinenie gosudarstvennykh izdatel'stv, 1946), p. 43. See also Natal'ja Lebedeva, "Österreichische Kommunisten im Moskauer Exil: Die Komintern, die Abteilung für internationale Information des ZK der VKP(b) und Österreich 1943–1945," in Stefan Karner and Barbara Stelzl-Marx, eds.,

Die Rote Armee in Österreich: Sowjetische Besatzung 1945–1955. Beiträge (Graz/ Vienna/Munich: Oldenbourg, 2005), pp. 39–60.

2. Foreign Policy Archives of the Russian Federation (hereafter AVP RF), f. 059, op. 1, p. 354, d. 2412, ll. 21–24. Reprinted in G. P. Kynin and J. Laufer, SSSR i germanskii vopros. 22 iyunya 1941g.-8 maya 1945. SSSR i germanskii vopros 1941– 1949, Vol. 1 (Moscow: Izdatel'stvo Instituta Mezhdunarodnykh Otnoshenii,1996), pp. 118–119, and in Stefan Karner, Barbara Stelzl-Marx and Alexander Tschubarjan, eds., Die Rote Armee in Österreich: Sowjetische Besatzung 1945–1955. Dokumente. Krasnaya Armiya v Avstrii: Sovetskaya okkupatsiya 1945–1955. Dokumenty (Graz/ Vienna/Munich: Oldenbourg, 2005), Doc. 1.

3. Karl Stuhlpfarrer, "Österreich—Mittäterschaft und Opferstatus," in Ulrich Herbert and Axel Schildt, eds., Kriegsende in Europa: Vom Beginn des deutschen Machtzerfalls bis zur Stabilisierung der Nachkriegsordnung 1944–1948 (Essen: Klartext-Verlag, 1998), pp. 301–317, here p. 307.

4. Kynin and Laufer, SSSR i germanskii vopros, p. 646.

5. AVP RF, F. 48z, op. 24a, p. 46, d. 1, l. 46.

6. Ibid., l. 49.

7. Kynin and Laufer; SSSR i germanskii vopros, pp. 301–303.

8. Ibid., p. 402.

9. Ibid., p. 407.

10. Ibid., p. 413.

11. Ibid., p. 416.

12. Ibid., p. 461.

13. Ibid., p. 464.

14. Ibid., p. 469.

15. Ibid., p. 488.

16. V. N. Beletskii, Sovetskii Soyuz i Avstriya. Bor'ba Sovetskogo Soyuza za vozrozhdenie nezavisimoi demokraticheskoi Avstrii i ustanovlenie s nei druzhestvennykh otnoshenii (1938-1960gg.) (Moscow: Izdatel'stvo Instituta Mezhdunarodnykh Otnoshenii, 1962), p. 104.

17. A. A. Roshchin, Poslevoennoe uregulirovanie v Evrope (Moscow: Mysl', 1984), p. 86.

18. Ibid., pp. 86–88.

19. Perepiska predsedatelya Soveta ministrov SSSR s prezidentami SShA i prem'er-ministrami Velikobritanii vo vremya Velikoi Otechestvennoi voiny 1941– 1945 gg., Vol. 1 (Moscow: Izdatel'stvo politicheskoi literatury, 1957), pp. 361–362.

20. V. M. Falin, Vtoroi front. Antigitlerovskaya koalitsiya. Konflikt interesov (Moscow: Tsentrpoligraf, 2000), p. 565.

21. Audrey Kurth Cronin, Great Power Politics and the Struggle over Austria 1945–1955 (Ithaca/New York: Cornell University Press, 1986), pp. 26–27.

22. Beletskii, Sovetskii Soyuz i Avstriya, p. 111.

23. Ibid., p. 65.

Chapter Three

Under Soviet Control

The Establishment of the Austrian Government in 1945

Stefan Karner and Peter Ruggenthaler

The pictures of the assumption of office of the Provisional Austrian State Government and the proclamation of the new, Second Republic of April 29, 1945, that show State Chancellor Karl Renner standing with Soviet soldiers in front of the Parliament aroused deepest mistrust and unease on the part of the Western powers.[1] They gave the impression that the Soviets had now installed a puppet government in Austria, as they had before in Bulgaria, Poland, Romania, and Hungary.

In Yalta, the Soviet dictator Iosif Stalin had succeeded in maneuvring the discussion toward the future of Eastern and Southeastern Europe in the context of the creation of sovereign states and, in the process, stymie the confederation plans of the British (with Vienna as a possible capital city).[2] This furthermore gave Stalin from this point on the opportunity to proceed in Eastern Europe in selective stages.[3] In one country after another the Communists ultimately assumed power. Americans and British did not initially accept the pro-Soviet governments installed in the Eastern European countries, while in the case of Austria they were likewise not prepared to approve a "puppet government" of Stalin and refused to recognize Renner's provisional cabinet.

Principally speaking, during the Second World War the Allies had, in London at the European Advisory Commission (EAC), merely agreed in their intentions toward Austria on the creation of a control mechanism, i.e., on the installation of a military government, the creation of an administrative apparatus, and the gradual transition from a military to a civilian administration. Only the British had developed more far-reaching proposals for the post-war period and presented them at the EAC. The Soviets, however, did not even give an official reaction in London.[4] For the negotiations in London, the Soviet representative, Fedor Gusev, merely received instructions for matters concerning the division of Austria into Allied occupation zones.[5] In fact, during the war the Soviet government had not come up with any concrete ideas on the individual composition of an Austrian government. In general, the following applied: as in the rest of Europe, in Austria it would at least be attempted to make the country communist step-by-step by means of the establishment of a national front. This corresponded to the general Soviet strategy of bringing about a socialist social order not through a revolutionary upheaval, but rather after a gradual development, evolutionary, after a period of at least thirty and at most fifty years.[6] The Soviet approach in Austria is, furthermore, to be viewed in the context of the Soviet global security policy, which aimed at maintaining long-term "peace" in Europe in the sense of a suppression of potential big power opponents (first and foremost Germany), in order to secure the Soviet Union's security.

Conceptually speaking, the Austrian Communists in exile in Moscow had admittedly not remained idle,[7] but the realization of their plans was given only very limited consideration by Stalin. The plans of Austrian expatriates in the West were not given any consideration at all by Moscow. At most, they merely gave Stalin the impulse to think about Austria himself: a person was needed who would be suitable for implementing in Austria the Soviet plans regarding the strategy of a "National People's Front," i.e., the national coalition of left-wing forces. Even if there must have been an awareness that Austria would not be under exclusive Soviet influence in its entirety, Austria was, of all places, a suitable testing ground, not least because it was here that capitalism and communism would stand in direct competition to one another after the war.

"WESTERN OPTIONS"

On March 10 and 25, 1945, Ernst Lemberger and Fritz Molden of the resistance movement "O5" in Paris approached the Soviet liaison officer of the Supreme Headquarters Allied Expeditionary Force (SHAEF) in an attempt to establish a representation of the Provisional Austrian National Committee (POEN) in Moscow.[8] The former head of the Comintern, Georgi Dimitrov, thereupon obtained information on the "O5" representatives. On April 6, 1945, he informed Stalin that Lemberger was a British spy.[9] A bourgeois government supported by the Western powers, as aimed for by Lemberger and Molden, was naturally at variance with the interests of the Soviet leadership. The "O5" representatives told the Soviets in Paris that their plans had been agreed on with the British. This must presumably have aroused Stalin's mistrust toward London, as agreement regarding the setting up of a government had been reached at the EAC to the effect that a "military government" would be jointly installed in Austria. Now, however, the British appeared to have deceived Moscow in this matter, which presumably prompted Stalin to subsequently proceed unilaterally in the question of setting up a government, without consulting the Western powers. It was at least agreed in Paris with the representatives of the Austrian resistance movement that the resistance movement would send an empowered representative, Ferdinand Käs, across the front line to Marshal Fedor Tolbukhin. An independent code was agreed on for this purpose.[10]

Under the later long-time Austrian Federal Chancellor Bruno Kreisky, the "Austrian Union" in Swedish exile had already much earlier taken up contact with the Soviet Embassy in Stockholm on several occasions and "signalised the readiness to take part in the reconstruction of Austria" and offered the Soviet government their services. The Soviets, however, saw the exiled Austrians in Sweden only as stooges of the British:

> The local Austrians, aside from the communists, are closely connected with the American and English mission. It is known to us that the English dictate that they make contact with the Austrian political emigrants working in the USSR [. . .]. For this reason, we must regard the establishment of contact with us on the part of the Austrians as being in line with the English policy toward Austria. The English, as can be seen, would like to bring themselves, via the local Austrians (first and foremost via the Social Democrats) into the "Austrian Liberation Front," which is under the influence of Austrian political emigrants working in the USSR.[11]

Furthermore, the ominous plans of Josef Dobretsberger, who had been in exile in Turkey and Egypt during the Second World War,[12] to put himself at the head of an Austrian government, were not in the interests of the Soviet Union, likewise alleged British plans to reactivate former Chancellor Schuschnigg, as recorded in a SMERSH report.[13] The visit to Tyrol in January 1946 of Otto Habsburg,[14] who had attempted in American exile during the war to establish a representative Austrian agency abroad by means of the Austrian National Committee,[15] also ran counter to Soviet ideas.

STALIN AND RENNER

At the end of March 1945, when the Red Army entered Austrian territory, the Austrian question moved in the Kremlin into Stalin's focus. Time was pressing when it came to dealing with the personnel question in Austria. A message arrived from Paris to the effect that the British had already set up a provisional government or were supporting the plans of the Austrian resistance movement.

Stalin's mistrust would be an obvious explanation for the question as to what was the decisive catalyst for undertaking the attempt to set up a national people's front government in Austria. Or would Stalin in any case have attempted to proceed unilaterally in Vienna when it came to the question of forming a government? The burning question was now: could an "Austrian Miklos"[16] be found? The required profile for a provisional head of government was clear: it had to be a recognized figure capable of unifying left-wing forces.

According to the memoirs of the Soviet army general, Sergei Shtemenko, Stalin apparently suddenly raised the question in a session of the State Defence Committee GOKO at the end of March 1945: "Where then is this social democrat Karl Renner, who was a pupil of Karl Kautsky?[17] He belonged for many years to the leadership of Austrian social democracy. And he was, if I'm not mistaken, president of the last Austrian parliament."[18] Both the Chief of the General Staff of the Red Army, Aleksei Antonov,[19] and Shtemenko supposedly maintained an embarrassed silence before Stalin continued: "One should not ignore the influential forces who take an anti-fascist stance. The Hitler dictatorship must have taught the social democrats something as well."[20] Stalin then apparently ordered the 3rd Ukrainian Front by telephone "to find out what has happened to Renner, whether he is still alive and where he is located."[21]

In the meantime, the Red Army fought on at great cost—over 30,000 Soviet soldiers lost their lives on Austrian territory[22]—and already prepared for the storming Vienna. On April 2, 1945, some time after the aforementioned GOKO session, Stalin—in search of a head of government for Austria—called for the leader of the Department for International Information of the Central Committee of the CPSU, Georgi Dimitrov. He instructed him "to select a few useful Austrians to be sent to the 3rd Ukrainian Front," which operated in Austria under Marshal Tolbukhin. According to what Stalin said to Dimitrov, the status quo of 1938 should be re-established in Austria.[23] On the next day, Dimitrov informed Stalin that he, together with the Central Secretary of the Communist Party of Austria (KPÖ), Johann Koplenig, had examined those Austrians, communists, and imprisoned "anti-fascists" located in the USSR.[24] As a result, he recommended to Stalin Koplenig himself, Ernst Fischer,[25] and other communists.[26] "Alongside these Austrians," according to Dimitrov, "there are still the Austrian comrades Franz Honner and Friedl Fürnberg in Yugoslavia." In addition to other recommendations, he requested further instructions. On the same day, Stalin issued Tolbukhin with the directive "to indicate to the Mayor of Vienna that the Soviet command will not work against the creation of a provisional government with the inclusion of the democratic forces in Austria, [though] to write nothing about this matter on the leaflets."[27]

Three days later, on April 5, Dimitrov apparently of his own accord—further instructions from Stalin to Dimitrov are not documented—sent Stalin another letter. Dimitrov furthermore recommended Fischer for "leadership work in any areas" and Fürnberg for "political leadership work."[28] Stalin had probably been made aware of Dimitrov's first report on April 3, but initially taken no further action.[29] On the following day, Dimitrov's letters of introduction in any case became invalid. Things were to turn out very differently.

On April 4, Stalin received a message from Tolbukhin regarding Karl Renner; and now he took up the sceptre himself and acted at once. During the first days of April until the departure of the Austrian communists on April 8, he did not issue any further instructions from Moscow to Dimitrov in Vienna regarding the Austrian matter.[30]

With the emergence of Renner, the position of the exiled communists in Moscow was also decisively weakened. After Stalin had decided in favor of Renner on April 4, the Austrian communists in exile were no longer in the running for setting up a government. Nevertheless, Koplenig and Fischer in Moscow continued over the following days to receive instructions to this effect from Dimitrov and Deputy People's Commissar for Foreign Affairs Vladimir Dekanozov,[31] who had also been appointed the political advisor to the commandant of the 3rd Ukrainian Front,[32] before their departure for Austria.[33] It is, therefore, no wonder that the Austrian communists were surprised upon their arrival in Austria to find that Karl Renner had already been tasked with forming a government. Although Fischer, when speaking with British representatives of the embassy in Moscow in 1944 during his Moscow exile, had already advocated working together with Renner, Körner, and other leading political figures of the inter-war period, the KPÖ leadership was less surprised about the fact that Stalin had pinned his hopes on Renner than about the attendant circumstances. Coming unsuspectingly from Moscow, upon their arrival in Vienna they were confronted with a fait accompli and Renner was introduced to them as the head of government. But let us not get ahead of ourselves. Eventful days were to pass before this moment was reached.

KARL RENNER'S FIRST CONTACT WITH THE SOVIETS

Karl Renner, born in southern Moravia and State Chancellor of the Republic of German-Austria from 1918 to 1920, had campaigned in 1938 for the Anschluss of Austria to the German Reich. During the war, however, he retracted this call and withdrew to his villa in secluded Gloggnitz in Lower Austria. On Easter Sunday, April 1, 1945, the first Soviet military units reached the town.[34] On this day, Renner was supposedly recognized in a local bunker by a Soviet officer, but this did not seem to concern the latter. He even removed Renner's golden wristwatch.[35] The officer may not yet have been aware of the (oral) order to locate Renner, which must have been issued the previous day.

After Gloggnitz had been captured militarily, the indigenous resisters requested the now seventy-five-year-old Renner to approach the local Soviet commandant in order to request protection for the populace. On April 3, Renner eventually called on the political officer of the 103rd Guards Rifle Division of the 9th Guards Army.[36] On the basis of the search warrant, the latter must immediately have been aware of whom he was dealing with. He explained that he could not issue orders on his own authority and invited Renner to accompany him to the Troop Command (of the headquarters of the 103rd Guards Rifle Division) in Köttlach.[37]

Many reasons favor the interpretation that Renner not only approached the Soviets with the request assigned to him to protect the indigenous population, but also already with political ambitions. On the previous evening, Renner apparently sat down with a former Czech "foreign worker," who was to serve as translator. Renner is said to have explained to the Czech that he wanted to "re-establish our homeland" and for that he needed the "Russians."[38] From Köttlach, Renner was ultimately brought to the headquarters of the Soviet 9th Guards Army in Hochwolkersdorf, where he first of all met with Colonel General Aleksei Zheltov,[39] who had immediately been informed in writing from Köttlach by the political officers Glagolov and Gromov.[40] Following an initial conversation with Renner, Zheltov made his way back to Tolbukhin. They then immediately put Stalin in the picture regarding the surfacing of Renner by means of a telegram:

> To Comrade Stalin, [. . .] on 3 April [. . .] Doctor Karl Renner appeared at the headquarters of the 103rd Guards Rifle Division. During the course of a debriefing in the army headquarters, Karl Renner declared that he had been the last president of the Austrian parliament dissolved in 1934 [*sic*; actually 1933] by the Dollfuss government. He had occupied this position in the years 1925 to 1934. In the period from 1918 to 1920 he was Primer Minister [State Chancellor] of Austria; from 1938 he lived in his home town of Gloggnitz, after he had withdrawn from political life. Since 1894 he has been a member of the Social Democratic Party and since 1907 a member of the Austrian Parliament. Dr Renner explained: "I am old, but I am willing to assist with words and deeds in the establishment of a democratic order. Communists and social democrats now have the same task—the annihilation of fascism. As the last president of parliament, I could call on parliament to install a provisional government for the post-war period. I will exclude Nazis from parliament. With that done, I could lay down my functions and retire." During the course of the discussion, Renner explained that ninety per cent of the population of Vienna were hostile to the National Socialists, but the Nazi regime and the bombardments had demoralised

the Viennese and they now felt disheartened and unwilling to take action. On the part of the Social Democrats, no measures were initiated for a mobilisation of the population for the struggle against Hitler's fascists. Until your directives have been issued, Doctor Renner will remain at our disposal. I request your directives. Tolbukhin, Zheltov.[41]

The news of Renner's appearance was presented to the supreme military command staff, the Stavka, in Moscow on April 4 at 6:50 p.m.[42] Stalin was supposedly surprised that "old Renner" was still alive.[43] Within minutes, Stalin directed Tolbukhin to grant Renner his trust:[44] "With regard to your report of 4.4 [. . .] the Stavka of the Supreme Main Command issues the following directives: Karl Renner is to be granted our trust. He is to be informed that the Headquarters of the Soviet Armed Forces will provide him with assistance in the resurrection of democratic order in Austria. He is to be informed that the Soviet armed forces have not crossed the borders of Austria for the purpose of occupying Austrian state territory, but rather in order to expel the fascist occupiers from Austria."[45]

Unfortunately, neither of the telegrams shed light on whether Stalin had actually issued an order to search for Renner. At the same time, they do not exclude such an order. They confirm at least two of Shtemenko's three basic statements regarding the session of the GOKO at which Stalin is supposed to have issued the order. In fact, the latter gave indications himself for a systematic search for Renner. He apparently spoke about this in the circle of his Party friends.[46] If this was indeed the case, then one can only come to the following conclusion: Colonel General Zheltov and Renner must have agreed that the latter would emphasize in public his own independent appearance before the Soviets in order—and this was admittedly in Renner's own interests—not to be regarded by the Western powers as a head of government "installed" by the Soviets. Renner himself repeatedly stressed that he had been the last freely elected President of the Austrian Parliament in order in this way to legitimize his position as provisional head of government and to emphasize the continuity between the Austria that was to be resurrected and the democratic era of the First Republic.

The basic aim of the Soviet leadership directly after the Second World War was the creation of a security zone (*cordon sanitaire*) and the strengthening of the Communist movement in the countries of Europe occupied by the Red Army. By 1945, the starting position was completely different to that, for example, in the 1920s and the 1930s. The Red Army had at least in a certain sense demonstrated that Communism could be victorious. For this reason, the starting position for a further expansion of Communism through Europe was never better than immediately after the Second World War. Stalin regarded Renner as the ideal man for the realization of his plans for Austria. Renner was for the lack of alternatives the only one who could unify all the parties and also come to an agreement with the exiled communists. The KPÖ should not have exclusive control from the outset.[47] The National People's Front for Austria seemed to Stalin to be embodied in Renner. It should be the ideal prerequisite for the later inclusion of all parties in the country. Attempts to unite the "anti-fascist" parties were not only made at the highest level. It can be demonstrated for Styria that Soviet political officers had the task immediately after their entry into Graz of approaching the Styrian party leaders of the KPÖ, the Socialist Party of Austria (SPÖ), and the Austrian People's Party (ÖVP) and obtaining a joint agreement on basic questions. In the case of Styria, it was Friedl Fürnberg who had been briefed for this by the Soviets. "Together with Fürnberg, we have carried out the work for the establishment of a united block of the democratic parties (Communists, Social Democrats, Christian Socials)." In Styria, the "principle of equality in government for all three parties" was achieved.[48]

STALIN'S HENCHMAN?

In Stalin's dealings with Renner, the strategic thinking of his predecessor, Lenin, is also visible, of finding "useful idiots" specifically among the bourgeois socialists, who were prepared to go along with things for an important part of the way. It is thereby clear that Stalin no longer viewed the seventy-five-year-old Renner as the final executor of the transition of Austria to socialism, but at most as the perfect switchman.

It cannot be assessed to what extent Renner's ingratiating letters to Stalin influenced the latter in forming his opinion. Perhaps Stalin, when reading the lines, saw himself confirmed in his considerations, according to which the socialists would also have learned from fascism[49] and regarded Renner as someone who had already mutated to communism and was taking the "correct path." At least Stalin could be fairly sure to have in Renner a conversation partner and not a politician who was not prepared to make any compromises.[50]

From the point of view of the Soviet power, Renner was certainly the most suitable chancellor of an "anti-fascist" government. Renner had even offered the Soviets a "de-faschistification" (the removal from the government of ÖVP members), surged ahead with this, and attempted to kill two birds with one stone: consideration of the supposed wishes of the Soviets and the dismantling of ÖVP personnel. This, however, was contrary to the general Soviet approach in the countries occupied by them. Beyond the pseudo-democratic disguise, the representation of all the "anti-fascist" parties in a provisional government was desired.

Renner also had other strategic advantages: his level of familiarity, the countless "dark spots" and "blemishes" in his biography (above all his explicit advocacy in 1938 of the Anschluss to Hitler's Germany), which could be used as a means of applying pressure.[51] Furthermore, there was the possibility of selling him to the Western Allies as an anti-Communist and a certain acceptance of him on the part of the political opponent, the ÖVP. Beyond that, Renner was already in the seventy-sixth year of this life and appeared to be more prepared to compromise in order, perhaps, to see his views realized during his lifetime.[52]

At 2 p.m. on April 5, 1945, Zheltov made Renner aware in the headquarters of the 9th Guards Army of the basic principles contained in Stalin's telegram. In the process, Zheltov apparently asked Renner to address a memorandum to the Red Army, which Renner, however, rejected so as not to have to appear as the agent of the Red Army.[53] He apparently promised, however, to present his proclamations to the Soviet side for inspection. Renner was then brought back to Gloggnitz by the political officer Colonel Georgii Piterskii, where Renner sketched out his proclamations to the Austrian people and the main features of his policies for the Soviets. As of April 9, Eichbüchl Palace, which had been restored by the Soviets during the interim, was placed at Renner's disposal for this purpose.[54] The period after this cannot be completely reconstructed. From April 15, Renner was under Soviet surveillance—for his own protection; the Staff of the 336th Border Regiment of the Internal Troops of the NKVD had supplied Renner, "for security," with "a Rifle Section of the 4th Line Security Unit consisting of 10 persons."[55] In this way, Stalin complied with the request by Tolbukhin and Zheltov to make a division of NKVD troops available for "surveillance of the government and cleansing Vienna of fascist elements."[56]

On April 15, Renner addressed his famous letter (the first of many) to Stalin, in which he effusively thanked him for his services to Austria and for the glorious exploits of the Red Army. In his memoirs, Shtemenko described the arrival of the letter at the General Staff in Moscow: "After the first few lines we were unable to refrain from smiling. [. . .] It was not easy to separate sincerity from self-serving flattery in Renner's enthusiastic comments on the liberating mission of the Red Army."[57]

Following the taking of Vienna (April 13, 1945) by the Red Army, Tolbukhin, Zheltov, and Andrei Smirnov[58] contacted Stalin on April 15 with the request to accelerate [!] the decision for the establishment of an Austrian provisional government. It is clear from a document from the Military Archives in Podol'sk near Moscow, which was completely unknown until 2005 and can be regarded as quasi the "birth certificate" of the Second Republic of Austria, that the Soviet leadership was anxious to quickly press ahead with the construction of an Austrian government. In contrast to the Communist

Party of Germany (KPD), the advantage of the Communist Party in Austria was undermined by the early issuing of a government contract to Renner. Tolbukhin, Zheltov, and Smirnov even submitted to Stalin Renner's offer to summon all living members of the last freely elected National Council and Federal Council (with the exception of National Socialists). Thus, four parties were to be represented in the new government in the following strength: Social Democrats, 35 percent; Communists, 30 percent; Christian Democrats, 20 percent; Revolutionary Socialists, 10 percent.[59] And: "Renner's proposal regarding the establishment of a provisional government in this fashion upholds the basis of the constitution in a certain sense and one could take it up if it does not strengthen the position of the Catholics, the Social Democrats and those groups adjacent to them."[60] Tolbukhin and Zheltov warned, however, that such a government would constitute a strong block which could considerably "hinder the growth of new democratic [i.e., communist] forces." The two of them suggested as a second option the establishment by Renner of an initiative group in which representatives of the different parties as well as independents would be integrated. These figures—the proposal envisaged former Federal President Wilhelm Miklas, among others—would make up a Provisional Austrian Government, draft an appeal to the Allies, and request all possible support, even for the establishment of an independent, democratic Austria. According to the proposal, the provisional government would exercise legislative and executive power and work under the control of the Allies until the holding of free parliamentary elections.[61]

FORMING THE PROVISIONAL GOVERNMENT

Two days later, on April 17, 1945, Stalin finally gave Tolbukhin the "green light" to order Renner to him and to commission him with the establishment of a provisional government.[62] After writing his letter to Stalin, Renner had left Eichbüchl Palace, seemingly without a Soviet entourage. The 4th Guards Army was then tasked with bringing Renner to Tolbukhin.[63] The young Lieutenant Colonel Yakov Starchevskii assumed this task. As no-one seemed to know where Renner by this time was,[64] Starchevskii began the search and heard from workers in Wiener Neustadt that he was at his home in Gloggnitz, where he did indeed find him.[65] On April 19, a Thursday, Renner was brought to Tolbukhin.[66] Renner was not the first to be received. Immediately before him, the Soviets had spoken with Koplenig, an unmistakable sign that there would be no way of avoiding the KPÖ.

The following Saturday, at 4:55 a.m., a coded telegram was sent to Stalin regarding the meeting with Renner, in which the former was told "that

Renner, in accordance with your coded telegram, [. . .] was presented with the proposal that he set up a Provisional Austrian Government. The proposal regarding the forming of a government with the participation of the most important democratic parties, the clericals among them, was accepted by Renner. He promised to submit to us as of 24 April[67] of this year a list for the composition of the government."[68]

Whether they liked it or not, the Austrian Communists had to declare to Tolbukhin their agreement with Renner heading the government and the KPÖ receiving the Interior and Education Ministries. After the meeting, the Soviets saw in Renner a "very active and content" man who agreed "with all our proposals and measures." He was "very optimistic and gave off an optimistic 'everything will be alright' vibe to the effect that Austria would be filled with new life and [break] once and for all with National Socialism."[69] On the following day, Renner immediately began the first talks with the heads of the other parties.[70]

REACTIONS IN THE SOVIET FOREIGN OFFICE

In the Soviet People's Commissariat for Foreign Affairs (NKID), diplomats now began to give some thought as to how one should behave toward the Allies after the "selection" of Renner by Stalin: "We do not regard it as conducive to achieving our objectives to solve the question of forming an Austrian government without prior notification of our allies and without consultation with them, for this could provoke unnecessary suspicions [sic] in connection with our policy in Austria. In our notification, the Allies should be informed that the Soviet government does not see any reason to reject Karl Renner's offer to form a Provisional Austrian Government. Before such a government is formed, however, the Soviet Union would gladly like to hear the views of the governments of Great Britain and the USA."[71]

In the NKID, some thought had now to be given to how Renner could be brought into play vis-à-vis the Western Allies without presenting him as the Soviets' own preferred candidate. The starting position did not seem to be without any prospect of success: one could point out that Renner seized the initiative and sought out the Soviets himself.

On the late evening of April 22, Political Advisor Mikhail Koptelov reported on the actual state of affairs. He stated that Renner had not so far engaged in any "concrete negotiations" with the Communists[72] and that both sides were of differing opinions regarding the allocation of the Interior Ministry, though Renner had ultimately given his agreement to the Interior Ministry being assigned to the KPÖ.[73] It was a compromise, for in the matter of appointing deputies to the State Chancellor, Renner had stood his ground: "Renner rejected deputies to the State Chancellor and does not want the latter to have any control over him."[74] An intervention in favor of the Communists may have come from the political officer Colonel Piterskii,[75] for which he would hardly have had to check with Moscow. The strategy in those countries occupied only by the Red Army was clear. The Interior Ministry—and with it the police—should be in Communist hands.[76] The dispute over the Interior portfolio also rested indirectly on statements made by the Soviets during the discussion on April 19. Of his own accord, Renner had proposed the following distribution of power within the government: three Social Democrats, two Communists, two Christian Socials, one representative of the Rural Federation, a representative of the Revolutionary Socialists and two independents. The Soviets responded to Renner "that he would have to speak to the leading figures within the democratic parties regarding the question of composition and distribution of seats and should determine the future composition on the basis of the results of the negotiations."[77] The Soviets gave Renner a free rein to put together a proposal; in the matter of the Interior portfolio, a line was admittedly drawn.

On April 24, Tolbukhin informed Moscow that Renner had completed the formation of a government and would announce his government lineup the following day.[78] The next day, Ivan Lavrov, the assistant to the Head of the 3rd European Department, made Deputy Foreign Minister Andrei Vyshinskii in a working paper "aware that the Provisional Government of Austria has already been formed and that, as Comrade Tolbukhin reported on 24.4, Karl Renner intends to announce this today, i.e. 25 April." He considered it necessary: "1. To accelerate the decision regarding the sending of information to the Allies concerning Karl Renner's intention to form a Provisional Austrian Government. 2. When this information is sent by us to our allies today, then Comrade Tolbukhin should be instructed to postpone the announcement of the formation of an Austrian Government for two or three days."[79]

This document is striking. It demonstrates that at least the Soviet diplomats were anxious to proceed in the case of Renner and the formation of a government in consultation with the United States and Great Britain. Renner's cabinet had already long ago been formed; the NKID, however, had not yet even informed the diplomatic representations of the Western powers of Renner's intention to form a provisional government. Events had ultimately come thick and fast. Renner had already formed his provisional government on April 24, a Tuesday. As very few positive reports had previously been received, this did indeed come as something of a surprise to the Soviet diplomats. At this point in time, the bureaucratic apparatus of the NKID had not yet drafted a note to the Western powers. According to the date stamp, the draft of a letter to the Western powers in this matter was not presented to the Deputy People's Commissar Vyshinskii until April 25, the day on which Renner already wanted to proclaim the formation of his government. A handwritten note was added to the letter, however, which gave the date of the note to the Western powers as April 24. The wording corresponded to the requests of the political strategists within the 3rd European Department: "Upon the Red Army's entry into Austrian territory, the former Chancellor of the Austrian Republic and last President of the National Council, Karl Renner, approached the Soviet command and declared that he is willing to assist the Allies in any way in the liberation and resurrection of an independent Austrian state." Vyshinskii concluded that "the founding of a Provisional Austrian Government can provide valuable help in the struggle of the Allies for a complete liberation of Austria from dependence on Germany" and that "the Soviet government considers it *possible* not to hinder Karl Renner and other politically active Austrians in their work for the formation of a Provisional Government of Austria."[80]

The British reaction to this is well known. They rejected the Soviet proposal.[81] As long as Austria was not completely liberated and a four-member Allied Commission installed in Vienna, no government should be established. The British Ambassador in Moscow, Frank Roberts, informed Vyshinskii "that my government needs time to examine the proposal that Dr Renner is to be permitted to form a provisional government. Such a step is in the interests of my government, the government of the United States and the Provisional French Government in equal measure, and likewise the Soviet government."[82] Roberts asked in the name of his government that the Soviet holders of power in Vienna be instructed to defer the recognition of any provisional government in Austria.[83] The British did not know at this point in time that Renner had already long ago formed a provisional government. He did not, however, present it to the public on April 25, as planned, but instead had to postpone this for the reasons mentioned until April 27. On April 28, 1945, Renner drafted an appeal to the Western powers to recognize his government. This notification, as Renner titled the composition, did not arrive in Washington, however, until May 11. Molotov had revised it personally.[84] The pictures of jubilation with which the Austrian population greeted the provisional government on April 29, 1945, during the march from the town hall to the parliament, flying the red-white-red flag, the symbolic action of the resurrection of the Republic of Austria, and which showed Renner together with Soviet military personnel standing in front of the parliament, had ultimately strengthened the mistrust of the Western powers, who refused to recognize the Provisional Austrian Government. A few days later, Marshal Tolbukhin instructed the Soviet commanders' offices "to assist to the greatest possible extent the government itself and its local authorities."[85] An instant loan of 200 million Reichsmark, which Moscow had immediately placed at the disposal of the provisional government, served as the basis for Renner's work.[86]

The population of Vienna, meanwhile, had entirely different worries. It was suffering from hunger and subjected to repeated violent attacks by Red Army soldiers. The rape of women was the order of the day. Orders that were designed to combat the marauding and plundering initially had little effect. The first concrete measures on the part of the Soviets affected not only the provisioning of the city. Stalin issued the order to the Red Army to make 7,000 tons of bread, 1,000 tons of peas, and other foodstuffs available.[87] Soviet representatives in Vienna also immediately attended to cultural life. During the course of the election campaign in the autumn of 1945, a million rubles were in addition provided for rebuilding the Vienna State Opera House.[88]

STATE CHANCELLOR RENNER AS THE FIRST POINT OF CONTACT FOR THE SOVIETS

From the outset Renner was very self-assured in his dealings with his Soviet dialogue partners. He took them up on their promises. Initially, the sphere of control of the Provisional Austrian Government did not even extend to all Austrian territory captured by the Red Army. North of the Danube, Marshal Malinovskii was in command (2nd Ukrainian Front). Right from the start Renner was anxious to expand governmental power to all Soviet-occupied territories.[89]

On April 20, 1945, Tolbukhin and Zheltov had decreed a "provisional ordinance regarding the military headquarters on the territory occupied by Soviet troops." According to the ordinance, "military headquarters were [established] in the regions of Austria occupied by Soviet troops [. . .] in the capital cities and cities under self-administration as well as in the larger towns." Each headquarters was headed by a commandant, who in turn installed provisional mayors. The military headquarters were directly subordinated to the Military Council of the 3rd Ukrainian Front. The ordinance continued: "The military headquarters are *not* to introduce any Soviet system. All necessary measures are to be taken by the mayors (municipal representatives) in consideration of the interests of the Red Army and by the civilian authorities established by the mayors."[90]

The dismantling not only of concerns which the Soviet occupying power assigned as German property but also those of purely Austrian origin weakened the Austrian economy immensely. Renner often mentioned the dismantling of industrial enterprises[91] and requested forbearance and that "Austria be allowed to compensate for the losses incurred by the Soviet Union by means of industrial goods" or "at least [. . .] that it be explained that the installations belong to Russia [*sic*] but are to be left in Austria for the time being." Tolbukhin thereupon explained to the representatives of the provisional government the intentions concerning the dismantling of a series of factories, though he added that foodstuffs, light industry and communal industry would "not be touched by us, aside from individual properties." Tolbukhin continued: "The armaments industry, which is a mixture of German- and Austrian-owned, is to be removed as booty, particularly the secret [weapons] production, but we are prepared to examine each and every objection and to consider a consultancy with Austrian specialists." According to Tolbukhin, "they [the members of the government] were in principle agreeable" to this response.[92] The reality, however, generally looked a little different.

At the beginning of July 1945, Marshal Ivan Konev, Soviet war hero and liberator of Prague, at last assumed command of the Soviet Occupation Zone in Austria, which in administrative terms very much accommodated the Austrian provisional government. Only a few days after his arrival in Vienna, he received Renner, Figl, and Koplenig. Renner first of all thanked Stalin for the considerable assistance which the Soviet leader had so far provided to the provisional government and Tolbukhin for solving the difficult day-to-day problems.[93] Konev commented to Renner that it was one of the tasks of the Soviet command to help the provisional government and the Austrian people in the establishment of an independent, democratic state. Therefore, according to Konev, it was indispensable that all matters be dealt with in close cooperation with the provisional government.[94] At the same time, Konev made reference to the government's most important tasks: reconstruction of industry, good organization of the harvest,[95] determined course of action against saboteurs. Moreover, the Marshal called for the creation of corresponding laws which should aim at the "annihilation of fascism." He called for an energetic course of action against war criminals and former leading National Socialists. In conclusion, Konev expressed his hope that Renner and the government would follow "a hard line" in order to regulate all areas of life in the country, and added that the Soviet Supreme Command "will initiate resolute measures in every single case for the prevention of breaches of order and unlawful conduct."[96] Renner also mentioned to Konev the fears of the Austrians regarding the Soviet occupying power. He initially asked politely whether he could speak openly. Konev answered in the affirmative. After Renner had made reference to the fears of the populace, the Marshal assured the Austrian State Chancellor that the Soviets were "far from a policy of revenge" and "had at their disposal decisive measures for the prevention of incidents of all kinds (violence, confiscations)."[97] In the Cabinet Council, Renner reported on this only in diluted form.[98]

The Western powers continued to deny the Renner government their recognition. The assessment of the American charge d'affaires in Moscow, George Kennan, led to the Americans persisting in their viewpoint. Kennan expressed his doubts first and foremost regarding the allocation of the Interior Ministry to the Communist Franz Honner and pointed to similar experiences in Poland, Czechoslovakia and Romania.[99] The United States and Great Britain believed Austria was running the risk of becoming communist, although the concerns of the United States rather boiled down to the all too obvious solo effort on the part of the Soviets in the formation of a government.[100] Yet the intensive efforts of all parties during the subsequent four or five months ultimately led to the recognition of the Renner government by the Western powers on October 20, 1945.[101] As a precondition, an important alteration in the composition of the government was achieved on September 24, 1945, at the *Länderkonferenz* (conference of deputies from all Austrian provinces) in Vienna. "Westerners," first and foremost Karl Gruber for the newly created Foreign Office, were brought into the government. Josef Summer assumed control of the new Permanent Secretariat for the Interior and had, in this capacity, to prepare the first elections. In this way, the British were able to save face. They characterized the minor reshuffle as the formation of a new government (Government Renner II).[102] Renner's appearance at the *Länderkonferenz* itself was described by the Soviets as "excellent." The willingness of the British to come around was sold as a diplomatic victory and one achieved not without the self-serving assistance of Renner. In a rather more personal report to the NKID, the Soviet political advisor Koptelov wrote regarding the *Länderkonferenz*: "The conference developed in the direction we had hoped. The Renner government was confirmed at the conference. When agreement was reached at the conference on an enlargement of the government [. . .], Renner resorted to a small trick: in front of all the conference participants he read out the composition of the entire government with the new members. The English seized on this and wrote of a complete reorganisation and reformation of the government. It is clear that they wanted at least to comfort themselves a little with that and sweeten things."[103]

By this point in time, the Soviets' mistrust toward Renner had already grown considerably and their hopes for him had already sunk. The Soviet political plenipotentiary allegedly stated to his British colleagues at the *Länderkonferenz* that they could "absolutely imagine a stronger man for Austria," "yet Renner is evidently the only one with the necessary prestige." This statement was meant quite seriously—and less a case of diplomatic calculation in order to accommodate the British. The statement of the Soviet diplomat, however, was clearly never put on record. Stalin himself was merely presented with a very "dryly" composed report from Vyacheslav Molotov, Lavrentii

Beriia, Georgii Malenkov, and Anastas Mikoyan on the Resolution of the Allied Commission for Austria on October 1, 1945, regarding the expansion of the competences of Renner's Provisional Government of Austria.[104]

"WE CANNOT IMPROVE ON HIM"—"HE IS SOMETIMES A SCOUNDREL": RENNER FROM THE SOVIET POINT OF VIEW

The Soviets very quickly realized that Renner was not the man that Stalin appears to have thought he was. Renner did not let himself become Stalin's puppet. He used the opportunity granted to him very well. The Soviet occupying power, which continually changed its opinion of Renner, also perceived this. This ultimately culminated in autumn 1947 in open tirades of hatred against Renner in the Soviet press. In the resolutions from its first session, Cominform presented him as a danger to socialism. The internal reports of the Soviet occupying power and the political sections of the Internal Troops of the NKVD demonstrate the Soviet change of opinion.

The first critical utterances about Renner can be found in Soviet files very early on. After Renner had proclaimed at the 4th Plenary Session of the provisional government on May 10, 1945, his wish to invite only cabinet secretaries to future gatherings, it became clear to the Soviets what such a step meant: "By doing this, Renner is seeking to get rid of the 9 Communist deputy permanent secretaries and just as many representatives of the People's Party, by means of which he intends to alter the proportion of votes so as to be favourable to the Social Democrats. [. . .] Renner's appearances have a clear tendency to limit the participation of all members of the government in the solving of fundamental questions and to eliminate from these matters first and foremost the Communists," as Lieutenant Colonel Merkulov reported to Moscow on May 11, 1945.[105]

On May 16, the leadership of the Communist Party and permanent secretaries of the Provisional Austrian Government, Koplenig, Fischer, and Honner, met with representatives of the Military Council of the 3rd Ukrainian Front for an open discussion. The Soviet side invited the Austrian Communists "to openly recount all difficulties." Koplenig complained to the political officer Colonel Zheltov that "a tendency [in the government] to create a coalition of some of the Social Democrats and some of the Catholics [was] noticeable" and that this was "often directed against the Communists."[106] Koplenig continued: "The basis for the coalition consists of the efforts of the coalition to consolidate certain positions in the posts of the government leadership." The SPÖ and the ÖVP strove to "obtain control over as many leadership posts as possible in all organs [. . .] in order to eliminate the influence of the Communists." Koplenig gave Renner a real roasting: "In accordance with the system introduced by Renner, the government can only accept unanimous resolutions. Now if there is no unity, the Chancellor makes the decision himself. We Communists have objected to this. Renner announced that, if you're not happy with it, draw your own conclusions. Renner has no desire to work with us. [...] Of late, a strained relationship has developed between Renner and [the] Communists. Renner does not consider us one bit."[107] Honner pointed out to the Soviets that Renner intended to remove the State Police from the agenda of the Interior Ministry in order to be able to preside over it himself. He stressed that this function had to remain in the hands of the Interior Ministry, likewise the supervision of the staging of elections to the National Council. Fischer in turn emphasized in conclusion that there was already success on the lower level when it came to implementing joint operations within the masses. He stated that a "drive for unity" could be observed, but pointed to the glaring lack of managers in the ranks of the Communist Party, which he hoped to solve by obtaining new people from Moscow, who were trained from anti-fascist prisoners of war.

The concluding remarks by the political officer Colonel Zheltov clearly demonstrate Moscow's strategy: the establishment of the Communist Party in public and the capture of as broad a stratum of the population as possible through the utilization of the "fig leaf" of a democratically composed government on the basis of a one-third equal share for each of the permitted democratic, anti-fascist parties. Renner, the members of his government and the ÖVP were to be shown up; the Communists, due to the inability of the government to solve problems, would ultimately gain political capital and profit from it. Zheltov made clear:

> [...] that the main task of the Communist Party must be to capture the masses. [...] The masses and not the government must be conquered. If the mass of the people are brought on to the side of the Communist Party, then it can also bring about in the government the situation it requires. One should not get involved in a real fight with Renner as long as the masses have not been won over, but just a catfight. One has to work more quickly, more broadly and more deeply within the masses, among the farmers, the Catholics and the Social Democrats. If the government is less active, this is to the advantage of the Communist Party. [...] Renner said that he does not have any new blood this year, no-one to whom he could transfer the post of premier if necessary. If that were to happen, we must raise some people and put them on display. Which position should the Communists assume in relation to Renner? We cannot improve him. What do we need? We need a practical working environment founded on the unity of all democratic parties. We support Renner. May he himself solve the problems facing us at this difficult moment, such as the question of reparations, the reestablishment of industry and other problems. The Communists must interact with the masses and you must remain authentic advocates of the democratic front. If the Social

Democrats, the Catholics and others gab a lot, you must be practically active and be the originators of all practical measures. The most important thing is [. . .] to retain at this present time the unity of all democratic parties and not to allow any disruption from within. One must keep in mind that the government is of a provisional nature and to use the situation that arises for the capture of further positions in the future government.

In conclusion, Zheltov declared that the KPÖ functionaries should retain close contact with the occupying power and not wait until they were "invited or called," but rather in cases of difficulty get in touch themselves. Zheltov assured the Austrian Communists his full support in this matter.[108]

Colonel General Zheltov, the exponent of Soviet political leadership circles and executive hand of Soviet policy in Austria, regarded Renner as a useful instrument of a government in which the Communists would prevail in a peaceful manner. The fact that lies and deception were concealed behind Renner's pro-Soviet behavior was not only hidden from him. When Colonel Piterskii was ordered to Moscow to report at the end of May 1945, he described Renner in a discussion with a colleague of the 3rd European Department of the NKID as being in a sense transparent: "Renner is interested in matters of material prosperity, not only that of the entire Austrian nation but also his own. Renner asks how the Austrians can live well and at the same time says that he does not have a good wristwatch and whether it would be possible to send him caviar from Moscow. One should not believe everything that Renner says; he is sometimes a scoundrel."[109]

PRESSURIZING THE WESTERN POWERS TO RECOGNIZE THE PROVISIONAL GOVERNMENT

The difficulties that arose for Renner's government as a result of the non-recognition on the part of the Western Allies and severely limited its scope for action were increasingly assessed by the Soviets as inactivity on the part of the government. From the Soviet point of view, they had been of the greatest possible help to Renner's government. From their perspective, following the Potsdam Conference and the expectation of recognition for Renner's government by the Western occupying powers, opportunities opened up for a more efficient way of working on the part of the provisional government; these opportunities were not, however, taken. While the Austrians were anxious well into summer 1945 to develop a smooth relationship with the Soviets, on the Soviet side the attitude of the government ("all [. . .] embarrassing reserve and discretion which we have expended for months for fear of bumping into anything at all")[110] was interpreted as "inactivity."

On September 1, 1945, a discussion of this matter took place between representatives of the State Chancellery Department for Foreign Affairs and Koptelov, Konev's political advisor. During the talk, Koptelov asked why the Austrian government was still lacking a Foreign Ministry. He was aware that at the time the provisional government was formed it had been Renner's wish to assume the role of foreign minister himself. Koptelov: "When the government was formed, the Chancellor told us that he wants to manage foreign affairs himself. Good. That's his business. That is no reason, however, for there not to be a ministry. We understood at the outset that you have organisational difficulties. But enough time has now passed and you still have no ministry." Koptelov furthermore expressed his astonishment about the fact that Austria had so far established diplomatic relations only with Prague.

The question of the recognition of Renner's government by the Western powers was a fundamental objective not only of Austrian policy but also of Soviet policy in Austria in 1945 and should be regarded as an integral part of Soviet plans for Austria (establishment of a people's front, unification of left-wing forces by the controversial Renner). With regard to the recognition question, political advisor Koptelov made it blatantly clear to the Austrians that they were undertaking too little to solve this problem. He simultaneously provided the impetus for an approach to the Western Allies. Koptelov did not accept the circumstance that no senior political representatives were in Vienna at this point in time:

> We give enough visas to people to enter the American Zone. You could also go there, if you wanted to. And by the way, there are already lots of very qualified experts for the Americans and the English who are authorised to engage in negotiations. But you don't make a move. You must work! Nothing happens by itself. We understand very well your difficulties and if the Americans and the English understand them less, then you'll just have to go and talk to them and explain things to them. For they have just as much interest as us Russians in establishing real foundations for a new Austria. But only you can know what you want.[111]

DID MOSCOW PUSH AUSTRIA INTO THE "ROLE OF VICTIM"?

After this chastisement by the political advisor of the Soviets, the conclusion was drawn in the Foreign Office in Vienna that the "absence of a Foreign Ministry appeared straightforward to be a characteristic sign of a lack of will, or at least eagerness, on the part of the state to assert and defend itself [and the] embarrassing reserve and discretion [. . .] was interpreted as inactivity, not to mention indolence."[112] Only a few days later, Koptelov gave representatives of the Foreign Office startling new advice. During informal talks at a dinner, he expressed his astonishment "at the limited extent to which the Austrians have highlighted their rape by Hitler's regime and the resistance that Austria demonstrated. The Russian side has [. . .] allowed all measure of freedom and possibilities for this, yet these have so far barely been used. [. . .] In Russia, countless inhabitants were deprived of their life and their property by Nazi troops; in Austria it was not much different. Thus, the highlighting of such facts would be met with complete understanding, particularly in the Soviet Union. [Otherwise] one could get the impression, for example in the Soviet Union, that Austrians fought in the ranks of German formations just as hard as the Germans did."[113]

A comparison of the exploitation of the Soviet Union by Nazi Germany with that of Austria is no doubt bold and is not tenable in terms of magnitude. As no Soviet record of this informal discussion exists, however, it is also a matter of debate which wording Koptelov in fact used. Nevertheless, it is certainly willingly heard and positively received by Austrians. To what extent the Soviet stimulus that forced Austria entirely into the role of victim is decisive for the well-known handling of its Nazi past requires further study. Koptelov, like Kiselev in Vienna, was the mouthpiece of the Soviet Foreign Office.[114]

It is well-known that de-Nazification was from the outset of the highest priority for the Soviet occupying power. In this respect, the first discrepancies with Karl Renner concerning the tracking down and arrest of National Socialists emerged as early as the session of the government at the end of April 1945. Renner ruled that the illegal National Socialists could be released from prison for good behavior after two or three years, while the Communists and representatives of the ÖVP demanded the death penalty. In a discussion between Fürnberg and Lieutenant Senin (responsible for the organization of the Party work of the 336th Border Regiment of the Internal Troops of the NKVD), Fürnberg described Renner for this reason as "the worst social democrat and a sly fox."[115]

FREE ELECTIONS

Parallel to the increasing mistrust on the part of Soviet representatives in Vienna toward Renner, hopes for a good result for the KPÖ at the first free elections in November 1945 may also have sunk. The Soviet leadership had hoped through grass-roots work, intelligence, and great dedication to help the Communists to a quasi democratic victory in all countries occupied by the Red Army. In the case of Austria, Stalin had placed great hopes in Renner succeeding in uniting the left. The Soviets soon realized that Renner had embarked on a path not desired by them, but they did not undertake anything against it. Immediately prior to the elections, Soviet diplomats in Austria were already aware that the Communists would not do well. Renner predicted during a discussion with the Political Advisor Evgenii Kiselev that the Communists would obtain a large proportion of the votes. Nikolai Lun'kov's[116] internal report commented: "Comrade Kiselev informed me that during a discussion with State Chancellor Renner, [. . .] the latter had voiced the opinion that the Communists were likely to receive 20 per cent of the votes. Kiselev added for his part that this figure was undoubtedly too high."[117] Furthermore, it had been heard before the elections that at the SPÖ's party congress at the end of October 1945, Renner had engaged in attacks on the Soviet Union and had described the Communists as "enemies of democracy."[118] The Soviets in Vienna probably expected around 10 percent of the votes, though this probably did not reflect the view of the Kremlin. Yet not even this minimal target was not achieved, in spite of the intensive election support for the KPÖ, the much-advertised assistance for Austria such as the donations of millions for the rebuilding of the Vienna State Opera House or the assumption of diplomatic relations with Austria on the part of the USSR—even before the official recognition of the provisional government by the Western powers.[119] With only 5.42 percent of the votes, the election turned into a disaster for the Communists. The ÖVP narrowly beat the SPÖ and Leopold Figl became the first Federal Chancellor of the Second Republic.

The relationship between Renner and the Soviet occupying power subsequently deteriorated drastically. The results of the free elections encouraged him to be even more self-confident in his dealings with Moscow and to give them from time to time a ticking-off. Now in the function of Austrian Federal President, he expressed his dissatisfaction about the current state of Austria. According to Renner, it was not clear whether Austria was a liberated or a defeated country; peace treaties were prepared with all countries, but with Austria nothing happened. For the first time, Renner now openly criticized the Soviet treatment of the SPÖ, though without saddling the Soviets with the blame for the election results:

> You Russians are not doing the right thing by only relying on the one Communist Party. The Communist Party did not have and still does not have any roots in Austria or the kind of influence that the Socialist Party has. It [the KPÖ] is regarded by Austrians as a foreign party. The main base of the Socialist Party of Austria is the working class, which views the Soviet Union with enormous friendliness and aligns itself only with it [the Soviet Union]. The Austrian workers are not looking to the West. The struggle that has recently unfolded between the Communist Party and the Socialist Party only benefited the People's Party

and leads to a schism in the Austrian working class. The Soviet Union would conduct itself better if it were to rely more on the policies of the Socialist Party, which is prepared to work together with it. That would bring more results.

Renner continued: "I must go to Moscow and enlighten Comrade Stalin personally as to the flawed dealings with the Socialist Party of Austria, which is the strongest workers' party."[120] The victory of the ÖVP may, admittedly, have hurt Renner; his manner toward the Soviets following the elections was in fact a tactical manoeuvre. He had initially predicted to the Soviets a promising result for the KPÖ; then he declared that the KPÖ had never had any roots in Austria and that its disputes with the SPÖ cost both parties votes and strengthened the bourgeois camp in Austria. In this way, Renner openly laid the blame on the Soviets for the defeat of the KPÖ. Now he had definitively emancipated himself from the Soviet occupying power.

At the latest by the time of the elections, the Soviets had seen through his maneuvering. While the SPÖ—without Renner being mentioned by name—was most vehemently criticized,[121] the Soviet holders of power in Vienna had finally "seen through" Renner and described the policies of the SPÖ, "which is led by Renner," as "duplicitous."[122] In their eyes, the SPÖ was one of the most right-wing and reactionary of Europe's social democratic parties. From now on, Renner, like the other leaders of the SPÖ, was accused of having "earlier worked with the Nazis."[123] The policies of Renner's government were "unprincipled," his domestic and foreign policy was pursued "without any backbone, serving the interests of the Austrian and foreign bourgeoisie."[124] The Soviets were still wary, however, of criticizing Renner openly. An open escalation did not occur until 1947. To begin with, the Soviet Foreign Ministry intimated to the Austrian envoy in Moscow, Norbert Bischoff, that the Austrian socialists were "reactionary" and that it was "as though their leadership [was] allied with 'American monopoly capitalism.'"[125]

In the final declaration of Cominform in September 1947, Renner was finally placed alongside other European "right-wing socialists" such as Clement Attlee, Ernest Bevin, Paul Ramadier, Léon Blum, and Kurt Schumacher. They were categorized as henchmen of the imperialists and accused of pursuing traitorous policies behind the "mask of democracy and socialist phraseology."[126] The following month a long article appeared in the *Literaturnaya Gazeta* on the "traitor Karl Renner, extinguisher of sparks."[127] In 1948, the Chief of the Section for Propaganda of the Soviet Element of the Allied Commission for Austria (SChSK), Colonel Dubrovitskii, described Renner and Adolf Schärf internally as "faithful minions of the imperialists who contribute to the decomposition of the working class and poison it."[128]

Tensions eased somewhat, however, at least pro forma. Already after the accession of Figl's government, Renner—in his henceforth representative position as Austrian Federal President—ceased to play a central role for the Soviets. On December 15, 1950, birthday wishes from the Soviet occupying power were printed in the *Österreichische Zeitung* on the occasion of Renner's eightieth birthday. Officially, Renner had done nothing but that which the Soviet occupying power had always officially announced: he had made a decisive contribution to the reestablishment of Austria as an independent state.

Renner was most accurately characterized during his lifetime by the British newspaper, the *Observer*. In October 1949, the *Observer* dedicated an essay to him:

> He appeared to be just the man that the Russians needed: old, very old, very popular, for a long time uninvolved in practical politics, a link to the past, a respectable facade for a "People's Front" government that would be rapidly seized by a few energetic young communists. But this time the Russians had chosen the wrong man. Renner was mild, friendly and engaging, also willing to leave some ministerial posts to the Communists, but also capable of retaining the reins in his own hands. [. . .] He meekly came to terms with being described by some of his foreign friends as a Russian puppet; he did not create any scandal for the occupying power, he was flexible, polite and charming. But the point on which he insisted with resolute calmness, was the necessity for general elections [. . .] and Renner threw the entire energy and fighting strength into this election campaign that had gathered during the long years of forced inactivity. [. . .] His party, the socialists, was marginally outperformed by the Catholic People's Party, but the Communists were completely annihilated. [. . .] There are few men who succeed in founding two republics during their lifetime, and there was hitherto no man who survived the decline of the first knowing with certainty that the second would last. If this Second Austrian Republic remains successful, however, then it will be a monument to Dr Renner.[129]

In 1949, Karl Renner was among the twenty-three candidates shortlisted for the Nobel Peace Prize.[130] On December 31, 1950, Karl Renner died as incumbent Federal President in the eighty-first year of his life. Together with Figl and Schärf, he had set the course for a stable Second Republic and had gone down in history as the founding father of the First and the Second Republic of Austria.

SUMMARY

Stalin's approach to Austria corresponded to that pursued in every Eastern European country occupied by the Red Army. For the realization of the "National Front" strategy, he required an enigmatic figure with "blemishes" in his past, a man with "little backbone" who, as a willing puppet of the Kremlin, possessed the necessary authority in his own country in order to first of all unite all "anti-fascist forces" and form a democratic government. Within this government, the Communists would gradually establish themselves. Stalin's approach in Eastern Europe was shaped by tactical calculations; if he was confronted by too much resistance from the Western powers, he backed off from the next step and waited for the right moment. With regard to Austria, the decisive question is what moved Stalin to proceed in Vienna in the same way as in Eastern Europe; had the plans to form a provisional government become known, the United States above all would have registered their misgivings.

In terms of post-war plans for Austria, Stalin had succeeded in pushing through his own position. Austria had again emerged as a small state occupied fourfold. Stalin ultimately adhered to all agreements, even though he had attempted to skilfully exploit the Allied entry into Vienna, the transfer of Styria to the British or the precarious situation in Carinthia as a game of poker with the Western powers. He also did not support the demands of Tito for an independent Yugoslavian occupation zone in southern Austria.[131] The question of forming a government had not been seriously discussed by the Allies at the EAC in London. The Western powers desired the democratic establishment of a government from below. What made Stalin opt for a unilateral approach?

Was it the appearance of Fritz Molden and Ernst Lemberger, who called on the Soviets in Paris in March 1945 and presented the government plans of the Provisional Austrian National Committee (POEN), the political arm of the resistance movement "O5," which was allegedly supported by the Americans? Did this strengthen Stalin's mistrust toward the Western Allies? This can be assumed. Did supposed, in fact nonexistent, Western plans for the formation of an Austrian government tempt Stalin to pursue his unilateral approach? What was decisive for Stalin in deciding to seize the initiative in the question of forming a government before the capture of Vienna? Did he want to preempt the Western powers and avert a pro-Western government? Was this the stimulus that made Stalin, for the first time, give some thought to Austria, select Karl Renner and have him tracked down? Subsequent remarks by Molotov to the effect that the Soviet leadership had early on decided "not to touch Austria"[132] suggest an ad hoc decision on Stalin's part. For Stalin, this seemed to be an ideal starting position. He could now inform the Allies that Renner had appeared and declared his willingness to form a provisional government. The Western powers, first and foremost the exponent of American diplomacy, George Kennan, Ambassador to Moscow, recognized the all too apparitional approach of the Kremlin. From now on, the West was not prepared to put up with a unilateral approach in Austria on the part of the Kremlin. Unperturbed, Stalin clung on to Renner and indeed granted him considerable freedom of action.

An argument against the necessity of a "stimulus" for a unilateral approach on the part of Stalin would be the fact that Stalin skillfully calculated and sounded out how far he could go. Precisely at this point in time, on April 12, 1945, the American President Franklin D. Roosevelt died, "at the time, when his suspicions of Soviet intentions began to clash with his desire for postwar cooperation." His death apparently mollified Stalin and Molotov.[133] Did Roosevelt in fact die at a propitious time for Austria?[134] Unable to calculate what might come, Stalin continued to place his hope in Renner and gave him all the freedom of a head of government, even if it was recognized at an early stage that Renner was "a scoundrel" and the Communists were unable to establish themselves in the provisional government or compete with the cohesion of the ÖVP and the SPÖ. Moscow stuck to the "practical basis for work," according to which people were to be "raised" who would, if necessary, be capable of assuming the office of head of government.

The question remains, however, whether Stalin only proceeded unilaterally in Austria in order to preempt the West and to avert a pro-Western government? Probably not. These two alternatives do not, however, rule each other out. Regardless of this, Stalin would almost certainly have proceeded unilaterally. The appearance of Molden and Lemberger may have solidified his plans for Austria; conclusive evidence is not available. From the Soviet perspective, the illusory "Renner experiment" ultimately went wrong. Karl Renner prevented the establishment of the Communists in his government and, together with Leopold Figl and others, paved the way for a stable Second Republic of Austria. For the Kremlin, this was not so bad. Officially, Moscow had never wanted anything else.

The expectations of the Soviets for the elections of November 1945 were, up until the elections in Hungary that is, by no means low; it was only directly before the elections that at least the diplomats stationed in Vienna realized that the KPÖ was fighting a losing battle. In November 1945, the KPÖ suffered a devastating election defeat. With the elections, the illusory hopes of the Kremlin burst like a bubble. Even if Moscow involved itself in the formation of the new Austrian government under Leopold Figl (ÖVP) and refused to agree to the appointment of some ministers (the later Federal Chancellor Julius Raab among them), it allowed the government a freer hand than, for example, the Hungarian, where a tougher stance was taken and Stalin had to be less and less considerate of the Allies. Nevertheless, the occupation of Austria subsequently remained of strategic importance for the Kremlin. In the burgeoning East-West conflict, it acquired within Soviet foreign policy an ever greater importance for the consolidation of the Eastern Bloc.

NOTES

1. The authors would like to thank Alex J. Kay for translating this article from German into English. In contrast to the longer, German original version of this text, the lengthy discussion in the footnotes of, above all, the Austrian historiography will be dispensed with. On this see Stefan Karner and Peter Ruggenthaler, "Unter sowjetischer Kontrolle: Zur Regierungsbildung in Österreich 1945," in Stefan Karner and Barbara Stelzl-Marx, eds., *Die Rote Armee in Österreich: Sowjetische Besatzung 1945–1955. Beiträge* (Graz/Vienna/Munich: Oldenbourg, 2005), pp. 97–140.

2. Vojtech Mastny, *Russia's Road to the Cold War: Diplomacy, Warfare, and the Politics of Communism, 1941–1945* (New York: Columbia University Press, 1979), p. 234. Manfried Rauchensteiner, *Der Sonderfall: Die Besatzungszeit in Österreich 1945 bis 1955* (Graz: Styria, 1995), pp. 15ff.

3. Donal O'Sullivan, *Stalins "Cordon sanitaire": Die sowjetische Osteuropapolitik und die Reaktionen des Westens 1939-1949* (Paderborn: Schöningh, 2003), pp. 237–242 and 306; Jost Dülffer, *Jalta, 4. Februar 1945: Der Zweite Weltkrieg und die Entstehung der bipolaren Welt* (Munich: dtv, 1998). Yalta enabled Stalin from this point on to proceed selectively in the individual Eastern European countries. It is possible that Stalin hoped for an easier approach toward Austria in order to bring it under Soviet influence after the war. See Günter Bischof, "Die Planung und Politik der Alliierten 1940–1954," in Rolf Steininger and Michael Gehler, eds., *Österreich im 20. Jahrhundert: Ein Studienbuch in zwei Bänden. Vom Weltkrieg bis zur Gegenwart*, Vol. 2 (Vienna/Cologne/Weimar: Böhlau, 1997), pp. 107–146, here p. 111. On the subject in general see above all Stefan Creuzberger and Manfred Görtemaker, eds., *Gleichschaltung unter Stalin? Die Entwicklung der Parteien im östlichen Europa 1944–1949* (Paderborn: Schöningh, 2002); Norman Naimark and Leonid Gibianskii, *The Establishment of Communist Regimes in Eastern Europe, 1944–1949* (Boulder: Westview Press, 1997).

4. On the British-Soviet exchange of blows regarding the memorandum on the post-war order in Europe, presented by the British, see Jochen Laufer, "Die UdSSR und die Zoneneinteilung Deutschlands (1943/44)," *Zeitschrift für Geschichtswissenschaft*, Vol. 43 (1995), pp. 309–331.

5. On the EAC see above all Hans-Günter Kowalski, "Die European Advisory Commission als Instrument alliierter Deutschland-Planungen 1943–1945," *Zeitschrift für Geschichtswissenschaft*, Vol. 19 (1971), pp. 261–293. Furthermore: I. C. B. Dear, ed., *The Oxford Companion to World War II* (Oxford: Oxford University Press, 1995), p. 342; Foreign Policy Archives of the Russian Federation (hereafter AVP RF), f. 07, op. 10, p. 13, d. 159, ll. 9–11, 18–21 and 82–84, "Report of the 2nd European Department of the People's Commissariat for Foreign Affairs of the USSR on the progress of discussions of matters relating to the occupation of Austria in the European Advisory Commission (EAC) for the period 8 May–6 September 1944," 17 September 1944. Reproduced in: Stefan Karner, Barbara Stelzl-Marx and Alexander Tschubarjan, eds., *Die Rote Armee in Österreich: Sowjetische Besatzung 1945–1955. Dokumente. Krasnaya Armiya v Avstrii: Sovetskaya okkupatsiya 1945–1955. Dokumenty* (Graz/Vienna/Munich: Oldenbourg, 2005), Doc. 4.

6. On this see the corresponding plans of the Maiskii Commission on the transition to communism in the whole of Europe. See Eduard Mark, "Revolution by Degrees: Stalin's National-Front Strategy for Europe, 1941–1947," CWIHP Working Paper No. 31, Washington, DC, 2001.

7. Natal'ja Lebedeva, "Österreichische Kommunisten im Moskauer Exil: Die Komintern, die Abteilung für internationale Information des ZK der VKP(b) und Österreich 1943–1945," in Karner and Stelzl-Marx, eds., *Die Rote Armee in Österreich*, pp. 39–60.

8. On this see Fritz Molden, *Fepolinski & Waschlapski: Auf dem berstenden Stern* (Vienna/Munich/Zürich: Molden, 1976), pp. 352–354; Rauchensteiner, *Der Sonderfall*, p. 68; Wilfried Aichinger, *Sowjetische Österreichpolitik 1943–1945: Materialien zur Zeitgeschichte*, Vol. 1 (Vienna: Eigenverlag der ÖGZ, 1977), pp. 160–161. Ernst Lemberger, alias Jean Lambert, immigrated to France in 1938 and was a leading member of the French resistance movement during the Second World War. After 1945 he was the Austrian Ambassador to Brussels, Washington, and Paris, among other places. As a resistance fighter during the Second World War, Fritz Molden, the son of the well-known lyricist and author of the current Austrian national anthem, Paula von Preradović, repeatedly made contact with the Allies. After the war, he initially worked as the secretary to Foreign Minister Karl Gruber and later at the Austrian General Consulate in New York. In 1948 he married Joan Dulles, who had become known in Austria above all as a publisher and newspaper editor and was the daughter of the later CIA head, Allen Welsh Dulles.

9. Russian State Archives of Socio-Political History (hereafter RGASPI), f. 495, op. 74, d. 25, ll. 7–8, Dimitrov to Stalin, 6 April 1945.

10. Molden, *Fepolinski & Waschlapski*, pp. 354–355. The reporting on the revolt planned by Major Szokoll can now also be documented using Soviet sources. Central Archives of the Ministry of Defence (hereafter TsAMO), f. 243, op. 2912, d. 146, ll. 118–120, "Report of the High Commander of the 9th Guards Army to the Chief of the General Staff of the Red Army on the uprising prepared in Vienna," April 5, 1945. Reproduced in: Karner, Stelzl-Marx and Tschubarjan, eds., *Die Rote Armee in Österreich*, Doc. 14.

11. AVP RF, f. 066, op. 25, p. 120, d. 27, l. 7, Report of the First Mission Secretary of the USSR in Sweden, V. Razin, to the 3rd European Department of the Soviet Foreign Ministry, December 19, 1944.

12. Dieter A. Binder and Karl Maria Stepan, *Josef Dobretsberger: Verlorene Positionen des christlichen Lagers* (Vienna: Karl-von-Vogelsang-Institut, 1992), pp. 39–43. Rumors were still circulating in the Foreign Office in May about a possible Dobretsberger government supported by the British. Austrian State Archives, Archives of the Republic (hereafter ÖStA, AdR), AA, II-pol. 1945, K. 1 (1-100), 13, May 5, 1945; on this see also Eva-Marie Csáky, Franz Matscher and Gerald Stourzh, eds., *Josef Schöner: Wiener Tagebuch 1944/1945* (Vienna/Cologne/Weimar: Böhlau, 1992), p. 165 (notes from April 18, 1945). A Soviet Secret Service report falsely reported in 1947 that Dobretsberger had long been in exile in the United States and had been groomed by the Americans for the post of the future chancellor. Central Archives of the Federal Security Service of the Russian Federation (hereafter TsA FSB RF),

f. 135, op. 1, d. 29, ll. 201–207, Report "On the pro-American Course of the ÖVP and Attempts to Form a Catholic Block in its Place" to the Supreme Commander of the Soviet Occupation Troops in Austria, May 27, 1947.

13. AVP RF, f. 066, op. 25, p. 118a, d. 5, ll. 10–16, SMERSH report from October 26, 1945.

14. RGASPI, f. 17, op. 128, p. 117, ll. 97–98, "From the report of the Propaganda Department of the Soviet Element of the Allied Commission on the Catholic Church and its influence as well as on the general situation in Austria," n.d. [no later than August 8, 1946]. Reproduced in Karner, Stelzl-Marx and Tschubarjan, eds., *Die Rote Armee in Österreich*, Doc. 96. On this see also in ibid. the comprehensive secret service report from May 17, 1947 on alleged Western plans with Habsburg. See TsA FSB RF, f. 135, op. 1, d. 29, ll. 117–147, Report of the secret service section of the SChSK "On the domestic situation in Austria" to the Soviet High Commissioner in Austria, May 18, 1947.

15. On this see above all Dokumentationsarchiv des österreichischen Widerstandes, ed., *Österreicher im Exil: USA 1938–1945. Eine Dokumentation*, 2 vols. (Vienna: Deuticke, 1995).

16. János M. Rainer, "Der Weg der ungarischen Volksdemokratie: Das Mehrparteiensystem und seine Beseitigung 1944–1949," in Creuzberger and Görtemaker, eds., *Gleichschaltung unter Stalin?*, pp. 319–352.

17. Karl Kautsky, 1854–1938, was the author of studies on political theory and history, head of the journal of the Second International, the *Neue Zeit* (New Times), and author of the draft "Erfurt Programme" of the Social Democratic Party of Germany. Influenced by Marxist theory, he strived for a socialist society but rejected the Russian path after 1917. In 1924, Kautsky moved to Vienna, from where he immigrated to the Netherlands in 1938, where he died the same year at the age of eighty-four.

18. On this see Sergej Matwejewitsch Schtemenko, *Im Generalstab*, Vol.1 ([East] Berlin: Militärverlag der Deutschen Demokratischen Republik, 1985), pp. 403–405; S. M. Shtemenko, *General'nyi shtab v gody voiny. Kniga vtoraya* (Moscow: Voenizdat, 1974), p. 356.

19. Aleksei I. Antonov, born 1896, was from December 1952 the First Deputy Chief of the General Staff and one of Stalin's most important military advisers. During the Second World War he was the Chief of Staff on several fronts, from February 1945 Chief of the General Staff. V. A. Torchinov and A. M. Leontyuk, *Vokrug Stalina: Istoriko-biograficheskii spravochnik* (St. Petersburg: FilFak SPbGU 2000), pp. 60–61.

20. Schtemenko, *Im Generalstab*, pp. 403–405; S. M. Shtemenko, *General'nyi shtab*, p. 356. Stalin had admittedly probably never met Renner personally, but he had read his publications on the nationalities question in the Austrian-Hungarian monarchy due to his "research trip" in 1912/1913. From Krakow, Lenin had sent him to Vienna for a few weeks in order to study the views of Austrian social democrats on the national self-determination of peoples. His treatise "The Nationality Question and Social Democracy" originated in Vienna. Stalin's academic works induced Lenin after the October Revolution to appoint Stalin to the government as People's

Commissar for Nationality Affairs. See Isaac Deutscher, *Stalin: Eine politische Biographie* (Berlin: Dietz, 1990), p. 163. Renner's publication "State and Nation" was also translated into Russian. Anton Pelinka, *Karl Renner zur Einführung* (Hamburg: Junius, 1989), pp. 126–127. A personal meeting between Stalin and Renner at this time is not documented. In his first letter to Stalin from April, 15, Renner admittedly "regrets" never having met him personally (in contrast to Lenin and Trotskii), but he supposedly told Lieutenant Startchevskii, who brought him to Tolbukhin in Vienna on April 19 (or perhaps already on April 18), during the journey from Gloggnitz that he "had had too few personal contacts with Stalin." Hugo Portisch, *Am Anfang war das Ende: Österreich II. Die Geschichte Österreichs vom 2. Weltkrieg bis zum Staatsvertrag*, Vol. 1 (Munich: Wilhelm Heyne Verlag, 1993), p. 229. What he meant by "personal contacts," however, remains unclear.

21. Shtemenko, *General'nyi shtab*, p. 356.

22. Peter Sixl, *Sowjetische Kriegsgräber in Österreich* (Graz: Verein zur Förderung der Forschung von Folgen nach Konflikten und Kriegen, 2005).

23. Admittedly, Stalin did not mean a restoration of the authoritarian corporate state. Ivo Banac, ed., *The Diary of Georgi Dimitrov 1933–1949* (New Haven/London: Yale University Press, 2003), p. 365.

24. After Dimitrov had been ordered to Stalin, he conferred with Koplenig and Khvostsev on April 2 and again on April 3 with Koplenig. On April 4, he also brought Fischer in on the consultations. See ibid.

25. On this see also Ernst Fischer, *Das Ende einer Illusion: Erinnerungen 1945–1955* (Vienna: Molden, 1973), p. 20. Fischer depicts the planned reconstruction of socialism in Austria in the following way: "[. . .] no leadership claim on the part of the Communist Party, but maximum efforts to obtain respect and trust through intelligence, altruism and political foresight." See also Banac, *The Diary of Georgi Dimitrov*, p. 366.

26. RGASPI, f. 495, op. 74, d. 24, ll. 1–2, Written communication from Dimitrov to Stalin, April 3, 1945.

27. TsAMO, f. 148a, op. 3763, d. 212, ll. 10–11, Directive of the Stavka from April 2, 1945. Reproduced in: Institut Voennoi Istorii, ed., *Krasnaya Armiya v stranakh Tsentral'noi Evropy i na Balkanakh: Dokumenty i materialy 1944–1945. Russkii Arkhiv. Velikaya Otechestvennaya Voina*, Vol. 3(2) (Moscow: Terra, 2000), pp. 221–222.

28. RGASPI, f. 495, op. 74, d. 24, l. 5, Dimitrov to Stalin, April 5, 1945.

29. At least no further instructions for Dimitrov are known. See RGAPSI, f. 495, op. 74, d. 24, 25.

30. See Banac, *The Diary of Georgi Dimitrov*, pp. 365–367.

31. Confirmed by the Politburo of the Central Committee of the VKP(b) on April 7, 1945 in his position as Political Advisor in Austrian Matters to the Commandant of the 3rd Ukrainian Front. His deputy was Andrei Smirnov. RGASPI, f. 17, op. 3, d. 1.052, Politburo Resolution 45 (108) from April 7, 1945.

32. Molotov was informed about Renner by Stalin. He received a copy of the telegram to Tolbukhin. It can be assumed that Dekanozov was in turn informed of this by Molotov. During their shared flight to Austria, however, they were both exceedingly

tight-lipped toward the KPÖ leadership. See Fischer, *Das Ende einer Illusion*, pp. 19–23.

33. Banac, *The Diary of Georgi Dimitrov*, pp. 366–367.

34. Regional Archives of Lower Austria (NÖLA), L. A. III/3-a-29/8-1961; Siegfried Nasko, ed., *Karl Renner—vom Bauernsohn zum Bundespräsidenten* (Vienna/ Gloggnitz: Österreichisches Gesellschafts- und Wirtschaftsmuseum, 1979).

35. Aichinger, *Sowjetische Österreichpolitik*, p. 123.

36. Supposedly Captain Garin; see Harry Piotrowski, "The Soviet Union and the Renner Government of Austria, April–November 1945," *Central European History*, Vol. 20 (1987), pp. 246–279, here p. 252.

37. TsAMO, f. 350, op. 6076, d. 32, ll. 244–246. This can also be found in the memoirs of the daughter of Karl Renner: "In Gloggnitz, he was told [. . .] that he should contact the commandant's office in Köttlach. There, a Soviet officer remembered the name Renner and immediately detained him until he received orders from Moscow for further assignment." *Salzburger Nachrichten*, May 10, 1975, p. 25.

38. Mastny called into questioned the systematic search for Renner; Mastny, *Russia's Road to the Cold War*, pp. 387–388. Schärf passed on Stalin's surprise at the news regarding Renner's appearance (see his discussions with the Soviet leadership in April 1955). Dallin puts these words in Mikoyan's mouth and Nasko in Khrushchev's. See David J. Dallin, "Stalin, Renner und Tito: Österreich zwischen drohender Sowjetisierung und den jugoslawischen Gebietsansprüchen im Frühjahr 1945," *Europa-Archiv*, Vols. 13–17 (1958), pp. 11,030–11,034, here p. 11,031. Siegfried Nasko, "Zur Rolle Dr. Renners im April 1945," in Siegfried Nasko, ed., *Gedenkraum 1945: Hier entstand Österreich wieder. Katalog zu "Gedenkraum 1945"* (Vienna/ Wiener Neustadt/Hochwolkersdorf: Österreichisches Gesellschafts- und Wirtschaftsmuseum, 1981), p. 339. Furthermore, Stalin supposedly said: "He [Renner] is precisely the man that we need!"

39. Until July 1950, Aleksei Zheltov (1904–1991) was deputy Soviet High Commissioner in Austria. His first advisor was Embassy Counsellor Kiselev. O. A. Rzheshevskii, N. B. Borisov and E. K. Zhigunov, eds., *Kto byl kto v Velikoi Otechestvennoi Voine, 1941–1945: Lyudi. Sobytiya. Fakty. Spravochnik* (Moscow: Respublika, 2000), pp. 96–97.

40. TsAMO, f. 350, op. 6076, d. 32, ll. 244–246, "Report of the Command of the 9th Guards Army to the Military Council of the 3rd Ukrainian Front on discussion with the former chairman of the Austrian Parliament, 3 April 1945." Initially, Renner had not been recognized by the Soviets in Köttlach. "No-one initially paid particular attention to him. But then one of the political employees realised whom he was dealing with." See Nasko, "Zur Rolle Dr. Renners im April 1945," p. 17.

41. TsAMO, f. 48, op. 3411ss, d. 196, ll. 309–311, Coded telegram no. 167376/sh from April 4, 1945 from Tolbukhin to Stalin.

42. The telegram was sent at 4:08 p.m. to the 8th Administration of the General Staff of the Red Army by the 3rd Ukrainian Front. It arrived in Moscow at 6:05 p.m. and had been decoded by 6:40 p.m. The seven printed copies of the telegram were sent to Stalin, Molotov, Bulganin, Beriia, Antonov, Shtemenko and the 4th Section at 6:50 p.m. TsAMO, f. 48, op. 3411ss, d. 196, ll. 309–311.

43. As Molotov or Mikoyan told Schärf in April 1955 in Moscow. Nasko, "Zur Rolle Dr. Renners im April 1945," p. 22.

44. TsAMO, f. 243, op. 2912, d. 146, ll. 113–114. Coded telegram no. 29904/sh from 4 April 1945 from Stalin to Tolbukhin. The telegram left the Stavka at 7:30 p.m. On this see also Schtemenko, *Im Generalstab*, p. 405.

45. A copy was sent to Molotov. The telegram was sent at 8:30 p.m. TsAMO, f. 243, op. 2912, d. 146, l. 269. The wording of the telegram is the same as that which the Soviets proclaimed at the beginning of April in the first appeal of the Red Army to the population of Austria. The texts of the first proclamations to Austria and appeals to the Austrian population can be traced back to Stalin himself. In a directive issued to Tolbukhin on April 2, 1945, he had instructed the latter to explain to the Austrian population the aims of the Red Army in Austria. TsAMO, f. 148a, op. 3763, d. 212, ll. 10–11, Directive of the Stavka from 2 April 1945. Reproduced in: Manfried Rauchensteiner, *Der Krieg in Österreich 1945*, new edition (Vienna: Böhlau, 1995), p. 491.

46. Aichinger, *Sowjetische Österreichpolitik*, p. 122.

47. Ernst Fischer also said the same in his memoirs. See Fischer, *Das Ende einer Illusion*, p. 20.

48. TsAMO, f. 243, op. 2914, d. 268, ll. 53–54, Report of Major Vasil´ev; TsAMO, f. 413, op. 10389, d. 46, ll. 1–8, Report of the Chief of the Political Section of the 57th Army, Major General Tsinev, June 5, 1945, reprinted in: Stefan Karner and Othmar Pickl, eds., *Die Rote Armee in der Steiermark: Sowjetische Besatzung 1945*, in cooperation with Walter M. Iber, Harald Knoll, Hermine Prügger, Peter Ruggenthaler, Arno Wonisch and Silke Stern (Graz: Leykam, 2008), Doc. 92.

49. See Shtemenko, *General´nyi Shtab*, p. 356.

50. "The last thing Stalin wanted in Austria was a politician who would take a similarly uncompromising position." Piotrowski, "The Soviet Union and the Renner Government," p. 260.

51. On this see, for example, the role of Gheorge Tatarescu in Romania. See O'Sullivan, *Stalins "Cordon sanitaire,"* pp. 250, 302 and 308.

52. Aichinger, *Sowjetische Österreichpolitik*, pp. 127–128.

53. In the reports from Tolbukhin and Zheltov to Stalin, there are no indications to this effect, though that is hardly surprising. TsAMO, f. 243, op. 2912, d. 146, ll. 123–125.

54. Aichinger, *Sowjetische Österreichpolitik*, p. 125; Nasko, "Zur Rolle Dr. Renners im April 1945," pp. 340–341.

55. Russian State Military Archives (hereafter RGVA), f. 38756, op. 1, d. 6, l. 201. The surveillance evidently came about at Renner's own request. "The other members of the government have not expressed the desire for a personal surveillance." Colonel Martynov, Commander of the 336th Border Regiment to Lieutenant Colonel Semenenko, Chief of Staff of the Internal Troops of the NKVD for the Protection of the Rear of the 3rd Ukrainian Front, May 5, 1941.

56. TsAMO, f. 243, op. 2912, d. 146, ll. 192–194, Tolbukhin and Zheltov to Stalin, April 28, 1945, on the reception of the Provisional Austrian Government on April 27, 1945. TsAMO, f. 243, op. 37385, d. 4, ll. 84–85, Regulation from Tolbukhin and Zheltov regarding assistance for the Provisional Austrian Government, May 5, 1945.

Reproduced in: Institut Voennoi Istorii, ed., *Velikaya Otechestvennaya Voina*, pp. 654–655.

57. Schtemenko, *Im Generalstab*, p. 414.

58. Smirnov was a senior Soviet diplomat in matters pertaining to Germany and, from April 1945, Dekanozov's deputy for Austrian affairs.

59. The Revolutionary Socialists were only founded in Czechoslovak emigration in 1934 in Brno/Brünn. On April 14, 1945, they again merged with the Social Democrats to form the Socialist Party of Austria. See, for example, Peter Pelinka, *Erbe und Neubeginn: Die Revolutionären Sozialisten in Österreich 1934–38* (Vienna: Europaverlag, 1981).

60. TsAMO, f. 48, op. 3411, d. 196, ll. 315–319, Coded telegram from Tolbukhin, Zheltov and Smirnov to Stalin, April 15, 1945. Decoded on April 15, 1945 at 12:50 a.m. The nine copies were sent to Stalin, Bulganin, Molotov, Antonov, Beriia, Malenkov, Dekanozov and the 4th Section of the 8th Administration.

61. Ibid.

62. TsAMO, f. 148a, op. 3763, d. 213, l. 84, Coded telegram from Shtemenko to Tolbukhin, April 17, 1945. Reproduced in: Karner, Stelzl-Marx, and Tschubarjan, eds., *Die Rote Armee in Österreich*, p. 24.

63. It can be assumed that the NKVD troops did not let Renner out of their sights following his departure from Eichbüchl Palace. An enquiry by Tolbukhin to the NKVD as to where Renner could be found would have been an embarrassment for the Marshal. This would explain the fresh search, as Starchevskii has passed it down and it has been reiterated by veterans of the 4th Guards Army. See Archives of the Ludwig-Boltzmann Institute for Research on War Consequences (AdBIK), Oral History Interview, VD-0282b/0283a, Vasilii Tyukhtyaev in Moscow on November 21, 2003. Interviewer: Ol'ga Pavlenko.

64. On April 17, Renner was "in the immediate vicinity of Wiener Neustadt" (letter from Renner to Schärf). Adolf Schärf, *Österreichs Wiederaufrichtung im Jahre 1945* (Vienna: Verlag der Wiener Volksbuchhandlung, 1960), p. 69. In another letter he stated that he was "holding himself in readiness." Adolf Schärf, *Österreichs Erneuerung 1945–1955: Das erste Jahrzehnt der Zweiten Republik* (Vienna: Verlag der Wiener Volksbuchhandlung, 1955), pp. 30–32.

65. Until now, this search for Renner has always been intermingled with the (presumed) search order from Stalin from the beginning of April. See Portisch, *Österreich II*, Vol. 1, pp. 228–229.

66. TsAMO, f. 148a, op. 3763, d. 213, l. 84 (as in note 62).

67. This is probably an error. According to the minutes of the discussion, Renner apparently promised to submit a list by April 23. AVP RF, f. 066, op. 25, p. 118a, d. 7, ll. 1–5, here l. 3, "Notification of the Deputy Political Advisor attached to the Commander-in-Chief of the 3rd Ukrainian Front, M. E. Koptelov, to the Deputy People's Commissar for Foreign Affairs of the USSR, V. G. Dekanozov, on the discussion with K. Renner regarding the formation of the Provisional Austrian Government," Vienna, April 19, 1945. Reproduced in: Karner, Stelzl-Marx and Tschubarjan, eds., *Die Rote Armee in Österreich*, Doc. 21.

68. Decoded on April 21, 1945 at 10:10 a.m. The nine copies were sent to Stalin, Molotov, Beriia, Malenkov, Antonov, Vyshinskii, Dekanozov and the 4th Section. TsAMO, f. 48, op. 3411, d. 196, l. 337. Mikhail Koptelov, the Deputy Political Advisor of the Commander of the 3rd Ukrainian Front, sent a detailed report on the discussion to the Foreign Office. AVP RF, f. 066, op. 25, p. 118a, d. 7, ll. 1–5 (as in note 67).

69. Ibid.

70. On this see, Rauchensteiner, *Der Sonderfall*, pp. 68–73; Portisch, *Österreich II*, Vol. 1, p. 230 on.

71. AVP RF, f. 066, op. 25, p. 118a, d. 7, l. 6, A. Smirnov and I. Lavrov to V. Dekanozov, April 20, 1945.

72. Ernst Fischer met with Renner for the first time on April 22. On this see his memoirs: Fischer, *Das Ende einer Illusion*, pp. 65–68. The first discussion took an unfortunate turn. Ernst Fischer was sharply reprimanded for his conduct by the Soviet political officer Piterskii. Piterskii made it clear to Fischer that Renner enjoyed Stalin's trust and would have to form a government as soon as possible in order to forestall the West.

73. AVP RF, f. 066, op. 25, p. 118a, d. 7, ll. 9–10, First version of the composition of the Provisional Government of Austria, April 23, 1945.

74. AVP RF, f. 066, op. 25, p. 118a, d. 7, l. 8, Telegram from Koptelov to Dekanozov, April 23, 1945.

75. His reports—as is typical for military reports—continue to be inaccessible, in contrast to the reports of SMERSH, which presented on April 25, 1945, a report on the formation of the Provisional Government. The report concluded by stating that the ÖVP supported the Communists. TsA FSB RF, f. 135, op. 1, d. 1, pp. 16–17, Report from the assistant of the Chief of the Main Administration for Counterespionage "SMERSH," Major General Bolotin, to his boss, Abakumov, April 25, 1945.

76. As happened later in, for example, Hungary. On November 10, Molotov recommended that the Interior Ministry in Budapest be insisted on. Rainer, "Der Weg der ungarischen Volksdemokratie," pp. 332–333. T. V. Volokitina, eds., *Sovetskii faktor v Vostochnoi Evrope 1944–1953, Vol. 1: 1944–1948. Dokumenty* (Moscow: ROSSPEN, 1999), pp. 243–245.

77. AVP RF, f. 066, op. 25, p. 118a, d. 7, l. 4 (as in note 67).

78. This was presented to Molotov on 25 April 1945. AVP RF, f. 06, op. 7, p. 26, d. 321, ll. 1 and 9.

79. AVP RF, f. 066, op. 25, p. 118a, d. 7, l. 19, Lavrov to Vyshinskii, 25 April 1945.

80. Ibid., ll. 17–18, Vyshinskii to Kennan, April 24, 1945. Emphasis by the authors.

81. Günter Bischof, *Austria in the First Cold War, 1945–1955: The Leverage of the Weak*, Cold War History Series (London/New York: Macmillan Press & St. Martin's Press, 1999), p. 46; Rauchensteiner, *Der Sonderfall*, pp. 72–73.

82. AVP RF, f. 066, op. 25, p. 118a, d. 7, l. 39, Roberts to Vyshinskii, April 27, 1945.

83. Rauchensteiner, *Der Sonderfall*, p. 73.

84. AVP RF, f. 066, op. 25, p. 118a, d. 7, l. 95, Notification from Renner (Russian translation), April 28, 1945. Renner originally intended to speak about "complete independence" (Molotov: autonomy) and about "different political parties" (Molotov: all political parties). In addition, Molotov deleted the direct form of address to the Allies (Renner: "the government informs you," Molotov: "the government announces"; Renner: "turns to you with the request," Molotov: "requests"). Molotov did not implement these corrections until April 30. Portisch rightly poses the question as to why the notification did not arrive in Washington until May 11. The consultation with Moscow would explain this delay. See Portisch, *Österreich II*, Vol. 2, p. 20.

85. TsAMO, f. 243, op. 2945, d. 18, ll. 44–45, Order of the Command of the 3rd Ukrainian Front from May 6, 1945.

86. Resolution in: TsAMO, f. 254, op. 19951, d. 2, l. 34. AVP RF, f. 066, op. 25, p. 119, d. 18, ll. 3–8. RGASPI, f. 644, op. 1, d. 415, l. 35, Resolution of the GOKO from 11 May 1945.

87. TsAMO, f. 243, op. 2912, d. 146, ll. 192–194, Tolbukhin and Zheltov to Stalin, 28 April 1945, on the reception of the Provisional Austrian Government on 27 April 1945. On this see also Barbara Stelzl-Marx, "Erbsen für Wien: Zur sowjetischen Lebensmittelhilfe 1945," in Stefan Karner and Gottfried Stangler, eds., *"Österreich ist frei!" Der österreichische Staatsvertrag* (Horn/Vienna: Berger, 2005).

88. TsAMO, f. 275, op. 28382, d. 32, l. 266. In addition, hundreds of tons of confiscated building materials were made available. TsAMO, f. 275, op. 426039, d. 4, ll. 13–14, Order of the Supreme Commander of the Central Group of Forces, I. Konev, regarding material assistance for the Austrian Provisional Government for rebuilding the Vienna State Opera House from October 8, 1945.

89. As on May 11, 1945. AVP RF, f. 06, op. 7, p. 26, d. 322, ll. 14–15, Memorandum from M. Koptelov, May 11, 1945. On this see Rauchensteiner, *Der Sonderfall*, pp. 65 and 106.

90. TsAMO, f. 243, op. 2922, d. 49, ll. 168–177. "Provisional ordinance of the 3rd Ukrainian Front on the military headquarters on Austrian territory taken by the Red Army," April 20, 1945. Reproduced in: Karner, Stelzl-Marx, and Tschubarjan, eds., *Die Rote Armee in Österreich*, Doc. 59.

91. TsAMO, f. 48, op. 3411ss, d. 196, ll. 370–372, Coded telegram from Tolbukhin and Zheltov to Stalin, May 17, 1945. Further requests were submitted by the Communist permanent secretaries Buchinger and Honner. On this see Karner, Stelzl-Marx and Tschubarjan, eds., *Die Rote Armee in Österreich*, Doc. 40, "Coded telegram from the Commander-in-Chief of the 3rd Ukrainian Front, F. I. Tolbukhin, and the member of the Military Council of the Front, A. S. Zheltov, to I. V. Stalin on a meeting with members of the Provisional Austrian Government," May 16, 1945.

92. TsAMO, f. 48, op. 3411ss, d. 196, ll. 370–372 (as in note 91).

93. TsAMO, f. 275, op. 353761, d. 1, ll. 856–866, Discussion minutes from the Military Council of the Central Group of the Troops, July 9, 1945; ÖStA, AdR, AA, II-pol. 1945, Kt. 1, 23-pol. 1945 [n.d].

94. AVP RF, f. 066, op. 25, p. 118a, d. 3, ll. 2–4, Communiqué regarding the reception of Renner and his deputies, Figl and Koplenig, by Marshal Konev, Vienna, July 11, 1945.

95. During the discussion, Figl pointed out that the "harvest is endangered due to the uncertainty of the work in the fields as a result of the incursion on the borders, the wandering marauders, etc." Konev contemplated "the provision of small arms to the rural security organs." ÖStA, AdR, AA, II-pol. 1945, Kt. 1, 23-pol. 1945 [n.d.].

96. AVP RF, f. 066, op. 25, p. 118a, d. 3, ll. 2–4, here p. 3, Communiqué regarding Konev's discussion with Renner, Figl and Koplenig on July 9 and 11, 1945; ÖStA, AdR, AA, II-pol. 1945, Kt. 1, 23-pol. 1945 [n.d.].

97. TsAMO, f. 275, op. 353761, d. 1, l. 866 (as in note 93).

98. Gertrude Enderle-Burcel, Rudolf Jeřábek and Leopold Kammerhofer, eds., *Protokolle des Kabinettsrates 29. April 1945 bis 10. Juli 1945: Protokolle des Kabinettsrates der Provisorischen Regierung Karl Renner 1945*, Vol. 1 (Horn/Vienna: Berger, 1995), p. 357.

99. US Department of State, *Foreign Relations of the United States* (FRUS), *Diplomatic Papers: 1945*, Vol. III: *European Advisory Commission—Austria—Germany* (Washington, DC: US Government Printing Office, 1968), pp. 105–106, Kennan to the Secretary of State, April 30, 1945.

100. The number of Communists in the government was too high for the British. Audrey Kurth Cronin, *Great Power Politics and the Struggle over Austria 1945–1955* (Ithaca/New York: Cornell University Press, 1986), p. 31.

101. The USSR also did not in fact recognize the Provisional Government de jure until 20 October 1945 following the recommendation of the Allied Council from 1 October. AVP RF, f. 66, op. 26, p. 32, d. 24, l. 3, Konev to Renner, October 20, 1945; Gertrude Enderle-Burcel and Rudolf Jeřábek, eds., *Kabinettsratsprotokoll Nr. 30 bis Kabinettsratsprotokoll Nr. 43. 12. September 1945 bis 17. Dezember 1945: Protokolle des Kabinettsrates der Provisorischen Regierung Karl Renner 1945*, Vol. 3 (Vienna: Verlag Österreich, 2003), Cabinet Minutes No. 36, October 24, 1945, p. 180. On the change of opinion toward Renner see the OSS reports, reprinted in Beer, "Wien in der frühen Besatzungszeit," p. 61.

102. Rauchensteiner, *Der Sonderfall*, pp. 124–125. On this see also the OSS reports on the enlargement of the Provisional Government with "a few men from western Austria." Beer, "Wien in der frühen Besatzungszeit," p. 54.

103. AVP RF, f. 066, op. 25, p. 118a, d. 2, ll. 49–50, Handwritten letter from Koptelov to Smirnov, Vienna, September 27, 1945.

104. RGASPI, f. 558, op. 11, d. 97, ll. 80–85, Telegram from Molotov, Beriia, Malenkov and Mikoyan to Stalin, October 19, 1945.

105. TsAMO, f. 243, op. 2914, d. 268, ll. 12–14, Report by Merkulov on the Fourth Plenary Session of the Provisional Government of Austria, May 11, 1945.

106. AVP RF, f. 066, op. 25, p. 118a, d. 7, ll. 64–69, Session minutes of the meeting of representatives of the Military Council of the 3rd Ukrainian Front with Communist members of the government, May 16, 1945, written by M. Koptelov. One month later, Koptelov stated that the Austrian Communists had "for a while alleged that the Socialists had formed a block with the Catholics against the Communists." TsAMO, f. 275, op. 353763, d. 1, ll. 113–117, "Report of the Deputy Political Advisor attached to the Commander-in-Chief of the 3rd Ukrainian Front, M. E. Koptelov, and the leading consultant of the 3rd European Department of the People's Commis-

sariat for Foreign Affairs of the USSR, G. N. Dzyubenko, on the KPÖ," June 10, 1945. Reproduced in: Karner, Stelzl-Marx and Tschubarjan, eds., *Die Rote Armee in Österreich*, Doc. 141.

107. AVP RF, f. 066, op. 25, p. 118a, d. 7, ll. 64–69, Report by Koptelov on the Session of the Military Council of the 3rd Ukrainian Front with the KPÖ members of the Provisional Government of Austria, May 16, 1945.

108. Ibid.

109. AVP RF, f. 066, op. 25, p. 118a, d. 8, ll. 10–11, Record of a discussion between Lavrov, an employee of the 3rd European Department, and Colonel Piterskii, Moscow, May 24, 1945.

110. ÖStA, AdR, AA, II-pol. 1945, Kt. 5, 959-pol. 45, Official memorandum on the discussion with Koptelov, September 2, 1945.

111. Ibid.

112. Ibid.

113. ÖStA, AdR, AA, II-pol. 1945, Kt. 5, 1077-pol. 45.

114. On January 20, 1946, Evgenii Kiselev of the Politburo of the Central Committee of the CPSU was appointed the Political Representative of the USSR in Austria. RGASPI, f. 17, op. 3, d. 1.056, l. 3, Politburo Resolution 246 (2), January 20, 1946.

115. Literally: "crafty wolf." RGVA, f. 32900, op. 1, d. 458, l. 141, Report on the political situation in Austria by the Political Section of the Internal Troops of the NKVD for the Protection of the Rear of the 3rd Ukrainian Front, May 14, 1945.

116. Nikolai Lun'kov, one of those from "the nursery" of Andrei Smirnov, as he described himself in 1944 when he was unexpectedly assigned to the diplomatic service of the 3rd European Department of the NKID straight out of the Higher Party School. In February 1945, he was sent to Tolbukhin's staff in Hungary. Until 1946, Lun'kov was Deputy Political Advisor to Tolbukhin and Konev. After his service as First Secretary in the Soviet Embassy in Switzerland, he returned to the diplomatic service in the 3rd European Department of the NKID. See Nikolai M. Lun'kov, *Russkii diplomat v Evrope: Tridtsat' let v desyati evropeiskikh stolitsakh* (Moscow: Nauchnaya kniga, 1999), pp. 10–11 and 58.

117. AVP RF, f. 066, op. 25, p. 118a, d. 2, ll. 61–62, Report by Lun'kov to Deputy People's Commissar Dekanozov.

118. TsA FSB RF, f. 135, op. 1, d. 21, ll. 100–113, Report from the Chief of the Propaganda Section of the SChSK, Pasechnik, to the Deputy High Commissioner, Zheltov, dated no later than November 23, 1945. The informant may have been Erwin Scharf, whose criticism of "Renner, like the other old men who pursue right-wing policies" is often cited in the report.

119. RGASPI, f. 17, op. 162, d. 37, ll. 154 and 163, Central Committee resolution from October 19, 1945, announced on October 23 in a letter from Konev to Renner. The letter was reprinted in *Österreichische Zeitung*, October 23, 1945, p. 1.

120. TsAMO, f. 275, op. 174769s, d. 1, ll. 262–264, Koptelov's record of the discussion, Vienna, December 28, 1945.

121. AVP RF, f. 066, op. 25, p. 118a, d. 2, ll. 71–73, Koptelov to Smirnov, December 24, 1945.

122. AVP RF, f. 066, op. 26, p. 121, d. 10, l. 20, Kiselev to Molotov, January 26, 1946.

123. AVP RF, f. 012, op. 7, p. 101, d. 80, l. 41, Memorandum from E. Kiselev "The Political Situation in Austria and the Tasks of our Politics," June 4, 1946. RGASPI, f. 17, op. 125, d. 392, ll. 62 and 73, Report of the Head of the Propaganda Section of the SChSK, M. Pasechnik, May 1946.

124. RGASPI, f. 17, op. 128, d. 117, l. 30, Political report from the Chief of the Propaganda Section of the Soviet element of the Allied Commission to Austria, Lieutenant Colonel Pasechnik, to the Central Committee of the CPSU, M. A. Suslov, Vienna, August 1946.

125. ÖStA, AdR, AA, II-pol 1947, Kt. 38 (Po-R), 107.686.

126. Declaration of the first session of Cominform, Minutes of the first session, in: *Soveshchaniya Kominforma 1947, 1948, 1949: Dokumenty i Materialy* (Moscow: ROSSPEN, 1998), pp. 243 and 664. On Cominform see above all Grant M. Adibekov, *Das Kominform und Stalins Neuordnung Europas: Zeitgeschichte—Kommunismus—Stalinismus. Materialien und Forschungen*, Vol. 1 (Frankfurt am Main: Peter Lang, 2002).

127. *Literaturnaya Gazeta*, 29 October 1947; Rauchensteiner, *Der Sonderfall*, p. 214.

128. RGASPI, f. 17, op. 132, d. 5, l. 62, "Report on the Conference with the Commander-in-Chief concerning Issues of Propaganda within the Population," May 15, 1948.

129. *Observer*, October 9, 1949, quoted from: Jacques Hannak, *Karl Renner und seine Zeit: Versuch einer Biographie* (Vienna: Europa Verlag, 1965), p. 671. Translated from the German translation back into English.

130. *Arbeiter-Zeitung*, February 24, 1949, p. 1.

131. On this see the chapter by Peter Ruggenthaler, "Soviet Policy toward Austria 1945 to 1955," in this volume.

132. Feliks Chuev, *Molotov: Poluderzhavnyi Vlastelin* (Moscow: OLMA-Press, 1999), p. 106. Molotov to Chuev, August 14, 1973.

133. Vladislav Zubok, *A Failed Empire: The Soviet Union in the Cold War from Stalin to Gorbachev* (Chapel Hill: University of North Carolina Press, 2007), p. 14.

134. Peter Ruggenthaler, "Warum Österreich nicht sowjetisiert werden sollte," in Karner and Stelzl-Marx, eds., *Die Rote Armee in Österreich*, pp. 61–87, here p. 63.

Chapter Four

Soviet Policy toward Austria 1945 to 1955

Peter Ruggenthaler

In all its official pronouncements the Soviet Union was at pains to present itself as the guarantor of the reestablishment of Austria as a sovereign state, at a time when Austria, militarily occupied by the Allies, was primarily regarded as a country that had to be liberated from the National Socialist regime, despite the fact that Austrians had been extensively involved in Nazi war crimes. In the terms of international law, Austria was an "exceptional case." Seen by the allies as a territory occupied by Hitler Germany and therefore as one—or, indeed, as the first—of Hitler's "victims," the Republic of Austria, which was about to be brought back to life, was not *prima facie* an enemy state which required a peace treaty, as was the case with Germany's satellite states: Austria needed a state treaty and the restoration of its full sovereignty after the withdrawal of the occupying forces and these two objectives would be the focus of the negotiations the Austrian government had to conduct with the four victorious powers.

Officially, again, the Soviet Union seemed to be committed to an early withdrawal from Austria and a swift conclusion of the state treaty. But was an early withdrawal and the release of Austria really in the best interest of Stalin's Soviet Union? Was the Soviet occupation zone not something in the nature of a pawn for the Soviet side in the rapidly escalating Cold War? Could it even have been the potential basis for a westward extension of the Soviet sphere of influence? Or was, conversely, the ten-year period of occupation being increasingly felt by Moscow as an albatross around its neck?

It has taken historians years of intensive research in Russian archives to obtain a look behind the scenes. Two things in particular have now become quite clear: in the initial stages of the Cold War, Austria was one of the major battlefields. And from the Soviets' point of view, Austria always ceded precedence to the German question, which they saw as infinitely more important. Having said this, an examination of the "Austrian question," rather than providing material for just another case study, holds out a significant key to an understanding of the origins of the Cold War and grants us important insights into Stalin's thinking and into the ways he proposed to expand his empire into Europe.

STALIN AND AUSTRIA

Stalin prevailed very early on over the other Allies to the effect that Austria would re-emerge as a small state (thus putting a stop to a new power center in the Danube region, as Winston Churchill, for example, had intended).[1] In October 1943, this aim was finally fixed in writing. From the Soviet perspective, herein lay the significance of the "Moscow Declaration" on Austria in 1943.[2]

Stalin pursued not only the aim of not allowing great power centers to emerge on the European continent but also first and foremost to prevent a rapid restrengthening of Germany after the war.[3] Germany should be permanently weakened and rendered harmless.[4] There was no master plan to achieve this, but there were strategies, which Stalin altered depending on the situation, which later allowed him to appear as a cunning tactician (assisted by his confidante Molotov). Stalin was aware that Germany could not be destroyed ("Hitlers come and go, but the German people, the German state will remain").[5] His experiences after the First World War, when Germany was politically and militarily devastated and yet within a few years became so strong again, were Stalin's most important motivation for demanding the dismemberment of the German Reich, from which Austria ultimately profited by becoming independent. Austria should be forced in any way possible—not least by means of preferential treatment as compared with Germany in the form of a public recognition of Austria as the "first victim"—to abandon the strongly held desire of the inter-war period to unite with Germany. The Soviet Union's vehement advocacy of an Austrian state runs like a red thread through all known internal Soviet plans during the Second World War. All other (Western) plans were rejected, as they were diametrically opposed to Soviet great power interests in central and central-eastern Europe.[6]

For Stalin, Austrians were Germans and Austria was to be treated as part of the whole German question, which means that the drawing of borders in Central Europe has to be seen through this prism.[7]

CONSOLIDATION OF SOVIET POWER
IN CENTRAL AND EASTERN EUROPE[8]

After the Soviet Union, without prior consultation and in violation of the agreements with the Allies, immediately arranged for the forming of a provisional government[9] following the entry of the Red Army into Austria[10]—which was propagated as a liberation mission, but generally looked different on a day-to-day level (murder, plunder, rape, arrests and abductions)—serious difficulties emerged in the question of the post-war treatment of Austria under the Allies.[11] The recognition of the government of Karl Renner by the Western powers was the decisive topic in the summer of 1945[12] and in this way ruled out—from the Western perspective—the beginning of negotiations for a treaty on Austria from the outset. The Soviet Union furthermore insisted first of all on the conclusion of peace treaties with the former satellite states of the German Reich. Austria did not fall into this category. There is much to support the view that the USSR systematically delayed the commencement of negotiations on the State Treaty,[13] as it was not interested in a swift withdrawal of its troops from Austria. In the peace treaties with Hungary and Romania, the Soviet Union was granted the right to station troops in both countries for the purpose of supplying its occupation troops in Austria.[14]

The significance of this arrangement was very clear to the Americans, and it was also a thorn in their side. At the Paris Conference of Foreign Ministers in 1946, the United States had at least to bring about a conclusion to a treaty on Austria, which would have led to a Soviet troop withdrawal in these countries as well.[15] However, the Americans had admittedly not expected that Stalin would jump on board. This tactical step had been far more an attempt to sound out Stalin's intentions in the German question in order to see whether he would be prepared to abandon his policy of spheres of influence.[16] With Molotov's formal demand for the revision of the Byrnes plan (for the demilitarization and neutralization of Germany for many decades), which was currently under discussion, and the tactic of propagating the Soviet Union as the defender of German unity, it had become clear to the Americans and British that Stalin did not seek an agreement with the Allies over Germany.

Initially, a tactical benefit was thus assigned to the Austrian question—both from the Western and from the Soviet perspective. With the repeated attempts in Paris to raise the Austrian question, the Western side attempted to uncover the Soviet cards.[17] For them it was first and foremost a question of discovering the true intentions of Soviet policy. With this strategy, they really did drive the Soviet Union into a corner. Foreign Minister Molotov was left with no option but to brusquely reject all talks on Austria. He no longer pointed out that Austria was not yet sufficiently "cleansed of fascists" and that the Austrians must be assisted in this matter; instead he allowed himself the following remarkable statement: "The USSR will leave its troops in Austria as long as it has the right to do so." Thus, from the Soviet perspective, the military presence in Romania and Hungary continued to be secured and an agreement on the German question was ruled out. This was finally clear to the Western powers in Paris.

Yet to the outside world, the Soviet Union could admittedly not oppose the commencement of negotiations on the State Treaty. After all, the re-establishment of an independent Austrian state had always been propagated. The public could be stalled with the conclusion of the Second Control Agreement of 1946, which widely granted the Austrian government internal freedom of action, and thus demonstrated a fundamental willingness to talk. Until the actual negotiations on a state treaty for Austria began at the beginning of 1947 as a result of the Soviet delaying strategy, one-and-a-half years had already passed since the end of the war.

By this time, the Soviet Union had already allowed a large proportion of the Austrian prisoners of war to return home. From 1947, they organized regular transports back to the homeland.[18] The USSR had never used the prisoner of war question as security (even if there were intermittent—yet unsuccessful—attempts to combine this question with the demand for the return of Soviet DPs still in Austria).[19] The mass sentencing of foreign prisoners of war from 1949 took place above all against the backdrop of retaining manpower, as a further retention of prisoners of war would have violated the Geneva Convention. The Soviet Union had admittedly never signed it, but the Western powers repeatedly complained to the USSR about the incomplete repatriation. From this point on, Moscow always pointed out that the convicts only remained in the Soviet Union due to war crimes or other offences.[20]

Yet was the Soviet Union at all prepared to withdraw from Austria following the commencement of negotiations? The military and strategic significance of the Soviet occupation of eastern Austria and the related maintenance of a military presence in Hungary and Romania—which appeared vital for a long-term implementation of Soviet system and rule—excludes a willingness on the part of the Soviets to conclude an Austrian state treaty with subsequent military vacation of the country by the Allies, at least for the early phase of the Cold War. From an intelligence point of view, the Soviet occupation zone in Austria was furthermore of considerable importance as a "gateway to the West."[21]

The strategic importance of Austria is evident in Soviet files for the first time in April 1945. In Moscow's Foreign Office (People's Commissariat for Foreign Affairs), the significance of the occupation of Austria for the maintenance of the Red Army's troop presence in south-eastern Europe was discussed.[22] In 1947, the Hungarian Communist leader Mátyás Rákosi was concerned about a possible withdrawal of Soviet troops from his country. Yet Molotov reassured him and assured him that a conclusion of an Austrian state treaty was not foreseeable in the near future.[23] And in October 1949, the question of troop presence in Hungary and Romania was the decisive reason why Stalin had the negotiations on the State Treaty broken off. Stalin was not prepared in 1949 to oblige Tito by signing a state treaty for Austria.[24] For Stalin interpreted the determination of the Western powers to withdraw from Austria as support for Tito. Tito's breach with Stalin had grave consequences for Soviet policy in south-eastern Europe and thus for Austria.

Alongside the troop presence in Hungary and Romania—which had increased in importance as a result of escalating relations between Moscow and Belgrade—and Stalin's hatred for Tito, a further aspect may have played a not insignificant role in Soviet strategy: the exterritorial "Soviet Mineral Oil Administration" (SMV), consolidated on the basis of former "German assets," which was already struggling with economic problems in 1948, discovered in March 1949 in Matzen near Vienna the then largest single oilfield in central Europe. By autumn 1949, further Soviet drilling brought the Soviets clarity regarding the considerable potential of these oil deposits. At the end of September 1949, when negotiations on the State Treaty were on the verge of a supposed conclusion, Vsevolod Merkulov, Chief of the State Administration of Soviet Assets Abroad (GUSIMZ), reported this to Stalin. This discovery had been concealed during the negotiations on the State Treaty. The outputs to be submitted to the Soviets according to the draft of the State Treaty from 1949 had been calculated based on the old oilfields in the region of Zistersdorf, whose productivity could not be compared to that of Matzen. From this point on until 1955, the Soviets were to extract 15 million tons of mineral oil with a then value of circa 260 million US dollars (for the purposes of comparison: from 1945 until 1949 it had been three million tons).[25] From an economic point of view, the occupation remained lucrative. The Administration for Soviet Property in Austria (USIA) recorded rising profits, which first ceased after 1952.[26]

Austria thus remained for Moscow, alone due to its mineral oil reserves, which were the largest in Europe after those of Romania, an (economic) asset. A withdrawal from Austria would admittedly have granted Moscow on-going drilling rights, but the Soviets would have had to pay taxes to the Austrian state for the privilege. The "eastern trade," so lucrative for Moscow (oil theft for supplying Czechoslovakia, the GDR, and Hungary, which received 90 percent of its crude oil from eastern Austria at the beginning of the 1950s), would no longer have been possible in this form.²⁷ From an economic point of view, from autumn 1949 Stalin could thus definitively not have had any interest in withdrawing from Austria.

The Soviet strategy must thus have been to maintain the state of uncertainty regarding the occupation of eastern Austria for political and economic reasons at least until a—from the Soviet point of view—stable consolidation of the eastern bloc. This interpretation is favored by Soviet opposition to KPÖ plans for the division of Austria. In 1948, the KPÖ leadership, on the recommendation of their Yugoslav comrades, had entertained such a scenario but had been severely reprimanded by Moscow (this was contrary, as explained above, to all Soviet interests in the German question—which included the treatment of Austria). From Moscow's point of view, moreover, no "Trotskyist" tendencies like those in Yugoslavia could be allowed in Vienna.²⁸ Furthermore, the support of Yugoslav territorial demands against southern Austria on the part of the USSR amounted to an impediment, which delayed the completion of the Austrian State Treaty, yet ceased to exist following the breach between Stalin and Tito and ultimately allowed for an intensification of negotiations on the State Treaty in 1949.²⁹ Soviet conduct during the so-called October putsch of 1950 and the assessment of these events in Moscow³⁰ also make it clear that the USSR must have been concerned during this phase to further maintain the occupation of eastern Austria without wanting to bring about an escalation. The Soviet power moreover pursued from the outset a strict yet not unbroken denazification policy; in contrast to the eastern European states, however, it never used this as cover for actions against all non-Communist opposition.³¹

REINFORCING THE DIVISION OF GERMANY SMOOTHED THE PATH TO NEUTRALITY

After Stalin withdrew from State Treaty negotiations on Austria in the fall of 1949, the Communist Party of Austria (KPÖ) began to push its own plans for a neutral Austria.³² There is no record of any instructions from Moscow. In fact, the Soviet Foreign Office dismissed such considerations in an internal memo dating to early 1950.³³

The KPÖ was allowed its head for a while, but in the end their propaganda fell into line with the prevailing public face of Soviet Union foreign policy. In Austria, the KPÖ drive for neutrality led to a public perception of neutrality as a communist offensive. This chimed with a real fear that Austria was heading for the same fate as neighboring people's democracies, so that even after Stalin's death in March 1953 there was still a long way to go before the State Treaty of May 1955 could be concluded. The first task for Austrian politicians was to sell the idea of neutrality to their own people.[34]

There was also the fact that, for the Soviets, the "Austrian Question" was always part of the "German Question." It owed this position "in the shadow of the German Question" to the Soviet perception that any concessions made to the West in Austria could not fail to have an impact on the expectations entertained by the German people—especially that part of it then resident in the SBZ/DDR. Any withdrawal of Soviet troops was likely to revive their hopes of liberation from the Communist Party dictatorship and thereby destabilize the SED regime, all of which drove Moscow's perception of the occupation of East Austria as a key element in the consolidation of Soviet power not only in Central and Eastern Europe, but also in eastern Germany.[35] It was an important factor in the Sovietization of neighboring countries and so had to be maintained until such time as their position had been fully consolidated.

From here on the Soviet Union embraced obstructionism on the "Austrian Question." Stalin left his special deputy at the meetings scheduled for January 1950 no margin for negotiation. Officially, they took the line that Austria was not yet sufficiently denazified or demilitarized. By linking Austria and Trieste—where the Western powers and Yugoslavia had combined to oust the USSR—the Soviets could put together a compelling legal case for putting any resumption of treaty negotiations concerning Austria very much on the back burner.[36] The 1951 internal measures to "strengthen Soviet influence in Austria" emphasize Moscow's unwillingness to pull out of the country. Stalin's policy leaned rather toward strengthening Soviet control over both central and local government in the Soviet occupation zone.[37]

In the fall of 1951, the three Western powers took the initiative on the "Austrian Question."[38] In the final communiqué of the conference of foreign ministers in Washington they noted that there was no reason for further delay on the issue of an Austrian State Treaty. They prepared a new treaty between themselves, the so-called "Short Treaty," as a basis for future negotiations. The military occupation of Austria was to end. No one thought that there was any chance of the Soviets engaging in negotiations on this basis; such was never their intention—the "Short Treaty" was a US propaganda maneuver, designed to test Moscow's readiness for talks on the "German Question."[39]

The files of the Soviet Foreign Ministry show that the Soviet leadership in late 1951 and early 1952 had no interest at all in any progressing of the treaty negotiations. All the Soviets wanted was to put the blame for any failure of further negotiations on to the Western powers. Seeing the possibility—or, as they saw it, the threat—that all matters still in dispute might be resolved, the Soviets decided on a total boycott of the next meeting in London.[40]

The British were alerted by their Indian sources that Moscow had got wind of the "Short Treaty" and had therefore decided against coming to London, bringing about an American reluctance to debate the matter.[41] Soviet sources show that this was not the true story. At this point, Stalin was simply not prepared to put withdrawal from Austria on the table. The Indian sources had done no more than pass on their own interpretation of Soviet policy.[42] The real position was that the Soviets had assumed from their own intelligence data that the Western powers might well be on the point of concluding an Austrian State treaty. So the "Short Treaty" was not, as it has been portrayed so often by Austrian historians, a ruse dreamed up by the Western powers that shocked the Soviet Union into derailing treaty negotiations. It was simply that Stalin, in early 1952, was categorically opposed to any discussion of the Soviet position in Austria.

The "Short Treaty" was conceived in the summer of 1951 at the "Austrian Desk" of the State Department, engendering alarm not only in Austrian diplomatic circles, but even in London and Paris. A negative reaction from Moscow was inevitable.[43] Nevertheless, between February 29 and March 15, 1952, Moscow was presented with the "Short Treaty" as a new proposal to resolve the "Austrian Question." Yet it must always be borne in mind that the "Short Treaty" was formulated from the outset in such a way that the Western powers were certain that Moscow would reject it. It even provided the option of a free choice of alliances for Austria, so that by signing up to the "Short Treaty" the Soviets would be paving the way for Austria to join NATO. The Americans hoped to use his expected rejection of the "Short Treaty" to demonstrate a lack of sincerity in Stalin's proposals for Germany.[44] A bizarre argument, but probably not far from the truth. On May 10, 1952, the still hidden "Short Treaty" was overtaken by a new initiative: Stalin sent a note to the Western powers proposing that Germany should be reunited—as a neutral state!

Broad-based studies of the Soviet source material in recent years have clearly demonstrated that Stalin in 1952, far from being willing to sacrifice the GDR, was using this offer of German neutrality to engender a kind of legitimacy for a tighter integration of the GDR to the Soviet bloc.[45] All blame for the affirmation of the division of Germany was passed to the Western powers and the signing of the general agreement with the Federal Republic in the May of 1952 was used to cement the border between the two German states. Besides, Moscow (and East Berlin) hoped that the Soviet propaganda machine could use this "fight against remilitarization" to capture the hearts and minds of the West German people and polarize opinion against Federal Chancellor Konrad Adenauer. There was, of course, a great deal more going on behind the "Stalin Note" but there is no time to go into detail here.[46]

As regards the "Austrian Question," any presentation of the "Short Treaty" as scheduled by the Western powers but not by Moscow, was thereby circumvented. Nevertheless, the first reaction was to forward the "Short Treaty" to Moscow officially with all possible speed. This was finally done on March 13, 1952, three days after the "Stalin Note" was received. This was likely to provoke a certain amount of irritation in the Kremlin. In the Soviet Foreign Ministry they put everything together and set to work. They analyzed the existing but hitherto secret information from the MGB and augmented it with what could be learned from the MGB spies at the French Foreign Ministry in Paris. One week later, the Soviet leadership was quite clear what it must do about the "Short Treaty." It was declared that "the Western powers had been trying to put the Soviet authorities in a 'difficult position.'"[47] And the Western powers had—however unintentionally—actually done this. At this stage in the proceedings, the USSR had no interest in resolving the "Austrian Question"; rather, they saw the maintenance of the Austrian occupation as an ongoing necessity. Their immediate preoccupation was with talks about Germany.

Even at that time, there were allegations that Stalin could have been using the supposedly lesser problem of Austria as a smokescreen for his wishes concerning Germany. This was in fact always the most important evidence that Stalin did not mean his offer about Germany to be taken seriously. Moscow now saw itself with no choice but to say nothing further about the Austrian Question for weeks on end. Had the Soviets been able to reach an agreement with the Western powers on the neutralization of Austria—something that was definitely not on Moscow's agenda at that time—they would inevitably have created a model for Germany. From then on the Kremlin showed no inclination to discuss the "Austrian Question." Notes on this subject from the Western powers went unanswered for months.

Privately, the Soviets acknowledged that there was a risk that such inactivity might lead to the Western powers going ahead with a unilateral declaration on Austria accompanied by a move to withdraw their troops from the Western zones of occupation. This was not seen as an opportunity for expansionary action; rather it was viewed as a risk that any such move would necessitate the withdrawal of Soviet troops from Eastern Austria.[48] It has become clear that similar fears were entertained by the Soviet Foreign Ministry about Germany—that a unilateral withdrawal of the Western military from Germany could have put pressure on the Soviet Union with consequences for the Soviet position there. They did not see such a situation as an opportunity to take the whole of Germany under Soviet control.[49] On the one hand, this argues that the USSR had no plans at this time for any westward expansion; on the other, it underlines Soviet determination to hold on to its conquests in Central Europe.

Moscow found itself unable to make any corresponding offer of neutrality to Austria at this time. Such an offer would have lent undue weight to Soviet willingness to discuss the German Question.[50] By 1952 it had become obvious that Austria was seen as no more than a pawn on the chessboard of Cold War world politics, to be used as required in the diplomatic maneuvers aimed at furthering the respective German policies of the Great Powers. The NATO alliance of 1949 brought with it a fundamental reshuffle of the Central European deck. There was no guarantee that the post-war borders within Austria would not become a permanent or even insurmountable boundary between the Western and the Soviet zones of occupation.[51]

In the fall of 1952, the "Battle of Notes" in Germany finally came to an end. Positions were deadlocked, and the Soviet power bloc in East Germany consolidated. But still Stalin could not "set Austria free": Austria could not be allowed to become a model case. Behind the scenes, however, the first informal Soviet-Austrian talks could begin. It was the final and official division of Germany that set the scene for Austria's neutrality—Stalin's death in 1953 was not the necessary precondition.

In February 1953, shortly before Stalin's death, meetings 259 and 260 of the special deputies for the Austrian State Treaty were held.[52] Soviet demands were unchanged. For Trieste, the USSR insisted on full compliance with the provisions of the peace treaty with Italy. Further deliberations at the beginning of March had to do without directives from Stalin. He was on the point of death. But a process had already been set underway, laying down a basis for talks. Julius Raab was the nucleus of a new leadership group in the (conservative) Austrian People's Party (ÖVP) that was willing to reach out to the USSR. Signals that Raab might be cast in the same mold as Finnish premier Urho Kekkonen were taken up. ÖVP politicians gave Moscow to understand that a solution that embraced neutrality might be acceptable so long as there was no question of Austria's becoming a "People's Democracy."[53] Neutrality was still despised in Austria as communistic.

The time would come when the new strongman in the Kremlin, Nikita Khrushchev, would be able to build on these contacts. However, official orthodoxy was maintained by the reinstated Foreign Minister Vyacheslav Molotov, at least where German policy was concerned (witness the 1953 uprising in the GDR), and Austria remained subordinate to this.[54] In the end, it was the prevention of a new "Anschluss" that provided the driving motivation for the State Treaty.[55] Molotov began by resisting withdrawal from Austria, but Khrushchev is said to have convinced him of the benefits of a State Treaty.[56] The geographical break inflicted on NATO—with the wedge of neutral Switzerland—proved a pleasant "by-product."[57] Economic reasons, namely the unprofitability of the Soviet companies in Eastern Austria after 1952, were another motive for finishing the ten-year-old occupation.[58] With Tito—probably the main reason for the negative attitude shown by Molotov—Khrushchev himself initiated a reconciliation. The improvement of Soviet-Yugoslav relations and the "new flexibility" of Soviet foreign policy are not to be underestimated as preconditions for the conclusion of the State Treaty.[59]

An overriding priority for the Soviet Union was that the separation of Austria and Germany should be permanent. To Moscow, this meant that the occupation of Austria was important for the consolidation of the Soviet bloc on two "fronts": its first purpose was to present an argument to the Western Powers for the Soviet military presence in Hungary and Romania; on the other hand, an Austria shared by all the Allies could not fail to endanger Soviet consolidation in the GDR.

The conclusion of the Austrian State Treaty in 1955 was regarded as a success by Khrushchev in various respects: the neutrality of Austria laid to rest all fears of an Anschluss with West Germany; economically, the maximum was obtained from the Soviet occupation zone; and the Austrian solution could be used propagandistically (with regard to the German question), but even more as a prime example for *Peaceful Coexistence* in practice.[60] The advantages of a neutral status between the blocs of countries like Austria or Sweden were supposed to animate NATO states to depart from the North Atlantic alliance. Moscow furthermore hoped, at least in the initial period after the signing of the State Treaty, that neutrality would be fertile ground for the establishment of socialism.[61]

THE SIGNIFICANCE OF AUSTRIA AS A CENTRAL THEATER OF THE EARLY COLD WAR AND IN THE CONCEPTION OF SOVIET FOREIGN POLICY IN THE HISTORIOGRAPHY

Austria was a central theater of the early Cold War in Europe. In the Anglo-American historiography, one of the central points of confrontation between West and East, be it in ideological, propagandistic, or, temporarily, also military respect, was barely mentioned, although the country at the Iron Curtain was accorded an increasing significance in line with the rollback policy. Austria, and with it Central Europe, was of the greatest importance for the policy of the Western powers.[62]

Austria was also of central importance for the Kremlin, however, in its conception of post-war politics. Vladislav Zubok and Constantine Pleshakov, who produced in 1996 the first study of Soviet foreign policy based on extensive research in Russian archives, emphasized the significance of the Soviet occupation of Austria in the conception of Soviet foreign policy: "The small country [. . .] remained a pawn on the chessboard of the Cold War. [. . .] The presence of Soviet troops in Austria, with which a link could be maintained via Hungary and Czechoslovakia, [constituted] an important flank in a future war against West Germany or Tito's Yugoslavia."[63] Lastly, Zubok stated that Soviet foreign policy (also with regard to Austria) during the final Stalin years served the preparation for war: "The detailed analysis of Soviet plans for Austria, which had long become a hostage of the German Question and Soviet military plans, also shows that Kremlin diplomacy at that time was just a camouflage for war preparations."[64]

On the basis of newly unlocked sources from Russian archives relating to Austria, the findings of Vojtech Mastny to the effect that the highest premise of Soviet Austrian policy was to prevent an Anschluss to Germany are to be endorsed.[65] This policy is to be seen in the overall conception of Soviet postwar policy, whose aim it was to permanently weaken Germany in order to rule out the possibility of a new invasion of the Soviet Union. In his monumental study of the history of the Austrian State Treaty, Gerald Stourzh described at length the negotiations of 1955 on the basis of Soviet sources and came—alongside the reasons already mentioned—to the conclusion that against the backdrop of the "new flexibility of Soviet foreign policy" under Khrushchev of finding a modus vivendi with the West, the armed neutrality of Austria as a guarantee that Austria would not fall into the hands of the West was an important motive for Moscow. "As long as there was the risk of Austria being admitted to NATO," the withdrawal of the Soviets could not be contemplated.[66]

The basic statements of Norman Naimark on Soviet–Austrian policy cannot be confirmed in the light of new Soviet sources. As demonstrated in this article, one can no longer talk of Austria as having been a burden for Stalin. "If he [Stalin] could have found a face-saving way to sign a State Treaty on Austria in 1946, in 1949 or 1952, he might well have done so. He understood completely that under occupation the Austrians and the Austrian state were more a burden than a benefit to Soviet interests. Khrushchev's view that the occupation did nothing but make the Soviets more unpopular among the Austrians was no doubt shared by Stalin. It is hard to know why Stalin did not sign a State Treaty."[67] As explained above, Stalin did not take the "chance" in 1949. At that point in time, the occupation of eastern Austria was still an important, indispensable factor in the conception of Soviet foreign policy. From an economic point of view, it was worth sustaining the occupation above all because of the rich discoveries of mineral oil. The advantages of a neutralization of Austria following the consolidation of the GDR at the end of the "Battle of Notes" in 1952, i.e., during Stalin's lifetime, were admittedly the same as afterward. The favorable outcome of the "Battles of Notes" for the Kremlin was in my view decisive for enabling a solution of neutrality for Austria. Before the March note of 1952 on Germany, Stalin was definitely not prepared to give up the Soviet occupation of Austria.

In light of Soviet sources and analyses of Soviet foreign policy since the Second World War, which have become available during the last two decades,[68] Rolf Steininger's speculative thesis to the effect that Stalin, with his repudiation of the Short Treaty, "missed the chance possibly to influence the West's policy on Germany in 1952" by making a "down payment" on the Austrian question, is to be rejected. As demonstrated, Stalin was not even interested in discussing Austria during the run-up to the Stalin note. Steininger, who is actually an expert on big power politics of the West, repeatedly draws conclusions about the aims and strategies of Soviet foreign policy under Stalin. He came to the conclusion that Soviet "offers concerning Germany and Austria, respectively, were intended to effect a change of course in the Western Allies' German policy, but always represented a case of too little, too late."[69] This is diametrically opposed to all solid research results on Stalin's policy on the basis of the holdings of Soviet archives on Soviet foreign policy after the Second World War.[70]

Detailed studies of the decision-making process on the Austrian question within the new Soviet leadership after Stalin's death (Mikhail Prozumenshchikov) and of Soviet economic policy in Austria (Walter Iber)[71] have revealed that economic reasons fundamentally tipped the scale for ending the ten-year occupation. Until then, the economic exploitation of the Soviet zone was exceedingly lucrative. By 1955, however, Soviet enterprises in eastern Austria had become unprofitable and increasingly a millstone around the neck.[72]

By 1955, Austria had fulfilled its role in the conception of Soviet foreign policy as an object for consolidating the Eastern Bloc. The overriding aim of the Kremlin, to permanently weaken Germany, had also been achieved with the restoration of Austrian independence and the consolidation of the German partition. In the "voluntary" acceptance of perpetual neutrality, the Kremlin's rulers saw a guarantee in 1955 for excluding an advance of NATO and a strengthening of its position in Central Europe. Austrian politicians, first and foremost Federal Chancellor Julius Raab and, later, also Vice Chancellor Adolf Schärf, had duly recognized the signs of the time and accommodated the feelers from Moscow.

The basic constants in Soviet foreign policy after the Second World War were fulfilled: no Anschluss to Germany; economic exploitation of the country (above all its mineral oil). As long as the Soviet occupation of eastern Austria was useful for the consolidation of the Eastern Bloc, it remained an important factor in the conception of Soviet foreign policy. Following the consolidation of the Eastern Bloc and, in particular, the stabilization of the German partition, Moscow, from its point of view, could dispense with the occupation of eastern Austria.

NOTES

This essay reflects the status of research on Soviet policy toward Austria, without direct references to the sources in Russian archives. For this see in detail Peter Ruggenthaler, *The Concept of Neutrality in Stalin's Foreign Policy 1945–1953*. Harvard Cold War Studies Book Series (Lanham, MD: Lexington, 2015) and Peter Ruggenthaler, "Warum Österreich nicht sowjetisiert wurde: Sowjetische Österreich-Politik 1945 bis 1953/55," in Stefan Karner and Barbara Stelzl-Marx, eds., Die Rote Armee in Österreich. Sowjetische Besatzung 1945–1955. Beiträge. (Graz/Vienna/Munich: Oldenbourg, 2005), pp. 649–726.

1. Günter Bischof, *Austria in the First Cold War, 1945–1955: The Leverage of the Weak* (New York: St. Martin's Press, 1999); pp. 20–29; Siegfried Beer, "Die 'Befreiungs- und Besatzungsmacht' Großbritannien in Österreich, 1945–1955," in Manfried Rauchensteiner and Robert Kriechbaumer, eds., *Die Gunst des Augenblicks. Neuere Forschungen zu Staatsvertrag und Neutralität* (Vienna et al.: Böhlau, 2005), pp. 23–74, here p. 25; Reinhold Wagnleitner, "Großbritannien und die Wiedererrichtung der Republik Österreich," Ph.D. Diss., University of Salzburg, 1975, pp. 14–35.

2. On the Moscow Conference of Foreign Ministers and Austria see Gerald Stourzh, *Um Einheit und Freiheit: Staatsvertrag, Neutralität und das Ende der Ost-West-Besetzung Österreichs 1945–1955*. Studien zu Politik und Verwaltung, Vol. 62. 5 (Graz et al.: Böhlau, 2005), pp. 11–28 and 34–35; recently see Stefan Karner and Alexander Tschubarjan, eds., *Die Moskauer Deklaration 1943. "Österreich wieder herstellen"* (Vienna/Munich: Böhlau, 2015).

3. Jochen Laufer, Die UdSSR und die Zoneneinteilung Deutschlands (1943/44), in *Zeitschrift für Geschichtswissenschaft 43* (1995), pp. 309–331, here p. 311.

4. On Soviet planning for Germany see, among others, Alexej Filitow, "Stalins Deutschlandplanung und -politik während und nach dem Zweiten Weltkrieg," in Boris Meissner and Alfred Eisfeld, eds., *50 Jahre sowjetische und russische Deutschlandpolitik sowie ihre Auswirkungen auf das gegenseitige Verhältnis* (Berlin: Duncker & Humblot, 1999), pp. 43–54; Jochen Laufer, "Der Friedensvertrag mit Deutschland als Problem der sowjetischen Außenpolitik. Die Stalin-Note vom 10. März 1952 im Lichte neuer Quellen," in *Vierteljahrshefte für Zeitgeschichte 52* (1/2004), pp. 99–118, here p. 103.

5. Aleksei M. Filitov, "SSSR i germanskii vopros: Povorotnye punkty (1941–1961gg.)," in N. I. Egorova and A. O. Chubar'yan, eds., *Kholodnaya Voina 1945–1963gg. Istoricheskaya retrospektiva. Sbornik statei* (Moscow: Olma-Press, 2003), pp. 223–256, here p. 225.

6. Aleksej Filitov, "Sowjetische Planungen zur Wiedererrichtung Österreichs 1941–1945," in Stefan Karner and Barbara Stelzl-Marx, eds., *Die Rote Armee in*

Österreich. Sowjetische Besatzung 1945–1955. Beiträge (Graz et al.: Oldenbourg, 2005), pp. 27–37; Peter Ruggenthaler, "Warum Österreich nicht sowjetisiert werden sollte," in ibid., pp. 61–87; Wolfgang Mueller, *Die sowjetische Besatzung in Österreich 1945–1955 und ihre politische Mission* (Vienna et al.: Böhlau, 2005); Barbara Stelzl-Marx, *Stalins Soldaten in Östereich. Die Innensicht der sowjetischen Besatzung 1945–1955* (Vienna et al.: Böhlau, 2012), pp. 33–39 and pp. 87–92.

7. See in detail Ruggenthaler, *The Concept of Neutrality in Stalin's Foreign Policy 1945–1953*; see also Stefan Karner and Peter Ruggenthaler, "Stalin und Österreich. Sowjetische Österreich-Politik 1938 bis 1953," in Jahrbuch für Historische Kommunismusforschung 2005, Berlin 2005, pp. 102–140.

8. See in detail Ruggenthaler, "Warum Österreich nicht sowjetisiert wurde: Sowjetische Österreich-Politik 1945 bis 1953/55," pp. 649–726; See also Stefan Karner and Peter Ruggenthaler, "Stalin, Tito und die Österreich-Frage. Zur Österreichpolitik des Kreml im Kontext der sowjetischen Jugoslawienpolitik 1945 bis 1949," in Jahrbuch für Historische Kommunismusforschung 2008, pp. 81–105.

9. Stefan Karner and Peter Ruggenthaler, "Unter sowjetischer Kontrolle: Zur Regierungsbildung in Österreich 1945," in Karner and Stelzl-Marx, *Die Rote Armee in Österreich*, pp. 97–140.

10. More than 30,000 Red Army soldiers lost their lives in Austria. See Peter Sixl, ed., *Sowjetische Tote des Zweiten Weltkrieges in Österreich. Namens- und Grablagenverzeichnis. Ein Gedenkbuch.* Veröffentlichungen des Ludwig Boltzmann-Instituts für Kriegsfolgen-Forschung, Sonderband 11 (Graz et al.: Verein zur Förderung der Forschung, 2010).

11. See above all Bischof, *Austria in the First Cold War*, pp. 43–52.

12. See the contributions by Ol'ga Pavlenko and Stefan Karner/Peter Ruggenthaler in this volume.

13. Wolfgang Mueller, "Anstelle des Staatsvertrages: Die UdSSR und das Zweite Kontrollabkommen 1946," in Rauchensteiner and Kriechbaumer, *Die Gunst des Augenblicks*, pp. 291–320, here p. 314.

14. Peter Ruggenthaler, "Warum Österreich nicht sowjetisiert wurde: Sowjetische Österreich-Politik 1945 bis 1953/55," in Karner and Stelzl-Marx, *Die Rote Armee in Österreich*, pp. 649–726, here p. 709.

15. Ruggenthaler, *The Concept of Neutrality*, pp. 232–234.

16. Hanns Jürgen Küsters, *Der Integrationsfriede. Viermächte-Verhandlungen über die Friedensregelung mit Deutschland 1945–1990* (Munich: Oldenbourg, 2000), p. 278.

17. For details see Ruggenthaler, *The Concept of Neutrality*, pp. 75–82.

18. Stefan Karner, *Im Archipel GUPVI. Kriegsgefangenschaft und Internierung in der Sowjetunion 1941–1956* (Vienna et al.: Oldenbourg, 1995), p. 198.

19. Stefan Karner and Peter Ruggenthaler, "(Zwangs-)Repatriierungen sowjetischer Staatsbürger aus Österreich in die UdSSR," in Karner and Stelzl-Marx, eds., *Die Rote Armee in Österreich*, pp. 243–273, here p. 267.

20. Stefan Karner and Harald Knoll, "Verurteilte Kriegsgefangene in der Sowjetunion. Zum Stand der Forschung," in Stefan Karner and Vjačeslav Selemenev, eds., Österreicher und Sudetendeutsche vor sowjetischen Militär- und Strafgerichten in

Weißrussland 1945–1950. *Avstriiskie i sudetskie nemtsy pered sovetskimi voennymi tribunalami v Belarusi 1945–1950. gg.* (Graz et al.: Verein zur Förderung der Forschung, 2007), pp. 36–47.

21. See Dieter Bacher and Harald Knoll, "Nachrichtendienste und Spionage im Österreich der Besatzungszeit," in Stefan Karner and Barbara Stelzl-Marx, eds., *Stalins letzte Opfer. Verschleppte und erschossene Österreicher in Moskau 1950–1953* (Vienna et al.: Böhlau, 2009), pp. 157–168, here p. 157. See the contribution by Dieter Bacher in this volume.

22. Stefan Karner and Peter Ruggenthaler, "Stalin, Tito und die Österreich-Frage. Zur Österreichpolitik des Kreml im Kontext der sowjetischen Jugoslawienpolitik 1945 bis 1949," in Jahrbuch *für Historische Kommunismusforschung* (2008), pp. 81–105, here pp. 87–88.

23. Wladislaw Subok and Konstantin Pleshakow, *Der Kreml im Kalten Krieg. Von 1945 bis zur Kubakrise* (Hildesheim: Claassen, 1997), p. 149.

24. Ruggenthaler, *Warum Österreich nicht sowjetisiert wurde*, pp. 678–681.

25. Walter M. Iber, "Erdöl statt Reparationen. Die Sowjetische Mineralölverwaltung in Österreich 1945–1955," in *Vierteljahrshefte für Zeitgeschichte 57* (2009), pp. 571–605.

26. Walter M. Iber and Peter Ruggenthaler, "Sowjetische Wirtschaftspolitik im besetzten Österreich. Ein Überblick," in Walter M. Iber and Peter Ruggenthaler, eds., *Stalins Wirtschaftspolitik an der sowjetischen Peripherie. Ein Überblick auf der Basis sowjetischer und osteuropäischer Quellen.* Veröffentlichungen des Ludwig Boltzmann-Instituts für Kriegsfolgen-Forschung, Vol. 19 (Innsbruck et al.: Studienverlag, 2012), pp. 187–207, here pp. 197–200; Stelzl-Marx, *Stalins Soldaten*, pp. 279–281.

27. See Walter Martin Iber, "Die Sowjetische Mineralölverwaltung (SMV) in Österreich, 1945–1955. Sowjetische Besatzungswirtschaft und der Kampf ums Öl als Vorgeschichte der OMV," Ph.D. Diss., University of Graz, Austria, 2008, pp. 86–87, 107–110, 119–120, 135–136 and pp. 163–165; Walter M. Iber, "Wirtschaftsspionage für den Westen. Erdölarbeiter im Spannungsfeld des Kalten Krieges," in Karner and Stelzl-Marx, eds., *Stalins letzte Opfer*, pp. 169–188, here p. 177.

28. Ruggenthaler, *Warum Österreich nicht sowjetisiert wurde*, pp. 670–673; Manfred Mugrauer, "'Teilungspläne' und 'Putschabsichten.' Die KPÖ im Gedankenjahr 2005," in *Mitteilungen der Alfred Klahr Gesellschaft 12* (4/2005), pp. 8–15; Wolfgang Mueller, "Die Teilung Österreichs als politische Option für KPÖ und UdSSR 1948," in *Zeitgeschichte 32* (2005), pp. 47–54.

29. On the influence of Yugoslav territorial demands on the Soviet negotiating position see Ruggenthaler, *The Concept of Neutrality*, pp. 112–118; for details see Stefan Karner and Peter Ruggenthaler, "'Eine weitere Unterstützung der jugoslawischen Gebietsforderungen bringt uns in eine unvorteilhafte Lage.' Der Artikel 7 des Österreichischen Staatsvertrags als diplomatischer Kompromiss mit Österreich und den Westmächten," in Stefan Karner and Andreas Moritsch, eds., *Aussiedlung—Verschleppung—nationaler Kampf.* Kärnten und die nationale Frage, Vol. 1 (Klagenfurt: Heyn-Hermagoras, 2005), pp. 99–118.

30. Ruggenthaler, *Warum Österreich nicht sowjetisiert wurde*, pp. 686–688.

31. Harald Knoll and Barbara Stelzl-Marx, "Wir mussten hinter eine sehr lange Liste von Namen einfach das Wort 'verschwunden' schreiben: Sowjetische Strafjustiz in Österreich 1945–1955," in Andreas Hilger, Mike Schmeitzner and Clemens Vollnhals, eds., *Sowjetisierung oder Neutralität? Optionen sowjetischer Besatzungspolitik in Deutschland und Österreich 1945–1955*. Schriften des Hannah-Arendt-Instituts für Totalitarismusforschung, Vol. 32 (Göttingen: Vandenhoeck & Ruprecht, 2006), pp. 169–219; Harald Knoll and Barbara Stelzl-Marx, "Sowjetische Strafjustiz in Österreich. Verhaftungen und Verurteilungen 1945–1955," in Karner and Stelzl-Marx, eds., *Die Rote Armee in Österreich*, pp. 217–321.

32. Stourzh, *Um Einheit und Freiheit*, pp. 267–268.

33. Ruggenthaler, "Warum Österreich nicht sowjetisiert wurde," pp. 684–685.

34. See Stourzh, *Um Einheit und Freiheit*.

35. See Peter Ruggenthaler, *Stalins großer Bluff. Die Geschichte der Stalin-Note in Dokumenten der sowjetischen Führung* (München 2007); Ruggenthaler, *The Concept of Neutrality*, pp. 241–249.

36. Karner/Ruggenthaler, "Stalin und Österreich," pp. 124–125.

37. Ruggenthaler, "Warum Österreich nicht sowjetisiert wurde," pp. 689–698.

38. Michael Gehler, "'Kurzvertrag' für Österreich? Die westliche Staatsvertrags-Diplomatie und die Stalin-Noten von 1952," in Vierteljahrshefte für Zeitgeschichte 42 (1994), pp. 243–278, here pp. 244, 248–250; Stourzh, *Um Einheit und Freiheit*, p. 183. Bischof, *Austria in the First Cold War*, pp. 123–129.

39. See Günter Bischof, "Recapturing the Initiative" and "Negotiating from Strength." The hidden agenda of the "Short Treaty" episode—The militarization of American foreign policy and the un/making of the Austrian Treaty, in Arnold Suppan et al., eds., *Der österreichische Staatsvertrag 1955. Internationale Strategie, rechtliche Relevanz, nationale Identität/The Austrian State Treaty 1955. International Strategy, Legal Relevance, National Identity* (Vienna: Böhlau, 2005), pp. 217–247.

40. Ruggenthaler, "Warum Österreich nicht sowjetisiert wurde," pp. 698–699.

41. Bischof, "Recapturing the Initiative," pp. 242–243.

42. In detail see Peter Ruggenthaler, "A New Perspective from Moscow Archives: Austria and the Stalin Notes of 1952," in Günter Bischof and Fritz Plasser, eds., *The Changing Austrian Voter*, Contemporary Austrian Studies, Vol. XVI (New Brunswick: Transaction, 2008), pp. 199–227.

43. Gehler, "Kurzvertrag," pp. 248–249.

44. Ibid.

45. See most recently Ruggenthaler, *The Concept of Neutrality*; Peter Ruggenthaler, "The 1952 Stalin Note on German Unification. The Ongoing Debate," in *Journal of Cold War Studies*, Vol. 13 (2011), No. 4, pp. 172–212; Jürgen Zarusky, "Die historische Debatte über die Stalin-Note im Lichte sowjetischer Quellen," in Nikolaus Lobkowicz et al., eds., *Die deutsche Frage im Ost-West-Geflecht—zum 20. Jahrestag der Öffnung der Berliner Mauer* (Cologne et al.: Böhlau, 2010), pp. 13–29; Ruggenthaler, *Stalins großer Bluff*; Gerhard Wettig, *Stalin and the Cold War in Europe: The Emergence and Development of East-West Conflict*. Harvard Cold War Studies Book Series (Lanham: Rowman & Littlefield, 2008); Jürgen Zarusky, ed., *Die Stalin-Note*

vom 10. März 1952. Neue Quellen und Analysen. Mit Beiträgen von Wilfried Loth, Hermann Graml und Gerhard Wettig (Munich: Oldenbourg, 2002).

46. Ruggenthaler, "The 1952 Stalin Note."
47. Ruggenthaler, *Stalins großer Bluff*, p. 122.
48. Ibid., p. 128.
49. Jochen Laufer and Georgij P. Kynin, eds., *Die UdSSR und die deutsche Frage 1941–1948. Dokumente aus dem Archiv für Außenpolitik der Russischen Föderation. Band* 3 (Berlin: Humblot & Duncker, 2004), p. LXXXIII.
50. As early as 1991 Günter Bischof highlighted the interdependence between the Stalin Note and the Western note containing the "Short Treaty," whose significance had up till then been totally neglected by historians. See Günter Bischof, "Karl Gruber und die Anfänge des 'Neuen Kurses' in der österreichischen Außenpolitik 1952/53," in Lothar Höbelt and Othmar Huber, eds., *Für Österreichs Freiheit. Karl Gruber— Landeshauptmann und Außenminister 1945–1953* (Innsbruck: Haymon, 1991), pp. 143–183, here pp. 147–149.
51. The Soviet High Commissioner in Austria, Vladimir Sviridov, found nothing in 1952 in neutralization scenarios for Austria to recommend them from a Soviet point of view. Neutralization was liable not only to lead to the country's orientation toward the West, which was already in full swing anyhow, but ultimately to its military integration into NATO. See Ruggenthaler, *The Concept of Neutrality*, p. 247.
52. Stourzh, *Um Einheit und Freiheit*, p. 183.
53. For details see Ruggenthaler, *Stalins großer Bluff*, pp. 26–128.
54. See above all Mark Kramer, "Der Aufstand in Ostdeutschland im Juni 1953," in Bernd Greiner, Christian Th. Müller and Walter Dierk, eds., *Krisen im Kalten Krieg* (Hamburg: HIS, 2008), pp. 80–126.
55. Stourzh, *Um Einheit und Freiheit*, p. 463.
56. On the conflict between Khrushchev and Molotov on Austria see ibid., pp. 455–462.
57. Vojtech Mastny, "Die NATO im sowjetischen Denken und Handeln 1949 bis 1956," in Vojtech Mastny, and Gustav Schmidt, *Konfrontationsmuster des Kalten Krieges 1946 bis 1956. Entstehen und Probleme des Atlantischen Bündnisses bis 1956. Band 3* (Munich: Oldenbourg, 2003), here p. 440.
58. Michail Prozumenščikov, "Nach Stalins Tod. Sowjetische Österreich-Politik 1953–1955," in Karner and Stelzl-Marx, eds., *Rote Armee*, pp. 729–753; Iber, *Sowjetische Mineralölverwaltung*.
59. Stourzh, *Um Einheit und Freiheit*, pp. 464–466, 480–485.
60. See therefore Wolfgang Mueller, *A Good Example of a Peaceful Coexistence? The Soviet Union, Austria and Neutrality, 1955–1991* (Vienna: Verlag der Österreichischen Akademie der Wissenschaften, 2011).
61. For more details see Peter Ruggenthaler, "On the Significance of Austrian Neutrality for Soviet Foreign Policy under Nikita S. Khrushchev," in Günter Bischof, Stefan Karner and Barbara Stelzl-Marx, eds., *The Vienna Summit and Its Importance in International History*. Harvard Cold War Studies Book Series. (Lanham et al.: Lexington 2014), pp. 329–348.

62. This point has always been made by Günter Bischof in his works. Even in most summary works on the early Cold War by well-known experts, Austria is rarely mentioned as a theater of the East-West conflict or even completely ignored. See, among others, Melvyn P. Leffler, *For the Soul of Mankind: The United States, the Soviet Union and the Cold War* (New York: Hill and Wang, 2007); John Lewis Gaddis, *We Now Know: Rethinking Cold War History* (Oxford/New York: Oxford University Press, 1998); John Lewis Gaddis, *Der Kalte Krieg. Eine neue Geschichte*, trans. Klaus-Dieter Schmidt (Munich: Siedler, 2007). While the Austrian historiography has hitherto comprehensively concerned itself with the first post-war decade on the basis of domestic, British, French and American sources, research into the Soviet Union lagged behind for a long time, even after the partial opening of Russian archives. References are limited here to the following works: Bischof, *Austria in the First Cold War*, and the magnum opus, Stourzh, *Um Einheit und Freiheit*, which is unfortunately only available in German; Erwin A. Schmidl, ed., *Österreich im frühen Kalten Krieg 1945–1958. Spione, Partisanen, Kriegspläne* (Vienna/Cologne/Weimar: Böhlau, 2000); Thomas Angerer, "Französische Freundschaftspolitik in Österreich nach 1945. Gründe, Grenzen und Gemeinsamkeiten mit Frankreichs Deutschlandpolitik," in Manfried Rauchensteiner and Robert Kriechbaumer, eds., *Die Gunst des Augenblicks. Neuere Forschungen zu Staatsvertrag und Neutralität* (Vienna/Cologne/Weimar: Böhlau, 2005), pp. 113–138.

63. Subok and Pleschakow, *Der Kreml im Kalten Krieg*, p. 226. Even during the nuclear era, Molotov remained in the grip of this mindset, which explains his resistance to relinquishing Austria.

64. Zubok, *A Failed Empire*, p. 83.

65. Mastny, "Die NATO im sowjetischen Denken und Handeln," p. 440.

66. Gerald Stourzh, "Der österreichische Staatsvertrag in den weltpolitischen Entscheidungsprozessen," in Suppan, Stourzh and Mueller, eds., *Der österreichische Staatsvertrag 1955*, pp. 965–995, here pp. 974 and 978.

67. Norman N. Naimark, "Stalin and Europe in the Postwar Period, 1945–53: Issues and Problems," *Journal of Modern European History*, Vol. 2 (2004), No. 1 ("Communist Regimes and Parties after the Second World War"), pp. 28–57, here p. 56.

68. See Zubok, *A Failed Empire*; Kramer, "Stalin, Soviet Policy, and the Consolidation of a Communist Bloc in Eastern Europe, 1944–1953."

69. Rolf Steininger, *Austria, Germany, and the Cold War: From the Anschluss to the State Treaty 1938–1955* (New York/Oxford: Berghahn Books, 2008), p. 100.

70. See above all Mark Kramer, "Stalin, Soviet Policy, and the Consolidation of a Communist Bloc in Eastern Europe, 1944–1953," in Vladimir Tismaneanu, ed., *Stalinism Revisited: The Establishment of Communist Regimes in East-Central Europe* (Budapest/New York: Central European University Press, 2009) pp. 50–102; V. O. Pechatnov, *Ot soyuza k kholodnoi voine. Sovetsko-amerikanskie otnosheniya v 1945–1947gg.* (Moscow: MGIMO, 2006); Norman Naimark and Leonid Gibianskii, eds., *The Establishment of Communist Regimes in Eastern Europe, 1944–1949* (Boulder, CO: Westview Press, 1997); Giuliano Procacci et al., eds., *The Cominform.*

Minutes of the Three Conferences 1947/1948/1949 (Milan: Fondazione Giangiacomo Feltrinelli, 1994) and many others.

71. See the contribution by Walter Iber in this volume; Walter Iber, *Die Sowjetische Mineralölverwaltung in Österreich. Zur Vorgeschichte der OMV 1945–1955* (Innsbruck et al.: Studienverlag, 2010).

72. See the contribution by Mikhail Prozumenshchikov in this volume.

Chapter Five

The Development of Soviet Policy toward Austria after Stalin's Death from 1953 to 1955

Mikhail Prozumenshchikov

On May 15, 1955, in an act of the greatest significance for the whole of post-war Europe, the Austrian State Treaty was signed in Vienna's Belvedere Palace. Seventeen years after the Anschluss of Austria to Hitler's Germany and ten years after the end of the Second World War, Austria obtained its independence as a state again. It was the first time that the former Allies in the anti-Hitler coalition, who had subsequently become bitter Cold War enemies, had succeeded in coming to an agreement on such an important issue. With the signing of the State Treaty an important political project, which was not geared toward an aggravation of the confrontation and a division of Europe but contributed rather to the mitigation of the tense international political situation, had been successfully put into practice for the first time.

Although the negotiations regarding the conditions for concluding the State Treaty spanned a decade,[1] and the decisive breakthrough was achieved only a few months before May 1955, March 5, 1953, can be regarded without a doubt as a landmark day for Austrian independence. It was on this day that Iosif Stalin, who had for three decades determined not only the domestic and foreign policy of the USSR but also exerted a decisive influence on the political development process across the globe, died. Stalin's successors attempted, sometimes inconsistently and not without contradictions, to find new approaches to solutions for those countless problems that had amassed at lightning speed during the preceding years. Among these problems was the issue of Austria.

When taking a closer look at the problems connected with the whereabouts and withdrawal of the occupation troops stationed in Austria, it must be kept in mind that political, economic, and military aspects were closely related when it came to this issue. In its oppositional stance toward the Western powers, the Soviet Union was guided first and foremost by issues of ideological expediency and national prestige. As early as the 1940s, Stalin had ruled out in the case of Austria, in contrast to a series of states in Eastern Europe, the conversion of the state (or some of its constituent parts) into a "people's democracy." Nevertheless, the USSR could not allow Austria, for whose liberation so many Soviet soldiers had given up their lives, to again become the bridgehead for a Blitzkrieg directed against the Soviet Union following the withdrawal of parts of the Soviet Army. Moscow even entertained serious fears of a merging of Austria and West Germany to form a united state (a new Anschluss). At any rate, a withdrawal of the USSR from Austria without a serious political reason would have been regarded in Moscow as a sensitive defeat for Soviet foreign policy.

The factor of a potential war scenario exerted even greater influence on the treatment of the Austrian question. Stalin assumed, like many of his Western opponents, that a Third World War was, if not unavoidable, then certainly very probable. In this respect, Austria, which was located in the center of Europe and at the point of contact for two antagonistic political camps, constituted an extremely important object of military considerations.

Finally, in a discussion of the Austrian question, economic factors must necessarily also be taken into account. The efforts of the Soviet Union to prevent Austrian participation in the Marshall Plan remained unsuccessful. Although Moscow constantly spoke of the enslaving character of the Marshall Plan and a subjugation of Austria by American monopolists, it rigidly remained the case that the Austrian economy continually grew and was able as early as 1949 to exceed its pre-war capacity. These circumstances, however, constituted merely the tip of the iceberg when it came to conflicts of interests between the occupying powers on economic matters.

In spring 1953, the change of power in the USSR gave the lethargic and de facto unsuccessful negotiation process regarding Germany and Austria a strong, new impetus. New proposals and initiatives had come from Moscow. The political leadership of the GDR was unequivocally ordered to not only hasten to proclaim the socialist character of East German society but also to exhibit the idea of a socialist GDR as soon as possible.[2] In the USSR, the prerequisites for a potential withdrawal of Soviet troops from Germany were even cautiously sounded out, if the Western countries were in return to guarantee the neutrality of Germany and a security border for the USSR and its allies. In Austria, such signals from Moscow were followed with great interest, especially since Austria correctly assumed that the solution of the German question would also pave the way for an Austrian State Treaty. The hopes for a State Treaty were further strengthened by the fact that a softening of the hitherto unbending Soviet position began to emerge in relations between the Soviet Union and Austria.

On June 9, 1953, the Soviet occupation forces abolished identity checks for the Austrian population along the demarcation line, as well as the inspection of the passage of goods. As of August 1, 1953, the USSR itself assumed all expenses for the maintenance of Soviet troops in Austria, censorship in the Soviet Occupation Zone was abolished, and the radio station of the *Radio-Verkehrs-AG* (RAVAG) was transferred to the Austrian government. As a sign of goodwill, the USSR decided to repatriate 610 Austrian prisoners of war who had been convicted by Soviet courts.[3]

Much that was put into practice on the international stage by the Soviet Union during this time was connected with the name of the Interior Minister and the First Deputy of the Council of Ministers of the USSR, Lavrentii P. Beriia, who can be regarded as one of the most important initiators of an openness to compromise in the treatment of the German and Austria questions. The ongoing power struggle among Stalin's successors prevented, however, the realization of all of his plans. The imprisonment of Beriia in summer 1953 and his conviction as a "spy and enemy of the people" disavowed all his actions and declarations, which were adjudged to be "treasonable" and "damaging to the state" (even though they had been endorsed by the entire Party leadership only a few days previously). And although some of the measures mentioned that impacted on Austria were carried out after his imprisonment, this was now done under compulsion and without dedication.

The aforementioned repatriation of 610 convicted Austrian prisoners of war can serve as an example of the Soviet stance toward Austria following the imprisonment of Beriia. The official diplomatic account of this was delivered to the Austrian Ambassador in the USSR, Norbert Bischoff,[4] on June 26, 1953, and shortly after published in the Austrian press together with a complete list of the repatriated persons. Subsequently, however, a definitive decision regarding the repatriation of the Austrian prisoners was repeatedly postponed and indeed, as the Soviet officials opaquely informed Norbert Bischoff, "for known reasons." In light of the thoroughly negative reaction observed in Austria to the fact that the amnestied Austrian citizens had to remain in the USSR, the Soviet Foreign Ministry addressed itself on August 25 of the same year to the Presidium of the Central Committee of the CPSU with the urgent request to come to a definitive decision on this matter as soon as possible. Not until September 26 (i.e., three months after the first decision) did the Party leadership grant their definitive consent for a repatriation of the Austrian prisoners of war.

This approach of Moscow's is not difficult to explain for the second half of 1953. Following the replacement of Lavrentii Beriia, representatives of an approach to international affairs that was unbending and did not shy away from confrontation returned to the forefront of the Kremlin's leadership;

Vyacheslav Molotov, one of the most faithful Stalinists, took over the office of Foreign Minister. With regard to Nikita Khrushchev, it should be pointed out that at this time his political weight and influence were not yet sufficient for a one-person rule of the state; he preferred to wait and maneuver without revealing his opinion on contested issues. These circumstances resulted in the USSR displaying very contradictory behavior on the global stage, which was particularly noticeable in preparations for the Conference of the Foreign Ministers of the USSR, the United States, Great Britain, and France, which was held in January and February 1954 in Berlin. The Berlin Conference of Foreign Ministers also addressed the German and Austrian questions.

On the eve of the conference, it was established during the discussion of special tasks for the Soviet delegation that the following two points should be placed on the agenda with top priority for the Soviet side: "Measures for easing the international state of affairs and the convening of a meeting of the foreign ministers of France, Great Britain, the USA, the USSR and the People's Republic of China" as well as "The German question and measures for maintaining European security." "The Austrian State Treaty" was only the third point listed, whereby the Soviet delegation was instructed in the event that the Western countries refused to put the first point on to the agenda to nevertheless insist "that this be dealt with after the German question and before the debate on an Austrian State Treaty." Furthermore, in the first version of the directives for the Soviet delegation, which Molotov had submitted to a session of the Presidium of the Central Committee of the CPSU for its perusal, the Austrian question was not even included as a separate point on the agenda. There was merely a very spongy formulation to the effect that the Soviet side would not object in the event that the Western countries wanted to deal with the Austrian question; the Soviet Union also intended, however, to use the Austrian question as a bargaining chip in order to encourage the negotiating parties to discuss the first point placed by the Soviets on the agenda.

Following some revisions and comments by members of the Party Presidium of the Central Committee of the CPSU, much more importance was granted to the Austrian question in the guidelines for the Soviet delegation. Clear progress was made in several hitherto contested questions. Thus, Moscow itself now advocated inviting a representative of the Austrian government to the Berlin Conference of Foreign Ministers and agreed not to make the fulfillment of the peace treaty with Italy regarding Trieste a precondition for the conclusion of the State Treaty with Austria. The USSR furthermore announced its consent for Austria making payments for former German assets in deliveries of goods.

Nevertheless, the most important and most painful problem for Austria remained unsolved; and according to the Soviet interpretation, a solution to the Austrian question was again to be dealt with in direct relation to a sought-after accord in the German question. It is not known what was intended by the Kremlin when two such contradictory points were included in the wording of the suggestions that were to have been announced by the Soviet delegation. On the one hand, it was suggested (in the first point) that a final draft text for an Austrian State Treaty be prepared within a three-month period, by means of which "Austria will be re-established as a sovereign, independent and democratic state [. . .], and through which the current Control Authority—the Union Commission for Austria and all its organs—will be dissolved and the occupation of Austria ended." On the other hand, it was established (in the second point) that "in order to avoid the receipt of Austria by one or the other power bloc, which would not be compatible with the conditions of an Austrian State Treaty, the troop withdrawal of the four victorious powers from their respective Austrian occupation zones is to be postponed until the finalisation of a peace treaty with Germany." All the empty phrases that followed, to the effect that the troops of the four victorious powers were not occupation troops and were accorded a special legal status, or that they did not interfere in the affairs of the Austrian administration and in the socio-political life of Austria, could not hide the fact that, in accordance with the Soviet proposals, foreign troop contingents had to remain stationed on the state territory of the "independent and sovereign Austria" for an indefinite length of time.

In view of these circumstances, it is clear that the Berlin Conference of Foreign Ministers would not be able to make even the slightest progress in solving the Austrian question; in the eyes of the international community of states and particularly from Austria's point of view, the main responsibility for this lay with the Soviet Union.[5] The statements made by Molotov after the conference to the effect that Moscow's stance was shaped by the West's endeavor to admit the FRG to the European Defence Community (EDC),[6] once more made it clear to Austria that the USSR made the Austrian question strictly dependent on a solution of the progressively more complex German problem. The course of events resulted in Austria in a strengthening of anti-Soviet tendencies and contributed to openly displayed pro-Western sentiment in the country.

It could not, meanwhile, have escaped Moscow's attention that several of the leading figures in the Austrian People's Party (ÖVP) had already in February spoken out in favor of the establishment of a neutral Austria[7] and, soon after the Berlin Conference of Foreign Ministers, began to advocate an exclusively Western orientation for Austria's trade and economic policies as well as Austrian foreign trade. At the same time, the leaders of the Socialist Party of Austria (SPÖ), who had taken up a very reserved position until the Berlin Conference of Foreign Ministers, voted at the Conference of the

Socialist International in Brussels on February 28, 1954, for the creation of the EDC. Increasingly, the statements of Austria's political leaders had negative connotations. In June 1954, Federal Chancellor Julius Raab openly stated that "some time must still elapse, however, until new efforts could be made; for it makes no sense to again take up the Austrian question immediately after the Berlin Foreign Ministers Conference."[8] All that the Austrian government hoped for in such circumstances was a further relaxation of the occupation regime, one small step after another. The whole of 1954 was de facto reserved for such "small steps": the USSR, Austria, and the Western countries exchanged diplomatic notes, which addressed the possibility of a conference of the ambassadors of the four occupying powers, the handling of contested issues in connection with the State Treaty, a potential replacement of the Union Commission with another organ, etc. All these activities were reminiscent of a standoff in a game of chess, where both players know that it is no longer possible to make another move that could decide the game.

Yet even if Moscow met the failure of the Berlin Conference of Foreign Ministers and subsequent declarations by Austrian politicians with comparative calmness, the political leadership of the USSR *was* unsettled by the reaction of the Austrian people. Anti-Soviet rallies, attended by the most varied strata of Austrian society, were completely unexpected by Soviet political grandees; they were still of the opinion that the Austrians would view the Red Army exclusively as liberator from Hitler's fascism and protector in the face of American imperialism. In Moscow, it was abjectly commented that the Austrians, after they had celebrated their liberation from the Nazi regime for eight years, now—in the ninth year—"staged a protest demonstration for us to liberate them from ourselves." The possibility of a further escalation in the situation in Austria, for instance, if Soviet troops were to be regarded by the Austrians no longer as liberators but as occupiers, produced even greater concern in the USSR. The response of the Soviet side was: "And what if tomorrow the Austrians throw stones at our soldiers; are we to shoot at them?"[9]

As members of the Presidium of the Central Committee of the CPSU confirmed, the political aspects of the Austrian problem remained the focus of the political leadership of the USSR during the entire second half of 1954.[10] The available documents, however, can by no means always illustrate the tenacious conflict waged by the Soviet leadership during this time, especially since much that was discussed at the highest level remains undocumented. Irrespective of this, it is to be assumed that two groups developed on this matter within the Presidium of the Central Committee, which can to some extent be designated "the orthodox" and "the moderates." While the first grouping continued to insist on a treatment of the Austrian question that did not take into account the political changes in Europe and in the world at large, the second group sought compromise solutions that allowed the Soviet Union to find a way out of the increasingly complex situation with dignity and without detriment to its interests. It would be wrong to exaggerate the extent of the diverging opinions in both groups, although it is beyond doubt that in the most senior Soviet Party circles the opinion was increasingly voiced during the course of 1954 that the policy hitherto pursued toward Austria had to be fundamentally changed.

It should be kept in mind that the Austrians themselves readily played into the hands of the Soviet "orthodox," who continued to regard the Austrian question in terms of a potential martial conflict between two opposed camps and were not prepared to make concessions when it came to a troop withdrawal and the conclusion of the State Treaty. While possible changes in the policy toward Austria were discussed in Moscow, one of the leaders of the Federation of Independents (VdU), Max Stendebach, advocated in a speech to the Austrian Parliament a merging of Austria with the FRG as soon as possible, during which he declared that "the border between Austria and the FRG must be invisible."[11] In Austria, a book by Julius Braunthal published in Great Britain, which in particular argued that the idea of an independent Austria was a "reactionary and daunting utopia,"[12] enjoyed great popularity, among others in high-level political circles. In conjunction with the declarations and actions of the United States and other Western powers, who strived to retain Austria as an active (not passive-neutral) member of the Western community, such statements were to the advantage of those leaders in the Kremlin who refused to believe in a peaceful and swift solution to the Austrian problem.

The reluctance of the Soviet Union to find a compromise solution to the Austrian question was not only due to prevailing political, ideological, and military doctrines. Economic problems, which were linked to a big extent with the Soviet military presence in Austria, also played an important role in the treatment of the Austrian question. While the Soviet leadership began to seriously deal with the political aspect of the Austrian question only in 1954, the economic aspect of the Soviet military presence in Austria had already been the subject of in-depth analyses a year earlier. The hope for a conclusion of a State Treaty in the near future, which the Soviet leadership had addressed in spring 1953, moved the USSR to examine the economic activity of Soviet firms in Austria more closely. That which came to light as a result generated little pleasure in Moscow.

Irrespective of the fact that the USSR, in its countless diplomatic notes to the Western nations, rejected the idea of a "Short Treaty" because, among other things, such a treaty was contrary to the economic interests of the USSR in Austria, the Soviet Union inflicted great damage on itself in economic matters. At the same time, political damage was evidently linked to the economic damage. Against the backdrop of the successes of Austrian and Western firms, the ineffective economic management of Soviet concerns, which found themselves in an ongoing crisis, conveyed to the Austrians a better picture of the "advantages" of the socialist economy than all political slogans could.

In economic terms, it was above all the firms of the USIA that confronted the USSR with considerable difficulties. For the Austrian side, the draft of the State Treaty envisaged with its signature the purchase of those firms in the hands of the USIA for 150 million dollars. In light of the course taken by negotiations regarding the Austrian question, which had reached an impasse at the intersection of the 1940s and the 1950s, however, both the signing of a State Treaty and the sale of the firms seemed improbable in the near future. Following the death of Stalin, Vienna approached Moscow with the request to negotiate the purchase of the Soviet firms prior to the conclusion of the State Treaty and made clear at an early stage their desire to be allowed to pay for the aforementioned sum with goods deliveries rather than freely convertible currency, as foreseen in the draft of the State Treaty.

Within the framework of the new political tendencies during the first half of 1953, the USSR initially responded to this request with understanding. At the beginning of May 1953, the Presidium of the Council of Ministers of the USSR tasked the relevant authorities with preparing a draft of a directive for the commencement of negotiations with the Austrian government, a positive decision regarding the Austrian enquiry being expected. However, the Presidium of the Council of Ministers of the USSR revised this decision only three weeks later during a session on May 22, 1953, and no longer regarded a sale of the Soviet firms as advantageous. It seems clear that such a change in the Soviet position cannot be ascribed only to political reasons, but rather in particular to economic considerations. As it turned out, the majority of the Soviet firms found themselves in a very strained economic state and their sale in this condition could have been regarded as an admission of Soviet inability to run the firms profitably. It was decided in the Soviet Union above all for this reason to reassess this matter.

In June 1953, the Council of Ministers of the USSR took a series of measures that aimed at resolving, at least partially, existing grievances. It was decided to shut down thirty-two firms that were in deficit, to considerably increase the capital investment in the USIA (during the next one and a half years, more funds should be pumped into them than in all previous years combined) or, for example, to set up a special fund for the improvement of conditions for workers and salaried employees. Additional funds were allocated to the accommodation fund of the USIA in order to erect new buildings and to renovate existing housing, which consisted of dilapidated buildings and rudimentary wooden barracks. The USSR decided furthermore to set up via the network of branches of Soviet businesses in the Soviet Occupation Zone a free retail industry for supply and industrial goods, the prices of which were 10 to 15 percent lower than those of Austrian businesses. Finally, the resources of the Soviet Military Bank in Austria, which had previously been unable for lack of financial means to guarantee financial aid to the firms of the USIA, were also replenished.

It should be kept in mind that some of the economic problems that were connected with Soviet firms in Austria arose from those ideological maxims that were under all circumstances strictly complied with in the USSR. The slogan, according to which the proletariat of Western countries would be the only ally of the socialist states on the way to a promising communist future, was also expressed in a curious fashion in the wage policy of the USIA. In accordance with top-secret Soviet statistics, the wage level of ordinary workers and assistants (i.e., the least qualified workers) in the firms of the USIA exceeded that of comparative workers in Austrian firms by 7 to 13 percent. The pay of the more qualified workers in the Soviet Zone was only 2.5 percent higher than in the rest of Austria, and the wage level of the salaried employees of the USIA or, in Soviet jargon, "the representatives of the petty bourgeoisie" was only 80 to 90 percent of the earnings of their colleagues in Austrian firms.

Also contributing to the idiosyncratic Soviet economic policy were the so-called "friends" of the Soviet Union, i.e., the representatives of the Communist Party of Austria (KPÖ), who regularly received financial allowances from Moscow and were obliged to synchronize their views with those of the USSR. The Austrian communists feared that as a result of the restructuring begun in the USIA firms the conditions of workers, who were for the most part Party members, could deteriorate, which would result in a further loss of prestige for the already not very esteemed KPÖ. For this reason, irrespective of the decision made in June 1953, several of those firms scheduled for closure had to be kept in operation at the request of the KPÖ. These firms brought the Soviet Union during the course of 1953 a loss of more than 100,000 rubles.

Nevertheless, the USSR was determined to turn seventeen of the firms in Austria belonging to her into model firms by the end of the year. When one considers that 144 USIA firms were located in the Soviet Occupation Zone alone, the restructuring of the firms according to the Soviet plan would have extended over the duration of at least two five-year plans. Unexpected unity prevailed within the Soviet leadership regarding the restructuring of the firms owned by the USIA. The "orthodox" still assumed that the Soviet military presence in Austria would be long-term and that sufficient time would, therefore, be available for the restructuring of the firms. The "moderates," who made an effort to present the firms under Soviet economic control in a better light to the international community of states, hoped to make at least a few of the USIA firms profitable before the signing of the State Treaty.

After the failed attempt to solve the Austrian problem at the Berlin Conference of Foreign Ministers, at which the possibility of selling USIA firms was also discussed in the framework of general questions, Austria again attempted to strengthen its activities in this direction. In March 1954, Julius Raab declared that he would insist toward the Soviet High Commissar "on the return of the USIA firms in accordance with the conditions of the State Treaty." At the same time as countless protests against a continued occupation of the country, which were condemned in the USSR as "hostile actions against the Soviet power and Soviet occupation troops in Austria," a boycott began in Austria directed against USIA firms[13] and the Austrian daily newspapers reported extensively on the tense situation in the USIA firms. In Moscow, the approach of the Austrian print media was described as "provocative and defamatory" but, for all the obvious political polemic, it could not be doubted that the reports of Austrian newspapers contained truthful information.

The Soviet Union had to recognize that the maintenance of the status quo in relation to the USIA firms was for the USSR neither politically nor economically advantageous. In the Kremlin, it became clear that through the embellishment of official statistics, by means of which one's own people could be deceived, the population of a country in which the USSR did not have complete ideological control or powerful organs of censorship could not be duped. The official figures differed clearly from those which the Soviet Union announced in their press reports.

According to official figures, the USIA firms brought the Soviet side during the occupation period a pure profit of 927 million rubles within the space of eight years. However, the USSR should in fact have paid almost half of this sum (450 million rubles) to Austria in the form of federal taxes. Under the pretext that Austria did not recognize the Soviet Union's right of ownership for these firms as former German assets and did not register them, the payment of taxes was refused. It is not difficult to guess that Austria, if it had recognized the Soviet Union's right of ownership for the USIA firms, would have delivered a decisive blow to their already precarious financial state. Moscow also failed to pay federal taxes for the goods turnover of the retail outlets opened by the USIA, which constituted a particularly crass breach of the law, especially since the latter had never been German property.

Due to the increase in investments in these firms on the part of the Soviets and because of the sales difficulties and the deteriorating economic climate, the profitability of the USIA increasingly dwindled. As early as 1953, the USIA only made 137 million rubles' profit, which was less than in the previous year by eighty million rubles. The actual return from the activities of the firms in fact only amounted to thirty-eight million rubles. The remaining ninety-nine million resulted from the evasion of federal taxes, customs duties and excise taxes (in other words, from offences against the law in force at the time). In view of the fact that the Soviet side only reckoned with a halved pure profit for 1954, it was clear that an Austrian demand to adhere to all laws (which would undoubtedly have been supported by the Western countries) would have led to the complete bankruptcy of the USIA firms.

It was thus no coincidence that the Presidium of the Central Committee of the CPSU reappraised the state of the USIA firms in April 1954 and classified them as absolutely unsatisfactory. Further measures for the improvement of their activities were suggested; for example, additional investments, the supply of the firms with contracts from the Soviet Union and the People's Democracies as well as an increase in the import of goods from USIA firms into the USSR as a reaction to the increasing sales difficulties for its production in Austria. Furthermore, the following social measures were planned: an annual holiday in the Soviet Union for twenty-five workers and salaried employees from USIA firms, housing loans for highly qualified specialists, the free lease of houses from the USIA accommodation fund to Austrian associations and citizens, and the like. The suggestions listed were presented to the Soviet leadership for its endorsement as early as May 1954.

A further idea had been developed parallel to these proposals. It is interesting that one of the longest-serving members of the Presidium of the Central Committee played a leading role in the emergence of both documents—the First Deputy of the Chairman of the Council of Ministers of the USSR, Anastas Mikoyan. Thus, on May 17, 1954, at the same time as the proposals listed above, which already bore the signature of the Soviet Premier Malenkov as well as that of Mikoyan and a whole host of further Party and government functionaries,[14] a note from Mikoyan with exactly the opposite content landed on the table at a session of the Central Committee. The note contained the proposal to immediately begin negotiations with the Austrian government for the sale of the USIA firms along the lines of the conditions in Article 35 of the draft State Treaty. Mikoyan justified this unexpected proposal with both political and economic considerations. With regard to the latter, he correctly pointed out that a continuation of the existing tendencies would reduce the profit from the USIA firms to a minimum or even lead to losses. Meanwhile, the USSR—in the event of a sale—would receive from Austria over the course of six years goods guaranteed to the value of 100 million rubles a year. The political expediency of such a decision, argued Mikoyan, was that it would help to counteract the powerful surge of the anti-Soviet campaign that had unfolded in Austria during the preceding years and which was directed first and foremost against the presence of Soviet troops and firms. Even Mikoyan, who belonged to the "moderates" group and reckoned on an early conclusion to the State Treaty, assumed that the continued presence of the Soviet occupying force would make it easier to ensure that the Austrians fulfilled their payment obligations to the tune of 150 million dollars, whereas following the conclusion of the State Treaty and particularly after the withdrawal of Soviet troops, Austria might attempt to sabotage the payment of this sum.

The only envisaged exceptions to the recommended sale were for the firms of the Soviet Petroleum Administration and the Danube Steam Navigation Company, which Moscow did not want to yield under any circumstances. The USSR was, like its allies in the "People's Democracies," very interested in the high-grade crude oil extracted in Austria, which was transported by ship to Batumi and reached Mukachevo in the province of L'viv by rail.

Mikoyan's initiative, however, failed to find any support in the highest leadership circles. Those forces within the Soviet leadership who did not believe in an early conclusion to the treaty and the related withdrawal of Soviet troops from Austria once again prevailed. The draft ordinance of the Central Committee of the CPSU submitted by Mikoyan, which was itself already of a compromise nature,[15] was considerably altered further. Ultimately, the point regarding measures for the improvement of work in the firms of the USIA moved to the top. This was followed by a laconic (but, for anyone initiated into the Kremlin's internal discord, thoroughly intelligible) formulation: "The appraisal of the proposals for a sale of Soviet firms in Austria is to be postponed by one month."

As was to be expected, this question was taken up again by the Presidium of the Central Committee neither after a month nor after half a year. Even when, in summer 1954, an increase in the extraction and processing of crude oil in the firms of the Soviet Petroleum Administration in Austria (precisely the one that Mikoyan had under no circumstances wanted to sell) was discussed, no one spoke anymore of the sale of the USIA firms.

Moscow often used the presence of the Soviet Army in Austria as the "final word," also for solving purely economic questions. As mentioned earlier, the Soviet leadership was afraid that, in the event of a withdrawal of military contingents, the Austrian government could refuse to pay for the sold USIA firms. The same applied to the discussion of the oil firms on Austrian territory. In accordance with the draft of the State Treaty, the Soviet Union would receive concessions for Austrian oil fields for thirty years; furthermore, the concessions for boring sites with the right to carry out drilling there for eight years and to extract crude oil for a period of twenty-five years starting on the day of the opening of a site.

As long as the oil firms were protected by the Soviet Petroleum Administration, they had no cause to fear for their future. The Soviet Petroleum Administration oversaw with particular vigilance the activities of the Anglo-American firms located in the Soviet Occupation Zone. All attempts by these firms to reach an agreement with representatives of the Soviet military on the division of expenses for the supervision of the monitored oil firms or reductions in the sales prices for crude oil always ended fruitlessly.

In the USSR, it had meanwhile become entirely clear that in the event of an early withdrawal of Soviet troops the time of privileges for the firms of the Soviet Petroleum Administration would be over and that they "would be exposed over a longer period to trade rivalry with capitalist firms." As in the case of USIA firms, however, the Soviet leadership had to recognize with regret that the technical standards of crude oil processing in Soviet firms in Austria did not allow for the manufacture of high-grade crude oil products that could hold their own against serious competition. The organization of production according to the socialist model was evidently inferior to the forms and methods of its capitalist competition. Under the conditions in an admittedly neutral but independent and capitalist Austria, this could only lead to the collapse of the Soviet enterprises. Here they had come full circle —Moscow needed the high-grade Austrian crude oil (the USSR planned an increase in the extracted amounts from 3.1 million tons in 1954 to 4.1 millions tons for 1957). The fact that this oil would end up in the Soviet Union for years to come guaranteed, on the other hand, the continued presence of the Soviet Army in Austria.

If there was something that the Soviet Union was happy to dispense with, then it was the former German assets that had passed over into their possession and brought neither political nor notable economic profit. In May 1953, the Soviet government transferred the assets of the hydroelectric power station Ybbs-Persenbeug to the Austrians, while the purchase price was included in the total sum of 150 million dollars. One year later, Moscow, responding to a request by Julius Raab, also declared itself ready to part with the completed parts of the Vienna–Salzburg motorway located in the Soviet Occupation Zone. The USSR was evidently not particularly concerned with the construction of new transport routes. After the USIA no longer operated these assets, they brought the Soviet side no profit whatsoever. Accordingly, the parting occurred easily enough, even under the conditions proposed by Vienna.

The difficult position of their firms in Austria compelled the Soviet leadership to continually keep Mikoyan's proposals at the back of their mind. During the course of 1954, Soviet representatives in Austria repeatedly recalled the possibility of a sale of the firms before the signing of the State Treaty. In this way, they raised hopes within the Austrian government and simultaneously fear within the KPÖ leadership. In January 1955, this question was surprisingly raised in a session of the Presidium of the Central Committee of the CPSU. This came about above all at the initiative of the KPÖ, which was troubled by news reaching it about an allegedly planned sale of Soviet firms in Austria. The Presidium of the Central Committee officially verified its position, according to which "negotiations with Austrian representatives over a sale of USIA firms to the Austrian government before the conclusion in due course of a State Treaty" were regarded as "inexpedient." At the same time, the Soviet High Commissioner in Austria was tasked with placating the leaders of the KPÖ and recommending to the Austrian friends that the work of the KPÖ in the USIA firms be better organized in order to strengthen the limited influence of the Party on the workers employed there.

The discussion in the session of the Presidium in January 1955 of the advisability of a sale of USIA firms coincided with the Plenary Assembly of the Central Committee of the CPSU at which Georgii Malenkov was not only harshly criticized but also removed from his posted as head of government.[16] This new flaring-up of power struggles within the post-Stalinist Soviet leadership had several far-reaching consequences for Austria. On the one hand, the position of Khrushchev, who was willing to compromise in the search for different ways to solve the Austrian problem, was considerably strengthened. On the other hand, during the course of the restructuring within the Kremlin leadership, Georgii Zhukov, who had achieved fame as a military commander, replaced Nikolai Bulganin as Minister of Defence, who for his part became the new Chairman of the Council of Ministers. If Bulganin, who had been Minister of Defence since 1950, had consistently pursued the political line laid down by Stalin, then Zhukov, who was popular in the army but had fallen out of favor with Stalin, had Nikita Khrushchev personally to thank for his new start. This was, in turn, not unimportant for Khrushchev, as it could not be clearly foreseen how army circles would react to a potential withdrawal of Soviet troops from Austria.

The repercussions of the changes within the Soviet leadership for Soviet policy toward Austria were not, however, limited to this. As early as January 19, 1955, the Presidium of the Central Committee had scheduled the ordinary congress of the Supreme Soviet of the USSR (formally the highest legislative organ in the country) for March 9 of the same year.[17] The affairs surrounding Malenkov, however, necessitated an amendment to this plan. After the congress had been hurriedly brought forward by a month, Vyacheslav Molotov proclaimed there of all places those new Soviet proposals regarding Austria that finally paved the way for a conclusion of the State Treaty.

To all appearances, the signing of the Paris Agreements of 1954 and the so-called "free" elections held in the GDR in autumn of the same year had also buried the prospects for an Austrian State Treaty along with hopes for a peaceful reunification of Germany. Equally unexpected were the USSR's new foreign policy initiatives at the beginning of 1955. And if, despite everything, the proposals on the future of Germany proclaimed shortly earlier by the Soviet leadership still smacked of the usual propaganda,[18] the declaration on Austria was simply "revolutionary."

Molotov's appearance doubtlessly took place on the one hand at the insistence of Khrushchev and his supporters in the Presidium of the Central Committee, but on the other hand against the backdrop that Molotov himself was at the time of his announcement of the new Soviet initiative in the Austrian question in no way convinced of the success of such an undertaking. It is no coincidence that contemporary publications which appeared during the era of a Khrushchev government indicate that Molotov held "further attempts on the part of the USSR to solve the Austrian question" for "futile,"[19] all the more so because only one point in the Soviet proposals was in fact new and "revolutionary." This was namely that in which Moscow declared its readiness to discuss the question as to whether a withdrawal from Austria of the troops of the four occupying powers could be realized without the prior conclusion of a peace treaty with Germany.[20] All other offers—both for early consultations between the four occupying powers as well as for Austrian participation in the negotiating process or the establishment of a guarantee against a new Anschluss—were, in a more or less clear form, already contained in earlier Soviet declarations. Yet now, for the first time, they were not conditional on a peaceful solution to the German question.

It is difficult to say whether the temporal concurrence of the new Soviet initiative with the dismissal of Malenkov was pure coincidence or whether these events were connected. Officially, Malenkov was called to account for mistakes in the organization of the people's economy (in particular the area of agriculture) and was furthermore accused of having accelerated the development of light industry at the expense of heavy industry. However, both in the discussion of the "Malenkov question" in the Presidium and afterward at the Plenary Assembly of the Central Committee indications were made to the effect that he had not "distanced himself from Beriia" or had even "admitted his closeness to Beriia" or something to that effect.[21] As can be seen from the notations of the head of the General Department of the Central Committee and the minutes of the Presidium of the Central Committee, reference was made to a close relationship between Malenkov and Beriia not only with regard to the question of reprisals but also in relation to the idea to solve the

German question by unifying both parts of Germany to form a united, neutral but capitalist state.[22]

Following the exclusion of Beriia, Malenkov mutated—as was not untypical in the framework of political struggles at the highest level of the Soviet leadership—into one of the most fervent advocates of a unification of Germany "on a genuinely democratic basis" (which meant in the language of Soviet ideology nothing other than the extension of the political system prevailing in the GDR to the rest of Germany). In this way, Malenkov unintentionally became one of the most important allies of Molotov, who continued to adhere to the old Stalinist guidelines[23] in his conduct on the international stage. When Malenkov suffered the loss of his status and his political star sank,[24] the Soviet Foreign Minister lost this comrade.

During the entire course of 1954, Molotov himself did not abandon the idea of making a solution to the Austrian question dependent on that of the German. At the same time, he attempted to convince the other members of the Presidium that a failure of the Western intention to establish a European defense union would improve the Soviet Union's negotiating position. When the French Parliament refused to ratify the agreement regarding the defense union, this was regarded as a victory for Soviet diplomacy and Molotov seemed to be confirmed in his course of action. Yet the signing of the Paris Agreements only a few months later showed that Molotov's politics had not been granted success in this matter. Against this backdrop, the Presidium of the Central Committee instructed the Soviet Foreign Ministry to present new proposals regarding Austria in time for the Plenary Assembly in January 1955, which did not however happen. If one can believe Anastas Mikoyan, he advised Molotov to submit the proposal at the congress of the Supreme Soviet to solve the German and Austrian questions independently of one another. If one considers the fact that Mikoyan was one of the most important supporters of a gradual withdrawal of the Soviet Union from Austria, which he then also—in the presence of Molotov, who did not object to this interpretation of events—reported to the Plenum of the Central Committee, then this evidently corresponds to the truth[25] just as much as the assumption that Mikoyan could not have presented this proposal to Molotov without prior approval from Khrushchev. Ultimately, it was not consistent with the conventions of the Soviet leadership to seize such initiatives without the knowledge of the Party leader.

Even after his declaration, Molotov further attempted to ensure that Moscow, in the event of a withdrawal from Austria, left symbolic troop contingents there or secured itself the right to station troops again in Austria at any time. He was unable, however, to attract a majority for these suggestions. On the one hand, the Soviet leadership did not want to experience the disappointment of the Berlin Conference of Foreign Ministers a second time and add fuel to the flames of unfulfilled Austrian expectations. On the other hand, the recognition of such a right would have led to the recognition of a corresponding right for the United States, Britain and France, which would have had barely foreseeable and dangerous consequences for the future. Molotov seems to have realized this and he returned to this topic neither in the negotiations with members of the Austrian government nor with the Western powers, and instead followed the united line of the Central Committee of the CPSU.[26]

Even though the entire Soviet leadership was more or less molded by the foreign policy dogmas of Stalin and none of the Party leaders intended to relinquish fundamental ideological principles, many of them, foremost Khrushchev, nevertheless recognized the necessity of finding new ways and means to disentangle the deadlocked situation. It was moreover almost characteristic for Khrushchev that he resorted to ideas (admittedly in new garments and under other conditions) of former rivals, whom he himself had toppled. He later—in somewhat modified form and furnished with the corresponding propagandistic packaging—successfully applied much that Beriia had said and which, therefore, had been banned in summer 1953.

It is doubtlessly to the Soviet leader's credit, however, that he proved himself capable of viewing any given situation from a new perspective. The Soviet initiative took the Western countries completely by surprise. They were accustomed to "Molotov diplomacy" and had not expected any radical changes in the Kremlin's course of action. It is not surprising, therefore, that they had no alternatives with which to counter Soviet proposals in the many subsequent declarations and commentaries. They merely directed warnings at the Austrian rulers to exercise "caution" during negotiations in Moscow, not to discuss any "concrete treaty conditions," and to limit themselves to discussing the Soviet proposals in more detail.

It is significant that even the Austrians themselves, mindful of the Austrian policy pursued up to that point by the Soviets, initially encountered Molotov's proposals with extreme reservation and scepticism. Vienna's official reaction was appropriately cautious—the Soviet proposals had been "registered with great interest and closely studied," but they were "not formulated clearly enough."[27] Even greater scepticism prevailed among the Austrian public. When the Austrian governmental delegates already prepared themselves for negotiations in Moscow in April 1955, hardly anyone believed that these would be successful. In the opinion of ordinary Austrians, "someone" was sure to be "against something"[28] again.

Only after consultations between the Soviet leadership and Norbert Bischoff in February and March 1955, during which Moscow had explained a series of questions to the ambassador, was Vienna convinced of the seriousness of Soviet intentions, at which point the tone of declarations made by the Austrian government significantly changed. When the official invitation to negotiations in Moscow then followed, this meant for Federal Chancellor Julius Raab and his government a unique opportunity that could not be missed. Even if there were still obstacles, they did not justify Austria passing up the possibility of obtaining its independence. For this reason, all Western attempts to convince Julius Raab not to sign any agreement if the USSR should insist that Austria—on the Swiss model—declare itself a neutral state remained without effect.[29] Austria was confronted with the choice between a continuation of the occupation by powers that were, moreover, hostile toward each other and an independence that was conditional, on the one hand, on neutrality and, on the other, on the duty not to enter into a union with the northern neighbor. The Austrian government preferred to opt for the latter.

For its part, the USSR made every effort to ensure that Vienna did not rethink this decision. The Soviet negotiators explained to the Austrian leadership that the ban on participation in coalitions and military alliances applied neither to economic, cultural, scientific, and similar cross-national associations or agreements nor to political unions that were not directed at third states and served the peaceful collaboration of nations. Moscow likewise avoided more strict formulations in those passages of the State Treaty which addressed the prevention of a new Anschluss.

The question of deadlines for the withdrawal of occupying troops from Austria played an important role. In the countless discussions on this subject that the USSR and the Western powers had held over the course of several years, the most varied periods of time—from ninety days to two years—had been proposed. Immediately before the arrival of the Austrian delegation in Moscow, Molotov presented the supreme Soviet leadership with suggestions from the Foreign Ministry for the negotiations with the Austrian government. He spoke of the necessity to shorten the duration of the occupation following the signature of the State Treaty. In his opinion, a longer-lasting presence of Soviet troops in Austria would not have brought the USSR any significant advantage but would—on the contrary—have supported the plans of the NATO states. These would have sought, "for military-strategic considerations," to protract "the withdrawal of their troops from Austria." Alongside this, a purely propagandistic aspect required consideration: Moscow rightly assumed that the Austrian people would be elated about an early end to the occupation and one could in this way once more demonstrate to the whole world the goodwill of the USSR. When this proposal was debated in the Presidium of the Central Committee, the Soviet rulers decided on an even more generous gesture. The final version of the "Instructions for Negotiations with the Austrian Government" already contained a reference to a six-month time limit for the withdrawal of all troop contingents from Austrian territory. In this way, the Austrian government was offered a highly enticing prospect: in the event of an early signature and ratification of the State Treaty by all sides, the Austrian government would be able to announce to its people the withdrawal of all foreign soldiers by January 1, 1956.[30]

The USSR's endorsement of a quick withdrawal of occupation troops from Austria emanated not only from the efforts to finally solve—even at the price of certain concessions—the Austrian problem. The admission of West Germany to NATO and the already planned creation by Moscow of the Warsaw Pact as a military-political counterweight had created a new geopolitical situation in Europe. After Moscow succeeded, thanks to the efforts of Khrushchev, to normalize relations with Austria's southern neighbor Yugoslavia (even if they were no longer so "fraternal" as they had been during the first years after the end of the Second World War, they were nevertheless friendly), which had been destroyed during Stalin's rule, the strategic distribution of forces in Central Europe had been given a new quality. A neutral Austria, even one that extended several hundred kilometres into the Eastern Bloc, was considerably more attractive for the Soviet military than for Western strategists, who would have liked to have turned the country into their "Alpine fortress."[31]

The simultaneous solution of the Austrian and the Yugoslav problems allowed the Soviet leadership to immediately announce a further foreign policy initiative. Using Austria as a precedent, Moscow had a belt of neutral states in Central Europe in mind, which would separate the two military blocs from each other and include a united and neutral Germany. These thoughts were met with unexpected support from the United States. President Dwight D. Eisenhower manifested his fundamental endorsement of the "creation of a chain of neutral states" that would "cross the whole of Europe from north to south," and American newspapers reported that the United States wanted to respond to the Soviet proposal with its own plan for a "neutral belt."[32] It later turned out that Washington, however, demanded from Moscow the "neutralization" of all Soviet allies in Eastern Europe in return for the inclusion of Germany in this belt. At the time, in May 1955, the USSR still expected a comprehensive relaxation in the situation.

An early conclusion of the State Treaty also benefited the USSR in economic terms. First, the presence of Soviet troops in Austria was combined with considerable costs, which—as mentioned earlier—Moscow alone paid for from 1953. Secondly, the USSR decided to part with all its firms in Austria, even those that it had in no way wanted to give up only a year earlier: namely the crude oil firms and the Danube Steam Navigation Company. The reason for this decision lay not only in the readiness of Soviet leaders to make concessions for the State Treaty.

Regardless of the increased investments from 1954, the situation in Soviet oil firms remained extremely problematic. The oil manufacturing installations were technically outdated, and fuel with a high octane rating and high-grade oils could not be produced at all.[33] As these firms would have been obliged following the signing of the State Treaty to pay the relevant taxes to the Austrian government, Moscow was confronted with the same dilemma as it had been with regard to the USIA firms: either invest high sums in the modernization and development of the firms over a period of several years, without any guarantee that they would not still go bankrupt as a result of capitalist competition, or sell them to the Austrians at a sensible price. Ultimately, elementary economic sense prevailed and the members of the Austrian delegation noted with astonishment that the Soviet Union was now proposing that which they themselves had for years not dared to suggest.[34]

The Moscow negotiations resulted in the USSR transferring to Austria all former German assets, including the USIA firms, the oil field and refineries, the joint stock company for trading with crude oil products, and the Danube Steam Navigation Company along with the shipyard at Korneuburg as well as the ships and harbor installations. In return, Moscow received the previously arranged sum of 150 million dollars, which was to be paid for entirely in the form of deliveries of Austrian goods. In addition, Moscow secured the rights for ten years to the annual receipt of a million tons of crude oil. The benefit of this agreement was plain to see—according to calculations by Soviet experts, in the event of the oil firms remaining under Soviet administration and allowing for taxes, necessary investments and the general technical state of the equipment, the USSR could have imported only 170,000 tons of crude oil from Austria each year.

The Soviet Union insisted on one point with much resoluteness: after the handover of German property in the Soviet Occupation Zone, Austria had to commit itself "to ruling out the transfer of these assets into the hands of foreign citizens." Moscow justified this demand by arguing that the acquisition of these assets by foreigners would promote Austria's economic dependence on West Germany. It was expected, namely, that the FRG would leave no stone unturned in its attempts to regain these property assets. The Soviet Union did not overlook their Austrian "friends" and obtained an official declaration from the Austrian government to the effect that it would "not allow any oppression or discrimination of Austrian citizens in connection with their employment in Soviet institutions and firms in Austria until the State Treaty comes into effect."

Events surrounding the signing of the State Treaty demonstrate once again the inconsistency and complexity of the processes that occurred in these years on the international stage. It was surprising for the world community that geopolitical components ranked above ideological ones on the Soviet leadership's list of priorities when it came to a solution to the Austrian problem. For all the divergence in views and judgments, it remains an incontrovertible fact that capitalist Austria had above all the efforts of the new Soviet leadership to thank for its independence. At the same time, Moscow blatantly sacrificed the interests of its Austrian communist friends who, so it seemed, had at some point reached the conclusion that the Soviet Army would remain in Austria until the victory of world communism. Yet the leaders of the KPÖ ultimately, for better or worse, had to support the idea of a State Treaty with particular enthusiasm, both as patriots of their country and as friends of the Soviet Union, from whom this initiative had come. In this way, during the preparation for the signing of the State Treaty all Soviet propaganda theories of a proletarian internationalism and a struggle for the seizure of power by "progressive (i.e., pro-communist) forces" in Austria had for the time being to take a back seat.[35]

The signing of the Austrian State Treaty, which took place only a month after the Soviet-Austrian negotiations in Moscow,[36] meant an unquestionable victory for Soviet foreign policy, which increased the international prestige of the USSR. It is significant that during the course of the subsequent internal struggle within the Soviet leadership, when the toppled leaders (Nikita Khrushchev among them) were accused of all kinds of real and imaginary sins, not the least criticism was voiced in relation to the signing of the State Treaty or the conditions for guaranteeing Austrian independence.

As a result of its declaration of neutrality and its refusal to house foreign military bases on its territory, Austria was spared an entanglement in the confrontations that took place during the most dramatic phase of the Cold War, particularly in those days when first the Hungarian and then the Czechoslovak tragedy played out on its borders.

The successful conclusion of the State Treaty demonstrated the possibility—even at the highpoint of the Cold War—of solving international disputes by peaceful and civilized means. The State Treaty for Austria became, moreover, a symbol for a gradual overcoming of the era of Stalinist diplomacy. The new Soviet leadership had demonstrated that it was capable of making sensible compromises and engaging in dialogue with diverse political forces.

NOTES

1. Calculations by experts led to the result that the issue of the Austrian State Treaty was discussed at thirty-three Foreign Minister Conferences of the USSR, the United States, Great Britain, and France as well as 260 meetings of the deputies of the foreign ministers of these countries and at eighty-five gatherings of the Vienna

Commission, although countless other bilateral and multilateral negotiations and talks have not been listed here. The paper was first published in German: Michail Prozumenščikov, "Nach Stalins Tod: Sowjetische Österreich-Politik 1953–1955," in Stefan Karner and Barbara Stelzl-Marx, eds., *Die Rote Armee in Österreich: Sowjetische Besatzung 1945–1955. Beiträge* (Graz/Vienna/Munich: Oldenbourg, 2005), pp. 729–753.

2. Russian State Archives for Contemporary History (hereafter RGANI), f. 3, op. 8, d. 26, ll. 67–69.

3. Under Iosif Stalin, the USSR also carried out the repatriation of convicted foreign prisoners of war. Thus, in December 1952, it was resolved at a session of the Presidium of the Central Committee of the CPSU to amnesty and repatriate twenty-seven convicted Austrian prisoners of war. If one takes a closer look at the prisoners who were released from Soviet prisons and camps during this period, a particular fact quickly becomes apparent: only nine of the twenty-seven prisoners had been members of the German Wehrmacht, police or gendarmerie, and they had served above all as junior ranks and were in 1952 already fifty or more years old. The remainder of those amnestied had already served a second prison term, for which they had been convicted in the years 1948 or 1949, i.e., when they were already in Soviet captivity, most of them for theft of foodstuffs and basic commodities from camp stocks.

4. Against the backdrop of its new policies, the USSR approached Austria with the proposal to replace the political representatives in the embassies in Vienna and Moscow. This proposal was followed in mid-1953.

5. If one considers the reactions to this on the part of the international community of states, it must be kept in mind that in the USSR and the Eastern Bloc countries official propaganda proclaimed a contrary outcome of the Berlin Conference of Foreign Ministers. In Soviet printed works, it was claimed that the United States "has used all possible means to avoid a settlement of the issues linked with the State Treaty," and that "the governments of the USA, Great Britain, France and, in part, Austria" were to blame for the failure of negotiations on the Austrian question. *Izvestiya*, February 19, 1954; I. G. Zhiryakov, *SSSR i Avstriya v 1945–1975 gody* (Moscow: Molodaya gvardiya, 1982), p. 18.

6. Ministerstvo inostrannykh del SSSR, ed., *SSSR – Avstriya*, p. 52.

7. Even before and also during the Berlin Conference of Foreign Ministers, the leading lights of the ÖVP constantly emphasized that "both the Federal Government and the Austrian people are determined to pursue a purely Austrian but neither Russophile nor pro-American policy" and that "the Austrians will never be either American or Russian lackeys." RGANI, f. 5, op. 28, d. 223, l. 90.

8. *Wiener Zeitung*, June 19, 1954.

9. RGANI, f. 2, op. 1, d. 159, l. 86. Reprinted in Stefan Karner, Barbara Stelzl-Marx and Alexander Tschubarjan, eds., *Die Rote Armee in Österreich: Sowjetische Besatzung 1945–1955. Dokumente. Krasnaya Armiya v Avstrii. Sovetskaya okkupatsiya 1945–1955. Dokumenty* (Graz/Vienna/Munich: Oldenbourg, 2005), Doc. 184, "From the Transcript of the Speech by A. I. Mikoyan at the July Plenary Session of the Central Committee of the CPSU in 1955 on the Differences of Opinion within the Presidium of the Central Committee on the Question of Withdrawing Soviet Troops

from Austria and on the Resistance of the Soviet Foreign Minister, V. M. Molotov, following the Signing of the Austrian State Treaty," July 11, 1955.

10. RGANI, f. 2, op. 1, d. 159, l. 84.

11. *SSSR v bor'be za nezavisimost' Avstrii* (Moscow: Politizdat, 1965), p. 146.

12. Julius Braunthal, *The Tragedy of Austria* (London: Victor Gollancz, 1948), p. 154.

13. In some regions of Lower Austria, strict administrative measures were introduced in accordance with a directive of the Interior Ministry against Austrians who had bought goods in USIA shops: the security organs confiscated the goods bought in the USIA shops and imposed a fine on the purchasers. RGANI, f. 5, op. 28, d. 222, l. 84.

14. Ivan Kabanov, Valerian Zorin, Mikhail Gribanov, Petr Nikitin, S. Zholnin, and the Secretary of the Council of Ministers, A. Korobov, were also involved in the composition of the draft ordinance of the Central Committee as well as related materials.

15. In contrast to the original variations, which were concerned merely with negotiations with the Austrian government over the sale of USIA firms, proposals appeared in the new draft under point 2 addressing the measures with which the work of the firms could be improved—though with the restriction that only those measures be addressed that could still be realized in 1954.

16. It is interesting that Khrushchev, following the Plenary Assembly of the Central Committee, whose resolutions were kept secret from the Soviet people and the rest of the world for another few days, declared without the slightest embarrassment at a meeting with the American publisher William Randolph Hearst Jr. that the rumors circulating in the West regarding an intensification of the power struggle within the Soviet leadership as well as regarding differences of opinion between him and Georgii Malenkov were nothing more than fairy tales or attempts to pass wishful thinking off as reality.

17. RGANI, f. 3, op. 10, d. 123, ll. 1–2.

18. The majority of Western countries rejected the new Soviet proposals for Germany above all because they de facto recognized the existence in the long term of two German states. Nevertheless, stormy debates broke out in the FRG between the ruling block of CDU and CSU on the one hand and representatives of the SPD on the other, who held the view that "the reaction of the Western powers and the German Federal Chancellor to recent proposals from Moscow [is] irresponsible." Konrad Adenauer, *Vospominaniya (1953–1955)* (Moscow: Molodaya gvardiya, 1968), p. 140.

19. See for example V. N. Beletskii, *Sovetskii Soyuz i Avstriya: Bor'ba Sovetskogo Soyuza za vozrozhdenie nezavisimoi demokraticheskoi Avstrii i ustanovlenie s nei druzhestvennykh otnoshenii (1938–1960gg.)* (Moscow: Izd. IMO, 1962), p. 219.

20. *Izvestiya*, February 9, 1955.

21. RGANI, f. 3, op. 8, d. 388, ll. 26–27.

22. In detail, Molotov recalled that in spring 1953 "Beriia's surrender-like proposal to create a unified, bourgeois Germany as an allegedly 'neutral' state was rejected by the overwhelming majority of the members of the Presidium of the Central Committee, upon which Beriia and Malenkov descended with threats on individual Presidium members after the session." RGANI, f. 3, op. 8, d. 195, l. 32.

23. Stalin's conception of foreign policy from the end of the 1940s to the beginning of the 1950s was based on the principle that every concession to capitalism would demonstrate to the whole world the weakness of the USSR and its allies and thus provoke the West to unleash a Third World War. Such a policy "on the verge of confrontation" permitted a maintenance of ones own people in a state of constant readiness for war and at the same time to ascribe errors and misapprehensions to the "intrigues of the imperialists" and the necessity of having to prepare for a new war. The same tactic was later successfully used by Mao Zedong, the leader of the Chinese Communist Party.

24. Although Georgii Malenkov was strongly criticized and removed from his post as Soviet head of government, he was subsequently appointed Minister for Power Stations and remained furthermore a member of the Presidium of the Central Committee.

25. RGANI, f. 2, op. 1, d. 159, l. 87.

26. Ibid., ll. 87–88.

27. *Neues Österreich*, February 11, 1955.

28. RGANI, f. 5, op. 28, d. 231, l. 136.

29. Neutrality was for a long time one of the most doggedly fought questions in negotiations on the future of Austria. In response to Soviet demands that Austria remain just as neutral as Switzerland had done, the American minister John Foster Dulles responded that Switzerland had decided of its own free will in favor of a policy of neutrality, whereas an attempt was now being made to impose this on Austria by force. In the months March and April 1955, the Western press was full of articles on the duplicity of an Austrian policy of neutrality, from intimidation of the Austrians (*New York Herald Tribune*, April 18, 1955) to persistent advice and recommendations to Austria (e.g., calls for Chancellor Raab to openly state that the Western powers were against Austrian neutrality and that he would himself stand up against the idea).

30. It is worth mentioning that only a few months earlier the deputies of the government parties stated during a session of the Austrian Parliament in November and December 1954 that Austria would be prepared to sign the State Treaty "on the condition of a simultaneous withdrawal of all occupation troops but with an extension of the time limit for withdrawal to two years." RGANI, f. 5, op. 28, d. 331, l. 72.

31. From 1950 to 1951, Western countries carried out maneuvres in which they imitated hostilities in Europe against Soviet armies (in accordance with the so-called Béthouart plan). This plan envisaged establishing a "fortified Alpine front" in the mountains of Salzburg and Tyrol and that Yugoslavia, which was at this time hostile toward the USSR, be persuaded to support the British in the defense of the right flank of the Western armies in Austria. *Vooruzhenie Avstrii. Dokumenty i fakty* (Moscow: Izd. IL, 1952), pp. 33–34.

32. *Washington Post*, May 19, 1955; *Newsweek*, May 16, 1955.

33. See the contribution by Walter Iber in this volume.

34. Just how the Austrians experienced this situation can be seen from a speech by Chancellor Julius Raab, which he held in Vienna after his return from Moscow: "We could hardly believe," he said, "that everything that we had barely dared to hope for had become reality." Quoted in: Beletskii, *Sovetskii Soyuz i Avstriya*, p. 227.

35. In the estimate of Soviet diplomats, many Austrian communists were of the opinion that the Soviet Union, in signing the State Treaty, had "left them to their fate." In spite of efforts by the KPÖ leadership, in autumn 1955 a wave of departures from the Party took place. The regional organization of the KPÖ in Lower Austria alone lost within a few months around ten percent of all its members. A similar tendency was also witnessed in the other organizations of the Party. RGANI, f. 5, op. 28, d. 330, l. 288.

36. Faced with a fait accompli, the United States, Great Britain, and France, even if they had declared to the USSR that before a definitive solution to the Austrian problem "a considerable amount of preparatory work" had still to be taken care of, nevertheless had to concede that this work concerned merely technical matters that could be negotiated in the framework of the Ambassadors' Conference of the four occupation powers with the participation of Austrian representatives.

Part III

ASPECTS OF OCCUPATION

Chapter Six

Occupation and Exploitation
Soviet Economic Policy toward Austria from 1945 to 1955/63

Walter M. Iber

The Soviet Union ultimately emerged from the Second World War, its "Great Patriotic War," as a great victor, enormously strengthened both domestically and internationally. This was, however, at a high price, as the war had cost millions of Soviet lives and the country had suffered considerable material damage. Soviet production in 1945 had admittedly at least recovered in certain branches in comparison to 1940, and reconstruction took place unexpectedly quickly,[1] but production losses in the meantime had been, in part, enormous. The invasion by Hitler's Germany in 1941 had thrown the country in the short term into an economic state of shock.

Table 6.1. Soviet Industrial Production 1941–1945 (in percent compared with 1940)

Industrial Branch	1941	1942	1943	1944	1945
Iron and Metallurgy Industry (including ore extraction)	105	62	70	88	89
Coal	94	43	54	71	88
Petroleum	102	61	63	72	68
Production of Electricity and Thermal Energy	97	62	67	81	91
Chemicals	115	79	104	133	92
Engineering and Metal Processing	112	119	142	158	129
Timber and Wood Processing Industry	88	48	51	55	55
Building Materials	79	26	29	35	41

Source: Segbers, *Die Sowjetunion im Zweiten Weltkrieg* (as in note 1), p. 275.

The Kremlin attempted after the war to compensate for these economic losses as best it could by means of economic exploitation of the occupied territories of Central and Eastern Europe on the part of the Red Army. Initially, it did this in the form of dismantling and ultimately, as a second step, through on the spot cultivation of confiscated businesses which operated largely exterritorially and were not at all or only partially subject to the tax jurisdiction of the respective state. The Soviet Union organized this occupation economy according to two different models.

First, Moscow, together with the government of the occupied state, established bilateral companies, which were, however, controlled de facto by the Kremlin. In this way, the Soviets could place the property confiscated by them (so-called "German property") into joint ventures, while the assignment of corresponding capital investments was intended for the "partner" states. Such bilateral companies were established, for example, in Hungary, Romania (SovRoms), Bulgaria[2] and—from 1954—also in the GDR (Soviet-German Stock Company "Wismut," SDAG).[3]

Secondly, from the mass of the confiscated "German property" Moscow established firms which were regarded as the exclusive property of the Soviet Union. Such concerns were set up in the Soviet Occupation Zone/GDR (the Soviet Stock Company, SAG,[4] which existed until 1953), in Austria (the most important being the Soviet Mineral Oil Administration, or SMV, and the Administration of Soviet Assets in Austria, or USIA), but also from the "German property" in Finland, which was not occupied by the Soviets (Administration of Soviet Assets, or USIF).[5]

Despite the similar structures, the occupation economy in the Soviet-occupied parts of Austria had a completely different political background to that in, for example, East Germany. Soviet economic policy in the later "People's Democracies" of Eastern Europe, which ostensibly served the "radical economic exploitation for the consolidation of Soviet reconstruction,"[6] constituted only one of many Sovietization components in the Kremlin's Eastern Europe strategy, which encompassed in its entirety political, social, cultural and ideological areas alongside the economy.[7] An ambivalent but in no way inconsistent strategy, which is known in the literature as the "revolutionary-imperial paradigm,"[8] formed the basis for the Sovietization of Eastern Europe pushed by Moscow after 1945: with the creation of a "security belt" through the establishment of satellite states in Eastern Europe, the Kremlin pursued security-political interests, but moreover never lost sight of its imperialist aims and the decisive "propagation of world revolution." Stalin's pragmatism went so far, however, that he never unconditionally strived for imperialism and the export of revolution but always made them dependent on the prevailing situation.[9] The "special case" of Austria clearly demonstrated this.

Soviet occupation policy in eastern Austria between 1945 and 1955 thus remained for the most part, in contrast to the Eastern European states, limited indeed to economic exploitation for reparations purposes. The establishment in Austria of a bilateral petroleum company (Sanafta), which the Soviets had strived for in the wake of the Potsdam Agreement, fitted very much in with this, for the Sanafta project could not be accompanied by continued attempts at Sovietization. From the Soviet point of view, it was an endeavor to bring about an extension of the profitability duration (and with it a maximization of reparations) by means of Austrian capital investments.[10] For all the political and ideological "side noises" which, at least until the elections of November 1945, hung in the air,[11] the "Sanafta" project was ostensibly an economic matter. This was not the case, however, for the British, the Americans, and the French, and—necessarily—for the Austrian Provisional State Government, which recognized a Sovietization concept behind Sanafta.[12] The project ultimately failed due to the veto of the Western powers, upon which the Kremlin decided to establish with the SMV its own, purely Soviet economic body and to exploit Austrian petroleum deposits alone.

Alongside the leitmotiv of economic exploitation, "positive" Soviet measures toward Austria, like Stalin's food donation ("pea donation") of May 1, 1945, or the donation for the reconstruction of the State Opera House made during the election campaign of 1945, received little attention. This was, among other reasons, because even this supposed reverse side of Soviet economic policy could not be separated from the economic bleeding of Austria (the "pea donation" came from looted supplies from the city of Vienna)[13] or because it had an obvious propagandistic veneer, as in the case of the State Opera House.[14]

The process of economic exploitation in Austria can of course only be viewed in the context of Soviet military-strategic premises with regard to Central and Eastern Europe and the overriding attempt to create an Eastern European *cordon sanitaire*. However, Austria was generally affected to a major extent by the Kremlin's economic considerations. At least the industrial plants in the "Ostmark" (from 1943 the Alps and Danube *Reichsgaue*) had played a significant role in armaments production in the "Third Reich," above all in the primary industries, engineering, steel and aircraft construction and the electrical and textile industries.[15] During the course of the Second World War, at the latest from 1943, Moscow was already very well informed about Austria's economic potential, its importance for the war economy in the "Third Reich," its natural resources, and the industrial focus in the east of the country. This knowledge was put to use when the "Armistice Commission," set up in 1943 in the People's Commissariat for the Foreign Affairs of the USSR ("Voroshilov Commission"), began to plan possible partition variations for the occupation zones in Austria. One of the proposals envisaged Burgenland and half of both Lower Austria and Styria as the Soviet zone.

According to the final report of the Commission to Stalin from June 12, 1944, this arrangement would have meant that a large proportion of the industrial plants were located in the Soviet zone.[16] The definitive partition into zones in July 1945 admittedly ultimately looked different—it established the Mühlviertel in Upper Austria, Lower Austria, Burgenland, and parts of Vienna as the Soviet sphere of influence—but one cannot dismiss that the Voroshilov Commission exerted a certain influence on the economic-geographic focus of the Soviet occupying power. The Soviets also became active in Styria, even though it did not ultimately constitute part of the Soviet zone: until the end of July 1945, Red Army troops remained stationed in Styria, where they controlled the important industrial centers and undertook dismantling operations in the large former armaments concerns until their withdrawal.[17]

During the final weeks of the Second World War, when the Red Army was already on Austrian soil, the Soviets obtained via its military intelligence services additional information that was often extremely detailed on individual industrial branches that they considered particularly relevant.[18] The fact that above all the Austrian petroleum deposits had quickly become the object of Soviet desire was anything but a coincidence. On the basis of the rapid expansion in the framework of the Nazi war economy, Austria was namely in 1945 Europe's biggest petroleum producer after Romania. In the meantime, the petroleum sector in the USSR had suffered particularly heavy losses on account of the war, while on the other side Anglo-American oil concerns often turned out to be the real victors in the war. The financial circumstances above all of American firms such as Standard Oil New York had developed especially favorably from 1938 to 1945. In the Middle East, the British and Americans controlled the richest petroleum deposits in the world. The United States, which had become the foremost petroleum power, already owned a percentage of 40 percent in these oil territories in 1946. The British were even more strongly anchored in the Middle Eastern extraction countries, not least because of their predominant position in Iran, where the oil industry was dominated by the Anglo-Iranian Oil Company.[19] With the capacities of their own oil fields, the Soviets were unable to keep pace with the economic expansion of the Western oil companies. As early as 1944, Stalin had personally envisaged the scenario of an armed conflict with his then allies the United States and Great Britain and had made reference to this significant weakness and, in doing so, provided the impetus for initial considerations and attempts to tap and exploit "black gold" outside the Soviet Union as well.[20] First Soviet attempts of this nature took place in northern Iran;[21] Austria was soon to follow.

At the end of the war in 1945 and in the first weeks and months of the post-war period, Soviet economic ambitions in Austria were initially not yet guided by the idea of an onsite cultivation of resources. It was more the case that these ambitions found their expression in comprehensive dismantling operations, which affected basically all industrial sectors, though to varying degrees.

SOVIET DISMANTLING OPERATIONS

Soviet dismantling operations began in April 1945, i.e., in the weeks before the end of the Second World War in Europe. In the industrial plants, machines and production installations were dismantled, while production goods were confiscated. The Soviets transported their war loot by train to the east, where it was to be redeployed in Soviet industry. The Soviet commandos tasked with the looting dismantled in Austria a total of 220 plants (more than 31,000 freight cars). This admittedly corresponded to a fraction of that which had been dismantled, for instance, in the Soviet Occupation Zone or in Poland, but it was at least considerably more than the extent of Soviet dismantling in Hungary and Czechoslovakia.

Table 6.2. Extent of Soviet Dismantling Operations in Europe as of May 1, 1947

	Intended for Dismantling		Actually Dismantled	
	Number of Concerns	Freight Cars in Thousands	Number of Concerns	Freight Cars in Thousands
Total	4,537	841.6	4,458	809.5
Germany (Soviet Occupation Zone)	3,024	550,8	2,955	518,5
Poland (in today's borders)	1,119	211.5	1,119	211.5
Austria	220	31.2	220	31.2
Hungary	16	2.8	16	2.8
Czechoslovakia	36	6.5	36	6.5

Source: Russian State Archives for Economics (hereafter RGAE), F. 1562, op. 329, d. 2580, pp. 1–2.

Despite numerous deficits—the problems ranged from faulty dismantling and careless treatment of the equipment to serious logistical errors[22]—the value of the dismantled goods and equipment for the reconstruction of the Soviet Union cannot be underestimated.[23] For the affected countries, the economic losses were of course considerable, including for Austria, where the value of Soviet dismantling was established in 1947 in an internal itemization at 51.6 million dollars.[24] At an exchange rate of one to twenty-six, this was equivalent to a sum of 1.3 billion schillings, i.e., 8.5 billion schillings (300 million dollars) at 1955 prices.[25]

At the Potsdam Conference of July/August 1945, where the victorious Allies Great Britain, the United States, and the Soviet Union set the political course for the future of Germany and handled the question of reparations as a major issue, a continuation of Soviet dismantling operations initially remained very much on the cards as a declared form of Austrian reparations payments. A corresponding proposal was made on July 30, 1945, by the Soviet delegation; within a year further installations from Austrian industrial plants were to be dismantled and removed.[26] The Soviet Foreign Minister, Vyacheslav Molotov, had previously already referred explicitly to Austrian co-responsibility for the war and the devastation in the Soviet Union. He demanded, therefore, reparations from Austria to the tune of 250 million dollars, starting on July 1, 1945, to be paid in instalments (in the form of goods deliveries) within six years and to be divided among the Soviet Union, Great Britain, the United States, and Yugoslavia. Ultimately, however, the Soviet Union distanced itself from all these reparations variations and declared—expressly in consultation with the United States and Great Britain—that it did not want any reparations from Austria. This admittedly required a discontinuation of the dismantling operations in Austria, but the Soviets obtained guarantees from the Western powers for other reparations payments which were in the long term more severe for Austria: access to "German property."[27]

NO AUSTRIAN REPARATIONS? THE POTSDAM FALLACY

In accordance with the outcome of the Potsdam Conference, the Potsdam Agreement of August 2, 1945, (Reich) "German property" in Central and Eastern Europe was to be drawn on for reparations payments, whereas the Allies reciprocally renounced their claims on "German assets" in the, respectively, other occupation zones. This put Moscow in the position of being able to dispose at will of German assets in East Germany as well as German foreign assets in eastern Austria, Bulgaria, Finland, and Romania.[28]

This Potsdam reparations settlement, however, had one decisive catch. It was namely not clear what exactly was meant by the term "German property." This was soon demonstrated in the case of the oil firms in Austria, specifically with regard to the validity of the "Bitumen Law," issued by the National Socialists in 1938 and entirely under the banner of the state-controlled war economy, according to which every petroleum plant that wished to continue operating in the *Ostmark* had to find oil on its free prospecting within twenty-three months. If no oil was found, the rights to free prospecting would lapse.[29] The law thus left those oil firms that possessed prospecting rights in Austria with two possibilities: either to increase the development activities or to sell the prospecting rights, i.e., it was up to the state to decide with which intensity the crude oil deposits should be exploited. Precisely herein lay the fundamental problem when it came to the matter of "German property": should those firms that had been transferred to German ownership after 1938—in the case of the Austrian oil sector, precisely on the basis of the "Bitumen Law"—be regarded as "German property" in 1945? This essential question remained unanswered in Potsdam. It remains to this day a matter of debate in the literature, whether this was a case of Anglo-American calculation (partition of spheres of interests, destruction of Germany's ability to wage war) or simply a negotiating error on the part of the Western powers.[30] Interesting in this respect is the barely heeded fact that months later the British and the Americans, together with the Soviets, issued in Law No. 5 (Acquisition and Registration of German Property Abroad) of the Allied Control Council in Germany a definition of this term that was, in comparison to Potsdam, admittedly more precise but still extremely flexible and which thus played further into Moscow's hands. Law No. 5 was signed on October 30, 1945,[31] i.e., at a time when Western intelligence services and occupation authorities in Vienna, on the basis of their level of information regarding the Sanafta negotiations and Soviet confiscations, must have been warned long before of the consequences of a too imprecise definition of "German property."[32]

Yet regardless of whether the policy of the Western powers was shaped by tactical calculation or incompetence (or even by a mixture of the two)—from the Austrian point of view one has to talk of a momentous lapse. The Soviets continued to skilfully exploit the legal grey area that resulted from the lack of clarity surrounding the term "German property." For them, all property was "German" that had been in German hands at the end of the war and had not been acquired without payment by its German owners.[33] Even cases of "Aryanization" where the dispossessed had in most cases received a small amount of "compensation," were largely ignored during the subsequent confiscations.[34] However, the Soviets remained with their interpretation of the term "German property" in most cases in the framework of the agreements made in Potsdam,[35] and in the looming differences of opinion with the Western powers they even had in this way—even by appealing to the aforementioned Law No. 5—a very coherent argument down to pat.[36] Soviet-occupied eastern Austria was thus particularly affected by the Potsdam reparations settlement as there were, according to the Soviet definition, more German foreign assets here at the end of the war than in any other country in the world. The Soviets calculated the value of "German assets"—Moscow only assumed the assets, though not the liabilities[37]—in eastern Austria in 1947 to be just under 130 million dollars.

Table 6.3. "German Foreign Property" in the Sphere of Influence of the USSR in Eastern-Central Europe (and Finland): Soviet Definition and Calculation, 1947

Country	Value (in millions of dollars)
Eastern Austria	129.6
Romania	43.0
Bulgaria	16.0
Hungary	89.5
Finland	46.8

Source: RGAE, F. 1562, op. 329, d. 4597, p. 13.

The confiscations undertaken from October 1945 in eastern Austria by the Soviet occupying power under reference to the Potsdam Agreement constituted "according to strict criteria of international law" not Austrian but German reparations payments. Yet even when one assumes that the Soviet Union, in view of the involvement of the Austrians in the Nazi system and their co-responsibility for the war, would have been entitled to a certain moral right to such removals, the aforementioned declaration at Potsdam, not to demand any reparations from Austria, was flimsy. By 1945, the Austrian economy had for a long time been inseparably linked to the "German property," although such a sudden increase in German shares—and with, in part, questionable methods—could only have come about as a result of the Anschluss in 1938. "The German Reich brought large enterprises, which were decisive for the Austrian economy, into its possession," as Federal President Karl Renner stated in 1946, "by increasing the share capital by Reich investments or investments from German financial institutions and thus acquired the majority." Furthermore, many German enterprises in Austria were established with money from the Austrian National Bank.[38]

German capital had not in fact played a dominant role in the Austrian economy prior to 1938. The German penetration of the Austrian economy ultimately led to the large Austrian banks, namely the Creditanstalt (CA) and the Länderbank, and a substantial proportion of industry being in German hands at the end of the war in 1945. If the German share of the equity capital had been 9 percent in 1937, it catapulted by 1945 to 57 percent.[39] Thus, one must de facto speak of the economic exploitation of Austria and hidden reparations (or payments equivalent to reparations),[40] as the confiscations of "German property" by the Soviet Union inevitably constituted a heavy blow to the Austrian economy.

The British, French, and Americans also confiscated "German property" in their respective zones, namely essentially that property which, in accordance with the Western understanding of the term, had already been in German hands prior to the Anschluss in 1938 or had fallen into German hands between 1938 and 1945 without the use of coercion. It was just these Western notions as to how the formula "use of coercion" should be understood, however, that diverged considerably from the narrow definition of the Soviets (on the basis of this definition, the Western occupying powers regarded the "Bitumen Law," for example, as null and void).[41] At any rate, the United States returned the confiscated assets to the Republic of Austria in July 1946 in the form of a trustee relationship, and in spring 1949 the Western powers declared their intention to relinquish to Austria "German property" located in their zones following the conclusion of a State Treaty.[42] The Soviet occupying power, meanwhile, placed the mass of assets confiscated in eastern Austria under the administration of the economic bodies SMV (the forerunner of the Austrian Mineral Oil Administration, ÖMV; since 1995 OMV) and USIA, both of which were run according to a planned economy and had been specifically established for this purpose.

OCCUPATION ECONOMY: SMV AND USIA

As a result, around 50 percent of the industrial plants in the Soviet Zone were under the administration of the occupying power. SMV and USIA together engaged, meanwhile, almost 60,000 employees; although the upper echelons and senior administrative posts were staffed with Soviets, in the lower (and, partially, the middle) echelons Austrian laborers, who belonged for the most part to the KPÖ, were engaged throughout.[43] Soviet businesses were subordinated in the first instance to the GUSIMZ (*Gosudarstvennoe upravlenie sovetskim imushchestvom za granitsei*, or State Main Administration for Soviet Foreign Assets) in Moscow. A central office with sole or main responsibility did not yet exist. In fact, there was a plethora of Moscow ministries and departments which intervened, to varying degrees of intensity, alongside the GUSIMZ in matters relating to Soviet businesses in eastern Austria.[44] The Soviet businesses had to deliver the profits they generated to the Soviet Military Bank (SMB) in Vienna, a branch of the Soviet State Bank established in 1946. From the credit, the Bank then supplied the businesses with the required equipment. If no credit was available, the SMB issued loans, an approach which resulted in not a few USIA firms running up considerable debts.[45]

If one looks at the entire period of their existence, the aims of SMV and USIA—as well as those of a series of further, smaller Soviet creations, which were economically and, in part, also administratively closely linked to SMV or USIA (e.g., the Soviet DDFG,[46] founded on February 2, 1946)—were evidently not located within a rational economic strategy. In fact, the aim was to report high production successes as quickly as possible to Moscow.[47] By 1955, the firms were run down and as a result of the State Treaty were transferred to Austria in return for one-off payments.

The SMV was established in September 1945,[48] and from October 2, 1945, it assumed possession of "German" oil firms under reference to the Potsdam resolutions.[49] The Soviet business controlled almost the entire Austrian petroleum industry; mineral oil and natural gas fields, refineries, tank farms, and petrol stations belonged to its assets. The SMV leased its approximately 300 petrol stations and several large tank farms to the Commerce PLC for Mineral Oil Products of Austrian and Russian Origin (OROP), which had been established with Soviet capital in September 1946 but traded as a business under Austrian law and which had a monopoly in the marketing of mineral oil in the Soviet Occupation Zone.[50] The SMV was by no means content with the exploitation of oil fields already opened up during the Nazi period around Zistersdorf; in fact, it began very early to carry out exploratory drillings in other regions.[51] In March 1949, it opened up in Lower Austrian Matzen the largest continuous deposits known in Central Europe until 1955, which were particularly prized by the Soviets due to the qualitatively high-value oil. As early as January 1950, it succeeded in opening up a further, notably productive oil field in the Aderklaa region, which was completely exploited during the following years. In addition, the oil region near Süßenbrunn was discovered in 1951.[52] In the barely ten years of its existence, the SMV extracted on its oil fields around 17.8 million tons of mineral oil as reparations payments. Of this, approximately 55 percent was removed from the country, while the so-called "domestic quota," i.e. that proportion sold to Austria, remained for a long time strictly limited.[53] According to Soviet records, the SMV generated in barely ten years a total profit of 3.8 billion schillings, equivalent to around 146 million dollars (1955 prices).[54]

Only a few weeks after the SMV began operating, the Commander-in-Chief of the Soviet Armed Forces in Austria, Marshal Ivan Konev, suggested to Foreign Minister Molotov the further identification and seizure of "German property in eastern Austria" and the conversion of the administration responsible for "war loot" residing directly with the High Command of the Soviet Troops in Baden (Central Group of Forces, or TsGV) into an "Administration for Matters of German Property in Austria."[55] On the basis of a resolution by the Council of Ministers, Konev's proposal was ultimately implemented in accordance with the Soviet Order No. 17 of June 27, 1946. The order regulated the transfer of all "German assets located in eastern Austria" to the ownership of the USSR.[56] The administration and management of this property was incumbent on the USIA.

When the USIA officially began operating on July 16, 1946,[57] a total of 436 concerns (of which 231 were industrial plants, 163 agriculture and forestry concerns, and 31 other firms) and 3,109 pieces of real estate were under its administration. The majority of the firms were small and medium-sized firms with outdated technical equipment (merely 84 of the 231 industrial plants engaged more than 100 workers),[58] which also explains why the USIA share of the entire industrial production of Austria, at around 5 to 8 percent, was fairly small.[59] With its few large concerns, however, the USIA played at least in its own sectors an influential, in part even market-dominating role, e.g., with the engineering firm Voith, the AEG-Union, Austro-Fiat, the Siemens-Schuckert Works, or the Wiener Brückenbau AG (Vienna Bridge-Building PLC).[60]

Alongside a central administration, the USIA had a share in several corporations for the administration of individual economic sectors, e.g., there were, similar to the East German SAG, trusts like "Avtovelo" (motor industry), "Marten" (steel industry), "Tekstil" (textile industry), and "Vkus" (luxury food industry). In addition, the Soviets also erected a chain of USIA shops in which Eastern goods were undersold by evading Austrian taxes and customs duties. The number of concerns varied considerably in subsequent years, as (sometimes temporary) closures and amalgamations often occurred. In the operational lists from 1955, at least, only 264 USIA concerns appear, including DDSG.[61] During its existence, the USIA recorded a total profit of around 7.5 billion schillings, equivalent to around 288 million dollars (1955 prices).[62]

The diplomats of the Western occupying powers in Vienna evidently only gradually became aware after 1946 of how useful the Soviet economic enclaves in eastern Austria actually were to the Kremlin—and in fact not just economically but, above all, strategically. Of primary importance were the oil wells concentrated in Lower Austria, which were located exactly at the intersection between East and West. Eventually, the British, American, and French intelligence agencies, which—against the backdrop of the Cold War—not infrequently recruited Austrian workers and employees in Soviet concerns as "economic spies," also registered this. The items of information obtained in this way were important pieces of the jigsaw puzzle that the Western powers tried to put together on the economic potential of the USSR.[63] The American envoy in Austria, John G. Erhardt, was supplied in August 1947 with information from intelligence sources on the Soviet occupation economy. He concluded: "The evidence of high-level and detailed planning for the inclusion of eastern Austria in the Soviet-controlled Eastern European economic bloc is overwhelming."[64] Indeed, it was above all the "black gold" from Austria—particularly from the end of the 1940s on, when there existed in the bipolar world not only a political but also an economic split due to the Marshall Plan and the Council for Mutual Economic Assistance (Comecon)—that benefited the economic sphere of the Soviet Union and its satellites. The SMV supplied the large refineries in Hungary and the Czech Socialist Republic[65] as well as hydrogenation plants in East Germany with crude oil. In the 1950s, a large proportion of the total lubricant requirements of the GDR were covered by mineral oil from Austria[66] and in 1953, according to CIA data, around 90 percent of the crude oil traded between the Communist countries of Eastern Europe came from SMV production in eastern Austria.[67] The USIA, which until 1950 had still sold more than 50 percent of its goods on the Austrian domestic market, also considerably intensified its trade with the Eastern European People's Democracies.[68]

To a comparatively large extent, the changed political framework following the beginning of the Stalinization of Eastern Europe was reflected in the deliveries from Austria during the first half of the 1950s. In Western-orientated Austria, the Kremlin did not foster any serious Sovietization plans and the Soviet concerns on the domestic market that were run according to a planned economy in any case gradually approached the end of their competitive capacity in view of the advance of market economic structures, which was forced by the United States because of Austrian participation in the Marshall Plan.[69] At this point in time, Austria could, therefore, be far more blatantly exploited than the "friendly" states of the Soviet Union's own bloc. The estimates of Jörg Fisch, according to which Austrian reparations-analogous payments after the Second World War were ultimately higher per head than, for example, Romanian or Bulgarian reparations,[70] fit seamlessly into this picture.

In the run-up to the final State Treaty negotiations with the delegation of the Austrian government in April 1955 (Moscow Memorandum), the Foreign Trade Ministry in Moscow calculated that a continued exploitation of the Austrian oil fields would no longer have been profitable for the USSR.[71] The Soviets now had the opportunity to "get rid of" the run down concerns and to once again make a considerable profit by means of inflated payment deliveries: only at the negotiating table with the Austrians did the Soviets spontaneously increase the one-off payment for the SMV[72]—ten million tons of crude oil (ultimately it was only six million tons)[73]—although Soviet delegation originally was sent into the negotiations with much lower instructions regarding payments, namely 4.1 million tons of crude oil.[74] The one-off payment for the USIA (150 million dollars) was not even discussed at the Moscow negotiations in 1955, although this sum had already been fixed in 1949 at a time when the USIA had not yet approached the highpoint of its productivity. By 1955, however, the concerns were drained and only worth around eighty million dollars.[75] In order to finally achieve the withdrawal of the Soviets, however, the Austrian government had accepted this price (and would, indeed, have paid even more).

HIDDEN REPARATIONS: TOTAL AUSTRIAN PAYMENTS TO THE SOVIET UNION, 1945–1955/63

If one takes stock of the total extent of the economic burden brought about by the Soviet occupying power, one comes to the following schilling sums in 1955 prices: 8.5 billion schillings as damages sum for dismantling operations; the largest sum of 11.3 billion was formed by the reparations from the ongoing production of Soviet concerns, i.e., the profits generated by USIA and SMV (although around 40 percent as unpaid taxes, which were entered into the books without further ado as "profits"); 7.3 billion in one-off payments[76] for Soviet concerns as the cost of the State Treaty, which were paid partially in cash but for the most part in the form of deliveries of goods and crude oil up to the end of 1963.[77] Thus, one comes to a figure of 27.1 billion schillings for the actual "reparations." In order, however, to measure the real transfer to the Soviet Union in its entirety, Austria's financial expenditure for the stationing of Soviet occupation troops must be included in the itemization. These occupation costs came to 9.7 billion schillings. This gives us a total figure of 36.8 billion schillings (ca. 2 percent of the accumulated GDP 1946–1955),[78] equivalent to 1.4 billion dollars. This figure, calculated predominantly on the basis of information in Soviet files, thus levels out relatively exactly between the "reparations" estimates of Günter Bischof and Hans Seidel.[79] The amount would have corresponded in 2008 (with schilling consumer prices in the period 1955–2008 multiplied by six)[80] to a figure of approximately sixteen billion euros.

Table 6.4. Austrian Real Transfer to the Soviet Union, 1945–1963

	Billion Schillings at 1955 Prices	Billion Dollars at 1955 Prices	Billion Euros at 2008 Prices
Dismantling Operations	8.5	0.3	3.7
USIA and SMV Profits	11.3	0.4	4.9
One-off Payments for State Treaty	7.3	0.3	3.2
Subtotal Reparations	**27.1**	**1.1**	**11.8**
Occupation Costs	9.7	0.4	4.2
Sum Total	**36.8**	**1.4**	**16.0**

Sources: Author's estimates; Bischof, *Austria in the First Cold War* (as in note 29), S. 87; Seidel, *Österreichs Wirtschaft* (as in note 14), pp. 465–476.

In terms of a positive real transfer, i.e., foreign aid, this figure was set against around 1.6 billion dollars, of which almost one billion came from the Marshall Plan.[81] Austrian "reparations" to the Soviet Union were, thus, effectively paid by the West or, put differently, the Americans and the British made things up to Austria for their failure at Potsdam. On the other hand, the United States, Great Britain, and France naturally created an economic burden for the Austrian state as well and indeed to the tune of around 10.5 billion schillings (equivalent to around 400 million dollars, of which over 90 percent was in occupation costs alone).[82] The comparison shows how firmly Soviet occupation policy was ultimately focussed on economic exploitation: of the total Austrian payments to the four occupying powers, a good 75 percent went to Moscow.

It should be mentioned, however, that the hidden reparations to the Soviet Union also contained positive aspects for Austria; of these, the most profound was the fact that it was the Soviet occupation economy that "helped" Austria in the medium term to establish its own mineral oil and natural gas industry. In the inter-war period, Austria had abandoned its—then admittedly little developed mineral oil regions—predominantly Anglo-American oil firms and only after 1938 was this branch of industry for the most part (i.e., approximately two-thirds) "Germanized" as a result of the "Bitumen Law."[83] Many of the old tenures of Western firms were no longer taken into account after 1945, however, due to the Soviet understanding of "German property." The SMV exercised almost complete control over the mineral oil sector during the occupation period, although the Soviets transferred this status in large part to Austria (only a few concerns were restored) with the handover of 1955. The government incorporated the mineral oil complex into the nationalized industry, where the ÖMV—today, as the partially privatized firm OMV, after all one of the leading oil and gas concerns in Central Europe—was formed from it in 1956. Such a development would not have been possible without the SMV, however bitter its presence and dominance may have been for contemporary Austria. If the Western powers had been in a position following the Second World War to accomplish vis-à-vis the Soviets a reestablishment of the land tenures from the inter-war period, big concerns like Shell or Mobil Oil would with certainty have positioned themselves much more strongly in Austria. An Austrian firm would hardly have been able to come into its own alongside multinational oil companies.[84]

AFTER 1955: AUSTRIA AS SOVIET ECONOMIC SATELLITE?

Following their transfer on August 13, 1955, the former Soviet concerns were integrated into the Austrian economy at considerable cost—due to the enormous backwardness of some concerns, this integration was, in part, only possible through rationalization methods (amalgamations);[85] in other sectors, on the other hand, it proceeded very successfully. The Soviet side also attempted to remain as far as possible informed regarding the development of the former SMV and USIA concerns. The USSR and Austria had, after all, reached corresponding agreements in 1955 in the course of the Moscow negotiations: the Austrian government had pledged itself to "make sure that no discriminatory measures are taken against those employed in the former USIA concerns, the concerns of the former Soviet Mineral Oil Administration, the OROP PLC and the DDSG."[86] Furthermore, "agreement" had been reached regarding "a trade treaty for the duration of five years,"[87] which was ultimately signed in October 1955. As Peter Ruggenthaler has demonstrated, this treaty, in conjunction with the release payments agreed in the Moscow Memorandum, gave the Soviet Foreign Ministry reason to hope to succeed in pressurising Austria into a relationship of economic dependency on the USSR following the State Treaty.[88] In misjudging the prevailing circumstances, however, the Soviets acted here "as though the Marshall Plan had been without any consequences for Austria."[89] Moscow soon had to acknowledge that this plan was not feasible. The fact alone that the former USIA and SMV workers left the KPÖ in droves after August 1955[90] for (ultimately unfounded)[91] fear of dismissal on the basis of their Party membership, demonstrates that the ten-year Soviet occupation was in no way capable of bringing about a sustainable strengthening of communism in Austria. The Soviet Union even remained light-years away from achieving the evidently contemplated aim of utilising the aforementioned trade agreement to at least weaken the "economic dependence of Austria on the Western powers."[92]

Due to the Marshall Plan and the—largely—negative experiences of the population with the Soviet occupiers, the Western orientation effectively stood on extremely solid ground by the end of the 1940s at the latest. Under these circumstances, Austrian economic dependency on the Soviet Union, as hoped for by the Kremlin, remained purely an illusion. Aside from the release deliveries until the end of 1963 and the—comparatively insignificant—exchange in the framework of the trade agreement, economic contacts to the Soviet Union were in fact only then relevant when Austria fostered them of its own free will. The USSR benefited here from the fact that the formerly occupied country interpreted its Western orientation after 1955 in no way dogmatically, particularly when it came to economics.[93] Traditionally strong Austrian trade with the Eastern states admittedly dropped off due to participation in the European Recovery Programme (ERP) and as a result of the "Iron Curtain," but economic contacts were de facto never completely broken.[94] Austria ultimately used its new role as a neutral bridgehead between East and

West not only to sharpen its profile abroad but also during the subsequent crises of the Cold War to position itself more strongly as a trading partner vis-à-vis Eastern Europe. It was thus anything other than coincidence that it was Austria which became the first European country outside Comecon to sign a long-term treaty with the Soviet Union for the delivery of natural gas, and that indeed in the middle of the international crisis year of 1968.[95]

* * *

Soviet economic policy toward Austria was determined by the premise of "occupation and exploitation." Its guiding theme was, after the victorious war, to lay claim to "victor's law" and to help itself to the economic resources of the vanquished (as was, in part, indeed done by the Allies and in particular the Soviet Union in the examined case of Austria, although it was officially regarded not as a defeated but as a liberated country). This approach can, of course, in no way be regarded as an exception in the sense of what was "typically Soviet." That which is defined in the context of military conflicts with the keywords "conquer," "occupy," and "exploit" was (and is) rather a rule, a basic principle which we encounter from case to case, from era to era in varying shapes and forms.[96]

In the concrete case of the Kremlin's economic policy in the Soviet-occupied countries of Central-Eastern Europe after 1945, it was a systematic, organized exploitation carried out by a political and military great power. The Soviet Union pursued a relatively clear line according to the motto "compensate and conceal." It was first and foremost a question of compensation for the losses incurred during the preceding war—the Second World War; in other words a contribution to the regaining of economic strength. Secondly, against the backdrop of a bipolar world, the great power USSR permanently visualized the scenario of a new great war, i.e., it was not least a question of demonstrating strength in order to conceal as best possible its weaknesses as compared with potential, in many respects economically superior, wartime enemies—one has in mind here the United States and Great Britain with their rich mineral oil resources.

The Austrian economy was affected by these economic objectives to a relatively large extent. If one considers the reparations-analogous payments made to the Soviet Union, then the blood-letting was even higher than in some Eastern Bloc states. Nevertheless, the "reparations" were, of course, still a comparatively small price to pay so that Austria—in contrast to its Eastern European neighbors—was largely spared Moscow's attempts at Sovietization and could, in 1955, finally regain its freedom.

NOTES

1. Hans Raupach, *Geschichte der Sowjetwirtschaft* (Hamburg: Rowohlt, 1964), pp. 100–101; see also Klaus Segbers, *Die Sowjetunion im Zweiten Weltkrieg: Die Mobilisierung von Verwaltung, Wirtschaft und Gesellschaft im "Großen Vaterländischen Krieg" 1941–1943* (Munich: Oldenbourg, 1987).
2. See at length Nicolas Spulber, "Soviet Undertakings and Soviet Mixed Companies in Eastern Europe," *Journal of Central European Affairs*, Vol. 14 (1954/55), pp. 154–173, here pp. 156–164. On Romania and Hungary see in detail: László von Taubinger, "Die sowjetisch-rumänischen Gesellschaften," *Osteuropa*, Vol. 2 (1956), pp. 145–149; Maria Muresan and Mariana Nicolae, "Die Sowjetisierung Rumäniens und die Folgen für die Wirtschaft des Landes," in Walter M. Iber and Peter Ruggenthaler, eds., *Stalins Wirtschaftspolitik an der sowjetischen Peripherie. Ein Überblick auf der Basis sowjetischer und osteuropäischer Quellen* (Innsbruck et al.: Studien-Verlag, 2011), pp. 127–152; László Borhi, "The Merchants of the Kremlin: The Economic Roots of Soviet Expansion in Hungary," in CWIHP Working Paper No. 28, Cold War International History Project, Washington, DC, 2000; idem., "Sowjetische Hegemonial- und Wirtschaftspolitik der Sowjetunion in Ungarn 1945–1956," in Iber and Ruggenthaler, eds., *Stalins Wirtschaftspolitik an der sowjetischen Peripherie*, pp. 111–126.
3. On the S(D)AG Wismut see the recent Rainer Karlsch, *Uran für Moskau: Die Wismut—Eine populäre Geschichte*, 3rd rev. ed. (Berlin: Ch. Links Verlag, 2008); idem. and Zbynek Zeman, *Urangeheimnisse. Das Erzgebirge im Brennpunkt der Weltpolitik 1933–1960* (Berlin: Ch. Links Verlag, 2007), pp. 141–255.
4. See, for example, Jan Foitzik, *Sowjetische Militäradministration (SMAD) in Deutschland 1945–1949* (Berlin: Akademie Verlag, 1999), pp. 180–186; Gerhard Wettig, "Die sowjetische Wirtschaftspolitik in der SBZ/DR vor dem Hintergrund der System- und Herrschaftsziele," in Iber and Ruggenthaler, eds., *Stalins Wirtschaftspolitik an der sowjetischen Peripherie*, pp. 73–98.
5. See Ruth Büttner, *Sowjetisierung oder Selbständigkeit? Die sowjetische Finnlandpolitik 1943–1948* (Hamburg: Verlag Dr. Kovac, 2001), pp. 306–307.
6. Donal O'Sullivan, "'Wer immer ein Gebiet besetzt . . .' Sowjetische Osteuropapolitik 1943–1947/48," in Stefan Creuzberger and Manfred Görtemaker, eds., *Gleichschaltung unter Stalin? Die Entwicklung der Parteien im östlichen Europa 1944–1949* (Paderborn: Schöningh, 2002), pp. 45–84, here p. 50.
7. See ibid. and Ol'ga Pavlenko, "Österreich im Kraftfeld der sowjetischen Diplomatie 1945," in Stefan Karner and Barbara Stelzl-Marx, eds., *Die Rote Armee in Österreich: Sowjetische Besatzung 1945–1955. Beiträge* (Graz/Vienna/Munich: Oldenbourg, 2005), pp. 566–601, here p. 596.
8. This term was coined in the 1990s by Vladislav Zubok and Constantine Pleshakov. Wladislaw Subok and Constantine Pleschakow, *Der Kreml im Kalten Krieg: Von 1945 bis zur Kubakrise*, trans. by Ulrich Schweitzer [original title: *Inside the Kremlin's Cold War: From Stalin to Khrushchev*] (Hildesheim: Claassen, 1996), pp. 32–33.

9. Peter Ruggenthaler, "Einleitung," in idem., ed., *Stalins großer Bluff: Die Geschichte der Stalin-Note in Dokumenten der sowjetischen Führung* (Munich: Oldenbourg, 2007), pp. 11–22, here p. 12.

10. It was not for nothing that the Soviets repeatedly attempted to win over the Austrian government for Sanafta, for example, precisely during the economically less profitable period of the SMV from 1946 to 1949. Similar impulses can be demonstrated for spring and winter 1946 and for January 1948. See Walter Martin Iber, "Die Sowjetische Mineralölverwaltung in Österreich, 1945–1955: Sowjetische Besatzungswirtschaft und der Kampf ums Öl als Vorgeschichte der OMV," Ph.D. Diss, University of Graz, 2008, pp. 137–139 and 158–159. idem., *Die Sowjetische Mineralölverwaltung in Österreich. Zur Vorgeschichte der OMV 1945–1955* (Innsbruck et al.: StudienVerlag, 2011), pp. 167–170, 192.

11. In contrast to Soviet diplomats on the spot, Stalin had eyed a stronger KPÖ before the election, which was viewed as a "test run" for the Soviet Occupation Zone. The poor election results for the Austrian communists, however, were ultimately of little significance for the Kremlin. See Peter Ruggenthaler, "Warum Österreich nicht sowjetisiert wurde: Sowjetische Österreich-Politik 1945–1953/55," in Karner and Stelzl-Marx, eds., *Die Rote Armee in Österreich*, pp. 655–663.

12. See Hans Seidel, *Österreichs Wirtschaft und Wirtschaftspolitik nach dem Zweiten Weltkrieg* (Vienna: MANZ'sche Verlag- und Universitätsbuchhandlung, 2005), pp. 433–434.

13. Barbara Stelzl-Marx, "Erbsen für Wien: Zur sowjetischen Lebensmittelhilfe 1945," in Stefan Karner and Gottfried Stangler, eds., *"Österreich ist frei!": Der österreichische Staatsvertrag 1955. Beitragband zur Ausstellung auf Schloss Schallaburg 2005* (Horn/Vienna: Berger, 2005), pp. 54–57, here p. 54.

14. Wolfgang Mueller, "Kulturpolitik und Propaganda der sowjetischen Besatzungsmacht in Österreich," in Karner and Stangler, eds., *"Österreich ist frei!,"* pp. 241–244, here p. 241.

15. See Rolf Wagenführ, *Die deutsche Industrie im Kriege: 1939–1945* (Berlin: Duncker & Humblot, 2006 [1954]), pp. 103–105; see also Norbert Schausberger, *Rüstung in Österreich 1938–1945* (Vienna: Hollinek, 1970).

16. Aleksej Filitov, "Sowjetische Planungen zur Wiedererrichtung Österreichs 1941–1945," in Karner and Stelzl-Marx, eds., *Die Rote Armee in Österreich*, pp. 27–37, here pp. 33–34.

17. Stefan Karner, *Die Steiermark im 20. Jahrhundert. Politik—Wirtschaft—Gesellschaft—Kultur* (Graz/Vienna/Cologne: Styria Verlag, 2000), pp. 322–323; Stefan Karner, Peter Ruggenthaler and Barbara Stelzl-Marx, "Die sowjetische Besatzung der Steiermark 1945," in Stefan Karner and Othmar Pickl, eds., *Die Rote Armee in der Steiermark: Sowjetische Besatzung 1945* (Graz: Leykam, 2008), pp. 9–42, here pp. 34–36 and the documents reproduced in ibid., pp. 392–411.

18. Russian State Archives of Socio-Political History (hereafter RGASPI), F. 17, op. 121, d. 395, ll. 1–3, Beriia to Malenkov: Report on Austria's Petroleum Industry, 13.4.1945. On this report see also Stefan Karner, "Zu den sowjetischen Demontagen in Österreich 1945/46: Ein erster Aufriss auf russischer Quellenbasis," in Michael Pammer, Herta Neiß and Michael John, eds., *Erfahrung der Moderne: Festschrift für*

Roman Sandgruber zum 60. Geburtstag (Stuttgart: Steiner, 2007), pp. 301–312, here p. 303, note 9.

19. *WIFO-Monatsberichte*, 1948, p. 135. The Soviets also attempted from 1944 to obtain access to the rich oil deposits in Iran, which naturally caused conflicts of interest with the British and the Americans. See the recent Jamil Hasanli, *At the Dawn of the Cold War: The Soviet-American Crisis over Iranian Azerbaijan, 1941–1946* (Lanham, MD: Rowman & Littlefield, 2006), pp. 46–59.

20. Vladislav M. Zubok, *A Failed Empire: The Soviet Union in the Cold War from Stalin to Gorbachev* (Chapel Hill, NC/London: University of North Carolina Press, 2007), p. 41.

21. See the recent Hasanli, *At the Dawn of the Cold War*, pp. 46–59.

22. See Bogdan Musial, "Modernisierung durch Demontagen? Zur Wirtschaftspolitik Stalins nach dem Zweiten Weltkrieg," in Wolfram Dornik, Johannes Gießauf and Walter M. Iber, eds., *Krieg und Wirtschaft: Von der Antike bis ins 21. Jahrhundert* (Innsbruck: Studienverlag, 2010); idem., *Stalins Beutezug. Die Plünderung Deutschlands und der Aufstieg der Sowjetunion zur Weltmacht* (Berlin: Propyläen, 2010).

23. Subok and Pleschakow, *Der Kreml im Kalten Krieg*, p. 81.

24. RGASPI, F. 82, op. 2, d. 104, ll. 1–2: State Planning Commission of the USSR to Molotov, 7 March 1947.

25. For the schilling-dollar conversions I use the exchange rate of twenty-six to one throughout. The revaluation in prices from 1955 has been carried out with the assistance of the Cost of Living Index for a four-person working-class family (with April 1945 taken as the basis of the index) on STATISTIK AUSTRIA, at: http://www.statistik.at/web_de/statistiken/preise/verbraucherpreisindex_vpi_hvpi/zeitreihen_und_verkettungen/index.html, accessed on June 17, 2009, at 11:40 a.m., using MS Internet Explorer.

26. US Department of State, *Foreign Relations of the United States, 1945* (FRUS), Vol. II: *Conference of Berlin (Potsdam Conference)* (Washington, DC: US Government Printing Office, 1960), p. 667.

27. William B. Bader, "Österreich in Potsdam," *Österreichische Zeitschrift für Außenpolitik*, Vol. 2 (1962), pp. 206–223, here pp. 210–217. See also Reinhold Wagnleitner, "Großbritannien und die Wiedererrichtung der Republik Österreich," PhD Diss., University of Salzburg, 1975, pp. 227–233; Waltraud Brunner, "Das Deutsche Eigentum und das Ringen um den österreichischen Staatsvertrag 1945–1955," Ph.D. Diss., University of Vienna, 1976, pp. 27–32; Reinhard Bollmus, "Ein kalkuliertes Risiko? Großbritannien, die USA und das 'Deutsche Eigentum' auf der Konferenz von Potsdam," in Günter Bischof and Josef Leidenfrost, eds., *Die bevormundete Nation: Österreich und die Alliierten 1945–1949* (Innsbruck: Haymon, 1988), pp. 107–126; Jörg Fisch, *Reparationen nach dem Zweiten Weltkrieg* (Munich: Beck, 1992), pp. 129–137; Günter Bischof, *Austria in the First Cold War 1945–1955: The Leverage of the Weak* (Basingstoke: Macmillan, 1999), pp. 36–41.

28. Otto Klambauer, "Staat im Staate: Sowjetisches Vermögen in Österreich 1945–1955," in Karner and Stangler, eds., *"Österreich ist frei!,"* pp. 182–187, here p. 182.

29. Law Gazette for the Country of Austria (*Gesetzblatt für das Land Österreich*, GBLÖ) 1938, No. 375.

30. Otto Klambauer and Jörg Fisch, for instance, make reference to the components of tactical calculation: Otto Klambauer, "Die Frage des deutschen Eigentums in Potsdam," *Jahrbuch für Zeitgeschichte*, 1978, pp. 127–174, here pp. 128–136; Fisch, *Reparationen nach dem Zweiten Weltkrieg*, pp. 131–132; for a contrasting view see the thesis of negotiating error advocated and/or emphasized by: Bader, "Österreich in Potsdam," p. 218; Bollmus, "Ein kalkuliertes Risiko?," pp. 119–120; Roman Sandgruber, "Das wirtschaftliche Umfeld des Staatsvertrages," in Manfried Rauchensteiner and Robert Kriechbaumer, eds., *Die Gunst des Augenblicks. Neuere Forschungen zu Staatsvertrag und Neutralität* (Vienna/Cologne/Weimar: Böhlau, 2005), pp. 359–377, here p. 362.

31. Control Council Law No. 5 (in German), 30.10.1945, at: http://www.verfassungen.de/de/de45-49/kr-gesetz5.htm, accessed on June 25, 2009, at 2:30 p.m., using MS Internet Explorer.

32. For example, the Soviet Sanafta treaty proposal, which listed in detail those oil firms interpreted by the Soviets as being "German property," was already made available to the British Element of the Allied Commission for Austria at the end of September 1945. At this point, the British had also long been informed by a "secret informant" about SMV confiscations in the Lower Austrian mineral oil region of Zistersdorf and with it the fact that Moscow did not even shy away from assets that had been Western-owned before 1938. TNA, FO 1020/3096 (ACA 323/66): Zistersdorfer Oil Concessions. Nixon (Headquarters of the British Military Government, Vienna) to Bennet (Allied Commission for Austria, Finance Division), 28.9.1945 and ibid., British City Commander's Office in Vienna to the British Troops Austria (BTA), Economic Division, 9.10.1945.

33. Seidel, *Österreichs Wirtschaft*, p. 402.

34. The Federal Ministry for Asset Protection listed in 1947 a total of fifty-two USIA businesses that had fallen prey during the Nazi period to "Aryanization" or "partial Aryanization," which would correspond to a proportion of around twelve percent of all confiscated industrial plants. Austrian State Archives/Archives of the Republic (hereafter ÖStA/AdR), BMfF, Sekt. Vermögenssicherung: Staatsvertragsakten, Kart. 4879, GZ 66/349, List of Aryanisations, 1947. This was, however, probably just an interim result, as, according to Klambauer, the proportion of "Aryanized" businesses actually came to 20 percent. See Otto Klambauer, "Die USIA-Betriebe," 2 volumes, PhD Diss., University of Vienna, 1978, pp. 267–268.

35. See Bader, "Österreich in Potsdam," p. 219.

36. ÖStA/AdR, BMfF, Sekt. Vermögenssicherung: Staatsvertragsakten, Kart. 4875, GZ 66/346, Conclusions of the Soviet Delegates at the 71st Session of the Austrian Treaty Commission, Vienna, September 2, 1947 (translated from Russian).

37. In the Vienna Treaty Commission of the four occupying powers which met for a total of eighty-five sessions from May to October 1947 in order to discuss all disputed aspects of a future Austrian State Treaty (and, in particular "German property"), the Soviet delegation remarked laconically: "The Soviet delegation bases this stance on the Potsdam resolutions, which, as is well-known, defined German assets as such

and not liabilities. [. . .] The Soviet delegation thinks that such liabilities should be borne by those who supported Germany in its war against the United Nations." ÖStA/ AdR (as in note 38).

38. ÖStA/AdR, BMfF, Sekt. Vermögenssicherung: Staatsvertragsakten, Kart. 4876, GZ 66/348, Renner to Figl, July 16, 1946 (copy).

39. See Seidel, *Österreichs Wirtschaft*, pp. 366–369.

40. Fisch, *Reparationen nach dem Zweiten Weltkrieg*, p. 136.

41. ÖStA/AdR (as in note 38).

42. Klambauer, "Staat im Staate," p. 184, and Seidel, *Österreichs Wirtschaft*, pp. 406–407.

43. Walter M. Iber, "Sowjetische Wirtschaftsenklaven in Österreich: USIA, SMV und die Handelsbeziehungen zur Tschechoslowakei, 1945—1955," in Stefan Karner and Michal Stehlik, eds., *Österreich. Tschechien. geteilt—getrennt—vereint. Beitragsband und Katalog zur Niederösterreichischen Landesausstellung 2009* (Schallaburg: Schallaburg Kulturbetriebsges.m.b.H., 2009), pp. 192–195, here p. 192.

44. See in detail Iber, "Die Sowjetische Mineralölverwaltung," pp. 51–52.

45. See Klambauer, "Die USIA-Betriebe," pp. 291–294.

46. The Soviet Danube Steam Navigation Company (*Donaudampfschifffahrtsgesellschaft*, DDSG) was subordinated to the organization of the USIA as of December 15, 1946, but retained the right to an independent administration. RGAE, F. 107, op. 3, d. 3, ll. 192–193, Order No. 429 of the Head of the USIA Borisov, 4 December 1946.

47. This production pressure doubtlessly belonged to the characteristics of the state socialist centrally planned economy, as practised in the USSR. Typical for a planned economy were also the considerable weaknesses that the USIA and the SMV manifested: e.g., the innovative drive, which was lacking because it constituted a risk for the fulfilment of the plan, or the low quality of the manufactured products, caused by the absent interfirm competitive pressure as a result of the pronounced monopolistic business structure. "Staatssozialistische Zentralplanwirtschaft," in *Gabler Wirtschaftslexikon, Sp–Z*, revised edition (Wiesbaden: Gabler, 1992), pp. 3075–3077, here p. 3077.

48. On September 30, 1948, the communist workers' newspaper *Der Erdölarbeiter* celebrated with a special issue entitled "Drei Jahre SMV" (Three Years of SMV). See *Der Erdölarbeiter*, No. 17, September 30, 1948.

49. ÖStA/AdR, BMfF, Sekt. Vermögenssicherung: Staatsvertragsakten, Kart. 4863, Beilage zu GZ 66/271, Deutsche Gasolin AG (German Petroleum Ether PLC) to BMfVuW, 16 January 1947: Confiscation of the German Petroleum Ether PLC by the Soviet Mineral Oil Administration for Austria.

50. ÖStA/AdR, BMfF, Sekt. Vermögenssicherung: Staatsvertragsakten, Kart. 4789, GZ 1274–261.498/433–35/55, Public administrators Mayrhofer and Degen to the BMfF, November 3, 1955.

51. Foreign Policy Archives of the Russian Federation (hereafter AVP RF), F. 66, op. 23, p. 24, d. 8, ll. 157–167, here l. 157, Alekseev to Kiselev: Report on the Crude Oil Industry in the Vienna Basin, November 26, 1945.

52. Ernst Bezemek, "Dokumentation der Betriebe des USIA-Konzernes," in idem. and Otto Klambauer, *Die USIA-Betriebe in Niederösterreich: Geschichte—Organisation—Dokumentation* (Vienna: Selbstverlag d. NÖ Inst. für Landeskunde, 1983), pp. 80–340, here p. 325.

53. Iber, "Die Sowjetische Mineralölverwaltung," pp. 96–106.

54. Iber, "Sowjetische Wirtschaftsenklaven," p. 195.

55. AVP RF, F. 06, op. 726, d. 322, ll. 100–101, Konev to Molotov, 14 December 1945. See also Wolfgang Mueller, *Die sowjetische Besatzung in Österreich 1945–1955 und ihre politische Mission* (Vienna/Cologne/Weimar: Böhlau, 2005), pp. 150–151.

56. On Order No. 17 see the recent Ruggenthaler, "Warum Österreich nicht sowjetisiert wurde," pp. 663–665.

57. Hubert Steiner, "Die USIA-Betriebe: Ihre Gründung, Organisation und Rückgabe in die Österreichische Hoheitsverwaltung," *Mitteilungen des Österreichischen Staatsarchivs*, Vol. 43 (1993), pp. 206–220, here p. 206.

58. Russian State Archives for Contemporary History (hereafter RGANI), F. 5, op. 28, d. 224, ll. 70–78, Report of the Head of the Department for Domestic Political Matters in the Apparatus of the High Commissioner in Austria, A. G. Kolobov, on some questions of political work within USIA and SMV concerns, [no later than June 9, 1954], reproduced in: Stefan Karner, Barbara Stelzl-Marx and Alexander Tschubarjan, eds., *Die Rote Armee in Österreich: Sowjetische Besatzung 1945–1955. Dokumente* (Graz/Vienna/Munich: Oldenbourg, 2005), Doc. 113, pp. 560–571, here p. 561.

59. Klambauer, "Die USIA-Betriebe," pp. 309–310.

60. RGANI, F. 5, op. 28, d. 224, ll. 70–78, Report of the Head of the Department for Domestic Political Matters in the Apparatus of the High Commissioner in Austria, A. G. Kolobov, on some questions of political work within USIA and SMV concerns, [no later than June 9, 1954], reproduced in: Karner, Stelzl-Marx and Tschubarjan, eds., *Die Rote Armee in Österreich*, Doc. 113, pp. 560–571, here p. 561.

61. ÖStA/AdR, BMF, Sekt. Vermögenssicherung: Staatsvertragsakten, Kart. 4781, GZ 66/380, USIA Operational Lists, August 5, 1955. There is, however, data that differs from this figure. In November 1955, A. K. Kurzamenko, the Deputy Head of the Administration of Soviet Property in Austria and Finland, gave a figure of 263 USIA concerns handed over to Austria (although only 213 concerns are listed in the attached itemization). RGANI, F. 5, op. 28, d. 331, ll. 328–345, Report of the Deputy Head of the Administration of Soviet Property in Austria and Finland, A. K. Kurzamenko, to the Central Committee of the CPSU regarding USIA concerns, 25 November 1955 (secret), partially reproduced in: Karner, Stelzl-Marx and Tschubarjan, eds., *Die Rote Armee in Österreich*, Doc. 116, pp. 598–603.

62. Iber, "Sowjetische Wirtschaftsenklaven," p. 195.

63. See in detail Walter M. Iber, "Wirtschaftsspionage für den Westen: Erdölarbeiter im Spannungsfeld des Krieges," in Stefan Karner and Barbara Stelzl-Marx, eds., *Stalins letzte Opfer: Verschleppte und erschossene Österreicher in Moskau 1950–1955* (Vienna/Munich: Böhlau, 2008), pp. 169–188.

64. National Archives and Records Administration (NARA), Record Group 84, Box 83, File 710: Research Section to Erhardt, August 7, 1947, Enclosure: Outline of Soviet Economic Penetration of Austria.

65. *WIFO-Monatsberichte*, Supplement 33 to No. 11, 1955: "Österreichs Wirtschaftsverkehr mit der Sowjetunion," p. 6.

66. Rainer Karlsch and Raymond G. Stokes, *Faktor Öl: Die Mineralölwirtschaft in Deutschland 1859–1974* (Munich: Beck, 2003), p. 329. See the recent Maximilian Graf, *Österreich und die DDR 1949–1990. Politik und Wirtschaft im Schatten der deutschen Teilung* (Vienna: ÖAW, 2016), pp. 82–87.

67. Provisional Intelligence Report: Soviet Bloc Trade in Petroleum and Petroleum Products: Intra Bloc and East-West 1947–53, April 6, 1955, pp. 16–17, at: www.foia.cia.gov, accessed on July 15, 2008, at 11:00 a.m., using MS Internet Explorer. Although the sequence used by the CIA could well be accurate, the figures are nevertheless imprecise or unrealistic. One example: in the memorandum for 1952, the exports were estimated at a total of around 1.6 million tons. Intelligence Memorandum: Flow of Petroleum in the Soviet Bloc European Satellites, 1952. CIA/RR IM-375, July 13, 1953, p. 3, at: www.foia.cia.gov, accessed on July 15, 2008, at 9:00 a.m., using MS Internet Explorer. This figure is, however, too high, if one keeps in mind that the estimate for the Austrian domestic quota was, at 1 million tons (in fact, it was around 1.2 million tons in 1952), too low. That means that a corresponding redistribution would give a (realistic) export figure of around 1.4 million tons.

68. RGANI, F. 5, op. 28, d. 224, ll. 70–78, Report of the Head of the Department for Domestic Political Matters in the Apparatus of the High Commissioner in Austria, A. G. Kolobov, on some questions of political work within USIA and SMV concerns, [no later than 9 June 1954], reproduced in: Karner, Stelzl-Marx and Tschubarjan, eds., *Die Rote Armee in Österreich*, Doc. 113, pp. 560–571, here pp. 561–562.

69. On the economic decline of Soviet concerns see the example of the SMV in Iber, "Die Sowjetische Mineralölverwaltung," pp. 109–117.

70. Fisch estimates Austrian reparations, including occupation costs, at 105 dollars per head. After deducting the occupation costs for the Western powers, according to Fisch's figures 97.1 dollars per head remain as Austrian "reparations" payments to the Soviet Union. Fisch estimates Romanian reparations, meanwhile, at 91.1 and Bulgarian at 35.7 dollars per head. In comparison, the reparation costs of the Soviet Occupation Zone (SBZ)/East Germany were, of course, much higher at 888.7 dollars per head (including occupation costs). Fisch, *Reparationen nach dem Zweiten Weltkrieg*, pp. 230–231 and 319, Table 25.

71. See the contribution by Mikhail Prozumenshchikov in this volume; Iber, "Die Sowjetische Mineralölverwaltung," pp. 161–167.

72. On the final Moscow negotiations in April 1955 see at length Gerald Stourzh, *Um Einheit und Freiheit: Staatsvertrag, Neutralität und das Ende der Ost-West-Besetzung Österreichs 1945–1955* (Vienna/Cologne/Graz: Böhlau, 2005), pp. 415–449.

73. During a personal discussion with the Soviet head of state Nikita Khrushchev in Villach in 1960, Federal Chancellor Julius Raab obtained a reduction in the payment demands from ten to six million tons. See Herbert Grubmayr, "60 Jahre mit den 'Russen': Erinnerungen an meine Zeit als Legationssekretär an der Österreichischen

Botschaft in Moskau," in Karner and Stelzl-Marx, eds., *Die Rote Armee in Österreich*, pp. 785–813, here pp. 794–796.

74. RGANI, F. 3, op. 10, d. 136, ll. 9 and 36–39, here l. 38, Resolution of the Presidium of the CC CPSU (P 115/XXVIII), April 8, 1955, Enclosure: Instructions for the Discussions with the Austrian Government.

75. Iber, "Sowjetische Wirtschaftsenklaven," p. 195.

76. Alongside payments for SMV and USIA, Austria also had to release the Soviet DDSG with a one-off payment of, converted, fifty-two million schillings and the loans of the Soviet Military Bank to the USIA concerns with a payment on account of around 509 million schillings. Added to this were the separate payments for the SMV Central Tank Farm (67 million schillings) and the farm of the USIA concerns (20 million schillings). Furthermore, the Soviet Union retained part of the liquid assets of the OROP "as currently unpaid profit." See Sandgruber, "Das wirtschaftliche Umfeld des Staatsvertrages," pp. 366–367, and Seidel, *Österreichs Wirtschaft*, pp. 463–465.

77. Whereas the goods deliveries (USIA one-off payment) were discontinued in 1961, the last delivery of crude oil (SMV one-off payment) left Austria on December 30, 1963. *Arbeiter Zeitung*, March 31, 1963, p. 2.

78. Plus a fictional GDP for 1945, whereby dismantling operations and occupation costs for 1945 are also included. For the 1945 GDP I have drawn on the 1937 value, upgraded to 1955 prices, and halved it, i.e., only "measured" the GDP for the six months from July to December 1945.

79. Rounded to two digits after the decimal point, my calculations result in a sum total of 1.41 billion dollars. Bischof estimates 1.33 billion and Seidel 1.45 billion dollars (less the payments to the Western occupying powers, which he includes). Bischof, *Austria in the First Cold War*, p. 87; Seidel, *Österreichs Wirtschaft*, p. 467.

80. STATISTIK AUSTRIA, Cost of Living Index.

81. Felix Butschek, *Die österreichische Wirtschaft im 20. Jahrhundert* (Stuttgart: Fischer, 1985), p. 89.

82. See Seidel, *Österreichs Wirtschaft*, pp. 468–470.

83. See Iber, "Die Sowjetische Mineralölverwaltung," pp. 28–33; idem, "Erdöl statt Reparationen. Die sowjetische Mineralölverwaltung in Österreich 1945–1955," in Vierteljahrshefte für Zeitgeschichte Vol. 57 (2009), No. 4, pp. 571–605, here pp. 580–583.

84. See ibid., p. 202.

85. See Sandgruber, "Das wirtschaftliche Umfeld des Staatsvertrages," pp. 371–372.

86. See, for example, the Memorandum on the Results of the Discussion between the Delegation of the Government of the Republic of Austria and the Delegation of the Government of the Soviet Union ("Moscow Memorandum," April 15, 1955), reproduced in: Stourzh, *Um Einheit und Freiheit*, pp. 667–670, here p. 667.

87. Ibid., p. 670.

88. Ruggenthaler, "Warum Österreich nicht sowjetisiert wurde," pp. 706–707.

89. Ibid., p. 707.

90. RGANI, F. 5, op. 28, d. 431, ll. 30–31, from the official diary of the Second Embassy Secretary V. I. Ugryumov, February 29, 1956: discussion with the Chairman of the Lower Austrian KPÖ, Robert Dubovsky, on February 23, 1956.

91. The example of the oil concerns shows that following the end of the SMV the Austrian government did not engage in any large-scale, politically motivated dismissals of communists. On the contrary, due to the pledge made in the context of the Moscow Memorandum to retain the SMV workers in employ, the number of workers on the ÖMV payroll at the end of 1957 was, at over 10,000 employees, even higher than in the later period of the SMV. *ÖMV-Geschäftsbericht*, 1957, p. 21.

92. RGANI, F. 5, op. 28, d. 432, ll. 10–20, here ll. 14–16, Expertise by Smirnov on Austria's economic dependency on the Western powers, November 30, 1955.

93. On economic relations between Austria and the USSR after 1955 see in detail Wolfgang Mueller, *A Good Example of a Peaceful Coexistence? The Soviet Union, Austria and Neutrality, 1955–1991* (Vienna: ÖAW, 2011), pp. 122–126.

94. Butschek, *Die österreichische Wirtschaft im 20. Jahrhundert*, pp. 132–134.

95. On this delivery treaty see Friedrich Feichtinger and Hermann Spörker, *ÖMV–OMV: Die Geschichte eines österreichischen Unternehmens* (Horn: Berger, 2005), pp. 151–152.

96. See the contributions by Ingomar Weiler, Johannes Steiner, Wolfram Dornik, and Gudrun Harrer in the edited collection Dornik, Gießauf and Iber, eds., *Krieg und Wirtschaft*.

Chapter Seven

Intelligence in Occupied Austria 1945–1955

The Soviet Side

Dieter Bacher

Accompanying the Allied armed forces upon their entry into Austria in 1945 were also numerous members of the Allied secret and intelligence services. Even before hostilities had ended, they unfolded their activities and continued them on a large scale during the occupation period. During the first years of the occupation, Austria assumed a key role in the rapidly escalating East-West conflict, both for the Western as well as the Soviet intelligence services. A report from British MI5 official Sir Philip Vickery from November 1950, for example, described Austria as a two-way intelligence "highway" between the blocks and as a "unique opportunity" for intelligence gathering.[1] This estimation was obviously also shared within Soviet services—Vitalii N. Nikolskii, an officer of Soviet GRU stationed in Austria between 1947 and 1955, stated in his memoirs that Austria would not only be an excellent place to observe Western services but also to prepare own operations in neighboring Western states like Italy or Western Germany.[2]

They both had their reasons for these estimations—situated directly at the "Iron Curtain," Austria's geographical location in Central Europe alone made the country, and especially its capital Vienna, an interesting operations area for both sides. Vienna was not only a good "meeting place" for intelligence service employees and their handlers on both sides, but also the ideal location for signals intelligence and radio propaganda. Advantageous at a later stage were also Austria's neutrality and Vienna's status as the headquarters of important international organizations (e.g., the International Atomic Energy Agency, or IAEA).[3]

Austria was regarded both as a "gateway" between the blocs and as the "first line of defense." Therefore, not only services whose main task lay in the collection of information and in "espionage" but also numerous agencies for counterintelligence and counterespionage were on the spot. This explains why so many intelligence agencies were active in Austria and why the country obtained a reputation as a "battle ground for secret services."[4] Even during the early occupation period, this reputation was co-opted by the film industry. In his thriller *The Third Man*, Graham Greene had Harry Lime (played by Orson Welles) smuggling medicine in the underground of occupied Vienna, pursued by Major Calloway as a member of British counterintelligence, who in turn repeatedly had to deal with his Soviet "colleagues."

The "main battle lines" between East and West in the intelligence arena already traversed Austria at a very early date, though they were not primarily directed against the state of Austria.[5] As a result of the problematic access to files, still relatively little is known about the activities, methods, and operative results of Soviet intelligence services, compared, for example, to the state of knowledge regarding American and British services. Owing to collaboration with Russian archives, at least some new facts have been brought to light in recent years.

Fundamentally, the Soviet side attached a similar importance to Austria as the American and British side did. The Soviet occupying power on Austrian territory was supported in its work by numerous intelligence services and their departments, and not only their own—for their objectives and interests in Austria the Soviet side also drew on the intelligence services of their satellite states. In Austria, this was primarily the services of neighboring states Czechoslovakia[6] (from summer 1948) and Hungary. As time went by, these two states increasingly assumed "responsibility" for intelligence operations on Austrian territory and indeed, as it was assumed in the West, under the guidance of the Soviet Union. This went so far that in June 1954, for example, the American Counter Intelligence Corps (CIC) in Vienna stated that the Czechoslovak services in Austria were now carrying out more operations than all other Eastern European services (including Soviet ones) combined.[7]

This article sheds light on the structures of the Soviet services operating in occupied Austria and their activities, which have become known during the course of research carried out in recent years in Russian archives.[8] In addition, individual works by journalists are of considerable importance.[9] Furthermore, publications on individual services and overviews of Soviet intelligence services with individual references to Austria provide further information.[10] Supplementing this, former intelligence service employees made statements in their published memoirs regarding their service on Austrian territory.[11]

GRU—MILITARY INTELLIGENCE

In principle, for the Soviet side, like for all three other Allied occupying powers, both civilian and military services were active in Austria. It is in some cases difficult, however, to draw a dividing line, especially where the Soviet services are concerned, because departments of the, in itself civilian, Ministry of State Security (*Ministerstvo gosudarstvennoi bezopasnosti*, or MGB) were subordinated or attached to the military, i.e., the Soviet army.[12]

On the military side, the GRU (*Glavnoe razvedyvatel'noe upravlenie*), founded in 1918, should be mentioned first of all. The GRU was subordinated to the General Staff of the Red, i.e., the Soviet, Army and had the task of coordinating the activities of the individual intelligence departments at the fronts and with the armies, divisions and regiments as well as planning and carrying out intelligence tasks in the military area.[13] To this end, the units subordinated to it included its own military special unit (GRU Spetsnaz), founded in 1950.[14] The GRU units stationed in Austria were subordinated in organizational terms from June 1945 to the Command of the Central Group of Forces (*Tsentral'naya gruppa voisk*, or TsGV) in Baden bei Wien.[15]

The tasks of the GRU in Austria initially encompassed the "classic" tasks of a military intelligence service such as counterintelligence and preliminary intelligence for the Soviet occupation troops as well as the securing of the Soviet occupation zone. However, according to statements made by Vitaliy Nikolskiy, who served as an officer for the Main Directorate for Intelligence within the Soviet General Staff in Austria, after 1945 a broad spectrum of intelligence tasks was added, which were directed against the occupation zones of the Western Allies in Austria, Western and Southern Europe and, partially, also against Austria itself: intelligence against the Western zones in Germany and against Italy, France, and Switzerland (with regard to military, political and economic affairs), information on planning and activities of the Western Allies within the Allied Commission for Austria and on planning and policies of the Austrian Interior and Foreign Ministries.[16]

According to Nikolskiy's portrayal, the GRU department attached to the TsGV in Baden bei Wien, for example, was able to register some victories against the American occupying power. Thus, it gained access via a recruited Austrian to instructions and papers of the American occupying power. This recruit had developed an unusual but simple and fruitful form of access to such information—at the behest of the GRU he bought waste paper on a large scale from an American office for, as he claimed, recycling purposes. The office entered into the transaction and, in this way, saved itself the trouble of disposing of the waste. For a long time, according to Nikolskiy, the office was not aware of the security risk entailed in using this method. The informant then sifted out papers that appeared interesting and forwarded them to the Vienna office of Nikolskiy, who paid him for these materials. In this way, the GRU received access to planning measures for the civil defense of Salzburg and other cities in the American occupation zones in Austria and West

Germany in the event of a Soviet attack with nuclear weapons. Furthermore, this information was obtained at a very low price—Nikolskiy described the informant as ideologically highly motivated and stated that he demanded only low fees for his work.[17] Simultaneously, the GRU in Austria could also acquire documents on the organization, arming, and operational tasks of US nuclear missile units and instructions for defense against nuclear, biological and chemical attacks.[18]

As for Austria itself, the secret measures of the Austrian government for establishing a future Austrian Federal Army were of special interest to the GRU. According to Nikolskiy, the Soviet side was very well informed about this plan thanks to the GRU informants in the Austrian Foreign and Interior Ministries and in the Western parts of the Allied Commission for Austria.[19] In the area of technical espionage, i.e., primarily the acquisition of new technical equipment and information on new patents, there was also great potential for the GRU in Austria, according to Nikolskiy, but this potential was not used. Thus, around 1948 an opportunity to acquire a new type of heart-lung machine was passed by. At the time, such apparatuses were virtually unknown in the USSR. Moscow headquarters rejected the proposal with the argument that Soviet medical technology was already very advanced and there was no use within the military for such an apparatus. Many opportunities were to remain unused for similar arguments.[20]

On the basis of Nikolskiy's statements, it is apparent that the GRU in Austria pursued a broad spectrum of tasks, which were not only of military interest. Thus, their tasks here as well went far beyond the "classic" tasks of military intelligence.

UKR SMERSH IN BADEN—
MILITARY COUNTERINTELLIGENCE

Worthy of mention here for the initial post-war period until 1946 is also the Main Directorate for Counterespionage SMERSH (*Glavnoe upravlenie kontrrazvedki "Smert' shpionam,"* or GUKR "SMERSH") as an organ of the military counterintelligence and counterespionage. During the period of its official existence from April 1943 to May 1946, it was subordinated to the People's Commissariat for Defence (*Narodnyi komissariat oborony*, or NKO) and thus Stalin himself as the relevant people's commissar.[21] Until the formation of the TsGV in June 1945, the SMERSH employees deployed in Austria were decentralized and subordinated to the respective Directorates for Counterintelligence (*Upravlenie kontrrazvedki*, or UKR) at the fronts and with the army groups and the Departments for Counterintelligence (*Otdel kontrrazvedki*, or OKR) with the individual armies, corps, and divisions. Thereafter and until its dissolution, the GUKR SMERSH was subordinated to the TsGV as a directorate (*UKR SMERSH TsGV*). This remained active in Austria until the dissolution of the GUKR SMERSH in May 1946.[22]

With its fourteen departments within the Main Directorate in Moscow and its directorates and departments with the individual military units, the SMERSH pursued with its activities different objectives. Its primary task consisted of searching for "spies" and "traitors" in the ranks of the army and the hunt for "dissidents" and political opponents of the Soviet regime within and outside of the Soviet Union. To this were added during the period of the Second World War defense against espionage by the wartime opponent Nazi Germany, procurement of information on and the infiltration of enemy intelligence services, debriefing captive Wehrmacht members and "traitors," securing and monitoring the territory behind the Soviet frontline as well as various tasks in the area of signals intelligence (SIGINT), including radio propaganda and counterpropaganda against Nazi German activities.

After the war, the SMERSH remained present in Austria as part of the Soviet occupation troops and, later, the TsGV. Its headquarters were in Baden bei Wien and it had departments in Vienna and Mödling.[23] Its tasks partially remained the same: surveillance, observation, and regular monitoring of army cohorts and those employed in the occupation administration, prevention of and action against desertion and anti-Soviet activities, and defense against espionage by enemy intelligence services. Additional new tasks were counterintelligence and active intelligence work against the Western Allies and measures against organizations classified as "anti-Soviet."[24]

There is only very little information on the concrete activities of the SMERSH in Baden, as is the case with the GRU. However, it evidently had a broad spectrum of tasks to fulfil. One was the search for, arrest, and debriefing of former National Socialists who had committed offences against the Soviet Union during the war, as well as people who, from the point of view of the Soviet occupying power in Austria, had conducted intelligence activities or propaganda against the Soviet Union.[25] As a rule, these "investigations," which sometimes lasted many months, ended with arrest and indictment by the Soviet Military Tribunal of Troop Unit 28990 in Baden and conviction in accordance with § 58 of the Criminal Code of the RSFSR.[26]

A former counterintelligence captain, Boris Baklanov, who served from 1945 to 1947 as a SMERSH officer and from March 1946 in the ranks of the MBG in Baden, defected while in Vienna in 1947 and published his memoirs in London in 1972 under the pseudonym A. I. Romanov,[27] reported in these memoirs on numerous activities. Alongside the search for "anti-Soviet elements," he cited the collection of information on the garrisons of the Western

Allies in Vienna and their occupation troops in the Western zones as the main task of his service, and indeed as early as the end of the war in 1945. The SMERSH in Baden resorted in this context to both "internal" and "external" surveillance. "Internal" meant the recruitment of Austrians working there as cleaners, translators or typists. They were recruited using so-called "keys," i.e., weaknesses and needs of the target person compiled in advance. One "key" used very often in Austria was to promise the recruitees that, in the event of collaboration, their relatives imprisoned as POWs or condemned civilians in camps in the Soviet Union would be released as soon as possible and be allowed to return home. In view of the fact that during the initial postwar period numerous families had at least one member in the USSR, this tactic functioned very effectively. Another good "key" could be the fostering of existing pro-Communist convictions.[28] For a time, SMERSH also succeeded in recruiting Allied personnel—according to Baklanov, this also depended primarily on the existence of "pro-Soviet" sentiments.[29]

Western counterintelligence agencies did not remain oblivious to such undertakings. Not least with regard to the Austrians they employed, they were very aware of the risk they posed, but evidently had to hazard the consequences. These employees were indispensable for the maintenance of the occupation administration and also its intelligence work, because the numbers of their own personnel were insufficient.[30]

According to Baklanov, the SMERSH in Vienna deployed above all two categories of recruited Austrians for the "external" surveillance of the "enemy": on the one hand, members of the Communist Party of Austria (*Kommunistische Partei* Österreichs, or KPÖ),[31] who were recruited with money or also with benefits for their families, and on the other former members of the NSDAP who had been encountered during the search for Nazi functionaries. If the latter were being considered for collaboration, an arrest was dispensed with and they were deployed for the Soviets' own purposes.[32] They were not only deployed as direct employees, as Baklanov continues; some of them living in the Soviet zone were also used as "hostages" in order to blackmail another person, for example a relative, into collaborating. SMERSH then monitored these people day and night—in order to prevent them fleeing the zone.[33] The SMERSH in Vienna also resorted to recruiting brothel owners, of whom it knew that soldiers and officers of the Western Allies often socialized there. SMERSH offered the owners a "financial subsidy" for their business—in exchange for their girls attempting to elicit information from their customers and then conveying this information to SMERSH in the form of a report.[34]

Alongside the active intelligence against the "West," SMERSH, also in Baden, also had to invest extensively in the surveillance and investigation of its "own people." It was primarily responsible for the "political reliability" of Soviet civilian and military personnel. This led as early as 1945/1946 to it repeatedly having to examine in particular the military personnel deployed in Austria at the behest of "headquarters" in Moscow for "undesirable elements." Here SMERSH merely had the task of carrying out an examination and providing an evaluation—a commission in Baden established especially for the task, and which included a SMERSH officer among its members, then decided on the "categorization" of the person concerned. If "demobilization" was envisaged, the person was dismissed from military service and brought back to the USSR via a reserve regiment in Slovakia. In less suspicious cases, a transfer to a "less important" function was also a possibility. If the person appeared to be unobjectionable, he was left in his current post.[35]

SMERSH also carried out similar, if stricter, examinations of Soviet "displaced persons" (DPs) in Austria. Hundreds of thousands of Soviet citizens had been brought to the "Ostmark" as civilian forced laborers or POWs during the Second World War and were still on Austrian territory as of 1945. In accordance with the resolutions of the Potsdam Agreement and the Soviet standpoint, they were all to be returned to the Soviet Union as soon as possible after the end of the war. From the point of view of the Soviet repatriation organs, it was irrelevant whether those concerned actually wanted to go back or not—if necessary, their return should be enforced.[36] All these DPs were to be tracked down by the Soviet military missions in the Western zones (which, as a rule, included SMERSH officers) and brought to the Soviet zone. Those that the military missions could get their hands on were gathered in numerous provisional camps in the zone (in former forced labor camps, former factories, schools, or also large farmsteads), guarded by NKVD/MVD troops and "screened."[37] "Enemies of the Soviet forces" were brought to forced labor camps as well as prisons in the USSR, and "relatively unobjectionable" people were sent home but continued to be monitored there by organs of state security. People who were classified as "unobjectionable" were either sent home or, in some cases, employed by the Soviet occupying power as gardeners, housekeepers, or translators. SMERSH itself even recruited some of them—as translators or employees. Baklanov mentions the case of a young Russian woman who had worked as a translator for an SS officer during the war and been deployed by SMERSH in Vienna as a "tipper," i.e., she was required to identify people who were under consideration as SMERSH employees and then, as the case might be, recruit them.[38]

When SMERSH was dissolved in March 1946, its powers and tasks were transferred to the newly established MGB, which also assumed and continued to implement the former's agendas with the TsGV in Baden.

JURISDICTION AND PROTECTION—
NKVD/MVD IN AUSTRIA

In some of these areas of responsibility, the activities of the GUKR SMERSH overlapped with those of the People's Commissariat for Internal Affairs (*Narodnyi komissariat vnutrennikh del*, or NKVD) and its Internal Troops in Austria, for which reason there were repeated rivalries between the departments.[39] Especially in the question of protecting the hinterland of the frontline and searching for "anti-Soviet agitators" and "dissidents," the NKVD and the troop units attached to it were deployed on Austrian territory from the end of April 1945. The units, which totalled more than 65,000 men, had the primary task in April/May of securing the ongoing military operations of the Red Army, above all behind the front, and stopping enemy intelligence and (feared) partisan activities. Similar to the GUKR SMERSH, however, their activities were not to be directed exclusively against the wartime opponents: the Internal Troops were also supposed to locate deserters and "marauders" from their own ranks and arrest them.[40]

Already at this stage, the tasks of Soviet state security were also implemented by departments outside of the NKVD: the Main Directorate for State Security (*Glavnoe upravlenie gosudarstvennoi bezopasnosti*, or GUGB) had already been separated off in 1943 and consolidated in its own People's Commissariat for State Security (*Narodnyi komissariat gosudarstvennoi bezopasnosti*, or NKGB)—thereafter, the NKVD was responsible above all for the internal consolidation of the Soviet regime, and the aforementioned Internal Troops, Border Troops, Blocking Troops and Convoy Troops as well as the two camp systems GULag and GUPVI were subordinated to it.[41]

These objectives marginally changed after the end of hostilities in May 1945—the protection of military formations and the territories in Austria occupied by the Soviet side remained on the agenda, but greater weight was attached to the search for and capture of high-ranking Nazi functionaries, NSDAP members, partisans, deserters, saboteurs, and also former Soviet DPs.[42] Parallel to this, the NKVD also fulfilled tasks of civilian counterintelligence, took action against "political opponents" of the Soviet occupying power and prepared legal proceedings against imprisoned people.[43] It is clear how much the competences of individual Soviet services in Austria overlapped.

Particularly the partisan activities of former Wehrmacht and SS formations (so-called "werewolves") were regarded by the Soviet side, and also by the American and British side, as a great threat. Acts of sabotage and other attacks did indeed occur, though on a far smaller scale than expected. Nonetheless, thousands of arrests were made in cases where the possession of Nazi propaganda material or weapons allowed for a conclusion of "resistance." In June

1945 alone, 15,374 people were arrested by NKVD Border Troops in Austria, many of them on the suspicion of partaking in "Werewolf" activities.[44]

In March 1946, sections of the Internal Troops were assigned to the newly-founded Ministry for Internal Affairs (*Ministerstvo vnutrennikh del*, or MVD). The MVD continued to implement the tasks of the NKVD in Austria, primarily with regard to the search for and arrest of people sought by the counterintelligence service or the protection of prisons and DP camps.[45] In the area of state security and, above all, the active collection of information on the Western occupying powers, MVD units increasingly played a comparatively minor role over the course of the occupation of Austria.[46]

"CIVILIAN" STATE SECURITY—NKBG/MGB AS THE PREDECESSOR OF THE KGB

Like their colleagues from the GRU, the SMERSH, and the NKVD, employees of the NKGB were also present in Austria from 1945. The NKGB was responsible for tasks in the areas of foreign intelligence (1st Directorate), counterintelligence and counterespionage (2nd Directorate), and encryption (3rd Directorate).[47] To this end, the NKGB already maintained, not only within the Soviet sphere of influence, numerous networks in 1945 with the main focus on "enemy intelligence" against the American and British occupying powers. Several NKGB employees also operated as members of the Soviet diplomatic corps in Vienna.[48] Here as well, therefore, an overlap existed with the areas of responsibility of the aforementioned Soviet services.

During the course of turning the people's commissariats into ministries from March 1946, the NKGB also became a ministry (*Ministerstvo gosudarstvennoi bezopasnosti*, or MGB).[49] It was not merely a matter of the renaming and partial internal restructuring of the service, however. Competences of its former "rival services" were also transferred to the MGB. Thus, in May 1946, as mentioned earlier, the SMERSH was dissolved as an organ of military counterintelligence and counterespionage and completely incorporated into the MGB as the 3rd Main Directorate (Military Counterintelligence).[50] Foreign intelligence remained in the MGB as the 1st Main Directorate until late May 1947—at which point it was separated off and incorporated into the Committee for Information (*Komitet informatsii*, or KI), which was directly attached to the Council of Ministers of the USSR under the control of Foreign Minister Vyacheslav M. Molotov, until the KI was again incorporated into the MGB in November 1951 as the 1st Main Directorate.[51] Like the GRU or SMERSH, the foreign intelligence service regarded Austria as the "gateway to the West," where it was easy to recruit informants and employees and collect information not only on Austria itself.

The activities of the UKR SMERSH attached to the TsGV in Baden continued from March 1946 as part of the 3rd Main Directorate of the MGB to focus on its agendas, specifically as UKR MGB TsGV with the formal designation "Troop Unit 32750."[52] The four departments of this directorate dealt with counterintelligence, the protection of the Soviet occupying power against infiltration and espionage attempts, the search for and arrest of enemy "agents" and "anti-Soviet elements" in the Soviet occupation zone in Austria and the investigation of their activities, and the examination of Soviet prisoners of war during the course of their return home, as well as treason, desertion, and conduct damaging to the Soviet occupying power.[53] The workload involved in the latter task was especially considerable: thus, between the end of the war in 1945 and autumn 1946, around 14,000 soldiers and officers deserted from the Soviet occupation zones in Germany and Austria and fled to one of the Western zones.[54]

In the context of this task, the counterintelligence service of the MGB took action against numerous "spies" and "anti-Soviet elements" in Austria. For the imprisonment and interrogation of suspects, the directorate in Baden had an "internal prison" at its disposal, in which these people, who included numerous Austrians, were incarcerated and questioned in some cases for months on end, before their case was addressed by the military tribunal in Baden.[55]

Another important objective of the UKR MGB of the TsGV was the retrieval, investigation and surveillance of the repatriation of Soviet DPs in Austria. Like the UKR SMERSH before it, the UKR MGB was supposed to collect information on their stay in Austria, question them on this, gather them in camps and quarters, and prepare them for their transfer to the homeland. Furthermore, MGB officers were appointed to the commissions that decided during the course of "screening" whether repatriates were to be accused of "anti-Soviet conduct" or classified as "politically reliable."[56]

The Committee for State Security (*Komitet gosudarstvennoi bezopasnosti*, or KGB), founded from the MGB in March 1954 and attached to the Council of Ministers of the USSR, was only of limited importance for the period of the Soviet occupation. The KGB assumed the agendas of the MGB both in the area of foreign espionage and also counterintelligence. For its future activities in Austria, it could already draw on an existing broad foundation of knowledge, know-how, and networks, which also allowed a continuation of its activities in Austria even after the signing of the Austrian State Treaty on May 15, 1955.

The tasks of the MGB differed scarcely from those of SMERSH, especially during the initial period. Baklanov's portrayal makes it clear, however, that firstly, activities against the Western Allies became more numerous over time. Thus, he describes the deployment of "special troops" from the ranks of former NKVD troops in the Soviet occupation zone, who were trained for special operations such as sabotage and subversion.[57] The increasing tensions between East and West were also felt by numerous Austrians who allegedly or in reality had contact with Western intelligence services—they were monitored, studied, and, ultimately, arrested by the MGB, interrogated in the MGB remand prison in Baden, sometimes for months on end, convicted, and then brought to the USSR to serve their sentence. Between 1950 and 1953, more than 100 Austrians were sentenced to death and executed in Moscow on the basis of such accusations.[58] The counterintelligence service of the MGB did not hold back even in the face of high-ranking Austrian officials, if it thought there was a reasonable suspicion that someone was collaborating with Western intelligence agencies. Worth mentioning here, alongside the examples of state police officers Anton Marek and Franz Kiridus,[59] is the case of Margarethe Ottillinger. As a close colleague and planning chief for Minister of Property Control and Economic Planning Peter Krauland, she was responsible on the Austrian side for, among other things, negotiating the Marshall Plan, and thus occupied a key position that made her not unimportant for Soviet economic interests in Austria. She was targeted by the MGB, among other reasons, because she had repeated contact to employees of the American intelligence service CIC and had assisted a Soviet steel specialist, Andrei I. Didenko, to flee to the West in 1946. On November 5, 1948, she was arrested in the presence of the minister while crossing the border to the Soviet zone near St. Valentin and brought to Baden as an "American spy." After interrogations and investigations by the MGB lasting almost four months, she was sentenced to twenty-five years of imprisonment in a camp and brought to the Soviet Union. Soviet officials openly informed the Austrian government that Ottillinger's arrest was a clear warning (against its too openly Western course) to the Austrian government. She was not released until the general amnesty of the Austrian State Treaty. In June 1955, after more than six years of imprisonment in a camp, she returned, sick, to Austria. The charges against her were dropped a year later.[60]

Secondly, the MGB tightened the checks against its own ranks. The continued investigations were combined with considerable propaganda endeavors by the MGB, in order to prevent their own soldiers from collaborating with Western intelligence services or "defecting." Thus, according to Baklanov, in late 1946, the MGB, for example, selected individual officers and NCOs from among the occupation troops, whom it then used to spread rumors among the soldiers that did not shed a good light on the Western occupying powers. According to one of these rumors, Harry S. Truman and Winston Churchill were only waiting for a convenient opportunity to launch a military attack on the USSR.[61] Using this and other measures, an attempt was made to instil in their own employees the conviction that there was no alternative to the Soviet Union and that the Western powers could not be trusted.[62] Nonetheless, contrary rumors also did the rounds among Soviet soldiers in Baden, for example regarding hard living conditions in the USSR itself. The MGB attempted to combat this "anti-Soviet propaganda," too—and if it was able to locate the "author" of these "rumors," he was arrested, interrogated in Baden and in most cases convicted of "provocative enemy propaganda."[63]

CONCLUDING REMARKS

On the basis of reflections on the Soviet intelligence services in Austria, it is clear that the structures of the agencies present there and their objectives are now relatively well known but that the information on their concrete activities, operational methods and results is incomplete. As a result of available studies, our understanding of the more than complex structures and interwoven competences is now relatively good. Aside from several memoirs, at the operational level, i.e., on the activities of the employees, informants, and lower ranks of the services, there are a number of gaps. Access to case files and records on concrete operations and planning is especially limited. This deficit impedes our assessment of Austria as an operations area for intelligence agencies during the early Cold War. It is beyond question that extensive and intensive activities took place here—what they looked like in concrete cases, however, is yet to be determined. The possibilities offered by the better access to files of the intelligence services of the Western Allies have not yet been completely exhausted, either—further insights in this area can most certainly be expected. Although it is now possible to provide a summary overview, the assessment of an employee of the British MI1 from 1951 with regard to counterespionage against Soviet informant networks in Austria can also apply as a reflection on the activities of the Soviet intelligence services: only the surface has been scratched; the true dimensions of these operations are not yet known.[64]

NOTES

1. See TNA, DEFE 21/33, Report on Intelligence Organisation Allied Commission for Austria (British Element), November 15, 1950, p. 5f.

2. Vitalii Nikolskii, *GRU v gody velikoy otechestvennoy voyny*. Moscow 2005, p. 286.

3. Harald Irnberger, *Nelkenstrauß ruft Praterstern. Am Beispiel Österreich: Funktion und Arbeitsweise geheimer Nachrichtendienste in einem neutralen Staat* (Vienna: Promedia, 1983), pp. 34–35; see also Dieter Bacher, "Die KPÖ und die sowjetischen Nachrichtendienste. Zweiseitige Kontakte im frühen Kalten Krieg," in Stefan Karner and Barbara Stelzl-Marx, eds., *Stalins letzte Opfer. Verschleppte und erschossene Österreicher in Moskau 1950–1953*. Kriegsfolgen-Forschung. Wissenschaftliche Veröffentlichungen des Ludwig Boltzmann-Instituts für Kriegsfolgen-Forschung, vol. 5 (Vienna/Munich: Böhlau, 2009), pp. 189–203, here pp. 189–190.

4. See Harald Knoll and Dieter Bacher, "Nachrichtendienste und Spionage im Österreich der Besatzungszeit," in Karner and Stelzl-Marx, eds., *Stalins letzte Opfer*, pp. 157–169, here pp. 157–163.

5. Irnberger, *Nelkenstrauß ruft Praterstern*, p. 26.

6. Prokop Tomek, "Die Struktur der Staatssicherheit in der ČSSR," in Pavel Žáček, Bernd Faulenbach and Ulrich Mählert, eds., *Die Tschechoslowakei 1945/48 bis 1989. Studien zu kommunistischer Herrschaft und Repression* (Leipzig: Leipziger Universitätsverlag, 2008), pp. 99–128; Stefan Karner, *HALT! Tragödien am Eisernen Vorhang. Die Verschlussakten* (Salzburg: Ecowin, 2013).

7. See NARA, RG 319, box 100, Report on Czechoslovak Intelligence, Service Operations in Austria, June 28, 1954, p. 5.

8. See, for example, Richard J. Aldrich, *The Hidden Hand: Britain, America and Cold War Secret Intelligence* (Woodstock/New York: Overlook Press, 2002), pp. 180–205; Nikita Petrov, "Die militärische Spionageabwehr in Österreich und die Todesstrafe. Struktur, Funktionen, Praxis," in Karner and Stelzl-Marx, eds., *Stalins letzte Opfer*, pp. 79–96; Knoll and Bacher, "Nachrichtendienste und Spionage im Österreich der Besatzungszeit."

9. Irnberger, *Nelkenstrauß ruft Praterstern*; Kid Möchel, *Der geheime Krieg der Agenten. Spionagedrehscheibe* (Vienna/Hamburg: Rasch und Röhring, 1997).

10. Viktor Suvorov, *GRU. Die Speerspitze. Was der KGB für die Polit-Führung, ist die GRU für die Rote Armee. Spionage-Organisation und Sicherheitsapparat der sowjetischen Militärs—Aufbau, Ziele, Strategie, Arbeitsweise und Führungskader*, 3rd ed. (Solingen: Barett, 1995); Vadim J. Birstein, *Smersh: Stalin's Secret Weapon. Soviet Military Counterintelligence in WWII* (London: Biteback Publishing, 2011), pp. 362–364; Christopher Andrew—Oleg Gordiewsky, *KGB. Die Geschichte seiner Auslandsoperationen von Lenin bis Gorbatschow* (Munich: Bertelsmann, 1990); in parts also Christopher Andrew and Wassil Mitrochin, *Das Schwarzbuch des KGB. Moskaus Kampf gegen den Westen* (Munich: Ullstein, 2001); A. I. Kokurin and N. V. Petrov, *Lubyanka. Organy VChK–OGPU–NKVD–MGB–MVD–KGB 1917–1991. Spravochnik* (Moscow: Izdatelstvo Yelskogo Universiteta, 2003); see especially Andreas Hilger, "Sowjetunion (1945–1991)," in Łukasz Kamiński, Krysztof Persak and Jens Gieseke, eds., *Handbuch der kommunistischen Geheimdienste in Osteuropa 1944–1991*. (Göttingen: Vandenhoeck & Ruprecht, 2009), pp. 43–141.

11. Nikolskiy, *GRU v gody Velikoi otechestvennoi voiny*; Peter Deriabin and T. H. Bagley, *KGB: Masters of the Soviet Union* (London: Robson, 1990); Peter S. Deriabin and Joseph C. Evans, *Inside Stalin's Kremlin: An Eyewitness Account of Brutality, Duplicity, and Intrigue* (Washington/London: Brassey's, 1998); see above

all Ladislav Bittman, *The KGB and Soviet Disinformation: An Insider's View* (Washington, DC, et al.: Pergamon-Brassey's, 1985).

12. See, for example, Kokurin and Petrov, *Lubyanka*, pp. 139–147; Petrov, "Die militärische Spionageabwehr in Österreich und die Todesstrafe," pp. 92–93; Hilger, "Sowjetunion (1945–1991)," pp. 44–52.

13. Suvorov, *GRU*; Helmut Roewer, Stefan Schäfer, and Matthias Uhl, *Lexikon der Geheimdienste im 20. Jahrhundert* (Munich: Herbig, 2003), pp. 179–181; see also Dieter Bacher and Peter Ruggenthaler, "Als GRU-Offizier in Österreich. Die Erinnerungen Vitalij Nikolskiys. 1947–1955," in *JIPSS*, vol. 5, no. 1/2011, pp. 139–155, here p. 140.

14. S. Kozlov, *Spetsnaz GRU. Ocherki istorii. Istoriya sozdaniya ot rot k brigadam 1950–1979 gg.* (Moscow: SPSL—Russkaya Panorama, 2009); see also Suvorov, *GRU*.

15. Nikolskiy, *GRU v gody Velikoi otechestvennoi voiny*, pp. 5–34.

16. Ibid., pp. 281–286; Bacher and Ruggenthaler, "Als GRU-Offizier in Österreich," pp. 145 and 150–151.

17. Nikolskiy, *GRU v gody Velikoi otechestvennoi voiny*, p. 278–281.

18. Ibid.

19. Ibid., pp. 281–286.

20. Ibid., pp. 286–287; Bacher and Ruggenthaler, "Als GRU-Offizier in Österreich," pp. 151–152.

21. Petrov, "Die militärische Spionageabwehr in Österreich und die Todesstrafe," p. 92; Birstein, *Smersh*, p. 3.

22. Petrov, "Die militärische Spionageabwehr in Österreich und die Todesstrafe," p. 92.

23. A. I. Romanov, *Nights Are Longest There: Smersh From the Inside* (London: Hutchinson, 1972), pp. 159–160.

24. Ibid., pp. 149 and 158–159.

25. See Petrov, "Die militärische Spionageabwehr in Österreich und die Todesstrafe," pp. 94–95; Birstein, *Smersh*, pp. 362–363.

26. See the contribution by Barbara Stelzl-Marx and Harald Knoll in this volume.

27. Romanov, *Nights Are Longest There*.

28. Ibid., p. 158.

29. Ibid.

30. On this see, for example, the report of the Command of British Troops Austria (BTA) to the Vice Chief of the Imperial General Staff, Sir Nevil Brownjohn, from November 1950, which states: "There are, however, large numbers of local employees working as clerks and this must be a continuing problem." TNA, WO 216/951, Memorandum on Security in Austria and Trieste, 4 October 1951, p. 1. See also Dieter Bacher, "Austrian 'Spies' in the Early Cold War: The Recruitment of Austrian Citizens by Foreign Intelligence Services in Austria from 1945 to 1953," in Wladyslaw Bulhak and Thomas Wegener Friis, eds., *Need to Know: Eastern and Western Perspectives* (Odense: University Press of Southern Denmark, 2014), pp. 229–244.

31. The possibility of members of the KPÖ being recruited as employees of Soviet intelligence services was a constant concern for the American and British agencies in

Austria. See, for example, Dieter Bacher, "Der Freund meines Feindes ist mein Feind. Die Kommunistische Partei Österreichs im Visier amerikanischer und britischer Nachrichtendienste 1945–1955," in *Jahrbuch für Historische Kommunismusforschung*, 2016 (Berlin: Metropol, 2016), pp. 163–180.

32. Romanov, *Nights Are Longest There*, p. 158.
33. Ibid., p. 159.
34. Ibid., p. 160.
35. Ibid., pp. 163–168.
36. See Pavel Polyan, *Zhertvy dvukh diktatur. Zhizn', trud, unizhenie i smert' sovetskikh voennoplennykh i ostarbaiterov na chuzhbine i na rodine* (Moscow: Rosspen, 2002); Peter Ruggenthaler and Walter M. Iber, eds., *Hitlers Sklaven—Stalins "Verräter." Aspekte der Repression an Zwangsarbeitern und Kriegsgefangenen: Eine Zwischenbilanz.* Veröffentlichungen des Ludwig Boltzmann-Instituts für Kriegsfolgen-Forschung, vol. 14 (Innsbruck: StudienVerlag, 2010).
37. On the screening and forced repatriation of Soviet DPs in Austria see Polyan, *Zhertvy dvukh diktatur*; Ruggenthaler and Iber, eds., *Hitlers Sklaven—Stalins "Verräter."*
38. Romanov, *Nights Are Longest There*, p. 175.
39. Birstein, *Smersh*, pp. 33 and 217–247.
40. Natal'ja Eliseeva, "Zum Schutz des Hinterlandes der Roten Armee. Der Einsatz der NKVD-Truppen in Österreich von April bis Juli 1945," in Stefan Karner and Barbara Stelzl-Marx, eds., *Die Rote Armee in Österreich. Sowjetische Besatzung 1945–1955: Beiträge* (Graz/Vienna/Munich: Oldenbourg, 2005), pp. 91–104, here pp. 91–92 and 96–97.
41. Kokurin—Petrov, *Lubyanka*, pp. 59–60; Nicolas Werth, "Sowjetunion (1917–1945)," in Kamiński, Persak and Gieseke, eds., *Handbuch der kommunistischen Geheimdienste in Osteuropa 1944–1991*, pp. 15–41, here pp. 38–40; Roewer, Schäfer, and Uhl, *Lexikon der Geheimdienste im 20. Jahrhundert*, p. 318.
42. Eliseeva, "Zum Schutz des Hinterlandes der Roten Armee," pp. 102–103.
43. On the NKVD's area of responsibility in the occupied territories in Germany and Austria see Nikita Petrov, *Die sowjetischen Geheimdienstmitarbeiter in Deutschland. Der leitende Personalbestand der Staatssicherheitsorgane der UdSSR in der Sowjetischen Besatzungszone Deutschlands und der DDR von 1945–1954: Biografisches Nachschlagewerk* (Berlin: Metropol, 2010), pp. 12–14.
44. Eliseeva, "Zum Schutz des Hinterlandes der Roten Armee," pp. 102–103.
45. Romanov, *Nights Are Longest There*, pp. 195–196.
46. Petrov, "Die militärische Spionageabwehr in Österreich und die Todesstrafe."
47. Kokurin and Petrov, *Lubyanka*, p. 138.
48. See the contribution by Ol'ga Pavlenko in this volume.
49. Kokurin and Petrov, *Lubyanka*, p. 140.
50. Ibid., p. 139.
51. Kokurin and Petrov, *Lubyanka*, pp. 141–145.
52. Petrov, "Die militärische Spionageabwehr in Österreich und die Todesstrafe," p. 92.
53. Ibid., p. 93.

54. Romanov, *Nights Are Longest There*, p. 235.

55. See the contribution by Barbara Stelzl-Marx and Harald Knoll in this volume; see also Barbara Stelzl-Marx, "Verschleppt und erschossen. Eine Einführung," in Karner and Stelzl-Marx, eds., *Stalins letzte Opfer*, pp. 21–78; Dieter Bacher, "Sowjetische Ermittlungen und Prozesse gegen österreichische 'Spione' (1950–1953)," in Csaba Szabó, eds., *Sowjetische Schauprozesse*. Publikationen der ungarischen Geschichtsforschung in Wien, vol. 13 (Vienna: Institut für ungarische Geschichtsforschung, 2015), pp. 299–316.

56. Polyan, *Zhertvy dvukh diktatur*; Romanov, *Nights are longest there*, p. 173.

57. Romanov, *Nights Are Longest There*, pp. 195–200.

58. See Karner and Stelzl-Marx, eds., *Stalins letzte Opfer*.

59. See the contribution by Barbara Stelzl-Marx and Harald Knoll in this volume.

60. See Stefan Karner, *Im Kalten Krieg der Spionage. Margarethe Ottillinger in sowjetischer Haft 1948–1955*, 2nd ed. (Innsbruck/Vienna/Bolzano: StudienVerlag, 2016).

61. Romanov, *Nights Are Longest There*, p. 196.

62. Ibid., p. 236.

63. Ibid., p. 223.

64. TNA, WO 216/951, Report from MI1 to the DMI, October 4, 1951.

Chapter Eight

Stalin's Judiciary in Austria

Arrests and Convictions during the Occupation

Harald Knoll and Barbara Stelzl-Marx

During the course of the occupation of Austria, Moscow exported its legal system into the eastern zone of the country for a total of ten years. As a result, Soviet organs arrested from 1945 to 1955 around 2,400 Austrian civilians, at least 1,250 of which were sentenced for war, state, and everyday crimes to mainly long prison terms by Stalin's military tribunals, whereas more than 150 were executed.[1] The Austrian people and public remained largely in the dark regarding the reasons for an arrest and the subsequent fate of the "abductees." The apparently arbitrary conduct of this "human robbery" coupled with the powerlessness of the Austrian authorities have been firmly embedded in the collective memory.

The reasons for the arrests which were carried out in broad daylight, during a stroll, on the pretext of official business at Soviet headquarters or in ones own apartment, were manifold and should often be seen against the backdrop of the Cold War. In this way, the Soviet occupying power reacted rigorously to everything that they regarded as a threat: espionage, unauthorized weapons possession, membership in "Werewolf" groups, disputes with members of the Red Army and criminal activities. Stalin's criminal justice in Austria also punished Nazi war crimes that had been committed during the war against Soviet citizens or on the territory of the Soviet Union.

Among those arrested were prominent personalities in public life and in the economy—like the head of the planning section in the Ministry for Asset Protection and Economic Planning under Minister Peter Krauland, Margarethe Ottillinger,[2] or the unofficial "secret service chief" Police Inspector Anton Marek[3] as well as the Gendarmerie official Franz Kiridus[4]—and likewise "the man on the street." At the point of arrest, the person in question disappeared for several years into a Soviet microcosm. In 1956, one year after the signing of the Austrian State Treaty, the last repatriation trains from the Soviet Union arrived.

Some, however, never returned to their homeland: either because they had died during their imprisonment or because they had been executed following the death sentence. Their relatives were left in the dark for years. Only in the last few years has it been possible to deduce the fate of these victims of Stalin.[5]

ON THE STATE OF EXISTING SCHOLARSHIP

Similar to Germany,[6] in Austria the subject of civilian convicts also constituted for a long time a research desideratum. This was primarily down to the comparatively poor access to source material.[7] Only since the—partial—opening of the Soviet archives at the beginning of the 1990s could access be obtained to personnel files of convicted Austrian civilians and prisoners of war as well as other file material. Having said that, neither in Austria nor in Russia is access to the files of security, secret service, and judicial authorities entirely free from restrictions.

The collection of sources on Margarethe Ottillinger[8] was followed by research on convicted Lower Austrians,[9] Styrian "Werewolf" activists and policemen[10] and on the criminal law system in the Soviet Union.[11] Alongside the prosecution of National Socialist war and violent crimes as a form of denazification,[12] it was also possible to highlight the fates of several individuals.[13] In the last two decades, new sources on Soviet criminal law in Austria were made accessible and analysed in the framework of several research projects.[14] Also the fates of the more than 100 Austrian victims of Stalin who were shot in Moscow and buried in a mass grave in Moscow's Donskoe Cemetery between 1950 and Stalin's death in 1953 were rehabilitated.[15] Detailed research on Austrian women in the GULag and the arrests in the first post-war years are yet to take place, as is the rehabilitation of those executed between 1945 and 1947.

SOVIET SENTENCING PRACTICES
TOWARD AUSTRIAN CIVILIANS

To this day, the abductions of "thousands by the Russians" are anchored in the collective memory of the Austrian population. Research has revealed an actual number of around 2,200 arrested civilians. For around half of them there exists information on the circumstances of the arrest and the subsequent conviction. This corresponds to around 0.1 percent of the population living in eastern Austria at the end of the war.[16] Not included in that number is a dark figure of those abducted by the Red Army in particular in 1945, about whom to this day nothing is known. The Soviet authorities transferred some of the victims before their conviction to Austrian bodies. This was the case if those arrested had not committed offences against the Soviet Union.

The number of those arrested reached its peak during the first four years of the occupation and successively declined until 1955. Several factors played a role here: on the one hand, arrests took place on the basis of information from the population above all during the first weeks after the war, while later arrests were conducted primarily following research by the relevant Soviet units or on the basis of wanted person lists.[17] On the other hand, the population initially evidently behaved too incautiously vis-à-vis the orders of the Soviet military headquarters, especially where unauthorized weapons possession was concerned.

During the arrests themselves, Soviet units cooperated in many cases with the Austrian authorities. Thus, Austrian gendarmes and police officers arrested locals on the instructions of the Soviet military headquarters and transferred them to the relevant Soviet department. The sentences themselves were passed either by the MGB Special Commission (OSO) in Moscow or by one of the military tribunals of the formations stationed on Austrian territory. The Soviet Military Tribunal of the Central Group of Forces[18] stationed in Baden near Vienna, i.e., Formation 28990, was responsible for almost half of these convictions of Austrian civilians.[19]

The further fate of the arrestees varied greatly: from a total of 2,367 recorded Austrian civilians, around 15 percent were released again relatively quickly or transferred to the Austrian authorities for further prosecution. Thirty-seven percent were able to return to their homeland following the serving of their sentences; the fate of around 32 percent remains unknown. More than 16 percent never saw their homeland again. If one assumes a total of 1,247 cases whose fate following sentencing is known, then the proportion of those repatriated climbs to 66 percent, of those who died in prison to over 18 percent, of those executed to more than 12 percent and of those who remained in the USSR to almost 2 percent.[20]

Ten, fifteen, and, above all, twenty-five years of imprisonment were the sentences passed most often, whereby the latter was the maximum penalty between April 19, 1947, and January 12, 1950, during which period the death penalty was suspended. From 1950 to 1953, at least 104 victims of Stalin from Austria were executed, among them several Soviet occupation soldiers, stateless people, and Germans who had been on Austrian territory at the time of their arrest. It was first and foremost the Military Tribunal of the Central Group of Forces located in Baden which passed the sentence. The Stalinist legal practice in Austria was characterized by the almost complete secrecy of the proceedings. "Early one morning, he left and never came back," recalls Anna-Maria Melichar from Vienna of the arrest of her brother, Emil Dallapozza.[21]

With their seizure, the arrestees "disappeared" quasi from view for those around them. Neither relatives nor the Austrian authorities received information regarding their fate.[22] Months and years of waiting and the oppressive uncertainty followed this "kidnapping,"[23] as the *Arbeiter-Zeitung* (Workers' Newspaper) characterized the arrests under mysterious circumstances. Anna-Maria Melichar was to learn only in 2007 which fate had befallen her brother. In spite of the tragedy, she is relieved: "One feels a liberation when one knows what happened. It is good that one can now come to terms with it."[24]

From the moment of arrest the mills of the Soviet judicial apparatus and the bureaucracy began to grind—and they ground thoroughly. Although most of the prisoners remained in Austria until their conviction, they belonged—hermetically sealed off from the outside world—to a Soviet microcosm with its own rules. Protracted examinations with countless interrogations, secret debriefings of witnesses and identity parades systematically demoralized the accused. The prevention of all contact to the outside world was a well-directed instrument. In most cases, a confession of one's own "guilt" was only a matter of time.

The procedure was similar in all cases: arrest in the Soviet occupation zone by MGB organs or on their behalf, taking down of personal details, body search, interrogations, identity parades with co-defendants, identification of potential witnesses or suspects, transfer of the case to the Military Tribunal of the Central Group of Forces (Formation 28990), indictment, in some cases decision regarding confinement in an MVD special camp, closed court proceedings in Baden, death sentence, appeal for clemency to the Presidium of the Supreme Soviet, transmission by the Department for Counterintelligence of the MGB, forwarding of the appeal to the Military Council of the Supreme Court of the USSR in Moscow, "suggestion" by the Supreme Court, decision by the Politburo of the Central Committee of the VKP(b) (from 1952: Presidium of the Central Committee of the CPSU) and dispatch via the Presidium of the Supreme Soviet, execution by shooting in Moscow's Butyrka Prison, immediate incineration in the crematorium of the Donskoe Cemetery, and burial of the ashes in the mass grave located there. The next of kin did not receive notification of death until the late 1950s, though with a falsified "natural" cause of death. The true circumstances only came to light five decades later.

ON THE REASONS FOR CONVICTION

Anti-Soviet espionage, crimes against the occupying power, and war crimes were among the primary accusations that led to an arrest in the Soviet zone of Austria. First and foremost, the decree of the Presidium of the Supreme Soviet of the USSR from April 19, 1943, known as "Ukaz 43," and Article 58 of the Criminal Code of the RSFSR or the corresponding article of the Criminal Code of the Ukraine served as the legal basis for the conviction of Austrian civilians. Sentences were passed most often in accordance with Article 58-6 for anti-Soviet espionage: this article was drawn on for 41 percent of men and as many as 67 percent of women. With the continuation of the occupation, the number of convictions for espionage also strikingly increased: from 1950, more than 75 percent of the Austrian civilians were convicted of espionage, whereas cases of "acts of terror" (58-8), "diversionary tactics" (58-9), or "membership in a counterrevolutionary organisation" (58-11) had already declined heavily from 1947 on.[25] During the Cold War, Vienna increasingly developed into a hub of espionage.[26]

ANTI-SOVIET ESPIONAGE

During the first post-war decade, foreign intelligence services had optimal working conditions in Austria. As Austria was occupied until 1955 by occupation troops from the United States, Great Britain, France, and the Soviet Union, there existed military structures of these four states which could be used by their intelligence services. Due to its geographical location, Austria increasingly developed into an area of operations "between the fronts" between West and East during the early Cold War. In the context of operations, Austria was less the "aim" than the "theater" of the incipient antagonism between the later Warsaw Pact and NATO, founded in 1949. Here the activities of the military intelligence services of France, Great Britain, and the United States on the one side and of the Soviet Union on the other clashed with one another.[27]

In the case of the Western intelligence services, emphasis was initially placed on denazification, which was gradually supplanted by the problem of DPs and contrasts with the Soviet occupying power. Each of the three sides struggled with personnel shortages and insufficient training of their staff and attempted to compensate for this in part by recruiting local informants and employees, whereby it was above all financial incentives which were used as "bait." Here the intelligence services benefited from the poor economic situation in post-war Austria: by passing on seemingly harmless information, those recruited could earn the additional money they required to live. Most informants were not aware to which extent one attracted in this way the attention of the counterintelligence of the opposing side and which punishment these activities could entail.[28]

The Soviets were well informed about the activities of the Western intelligence services, above all those of the American CIC (Counter Intelligence

Corps), and monitored the recruited Austrian agents, in some cases for years.[29] They reacted particularly sensitively when the espionage activities affected the following areas: the stationing and transfer of Soviet occupation troops in eastern Austria and Hungary, the activities of the military headquarters or censorship offices, the surveillance of borders and zone intersections, the Communist Party of Austria (KPÖ), the Administration for Soviet Property in Austria (USIA), and the Soviet Mineral Oil Administration (SMV). Even rummaging through rubbish dumps near Soviet troop facilities or the debriefing of former prisoners of war who had been in Soviet custody were regarded as acts of espionage.[30] In the worst case, the death penalty could be passed.

Sometimes, love affairs between Austrian women and Soviet occupation troops proved to be particularly dangerous.[31] The women concerned were confronted with the accusation that they had used their personal contacts on behalf of Western intelligence agencies in order to obtain secret information or to bring about the desertion of Soviet military personnel. As early as July 1945, the Political Section of the NKVD Troops criticized relationships between Soviet officers and foreign women as "politically momentous" and the men in question as "morally unstable." Moscow regarded the Austrian women as a high risk factor, as they sought to elicit military and state secrets from the "captivated" Red Army soldiers by means of their "intimate relations."[32] Traditional Stalinist ways of thinking and concepts of the enemy took effect here. A decisive role was also played, however, by the reality of the Cold War.

The information passed on to Western intelligence services concerned for the most part areas which were generally accessible.[33] By today's standards, they constituted neither military nor state secrets. Even during the occupation period, many of the so-called "agents" underestimated the potential consequences of their activities. Thus, Isabella Lederer, who was sentenced to death and executed in October 1952, declared: "I plead not guilty of having allegedly committed espionage, as the information which I obtained was already well-known in Graz."[34] Michael Maczejka, who was shot in Moscow in May 1951, also stated with regard to his "espionage activity" via a USIA store in Baden near Vienna: "These questions as well as my answers to them appear to me to be completely harmless after all these things had been witnessed in public and were also well-known."[35]

As mentioned above, the seemingly easy money seduced many of those convicted. The Austrian post-war economy was in the doldrums, the black markets had mushroomed and bore no relation to wages, while the housing shortage was substantial. Famine threatened Vienna in 1945. An egg cost 230 shillings on the black market, one-third of Stefan Buger's monthly income. Following his conviction for anti-Soviet espionage, the station inspector of the Austrian Railway set out, therefore, his "financial and material hardship" which a French Secret Service officer had "meanly and shamefully" exploited in 1946: "I had a monthly income of 690 shillings, received nothing on food ration cards, everything only on the black market. 1 kg lard: 400 shillings; sugar: 220 shillings. Flour: 45 shillings; a piece of egg: 230 shillings; meat: 300–350 shillings. Our farmers only exchanged things for a lot of money. My family: undernourished; children were hungry and there were not even the required amounts of bread and fat at home. [. . .] This spy Fucsek[36] gave me 100 shillings as a present the second time we met, the third time 50 shillings, until I succumbed at the fourth meeting."[37]

In return for information on the frequency and cargo of Soviet goods trains on the Eastern Railway Line, Buger allegedly received "4000–5000 shillings in the form of money or as commodities such as lard, flour, sugar etc. at the contraband price."[38] In 1948, following the "disappearance" of Fuczik, he broke off all contact with the Secret Service. What he did not know was that Fuczik had already been sentenced for espionage to twenty-five years in a GULag Corrective Labor Camp (ITL) and had testified against him.[39] Four years later, Buger appeared before the Soviet Military Tribunal in Baden. His execution took place on July 11, 1952.[40]

"WEREWOLF" ACTIVITIES AS A FORM OF "DIVERSIONARY TACTIC" AND "TERRORISM"

While the convictions for espionage continually increased during the course of the occupation period, Soviet military tribunals punished membership in "Werewolf" organizations above all in 1945.[41] The official programme of these groups consisted predominantly of hostilities against the Red Army, assistance in delaying the end of the war, illegal weapons possession following the war, anti-Soviet propaganda as well as acts of sabotage behind the frontline. Stalin's military tribunals subsumed such actions under the terms "diversionary tactics" and "terrorism." Most of the internments of "Werewolf" members took place in Styria, which was only occupied by the Soviets until July 23/24, 1945: here almost 70 percent of all such arrests known in Austria till that point in time took place. In total, the Soviet occupying power sentenced 122 Austrians on the basis of this offence, from which three were executed, seventy-five repatriated or released, and thirty-three died. In eleven cases the fate is unknown.

The small Styrian town of Admont emerged as the center of these activities, where from April 16 to May 5, 1945, a course especially for "Werewolves" was held. This constituted training for the so-called "Freikorps Adolf Hitler," which had been set up on Hitler's orders on March 28, 1945.[42] The participants received rifles and machine guns in order to carry out "diversionary and terror work" in the rear of the Red Army. Although there was no verifiable realization of the planned operations, in May and June 1945 a wave of arrests of former participants of the "Werewolf" course took place. In the arrest of these people, who were termed "saboteurs and terrorists," the 91st Belgorod Border Regiment of the NKVD cooperated with the local population, who in some cases provided concrete clues. Furthermore, a list of participants had evidently fallen into the hands of the Soviet organs: alone on May 30, 1945, one section of the 17th Border Regiment of the NKVD Troops arrested sixteen people who—as was to come out during the interrogations—had likewise been trained on the special courses in Admont on operations in the rear of the Red Army.[43]

ILLEGAL WEAPONS POSSESSIONS IN THE POST-WAR PERIOD

Fear of attacks on Soviet military personnel characterized in particular the early occupation period. The arrest of several Austrian civilians for unauthorized weapons possession is also to be viewed against this backdrop. These people had not handed in their weapons as required due to a need for personal security, anti-Soviet political conviction or because of the unclear regulations on hunting weapons. It was in particular in the context of this offence that anonymous complaints were made repeatedly to the Soviet military headquarters, which then carried out searches of properties. From 1948, such cases sharply declined. For one thing, the population had begun to be more cautious in the way it dealt with this ban; for another thing, from this time on, the investigation of unauthorized weapons possession was increasingly transferred to Austrian authorities.

A particular sensation was caused by the arrest of the Lower Austrian state parliamentarian Franz Gruber, who was convicted in September 1946 of unauthorized weapons possession in accordance with Article 58-14 (Counterrevolutionary Sabotage) and taken to the Soviet Union, where he died in prison in January 1949. The *Arbeiter-Zeitung* in particular devoted itself to this imprisonment, which also caused considerable unrest among the population. The party organ of the Social Democratic Party of Austria (SPÖ) emphasized that although "one or two revolvers" had been found at Gruber's place, the incident constituted "hardly a grave offence in view of the security situation in Lower Austria."[44] The *Arbeiter-Zeitung* furthermore raised the issue of immunity for the delegate,[45] about which the Political Administration of the Central Group of Forces also reported internally in August 1946. According to Soviet sources, however, a positive arsenal had in fact been found at Gruber's place.[46]

The majority of convictions for this offence were initially secured on the basis of Article 58-2 (Revolt, Aggression of Armed Groups) and 58-14 (Counterrevolutionary Sabotage) of the Criminal Code of the RSFSR. This is noteworthy in the sense that today Moscow's Main Military Public Prosecutor frequently does not institute a rehabilitation in such cases but rather a commutation of the sentence—namely in accordance with Article 182-1 (Manufacture, Storage, Purchase and Sale of Explosive Articles or Projectiles as well as Firearms—aside from for Hunting Purposes). The Supreme Court of the Russian Federation, for example, reduced the original sentence of Karl R. to ten years ITL in accordance with Article 58-2 to a sentence of five years ITL on the basis of Article 182-1.[47] Even in the case of Leopold T., who had illegally been in possession of a pistol and sentenced to ten years ITL in accordance with Article 58-14, the Supreme Court retroactively converted his conviction in January 2000 to five years Corrective Labor Camp in accordance with Article 182-1.[48] Gruber was not rehabilitated.

DEATH-INDUCING ALCOHOL AND CAR ACCIDENTS: "CRIMES AGAINST THE OCCUPYING POWER"

Under "Crimes against the Occupying Power," the Austrian Interior Ministry subsumed various offences which were directed—in the widest sense—against Soviet organs in post-war Austria and resulted in an arrest. Serving alcohol injurious to the health counted among these offences, as did affrays with members of the Red Army or traffic accidents which resulted in the death of Soviet military personnel. Even train accidents were in some cases met with convictions by Soviet tribunals. All these offences declined the longer the occupation continued and barely occurred after 1950.[49]

The sale of harmful spirits, like murder in an ambush, was regarded in the eyes of the NKVD as an act of terror.[50] At the end of May 1945, the NKVD Troops warned "that inhabitants of Austria [were] displaying poisonous essences as spirits and selling these to members of the Red Army." The tip-off for this accusation had been provided by the Military Public Prosecutor of the 61st Rifle Division after eighteen soldiers had died of alcohol from a Graz woman. Yet the poisoning was also to have grave consequences for the woman: "The seller of the poisoned alcohol was arrested and is now in the hands of the Section for Counterintelligence of the 61st Rifle Division," as the Commander of the 17th NKVD Border Regiment reported.[51]

A car accident caused by Robert R. and Johann B. on December 4, 1947, in Wiener Neudorf, in which a Soviet car was involved, will serve as an example of convictions following traffic accidents. While the two Austrians remained unhurt, the Soviet vehicle occupants—a city commandant from Vienna among them, allegedly—were injured. The driver of the car, Johann B., reported the incident to the Austrian police and was then transferred to the Soviet authorities. On January 7, 1948, the Military Tribunal of the Central Group of Forces sentenced him in accordance with Article 59-3 of the Criminal Code of the RSFSR for the "violation of discipline at work (violation of traffic law)" to three years ITL.[52] B. did not return, however, until December 1956, five years after serving his original sentence.[53]

His fellow passenger, who had initially remained at the scene of the accident, was arrested by Soviet organs on the spot and taken to the military headquarters. When R. attempted to flee from the military headquarters on December 11, 1947, he threw himself on the Soviet sentry and hit him over the head with a bottle. The Military Tribunal of the Central Group of Forces then sentenced him on December 31, 1947 in accordance with Article 58-8 to fifteen years ITL. R.'s rehabilitation was rejected in 1997 on the grounds that his conviction had been lawful.[54]

WAR CRIMES AND NAZI VIOLENT CRIMES

Around a quarter of the convictions were for offences which had already been committed during the Second World War. Among them were above all the mistreatment of Soviet forced laborers during the Nazi period or crimes against the Soviet civilian population: of the 1,279 civilian convicts whose reason for conviction is so far known, 99 alone were arrested for offences against *Ostarbeiter* (eastern workers) or Soviet prisoners of war and 108 for other war crimes committed on the territory of the Soviet Union.[55] Added to these were an additional sixty former policemen who had carried out killings and maltreatment of Jews in the region of Galicia.[56] In the case of Austrian prisoners of war in Soviet hands, such allegations in fact constituted the most frequent reason for conviction in consequence of their military deployment during the war.

The overwhelming majority of war or Nazi violent crimes were punished in accordance with "ukaz' 43" from April 19, 1943, with the symptomatic title "On Measures for the Punishment of German-Fascist Wrongdoers Who Are Guilty of the Murder and Maltreatment of the Soviet Civilian Population and Captive Red Army Soldiers, as well as the Spies and Traitors among the Soviet Citizens and Accomplices." The "ukaz' 43" had been established only weeks after the Soviet victory in the battle of Stalingrad, when the Soviet Union reckoned on an imminent retaking of the lost territories and the seizure of large contingents of Wehrmacht soldiers as well as "renegade" Red Army soldiers.[57] In this way, the decree threatened in Article 1 not only "German-fascist wrongdoers" who had committed "acts of murder and mistreatment against the Soviet civilian population and captive Red Army soldiers" but also "spies and traitors among the Soviet citizens" with death by hanging. As the death penalty was discontinued between 1947 and 1950, death by hanging was replaced during this period by twenty-five years imprisonment.[58]

An example of such a conviction is the case of Johann E., whom the 95th Rifle Division sentenced on February 27, 1948, to twenty-five years ITL for offences against Soviet prisoners of war in Stalag XVII B Krems-Gneixendorf,[59] the largest prisoner of war camp in the *"Ostmark."*[60] His file in the Austrian Embassy in Moscow reads: "According to a statement by the Russian authorities, the named person is suspected of maltreating Russian prisoners of war and aggrieving their human dignity by exploiting his official power on the occasion of his activity as company leader in the former prisoner of war camp Gneixendorf (Stalag XVII B) during Nazi rule. The named person, who according to his own statement was a member of the NSDAP from 1938, disputed the crimes of which he was accused and claimed that he was transferred to the aforementioned camp as punishment and that he had always treated the prisoners of war humanely, indeed he strove to improve their conditions. On October 25, 1947, E. was taken from Krems by Soviet organs."[61] E. returned to Austria in June 1955 with the 70th repatriation transport.[62] The application for rehabilitation was rejected because of alleged "barbarous treatment of prisoners of war."[63]

Former commanders of POW installations were systematically searched for, as the arrests of, among others, Brigadier Hugo Schäfer,[64] the former commander of POW administration in the Military Districts XXI and XVII, as well as Gustav Grachegg, the former commander of POW administration in the Military District VII, demonstrate. A Soviet military tribunal sentenced the former in September 1945 to death and the sentence was implemented by shooting two months later.[65] At the beginning of 1956, the Soviet Foreign Ministry (MID) gave the official cause of death as "cerebral haemorrhage."[66] A death penalty is also likely in the case of Gustav Grachegg. He is still missing to this day.[67]

More than fifty Austrian policemen, furthermore, were arrested for war crimes[68] and sentenced in accordance with "ukaz' 43," Article 1, to twenty-five years imprisonment for the murder of Soviet citizens of, for the most part, Jewish "nationality" in Galicia.[69] The Vienna District Court had transferred them to the Soviet authorities between 1947 and 1950 for crimes committed in the region of Galicia, in particular in Drohobych, Kolomyia, Ternopil, Boryslav and Ivano-Frankivs'k/Stanyslaviv. Five of them died in prison, two were executed, and the remaining thirty-three were repatriated mostly in the mid-1950s.

In the case of the policeman Josef Gabriel, for example, the reason for the convictions read as follows: "Gabriel Josef, an active Nazi, served from 1940 in occupied Poland in the function of a representative of the Gestapo with the Security Police. In July 1941, Gabriel joined the section of the Security Police and the SD in Drohobych. As consultant within the Jewish department, Gabriel assumed control of mass raids of Soviet citizens of Jewish nationality. In the period 1941 to 1944, tens of thousands of Soviet citizens in Drohobych and in the *rayons* of the region were shot, hanged and transported to camps with the direct participation of Gabriel and under his command. On several occasions, Gabriel took part personally in the shooting of the civilian population in Boryslav. The entire stolen property and the valuables were taken away from the apartments of those arrested and that which had been confiscated from the doomed was shipped on the instructions of Gabriel."[70] Some of these former policemen were against sentenced to terms of imprisonment in two trials before Austrian juries following their return from the Soviet Union.[71]

"MY COUSIN ADOLF HITLER": RELATIONS AS A REASON FOR CONVICTION

Finally, reference should be made to those persons who were only arrested because they were related to Hitler or in a relationship with his relatives. Among them was Otto H., born in 1889 in the Mühlviertel, who was "picked up from his apartment by Soviet organs in plain clothes allegedly to receive information from the Soviet military commander"[72] on May 24, 1945, in Vienna. As a reason for the incident, the Federal Chancellor's Office for Foreign Affairs points to Otto H.'s connection to Hitler's relations: "Otto H. was charged with having been the lover of Adolf Hitler's sister, Paula Hitler. In fact, H. knew Paula Hitler personally for approx. 40 years, as she also came from P. and was a friend of his sister from their schooldays."[73] Otto H. was sentenced in December 1945 to twenty-five years of forced labor in accordance with Control Council Law No. 10. He returned to Austria in June 1955 with the 70th transport.[74]

A similar fate befell the Schmidt family from Spital near Weitra as well as Maria and Ignaz Koppensteiner from Langfeld, cousins of Adolf Hitler.[75] Their then five-year-old son, Adolf, who remains to this day afraid that "the Russians" will "come and get" him, recalls the arrest at the end of the war:

"It was 1945 and immediately after the collapse; the Russians marched into the Waldviertel. [. . .] Suddenly, the Russians were at the door and picked up mother and father. They said they had to bring my parents to Vienna so they could make a statement—I never saw them again; I don't know how they died; I don't even know where they are buried; no letter, not a single message, we heard nothing. Not a day passes that I don't think about my parents at least once."[76]

Maria Koppensteiner was sentenced as a "German-fascist criminal" for "crimes against humanity" to twenty-five years imprisonment. The verdict read: "Court examinations have established that Maria Koppensteiner, relation of Reich Chancellor A. Hitler, approved of his plans directed against the Soviet Union."[77] Some time later, the indictment was altered to "exploitation of Russian prisoners," although no evidence for a deployment of Soviet prisoners of war of civilian workers on the Koppensteiners' farm existed. On August 6, 1953, Maria Koppensteiner died in Soviet imprisonment of "decompensated heart failure." Her husband, Ignaz, had already lost his life on July 5, 1949, due to tuberculosis and failure of the heart vessels. Their only "guilt" was, from the Soviet point of view, being related to Hitler.[78]

RELEASE AND REPATRIATION OF AUSTRIAN CIVILIAN CONVICTS

The fate of a person following their arrest by the Soviet authorities could vary greatly. Many died in the Soviet prisons and camps; in the case of others, more than ten years passed before their repatriation. On occasion, even a release did not necessarily mean a return home. One example of this is the Lower Austrian Herbert Killian, who had been sentenced to three years in the GULag for the several slaps he had given the son of a Soviet occupation officer as a then nineteen-year-old. After serving his sentence, he had to spend another three years as a "freeman" on Kolyma and could only return to Austria following Stalin's death on 1953. The MVD had made the young man the offer of going "on holiday" to Vienna immediately if he assumed Soviet citizenship or being repatriated immediately if he were prepared to work in Austria as a spy. As Killian rejected both, his return was evidently regarded as "not desirable." He remained "imprisoned in liberty" until October 1953.[79]

The Soviet Union amnestied, on the other hand, several of the Austrian civilian convicts and repatriated them to their homeland before they had served their sentence: in April 1948, the Soviet High Commissioner in Austria, Lieutenant General Vladimir Kurasov, proposed an amnesty for a group of civilian convicts from Austria, as "the facts of the crimes committed during this period in the meantime no longer possess any significance in a political sense, but rather, on the contrary, [offer] Austrian as well as American and English reactionary circles the opportunity for negative propaganda against the Soviet element" of the Allied Commission.[80] On April 29, 1948, the Politburo of the Central Committee of the VKP (b) decided to agree to the amnesty of forty-nine Austrian citizens who had been convicted by Soviet military tribunals in Austria for "common crimes"—theft, hooliganism, causing car accidents, or unauthorized weapons possession. The Presidium of the Supreme Soviet of the USSR examined all cases once more and then agreed on December 15, 1948, to the amnesty of a total of thirty-three of these civilian convicts.

The Soviet Foreign Ministry did not remain in the dark either as to the negative effect of arrests on the attitude of the Austrian population toward the occupying power and above all the related news coverage in the Austrian press: "There is no doubt that the arrests of Austrian citizens on the basis of unimportant or unsubstantiated crimes are to the detriment of our policies in Austria,"[81] stated the head of the 3rd European Department of the MID, Andrei Smirnov, in December 1948. In this context, Stalin was informed that a total of 500 Austrian citizens had been convicted by military tribunals since Soviet troops entered Austria, 200 of them for so-called common offences which were not directed against either the Soviet Union or Soviet troops.[82]

A total of seventy-eight official "repatriation transports" with around 65,000 liberated Austrian prisoners of war and civilian convicts were put together during the period from 1947 to 1956.[83] The 60th transport—the first big repatriation train with convicted civilians—arrived in Wiener Neustadt on October 14, 1953, over half a year after Stalin's death. It was striking with regard to the transports carried out from 1953 onward (nos. 60 to 78) that the individual trains consisted of specific categories of prisoner—for example "sick civilians" or those convicted of war crimes. Particular attention was garnered by the 70th transport, with which prominent people like Margarethe Ottillinger, Anton Marek or the former deputy Gauleiter of Vienna, Karl Scharitzer, returned to Austria. All official transports—with the exception of the 73rd (not amnestied) and the 75th (those convicted of war crimes)[84]—were met at Austrian train stations with music and flowers, on which the newspapers generally reported at length in advance.

The repatriation transports arrived until June 25, 1955, in the Austrian "*Heimkehrerstadt*" (repatriation town) of Wiener Neustadt, where a memorial now commemorates the often moving reunion with relatives and friends. After that, only small transports were sent to Austria. The transfer to the Austrian authorities was from now on conducted via the train station at Bad Vöslau. The last regular repatriation train arrived in Austria just before Christmas 1956. Exactly forty years later, Russia began to roll out the sentences passed against Austrians and re-evaluate them.

ON REHABILITATION

In November 1996, the then Foreign Minister of the Russian Federation, Yevgenii Primakov, and the Foreign Minister of the Republic of Austria, Wolfgang Schüssel, agreed to the rehabilitation of Austrian civilians and prisoners of war wrongly convicted in the Soviet Union. For the first time, Russia thus officially recognized the unjust convictions of Austrians (emigrants, members of the *Schutzbund*, communists, prisoners of war, abductees) from the period between 1930 and 1955. In the event of rehabilitation, there was no material but certainly a—at least to a certain extent—moral compensation.

Rehabilitation took place in particular for sentences passed for espionage in accordance with Article 58-6. Even those convicted for acts of terror (58-8) and diversionary tactics (58-9) were frequently rehabilitated. It is striking, on the other hand, how few were rehabilitated in the case of offences punished in accordance with "ukaz' 43." This is linked to the fact that from 1998 practically no rehabilitation took place in the case of these convictions, which were originally for war crimes and not politically motivated crimes.[85] In contrast, all Austrians convicted in accordance with Control Council Law No. 10 were rehabilitated, the aforementioned "Hitler relatives" among them.

It is precisely the rejection of applications for rehabilitation that demonstrates that among the groups discussed here there were without doubt people who had committed very serious crimes. By no means all judgments passed by Soviet authorities were blanket politically motivated miscarriages. One can cite as an example the negative notification of rehabilitation for the aforementioned former policeman Gabriel, for whom a personal role in the shooting of Jews in Boryslav can be proven. Having said that, a connection cannot always be made between rehabilitation and a wrongful conviction or innocence, and vice versa. Formal juridical criteria, among other things, are too multilayered here.

In 1956, the last Austrian civilian convicts returned to their homeland, among them some persons who had been sentenced to death but pardoned after Stalin's demise. In this year, the relatives of those executed received the first notification of death from the Soviet Union—with falsified causes of death. The post-Stalinist system also attempted for decades to camouflage the wrongful convictions. Yet even the circumstances of the arrests and the convictions of the roughly one thousand Austrian civilian convicts as well as the fastidious records made during the time spent in the prisons and camps of the GULag could not be allowed to get out. Only through the partial opening of the Russian archives at the beginning of the 1990s did it become possible to shed light on this dark chapter of the Soviet occupation of Austria.

STATISTICAL ANALYSES

Table 8.1. Place of Arrest of Austrian Civilians According to Federal State and Year (based on information from 1914 cases)

Year	Vienna		Lower Austria		Burgenland		Mühlviertel (Upper Austria)		Styria (Occupied by the Soviets until July 1945)		Total	Female	Male
	Female	Male	Female	Male	Female	Male	Female	Male	Female	Male			
1945	12	154	6	212	3	32	1	51	6	237	714	28	686
1946	9	51	14	181		18	2	13			288	25	263
1947	8	83	5	63		13	1	9			182	14	168
1948	21	83	21	86		8	3	16			238	45	193
1949	8	37	10	47	3	11	1	15			132	22	110
1950	14	52	32	92	2	9	6	29			236	54	182
1951	5	22	2	21		2	1	5			58	8	50
1952	3	15	1	6							25	4	21
1953		15	3	6							24	3	21
1954		4		4			3	3			14	3	11
1955		2				1					3		3
Total	80	518	94	718	8	94	18	141	6	237	1914	206	1708

Source: AdBIK, Database of Austrian Convicted Civilians in the USSR.

Table 8.2. Authority Responsible for Conviction of Austrian Civilians

Court	Number	Proportion in Percent
War's end, 1945 (2nd Ukrainian Front)	18	2
War's end (Southern Group of Forces/3rd Ukrainian Front (26th, 27th, and 57th Armies)	92	9
Soviet Occupation Zone 1945 to 1955	673	68
Other Army departments	27	3
Soviet Union: MGB (NKVD-MVD), mostly in Moscow	180	18
Total	**990**	**100**

Table 8.3. Fate of Austrian Civilians Following Their Arrest by Soviet Organs, 1945 to 1955

Fate Following Arrest	Female	Male	Total
Arrested on the orders of the Soviet Union, but never handed over	15	4	19
Released before being transferred to the USSR	31	169	200
Probably released	14	74	88
Transfer from Soviet bodies to Austrian authorities verified	5	43	48
Repatriated following imprisonment	99	732	831
Died in imprisonment	7	225	232
Executed	11	148	159
Remained in the USSR following imprisonment	7	18	25
Still missing today	79	685	764
Total	**268**	**2,098**	**2,366**

Table 8.4. Extent of Sentence against Convicted Austrian Civilians (based on information from 1,130 cases)

Extent of Sentence	Female	Proportion in Percent	Male	Proportion in Percent
Acquittal/Probation	0	0.0%	4	0.4
2 to 9 years	16	14.7%	157	15.4
10 to 14 years	20	18.3%	279	27.3
15 to 19 years	17	15.6%	104	10.2
20 years	4	3.7%	51	5.0
25 years	40	36.7%	241	23.6
Death penalty (repealed)	1	0.9%	37	3.6
Death penalty	11	10.1%	148	14.5
Total	**109**	**100%**	**1,021**	**100**

Table 8.5. Convictions of Male Austrian Civilians According to Selected Charges (based on information from 1279 cases)

Reason for Conviction (Male Detainees)

Year	Espionage	"Werewolf"	Weapons Possession	Former "Citizen" of the Soviet Union	Maltreatment of "Eastern Workers" or POWs	Other War Crime	Criminal Activity	Violent Crimes / Affray	Policemen Involved in Persecution of Jews in Galicia	Alcohol	Number
1945	56	191	31		54	22	4	23		10	391
1946	17		64		23	26	27	42	1	1	201
1947	32	1	22	1	6	23	18	28	22	1	154
1948	76	1	13	9	4	19	17	4	15		158
1949	40		1	3	6	11	8	2	14		85
1950	51		20	1	4	7	8	6	8		105
1951	37				1		3				41
1952	16										16
1953	15		2				1				18
1954	1						2				3
1955	2										2
Total	343	193	153	14	98	108	88	105	60	12	1174

Table 8.6. Convictions of Female Austrian Civilians According to Selected Charges (based on information from 1279 cases)

				Reason for Conviction (Female Detainees)							
Year	Espionage	"Werewolf"	Weapons Possession	Former "Citizen" of the Soviet Union	Maltreatment of "Eastern Workers" or POWs	Other War Crime	Criminal Activity	Violent Crimes / Affray	Policemen Involved in Persecution of Jews in Galicia	Alcohol	Number
1945	5			1	1			1		1	11
1946	5		2	2			1				10
1947	7			1			1				9
1948	23			5			3				32
1949	8		1	3			2	1			14
1950	22			2							24
1951	2										3
1952	2										2
1953											
1954											
1955											
Total	74		3	14	1		8	2		1	105

Table 8.7. Release or Repatriation of Convicted Austrian Civilians in Soviet Imprisonment, 1945 to 1956 (based on information from 898 cases)

Year	Number
1945	55
1946	24
1947	1
1948	17
1949	37
1950	12
1951	1
1952	15
1953	237
1954	24
1955	422
1956	53
Total	**898**

Table 8.8. The Official Austrian Repatriation Transports from the Soviet Union 1953 to 1956. Information provided by the Austrian Ministry of the Interior

The Official Austrian Repatriation Transports in the Years 1953–1956

Date of Repatriation	Transport Number	Characteristics of the Transport	Civilians	Prisoners of War
14.10.1953	60	Largest transport since January 1950	210	420
1954	61–64	Small transports with civilians and convicted prisoners of war	11	12
28.12.1954	65	Ethnic Germans ("Volksdeutsche")	55	0
03.02.1955	66	Small transport with sick civilians	4	0
29.04.1955	67	First transport following the State Treaty; civilians	15	0
04.06.1955	68	Large transport with convicted prisoners of war	0	250
20.06.1955	69	Civilians, convicted prisoners of war	142	42
25.06.1955	70	Mass of civilians, "notables," a few convicted prisoners of war	180	6
08.07.1955	71	Civilians who had been forcibly settled in the USSR after serving their sentences	16	0
21.07.1955	72	Ethnic German prisoners of war and civilians	25	1
06.08.1955	73	Not amnestied	70	3
01.09.1955	74	Small transport with civilians and convicted prisoners of war	7	2
16.11.1955	75	Handed over to the Austrian authorities without an official welcome. Primarily convicted war criminals, inc. policemen in Galicia	48	2
18.12.1955	76	Small transport with civilians and convicted prisoners of war	3	14
25.04.1956	77	Small transport with civilians and convicted prisoners of war	4	3
23.12.1956	78	Small transport with civilians; many non-Austrians	19	0
Total			809	755

Table 8.9. Stations at Which the Official Austrian Repatriation Transports from the Soviet Union Arrived, 1953 to 1956

Transport Number	Station
60–70	Wiener Neustadt
only 64	Vienna, Ostbahnhof
71–75	Bad Vöslau
76	Salzburg
77	Rattersdorf in Burgenland
78	Vienna, Ostbahnhof

Table 8.10. Results of Rehabilitation Proceedings for Austrian Civilian Convicts to Date (based on information from 651 cases)

Result of Rehabilitation Proceedings	Number	Percentage
Rehabilitated	481	73.9
Commutation of original verdict	28	4.3
Not rehabilitated	102	15.7
No decision due to incomplete records	40	6.1
Total	651	100

NOTES

1. Archives of the Ludwig Boltzmann Institute for Research on Consequences of War (hereafter AdBIK), Database of Austrian Civilian Convicts in the USSR. This contribution is based on: Harald Knoll and Barbara Stelzl-Marx, "Sowjetische Strafjustiz in Österreich. Verhaftungen und Verurteilungen 1945–1955," in Stefan Karner and Barbara Stelzl-Marx, eds., *Die Rote Armee in Österreich. Sowjetische Besatzung 1945–1955. Beiträge* (Graz/Vienna/Munich: Oldenbourg, 2005), pp. 275–321. Thanks to further information from Russian archives, the number of Austrian civilian convicts could be concretized further.

2. See, among others, Stefan Karner, ed., *Geheime Akten des KGB. "Margarita Ottillinger"* (Graz: Leykam, 1992); Stefan Karner, *Im Kalten Krieg der Spionage. Margarethe Ottillinger in sowjetischer Haft 1948-1955* (Innsbruck/Vienna/Bolzano: StudienVerlag 2016).

3. See, among others, Harald Knoll and Barbara Stelzl-Marx, "Die Fälle Marek und Kiridus. Zur sowjetischen Strafjustiz in Österreich," in Stefan Karner and Gottfried Stangler, eds., *"Österreich ist frei!" Der Österreichische Staatsvertrag* (Horn/Vienna: Berger, 2005), pp. 143–147.

4. Gerald Stourzh, *Um Einheit und Freiheit: Staatsvertrag, Neutralität und das Ende der Ost-West-Besetzung Österreichs 1945–1955*, Vol. 62 of Studien zu Politik und Verwaltung series, 4th completely revised and expanded edition (Graz/Vienna/Cologne: Böhlau, 1998), pp. 140–142. Manfred Fuchs, *Der österreichische Geheimdienst. Das zweitälteste Gewerbe der Welt* (Vienna: Ueberreiter, 1994), pp. 133–135.

5. Stefan Karner and Barbara Stelzl-Marx, eds., *Stalins letzte Opfer. Verschleppte und erschossene Österreicher in Moskau 1950–1953* (Vienna/Munich: Böhlau, 2009).

6. See, among others, Andreas Hilger and Mike Schmeitzner, "Einleitung: Deutschlandpolitik und Strafjustiz: Zur Tätigkeit sowjetischer Militärtribunale in Deutschland 1945–1955," in Andreas Hilger, Mike Schmeitzner and Ute Schmidt, eds., *Die Verurteilung deutscher Zivilisten 1945–1955. Sowjetische Militärtribunale*, Vol. 2 (Cologne/Weimar/Vienna: Böhlau, 2003), pp. 7–34.

7. Initial indications of the problem of abductions by Soviet organs can be found in: Manfried Rauchensteiner, *Der Sonderfall. Die Besatzungszeit in Österreich 1945 bis 1955* (Graz/Vienna/Cologne: Böhlau, 1995); Manfried Rauchensteiner, *Stalinplatz 4. Österreich unter alliierter Besatzung* (Vienna: Edition Steinbauer, 2005); William L. Stearman, *The Soviet Union and the Occupation of Austria: An Analysis of Soviet Policy in Austria, 1945–1955* (Geneva: Siegler, 1961).

8. Karner, *Geheime Akten*.

9. See, among others, Edda Engelke, "Zum Thema Spionage gegen die Sowjetunion," in Erwin A. Schmidl, ed., *Österreich im frühen Kalten Krieg 1945–1958. Spione, Partisanen, Kriegspläne* (Vienna/Cologne/Weimar: Böhlau, 2000), pp. 119–136.

10. See, among others, Stefan Karner, "'Ich bekam zehn Jahre Zwangsarbeit.' Zu den Verschleppungen aus der Steiermark durch sowjetische Organe im Jahr 1945," in Siegfried Beer, ed., *Die "britische Steiermark." Forschungen zur geschichtlichen Landeskunde der Steiermark*, Vol. 38 (Graz: Historische Landeskommission, 1995), pp. 249–259.

11. Stefan Karner and Barbara Stelzl, "Strafrechtssystem und Gerichtspraxis in der Sowjetunion 1941–1956. Teilstudie des Projektes 'Die Nachkriegsgerichtsbarkeit als nicht-bürokratische Form der Entnazifizierung: Österreichische Justizakten im europäischen Vergleich,'" unpublished manuscript, Graz, 1998; Stefan Karner, "Die sowjetische Gewahrsamsmacht und ihre Justiz nach 1945 gegenüber Österreichern," in Claudia Kuretsidis-Haider and Winfried R. Garscha, eds., *Keine "Abrechnung." NS-Verbrechen, Justiz und Gesellschaft in Europa nach 1945* (Leipzig/Vienna: Akademische Verlagsanstalt, 1998), pp. 102–129.

12. Barbara Stelzl-Marx, "Entnazifizierung in Österreich: Die Rolle der sowjetischen Besatzungsmacht," in Wolfgang Schuster and Wolfgang Weber, eds., *Entnazifizierung im regionalen Bereich* (Linz: Archiv der Stadt Linz, 2004), pp. 431–454.

13. See, among others, Stefan Karner, "Schuld und Sühne? Der Prozess gegen den Chef der Gendarmerie von Černigov von 1941–1943: Karl Ortner," in Stefan Karner, ed., *Graz in der NS-Zeit 1938–1945*, Special Vol. 1 of Veröffentlichungen des Ludwig Boltzmann-Instituts für Kriegsfolgen-Forschung series (Graz: Selbstverlag, 1999), pp. 159–178; Barbara Stelzl-Marx, "Kolyma—Jahre in Stalins Besserungsar-

beitslagern," in Norbert Weigl, ed., *Faszinationen der Forstgeschichte. Festschrift für Herbert Killian*, Vol. 42 of Schriftenreihe des Instituts für Sozioökonomik der Forst- und Holzwirtschaft (Vienna: Eigenverlag, 2001), pp. 147–160.

14. On this see, among others, Nikita Petrov, "Die Inneren Truppen des NKVD/ MVD im System der sowjetischen Repressionsorgane in Österreich 1945–1946," in Karner and Stelzl-Marx, eds., *Die Rote Armee in Österreich*, pp. 219–242; Ol'ga Lavinskaja, "Zum Tode verurteilt. Gnadengesuche österreichischer Zivilisten an den Obersten Sowjet der UdSSR," in Karner and Stelzl-Marx, eds., *Die Rote Armee in Österreich*, pp. 323–338; Barbara Stelzl-Marx, *Stalins Soldaten in Österreich. Die Innensicht der sowjetischen Besatzung 1945–1955*. (Vienna/Munich: Oldenborg/ Böhlau, 2012), pp. 353–466, 487–465.

15. Karner and Stelzl-Marx, eds., *Stalins letzte Opfer*; Barbara Stelzl-Marx, "Death to Spies. Austrian Informants for Western Intelligence Services and Soviet Capital Punishment during the Occupation of Austria," in: *Journal of Cold War Studies*, Vol. 14, No. 4, Fall 2012, pp. 167–196.

16. This figure was calculated on the basis of a population of 2,091,215 people living in the Soviet zone of Austria in 1946, whereby the percentage of arrestees relates to the entire period from 1945 to 1955 and not just the year 1946. The total number results from 2,039,500 people who lived in the Soviet zone of Austria in 1946 and 51,715 people who lived in the Soviet zone of Vienna during the same year. The population figure for the whole of Austria in this year came to 6,999,500 people. See "Die wirtschaftliche Lage Österreichs am Ende des ersten Nachkriegsjahrzehntes," in *Monatsberichte des österreichischen Institutes für Wirtschaftsforschung*, Vol. XIX, No. 1–6, issued on July 31, 1946, pp. 5 and 50.

17. Karner, *Schuld und Sühne*, pp. 164–165.

18. Ol'ga Lavinskaja, "Das Militärtribunal der Zentralen Gruppe der Sowjetischen Streitkräfte und die Verurteilung von Personen nicht-österreichischer Staatsangehörigkeit," in Karner and Stelzl-Marx, eds., *Stalins letzte Opfer*, pp. 205–224.

19. AdBIK, Database of Austrian Civilian Convicts in the USSR.

20. Ibid.

21. Tessa Szyszkowitz, "Stalins letzte Opfer," *Profil*, February 12, 2007, pp. 34–41, here p. 34.

22. On the analogous approach in Germany see Andreas Hilger, "Strafjustiz im Verfolgungswahn. Todesurteile sowjetischer Gerichte in Deutschland," in Andreas Hilger, ed., *"Tod den Spionen!" Todesurteile sowjetischer Gerichte in der SBZ/DDR und in der Sowjetunion bis 1953* (Göttingen: V&R unipress, 2006), pp. 95–156, here p. 97.

23. "Doppelter Menschenraub in Wien," *Arbeiter Zeitung*, April 8, 1951, p. 3.

24. AdBIK, Anna-Maria Melichar, with thanks for the information provided to Barbara Stelzl-Marx, Vienna 17.3.2008.

25. AdBIK, Database of Austrian Civilian Convicts.

26. Erwin A. Schmidl, ed., *Österreich im frühen Kalten Krieg 1945–1958. Spione, Partisanen, Kriegspläne* (Vienna/Cologne/Weimar: Böhlau, 2000); Harald Irnberger, *Nelkenstrauß ruft Praterstern. Am Beispiel Österreich: Funktion und Arbeitsweise*

geheimer Nachrichtendienste in einem neutralen Staat (Vienna: promedia, 1983); Fuchs, *Der österreichische Geheimdienst.*

27. On this see, for example, Günter Bischof, *Austria in the First Cold War, 1945–1955: The Leverage of the Weak* (London/New York: Macmillan Press/St. Martin's Press, 1999); Dieter Bacher and Harald Knoll, "Nachrichtendienste und Spionage im Österreich der Besatzungszeit," in Karner and Stelzl-Marx, eds., *Stalins letzte Opfer*, pp. 157–168.

28. Dieter Bacher and Harald Knoll, "Spione und Stalinopfer. Die Rolle österreichischer Zivilisten in den Aktivitäten ausländischer Nachrichtendienste in Österreich 1950–1953," in ACIPSS, ed., *JIPSS (Journal for Intelligence, Propaganda and Security Studies)*, Vol. 2 (2008), No. 2 (Graz: ACIPSS, 2008), pp. 99–108.

29. Thus, Herbert B., for example, was already mentioned in a secret service report from March 1948 in connection with the CIC-430. He was arrested five years later, in February 1953, and sentenced by the Military Tribunal of the Central Group of Forces in Baden. On this see: Central Archives of the Federal Security Service of the Russian Federation (hereafter TsA FSB RF), F. 135, op. 1, d. 37, ll. 100–106.

30. Discarded envelopes belonging to Soviet military personnel ultimately provided information on the names of occupation soldiers or the numbers of troop units. This "espionage activity" was to prove the undoing of at least two Austrians— Wilfried Hejl and Roman Ryzewski.

31. On this see: Stelzl-Marx, *Stalins Soldaten in Österreich*, pp. 487–495.

32. Russian State Military Archives (hereafter RGVA), F. 32902, op. 1, d. 11, ll. 158–159, Directive No. 00811 from the head of the Political Section of the NKVD Troops for the Protection of the Rear Area of the 3rd Ukrainian Front on an improvement in educational work within the ranks, 4.7.1945, reprinted in: Stefan Karner, Barbara Stelzl-Marx and Alexander Tschubarjan, eds., *Die Rote Armee in Österreich. Sowjetische Besatzung 1945–1955. Dokumente* (Graz/Vienna/Munich: Oldenbourg, 2005), Doc. 64.

33. See in detail Stelzl-Marx, "Death to Spies."

34. State Archives of the Russian Federation (hereafter GARF), F. 7523, op. 76, d. 108, ll. 140–147, here l. 146, Statement by the Supreme Court on the Appeals for Clemency by Isabella Lederer and Rold Ravenegg, 23.8.1952.

35. GARF, F. 7523, op. 76, d. 15, ll. 157–158, here l. 158, Appeal for Clemency by Michael Maczejka, 19.1.1951.

36. Actually "Fuczik."

37. Quoted from: Barbara Stelzl-Marx, "Verschleppt und erschossen. Eine Einführung," in Karner and Stelzl-Marx, eds., *Stalins letzte Opfer*, pp. 21–78, here p. 69.

38. GARF, F. 7523, op. 76, d. 95, ll. 74–76, Appeal for Clemency by Stefan Buger, 1.4.1952.

39. GARF, F. 7523, op. 76, d. 95, ll. 66–68, here l. 67, Statement by the Supreme Court on the Appeal for Clemency by Stefan Buger, 1.4.1952.

40. Edith Petschnigg, "Stimmen aus der Todeszelle. Kurzbiographien der Opfer," in Karner and Stelzl-Marx, eds., *Stalins letzte Opfer*, pp. 301–588, here pp. 333–335.

41. On the "Werwolf": Perry Biddiscombe, *The Last Nazis. SS Werewolf Guerilla Resistance in Europe 1944–1947* (Stroud: Tempus, 2004); Volker Koop,

Himmlers letztes Aufgebot. Die NS-Organisation "Werwolf" (Vienna/Cologne/ Weimar: Böhlau, 2008).

42. "I decree the formation of a Freikorps 'Adolf Hitler,' which is to consist of activists from the movement, volunteers from the *Volkssturm* [home guard] and volunteers from the *Werkschar* [works troop]. Everyone who is over 18 years of age and volunteers must be released by the Party, the *Volkssturm* and by businesses. I entrust the Reich Organisation Leader of the NSDAP, Party Comrade Ley, with the formation of this volunteer corps and its leadership." Quoted from: Martin Moll, ed., *"Führer-Erlasse" 1939–1945. Edition sämtlicher überlieferter, nicht im Reichsgesetzblatt abgedruckter, von Hitler während des Zweiten Weltkrieges schriftlich erteilter Direktiven aus den Bereichen Staat, Partei, Wirtschaft, Besatzungspolitik und Militärverwaltung* (Stuttgart: Franz Steiner, 1997), pp. 488–489.

43. Natal'ja Eliseeva, "Zum Schutz des Hinterlandes der Roten Armee. Der Einsatz der NKVD-Truppen in Österreich von April bis Juli 1945," in Karner and Stelzl-Marx, eds., *Die Rote Armee in Österreich*, pp. 91–104; Karner, "'Ich bekam zehn Jahre Zwangsarbeit.'"

44. Quoted from: Herbert Killian, "Im GULAG von Kolyma. Betroffene erzählen," in Harald Knoll, Peter Ruggenthaler and Barbara Stelzl-Marx, eds., *Konflikte und Kriege im 20. Jahrhundert. Aspekte ihrer Folgen* (Graz: Eigenverlag, 2003), pp. 73–90, here p. 85. On the fate of Gruber's daughter, Helene Gruber, married Elena Bondarewa, who was arrested in 1946 for "cognisance" and only returned with her three children to Austria from the Soviet Union in 1960 see ibid., pp. 85–89.

45. "Die Verhaftung des Abgeordneten Gruber," *Arbeiter-Zeitung*, July 17, 1946, p. 2.

46. Russian State Archives for Socio-Political History (hereafter RGASPI), F. 17, op. 128, d. 118, ll. 216–218, reprinted in: Karner, Stelzl-Marx and Tschubarjan, eds., *Die Rote Armee in Österreich, Dokumente*, Doc. 99.

47. Supreme Court of the Russian Federation (hereafter VSRF), Notification 1n-01812/p-52, Karl R. Moscow 13.1.2000.

48. VSRF, Notification 1n-02279/p-52, Leopold T. Moscow 13.1.2000.

49. On this see also Stelzl-Marx, *Stalins Soldaten in Österreich*, pp. 454–466.

50. RGVA, F. 32900, op. 1, d. 211, ll. 169–172, Working Plan for the Administration of NKVD Troops for the Protection of the Rear Area of the 3rd Ukrainian Front for July 1945, confirmed by the Deputy Head of the NKVD Troops for the Protection of the Rear Area of the 3rd Ukrainian Front, Colonel Semenenko, 3.7.1945, reprinted in: Stefan Karner and Othmar Pickl, eds., *Die Rote Armee in der Steiermark. Sowjetische Besatzung 1945* (Graz: Leykam, 2008), Doc. 103.

51. RGVA, F. 32902, op. 1, d. 104, l. 240, Operational Daily Report No. 00146 from the Commander of the 17th NKVD Border Regiment, Colonel Pavlov, 30.5.1945, reprinted in: Karner and Pickl, eds., *Die Rote Armee in der Steiermark*, Doc. 82. See Siegfried Beer, "Das sowjetische 'Intermezzo.' Die Russenzeit in der Steiermark 8. Mai bis 23. Juli 1945," in Joseph F. Desput, ed., *Vom Bundesland zur Europäischen Region. Die Steiermark von 1945 bis heute* (Graz: Historische Landeskommission, 2004), pp. 35–59, here p. 49. Stelzl-Marx, "Die Innensicht der sowjetischen Besatzung," p. 319.

52. Main Military Public Prosecution Office of the Russian Federation (hereafter GVP), Notification of Rehabilitation 5uv-835-97, Johann B. Moscow 9.9.1997.
53. Austrian Embassy in Moscow (hereafter ÖBM), Personnel File Johann B.
54. GVP, Notification of Rehabilitation 41-N, Robert R. Kaliningrad, 19.8.1997.
55. Marschall sums up offences committed against prisoners of war and "*Fremdarbeiter*" (foreign workers) before the end of the war as "violations of the international laws of war." Karl Marschall, *Volksgerichtsbarkeit und Verfolgung von nationalsozialistischen Gewaltverbrechen in Österreich* (Vienna: Bundesministerium für Justiz, 1987), pp. 76–77. On forced labour in Austria see, among others, Stefan Karner and Peter Ruggenthaler, *Zwangsarbeit in der Land- und Forstwirtschaft auf dem Gebiet der Republik Österreich 1939–1945*. Veröffentlichungen der Österreichischen Historikerkommission. Vermögensentzug während der NS-Zeit sowie Rückstellungen und Entschädigungen seit 1945 in Österreich). Vol. 26/2. (Vienna/Munich: Oldenbourg, 2004).
56. AdBIK, Database of Austrian Civilian Convicts.
57. Andreas Hilger, Nikita Petrov and Günther Wagenlehner, "Der 'Ukas 43': Entstehung und Problematik des Dekrets des Präsidiums des Obersten Sowjets vom 19. April 1943," in Andreas Hilger, Ute Schmidt and Günther Wagenlehner, eds., *Sowjetische Militärtribunale. Band 1: Die Verurteilung deutscher Kriegsgefangener 1941–1953* (Cologne/Weimar/Vienna: Böhlau, 2001), pp. 177–209.
58. Stefan Karner, *Im Archipel GUPVI. Kriegsgefangenschaft und Internierung in der Sowjetunion 1941–1956* (Vienna: Oldenbourg, 1995), p. 176.
59. On the history of the Stalag XVII B Krems-Gneixendorf see, among others, Barbara Stelzl-Marx, *Zwischen Fiktion und Zeitzeugenschaft. Amerikanische und sowjetische Kriegsgefangene im Stalag XVII B Krems-Gneixendorf* (Tübingen: Gunter Narr, 2000); Barbara Stelzl-Marx, ed., *Unter den Verschollenen. Erinnerungen von Dmitrij Čirov an das Kriegsgefangenenlager Krems-Gneixendorf 1941 bis 1945*, Vol. 43 of Schriftenreihe des Waldviertler Heimatbundes (Horn/Waidhofen/Thaya: Waldviertler Heimatbund, 2003); Hubert Speckner, *In der Gewalt des Feindes. Kriegsgefangenenlager in der "Ostmark" 1939 bis 1945*, Vol. 3 of Kriegsfolgen-Forschung series (Vienna/Munich: Oldenbourg, 2003), pp. 228ff.
60. Barbara Stelzl-Marx, "Ein ganz normaler Kriegsverbrecher? Der Prozesse gegen den ehemaligen Lagerkassier des Stalag XVII B Krems-Gneixendorf," in Stefan Karner and Vjačeslav Selemenev, eds., *Österreicher und Sudetendeutsche vor sowjetischen Militär- und Strafgerichten in Weißrussland 1945–1950. Avstriiskie i sudetskie nemtsy pered sovetskimi voennymi tribunalami v Belarusi 1945–1950 gg.* (Graz/Minsk: Selbstverlag, 2007), pp. 368–406.
61. ÖBM, Personnel File Johann E.
62. AdBIK, Database of Austrian Civilian Convicts.
63. GVP, Notification of Rehabilitation 5uv-6188-48, Johann E. Moscow 8.7.1998.
64. Marcel Stein, *Österreichs Generäle 1938–1945 im Deutschen Heer. Schwarz/Gelb—Rot/Weiß/Rot—Hakenkreuz* (Bissendorf: Biblio, 2002), p. 94.
65. AdBIK, Database of Austrian Civilian Convicts.
66. ÖBM, Personnel File Hugo Schäfer.
67. AdBIK, Database of Austrian Civilian Convicts.

68. Ibid.

69. On the murders of Jews in Galicia see, among others: Dieter Pohl, *Nationalsozialistische Judenverfolgung in Ostgalizien 1941–1944. Organisation und Durchführung eines staatlichen Massenverbrechens* (München: Oldenbourg, 1996); Thomas Sandkühler, *"Endlösung" in Galizien. Der Judenmord in Ostpolen und die Rettungsinitiativen von Berthold Beitz 1941–1944* (Bonn: Dietz, 1996).

70. RGVA, F. 461, Personnel File No. 190400, Josef Gabriel.

71. On July 26, 1956, Leopold Mittas was sentenced to life imprisonment and Josef Pöll to twenty years imprisonment. Four additional defendants in this trial were acquitted. See Marschall, *Volksgerichtsbarkeit*, pp. 158–164.

72. ÖBM, Personnel File Otto H.

73. Ibid.

74. AdBIK, Database of Austrian Civilian Convicts, Otto H.

75. Wilhelm Romeder, *Das Jahr 1945 in Weitra und Umgebung. Ereignisse. Erlebnisse. Schicksale. Mit einem ausführlichen Beitrag über die Hitler-Verwandten* (Horn: Berger, 2003), pp. 99–128; Wolfgang Zdral, *Die Hitlers. Die unbekannte Familie des Führers* (Frankfurt am Main: Campus, 2005); Jean-Paul Mulders, *Auf der Suche nach Hitlers Sohn. Eine Beweisaufnahme* (Munich: Herbig, 2009).

76. "Hitlers letzte Verwandte," *News*, 08/2010, pp. 34–39, here p. 38.

77. Quoted from: Romeder, *Das Jahr 1945 in Weitra*, p. 71.

78. Ibid.

79. See Stelzl-Marx, "Kolyma," pp. 156–157; Herbert Killian, *Geraubte Freiheit. Ein Österreicher verschollen in Nordostsibirien* (Berndorf: Kral, 2008); Herbert Killian, *Geraubte Jahre. Ein Österreicher verschleppt in den GULAG* (Vienna: Amalthea, 2005); Herbert Killian, *Geraubte Jugend. Ein Österreicher kehrt zurück aus Sibirien* (Berndorf: Kral, 2010).

80. Foreign Policy Archives of the Russian Federation (hereafter AVP RF), F. 066, op. 29, p. 137, d. 15, l. 103, reprinted in: Karner, Stelzl-Marx and Tschubarjan, eds., *Die Rote Armee in Österreich, Dokumente*, Doc. 107.

81. AVP RF, F. 066, op. 29, p. 137, d. 15, l. 102, reprinted in: Karner, Stelzl-Marx and Tschubarjan, eds., *Die Rote Armee in Österreich, Dokumente*, Doc. 108.

82. RGASPI, F. 17, op. 3, d. 1071, Politburo Resolution No. P 64 (95) of the Central Committee of the VKP(b) from 29.6.1948, Ruling of Amnesty for 49 convicted Austrians; RGASPI, F. 17, op. 163, d. 1513, ll. 34–35, Proposal by Molotov to Stalin to amnesty the 49 Austrians, reprinted in: Karner, Stelzl-Marx and Tschubarjan, eds., *Die Rote Armee in Österreich, Dokumente*, Doc. 107.

83. Federal Ministry of the Interior, Repatriation Lists. On the repatriation of Austrian prisoners of war from the USSR see Karner, *Im Archipel GUPVI*, pp. 187–201.

84. "73 kehrten aus Schweigelagern heim," in *Kleine Zeitung*, August 7, 1955.

85. VSRF, Notification 2-001/48, Walter H. Moscow 17.2.1998.

Chapter Nine

Ivan's Children

The Consequences of Sexual Relations between Red Army Soldiers and Austrian Women

Barbara Stelzl-Marx

"Children of Occupation: A Global Problem" (*Besatzungskinder – ein Weltproblem*) was how the *Arbeiter-Zeitung* titled an article from November 1955 and declared: "Wherever foreign soldiers—as allies or as conquerors—make contact with the population of a country, illegitimate children are born. That was the case at the time of the Roman legions and nothing will change in this respect for a long time to come."[1] The occasion for this publication was the material poverty and moral difficulties in the form of discrimination and stigmatization which "half-breed children" in Austria had to suffer. This was abetted, however, by the article itself through its emphasis on their "otherness": "The coffee-brown Lizzi from Linz" read the subheading and it continued: "Lizzi was born nine years ago in Linz; as the child of an Austrian mother and a coloured soldier of the occupying power. She was born with all the characteristics of a jigaboo: milk coffee-brown skin, big, dark saucer eyes and a black frizzled shock of hair. Her mother never knew her."[2]

So-called children of occupation (*Besatzungskinder*) were born in all four zones in Germany and Austria: as a result of voluntary sexual relations between local women and members of the occupation forces, but also as a result of rape. They were in many cases regarded as "children of the enemy,"[3] although the fathers were de jure no longer enemies, and were generally subjected to different forms of discrimination. Their "shame" not only consisted of having been born illegitimately or out of wedlock, but also of having had the "wrong" father. Often they constituted in this way an "ideal" contact surface for racial, ideological, and moral prejudices. "Russian child" (*Russenkind*) or "Russian brat" (*Russenbalg*) were still commonplace swearwords in the 1960s.[4] Children of occupation soldiers, who were—and still are—born in all occupied countries, are frequently regarded as "occupation damages."[5]

SEXUAL RELATIONS AND THEIR CONSEQUENCES

In particular at the end of the war and during the early post-war period, Soviet soldiers were all but omnipresent in their occupation zone. As the victors, they dominated public life, intruded into the private sphere and regarded—at least to a certain extent—women as their "booty." Furthermore, there existed every form of professional and semi-professional prostitution, whereby in view of the material asymmetry between soldiers and local women, the borders between free will and force can no longer be clearly drawn. Parallel to this dark side of everyday life under occupation, a broad spread of erotic approaches between local women and Soviet army personnel developed, which ranged from flirts via love attachments for the duration of deployment to—in exceptional cases—marriage.[6]

Sexual relations between local women and occupation soldiers constituted a significant phenomenon of the post-war period with very different rules: the French authorities were most generous in their approach to this by-product of troop deployment abroad. They regarded—as opposed to the American and British occupiers—Austria as a "liberated" and not a "defeated" nation. There was thus from the outset no "ban on fraternization" for French and—as part of the French Army—Moroccan soldiers. In contrast, the Anglo-American headquarters issued on May 13, 1945 a strict "ban on fraternization," which it relaxed in the summer of 1945 and ultimately rescinded in the autumn of the same year. Even marriage, which had initially been regarded from a security point of view as "exceedingly dangerous" and had been banned as the "most intimate and extreme form of fraternization" was later permitted.[7] In Germany, the ban on marriage between German women and American GIs was repealed in December 1946, i.e., more than a year after the end of the ban on fraternization.[8] Countless women migrated due to these relations to France, Great Britain, or the United States; occupation personnel from these nations also remained permanently in the land of their erstwhile deployment.

In Germany, the Soviet military leadership ordered in summer 1945 that all intimate relations were to be avoided under threat of punishment. Only professional contacts, which were to be reduced to a minimum, were henceforth permitted. Although Soviet propaganda had systematically fueled the hatred for "Hitler's Germany" for years and numerous revenge acts against the now defeated enemy had taken place after the war, numerous love attachments had nonetheless developed. These guidelines were later relaxed and in the GDR—in contrast to Austria—German-Soviet marriages were even to become de jure possible after 1953. In actual fact, however, they remained the exception.[9]

The attitude of the Soviets toward Austria constituted in this respect a special case. On the basis of the Moscow Declaration from 1943, Austria was regarded as a "liberated" country whose "peaceful people"—in contrast to the "German subjugators"—were to be "protected."[10] Officially, there existed from the outset, therefore, no "ban on fraternization." The Kremlin nevertheless regarded sexual relations between Soviet military personnel and non-Soviet women abroad as "politically reprehensible." Here both ideological considerations as well as the fear of espionage and treason played a role. From this ambiguity there developed double standards with far-reaching consequences: love attachments between occupation soldiers and Western women were thus often implicitly tolerated—as long as they remained reasonably discreet.[11]

When relationships took on a more official form, however, this simultaneously meant the end of all contact. Thus, the announcement of a pregnancy or the desire to marry mostly unintentionally provided the impulse for a transfer of the relevant member of the military to another station or back to the Soviet Union. In the process, the possibility existed neither to take the woman to the Soviet Union nor to marry her. Even written correspondence was for many decades the exception. Ultimately, connections with the West were still regarded long after Stalin's death as suspicious. A "happy ending" to love attachments between Soviet occupation soldiers and Austrian or German women could, therefore, more or less be ruled out.

Rape

In May 1945, approximately 700,000 Allied occupation soldiers were located in Austria, around 400,000 Red Army soldiers among them. For autumn 1945, their total strength was estimated at 180,000 to 200,000 Soviet,[12] 75,000 British, 70,000 American, and 40,000 French members of the military.[13] Ten years later, there were still more than 50,000 Soviet soldiers, family members, and employees of the army stationed in eastern Austria.[14] This, in the given situation, particularly "woman-hungry" male potential in its prime was pitted against a striking lack of men of the so-called productive ages: 380,000 Austrian men had not returned home from the European battlefields. To this can be added the death toll of those Austrians murdered by the Nazi regime in prisons and concentration camps as well as the hundreds of thousands of Austrian prisoners of war, about whose fate relatives knew nothing exact for years. Even in 1948, it was calculated according to the *Wiener Wochenpost* that for 100 Austrian women there were on average only seventy men. This numerical discrepancy alone gives an indication of the social and mental cause for conflict in the post-war years.[15]

Testaments to the cases of rapes fill entire filing cabinets. They confirmed the image of the "Russians" molded by prejudices and Nazi propaganda and anchored it deep in the collective memory of the Austrian population: the Soviet Union as "the refuge of evil," "inhabited" by "Slavic sub-humans" and infested by "Jewish Bolshevism."[16] Rumors and warnings from the Wehrmacht soldiers engaged on the eastern front, who had carried out attacks on the civilian population themselves or observed them, strengthened these stereotypes still further. Thus, even before the entry of the first Red Army troops, there was petrified fear of the "wild hordes from the East." Furthermore, anti-Slavic reflexes from the monarchy combined here with current anti-communist tendencies. The slogan "strength through fear" was intended to strengthen the German will to resist.[17]

Rumors of rape spread like wildfire and preceded the advancing Soviet soldiers as the war approached its end. These rumors fell on the fertile ground of the Nazi concept of the enemy drawn from anti-Communist, racist and anti-Semitic ideas. In the process, German propaganda also systematically fuelled the fear of assaults by the Red Army in order to make the calls to stand fast more effective. The call "The Russians are coming!" became a synonym for horror and terror. This combination of actual and traditional experiences, latent anti-Slavism with its roots in the nineteenth century, long-lasting indoctrinated ideas about "Slavic sub-humans" and a certain craving for sensationalism led to the Soviet occupying power in Austria having, even today, a disproportionately negative connotation.[18]

The numerical data are to be handled with particular care, not least due to a high number of unknown cases: Günter Bischof estimates the number of rape cases for Vienna on the basis of contemporary sources at 70,000 to 100,000.[19] With regard to Vienna and Lower Austria, Marianne Baumgartner assumes around 240,000 assaults. Cases of venereal disease allow, furthermore, certain conclusions to be drawn: Lower Austria reported for 1945 a total of 47,000 new cases of gonorrhoea (from 70,000 cases in the whole of Austria).[20] According to official records, approximately 10,000 women in Styria suffered this fate during the short period of Soviet occupation, around four-fifths of these in eastern and southern Styria alone.[21] Total figures for Burgenland are not available.[22] It can be assumed, however, that in this, the first territory the Red Army entered, the assaults were particularly frequent and that there were thus at least 20,000 cases of rape.[23] According to information from the District Administrative Authority (*Bezirkshauptmannschaft*), approximately 900 cases were registered In the Mühlviertel from May 1945 to March 1946.[24]

The numerical relationship between occupation soldiers and rape victims is in Austria similar to that in Germany: the ratio is—statistically-speaking—approximately 1:2. Thus, purely on paper, at 270,000 cases of rape, every second of a total of 400,000[25] occupation soldiers stationed in eastern Austria at the end of the war committed rape at least once. In reality, the proportion can be adjusted: relatively speaking, fewer soldiers were each responsible for several assaults.

Attractiveness from the Female Point of View

In spite of the sexual assaults, numerous voluntary love attachments between local women and occupation soldiers also developed in the Soviet zone. As a result of the almost comprehensive deployment of occupation soldiers in eastern Austria, there were countless opportunities for them to get to know each other: at theater visits, dance events, at the market, at work, in private quarters, or in the garden. At those locations where troops were stationed, a particularly large number of relationships of course developed. Baden, near Vienna, where the headquarters of the Central Group of Forces was located, may have been the absolute front runner in this respect.

The situation in the Soviet Occupation Zone in Germany was similar. Especially in the first few years there were—despite the regimentation mentioned earlier—numerous points of contact. Occupation personnel were to be found in practically all quarters of a city. They had taken over schools, villas, health resorts, and cinemas as well as military installations previously used by the Wehrmacht. In the summer, not only local residents swam in the outdoor swimming pools but also Soviet military personnel. They also willingly attended theater and other cultural events.[26] Regardless of the widespread, negative "image of the Russians," which had been established not least as a result of the numerous cases of rape especially at the end of the war and in the immediate post-war period, voluntary love attachments did develop.

In both countries, the occupation soldiers in general frequently served as the source of vital foodstuffs, from which entire families profited. Soviet occupation soldiers, as opposed to Western ones, in any case had more difficulty coming up with classical luxury goods and those of which there was a shortage: Cadbury chocolate, chewing gum, or stockings were barely available to them. The exception was the thin stratum of officers who had perks of power, such as papers, permits, or the granting of permission to travel as well as a greater selection of foodstuffs, cigarettes, tobacco, and spirits.[27] Nevertheless, even basic foodstuffs such as bread and potatoes were coveted goods in the post-war period. The boundary between a purely erotic/sexual relationship and one that was at least in part material or dialectical was thus not always easy to discern.[28]

Attractiveness from the Occupiers' Point of View

The reasons as to why occupation soldiers found Austrian or German women attractive were often not identical with the motives of the latter. In the case of the former, housewife, communicative, and sexual "services" were at the forefront.[29] It was enticing for military personnel to offload areas of housework such as cooking, washing, ironing, or cleaning on Austrian women. They typically paid for such chores with foodstuffs, cigarettes, or other commodities in short supply.

After the hard years of the war, many of the occupation soldiers also simply felt the need to live and love in a comparatively carefree way. They regarded deployment in the West to a certain extent as a period of recuperation. Romantic love stories constituted a fixed component of the post-war period. Spring in Vienna, sunshine, trees in bloom, beautiful girls, and music condensed into a compact chain of associations, fulfilled by the joy of having survived the war.[30] Particularly in retrospect, deployment in Austria and Germany is nostalgically idealized in the tradition of a cavalier's tour of duty, especially since it was often the only stay abroad in their lives.[31]

Reactions in the Milieu

Even during the war, "loose" women who had entered into relationships with foreign forced laborers and prisoners of war during the "Third Reich" incurred ill-feeling and punitive measures. From a "nationhood and racial policy" point of view, the "purity of German blood" should not be tarnished. As "the epitome of the German soul," a woman personified a "bulwark against the other, the stranger, the enemy."[32] As Helke Sander emphasizes, it is "indeed an irony of history that the war which had been fought, among other things, for racial unity should have laid the foundations for an interbreeding of gigantic proportions and that the Europe of today in fact looks different to fifty [now seventy-five] years ago."[33]

The discrimination of local women who had become "involved with the enemy" was not, however, a singular phenomenon of the Third Reich. In the Netherlands, for example, women and girls who had entered into relationships with German soldiers were accused of treason after the end of the German occupation.[34] Analogous to this, around 20,000 women in France were shorn of their hair—half of them due to collaboration with the Germans or denunciations, the other half due to sexual relations with the enemy.[35]

In Germany and Austria, the conceptual world of National Socialism had an effect long after the war had ended. Sexual relations with occupation soldiers of the former enemy often contained, therefore, a racial-ideological component. Affairs with "completely foreign" men were regarded as particularly reprehensible: with black GIs, with Moroccans, with "Mongolians," but also—across the board—with the "Russians."[36] The Nazi image of the enemy as one of "wild hordes from the East," which was intensified as a result of assaults by the Red Army at the end of the war, led in many cases to a discrimination of "Russian sweethearts."

Among the conditions for the "downfall," the "national" infringement increasingly joined the "racial" infringement. The way of life designated "occupation bride" was regarded from the perspective of the population as treason against the "national community" (constituted under or by National Socialist rule), a model to which the people had emotionally only just begun to say goodbye. In the process, the segmentation of "us and them" or "us and the others," which had been cultivated during the Nazi period, continued to have an impact.[37]

Against this backdrop, the relationship triangle between local women, local men, and the occupation soldiers was particularly emotionally charged. Military defeat had deeply injured numerous former Wehrmacht soldiers in terms of their self-worth and their male identity. They interpreted relations between foreign military personnel and "their women" as a destruction of their last power position, as the loss of "hereditary property rights."[38] This in turn called into question their sexual potency, which constituted a profound insult. After all, the spotless reputation of those women for which he felt responsible was part of a man's honor. It humiliated him if their chastity was called into question, as the normal social value of a woman consisted of respectability, chastity and virtue or a monogamous love life with the "right" man. The "us group" insulted women who entered into a relationship with a man from the "them group" as "a loose girl," "trollop," or "whore."[39]

Verbal forms of discrimination against women in relationships with Soviet occupation soldiers were, for example, "Russian soldier's sweetheart," "Russian slut," or "Russian whore." This pejorative appraisal is still to be found in everyday perception and memory.[40]

The stigmatization—or the fear of it—led to some women attempting to conceal their relationship with an occupation soldier. In other cases, only the closest relatives were let in on it. Frequently, however, even one's own family was against the attachment to an occupation soldier and attempted in a way to rescue the daughter.

Reaction on the Soviet Side

Precisely against the backdrop of the Cold War, sexual relations between Soviet military personnel and foreign women were regarded from Moscow's point of view as reprehensible. The women were classified across the board as "politically questionable," for which reason intimate contacts with them on the part of Soviet officers and Red Army soldiers were undesirable.[41] So-called "cohabitations with politically questionable women" fell into the same category—that of "immoral occurrences"—as rape, murder, assault, plunder, alcoholism, or the causing of traffic accidents.[42] It was expressly forbidden for Soviet military personnel stationed in Austria to enter into marriage with foreign women. The political officers had the task of instructing the regular officers as to the inappropriateness of such marriages.[43] Officers and soldiers were also advised—admittedly often to no effect—that relationships with foreign women were undesirable.[44] The situation in the GDR was comparable: here German-Soviet marriages had been de jure possible since 1953. Aside from a few exceptions, however, they were de facto prevented until the end of the GDR.[45]

The Kremlin feared foreign women as, among other things, an "epidemiological weapon" in the hands of the "enemy," which would weaken the morale and fighting power of Soviet military personnel by infecting them with sexually transmitted diseases. Women were also regarded as dangerous tools of Western secret services, as they could spy on military and state secrets "undercover" as well as persuading Red Army soldiers to defect.

Yet even without the intent to spy, women—according to the internal evaluation—seduced Soviet military personnel into carrying out grave offences such as desertion and treason, for example by harboring them or encouraging them to emigrate together to the West. Thus, the People's Commissariat for Internal Affairs of the USSR (NKVD) observed in summer 1945 "numerous cases in which members of the Red Army [would] desert from their units, remain resident in Austria and marry Austrian women."[46] A particularly high proportion of cases of absence without leave could also be traced back, according to the NKVD, to associations with local women.[47]

Despite the efforts of the military leadership, love attachments between local women and Soviet military personnel were part of everyday life during the occupation. In the process, the women sometimes attracted the animosity of the wives of the Soviets both in the occupied territory and back home in the Soviet Union.[48] Sometimes the jealousy of the "bourgeois, capitalist women" continued beyond the direct period of deployment in Austria and Germany. Some former occupation soldiers preferred for this reason, among others, not to reveal anything at home about their (former) relationship with a Western woman. They did not want to unnecessarily attract the suspicion of their wives. Only decades later did some mention this private aspect of the occupation deployment in the West, which sometimes included the birth of a child.

CHILDREN OF THE OCCUPATION

According to official figures, around 8,000 "soldiers' children" (*Soldatenkinder*), as a contemporary term goes, were born in Austria between 1946 and 1953.[49] The total number of the children of occupation born until 1955 may well be at least 30,000, however. Many mothers after all stated at the birth "father unknown."[50] Definite figures are also lacking for Germany. Sometimes the figure of at least 100,000 children of occupation soldiers is cited.[51] Silke Satjukow assumes that about 400,000 children were born in Germany whose fathers were occupation soldiers and whose mothers local women.[52] In 1946, the proportion of "occupation babies" was estimated for the Western zone at a sixth of all illegitimate births; in the Soviet zone the percentage may have been higher. After 1948, when the number of rape cases decreased and the military authorities dealt more rigorously with love attachments to German women, the ratio was in all probability inverted.[53] According to a census from 1955, more than 66,000 illegitimate children of occupation were counted in West Germany, of which more than half had American fathers.[54]

It will also remain unknown how high the proportion of "children of rape" is.[55] Many women decided to deliver the child although the ban on abortion defined in paragraph 218 of the criminal code in the Soviet Occupation Zone of Germany was overruled in the case of rape.[56] In accordance with paragraph 144 of the criminal code, reinstated in June 1945, the discontinuation of pregnancies was forbidden in Austria. At least in Styria, which stood under Soviet occupation until July 24, 1945, the Provisional Styrian State Government released on May 26, 1945, "On the Relief of a State of Emergency," by which assaults by Red Army soldiers were meant.[57] In many cases, however, women undertook an illegal abortion—likewise women who were expecting a "Russian child" as a result of a voluntary love attachment.

In spite of their large numbers, those affected were—and to a certain extent still are—at the same time invisible. They were often forced on to the periphery of society and family, grew up with foster parents or grandparents and were surrounded by a strange mixture of tabooing and mysterious references by outsiders. Many of them were ashamed to speak about their origins or were met themselves with a wall of silence. To this day there is neither in Germany nor in Austria a state organization that deals with the concerns of those affected.[58]

"As a Russian Child I Was the Lowest of the Low": Reactions

Children of occupation were subjected to different forms of stigmatization and discrimination. Hidden references to their appearance or their "otherness" were part of this, as well as harassment at school, open rejection by family and neighbors, or beatings and insults. Many suffered from knowing very little or nothing about their father or even suspecting that he was one of the "hated Russians." Even official bodies such as welfare regarded them as a problem. For the broader public, those affected constituted a popular cliché of mock moral outrage.[59]

The term "Russian child" was still a widespread swearword among youths and children in the 1960s. They had adopted this phrase from their parents as a synonym for something particularly contemptible, often without knowing exactly what kind of abuse lay behind it.[60] Ferdinand Rieder, born in February 1947, thus reported that he—as the son of Soviet soldier—was not welcome in the homes of his friends: "As a 'Russian child' I was the lowest of the low. The parents of my friends chased me out of their homes."[61] His peers from the village seized on the tag "Russian child" used pejoratively by adults and used it as a swearword.

Rieder cites two reasons as to why "the Russians"—his father among them—were so unwelcome in the village in general and in the house of his mother's parents specifically: on the one hand the cases of rape at the end of the war and on the other hand the high proportion of committed "Nazis." In the small community of the village, where everyone knew everyone and wanted to know about everything, the negative image of the Russian shaped by Nazi propaganda was passed on to those women who had entered into a relationship with an occupation soldier. As a result, the "racial shame" and the "national betrayal" were passed on to those children who were subsequently born. This stigmatization consigned two of the three "Russian children" in his home village to alcoholism, says Ferdinand Rieder.

Rieder's mother told her later Austrian husband that she had been raped by a Soviet soldier. Her—assumed—role as victim was evidently regarded as less tainted with shame than the instance of having entered into a voluntary relationship with a Soviet soldier. In spite of this official disassociation from the Red Army soldier, Rieder found following the death of his mother a photo of his biological father in her identity card case. The outward renunciation of this apparently happy period of her life with the occupation soldier was evidently not followed by an inner disassociation.[62]

Some children of occupation also experienced open rejection at the hands of their own family. Rosa K., born in 1947 in Salzburg, thus remembers having been referred to by her uncle as a "Polack child": "As a result of the comments of my uncle, I found it as a child a great disgrace to have a father of Soviet origins. This was also the reason why I did not question my aunt for further details about him." Her father, who deserted from the Red Army and fled to France in 1947, thus constituted a taboo within the family.[63]

Against this backdrop, it is hardly surprising that numerous children of occupation report psychological, psychosomatic, and also physical problems, which in many cases already manifested themselves during childhood, but could in some cases only be explained in adulthood. Alongside the stigmatization, there was a further cause for this in the often difficult family surroundings or in the childhood spent in homes or with foster parents. Many had a latent or open feeling of essentially not being wanted. These problems can also be seen with children of German Wehrmacht soldiers who were conceived with local women during the occupation in countries such as Norway, Denmark, the Netherlands, and France.[64]

Childhood with Aunts and Foster Parents

Children of occupation often grew up with grandparents, other relatives, foster parents, or in homes such as the famous Catholic home in Berlin-Wilmersdorf, in which "Russian babies," as they were known, were welcome.[65] This was the case when, for example, the single mother went to work or the (future) stepfather rejected the children. Some even speak of having been engulfed by hatred. Anna E., a "child of rape," thus went to foster parents following the return of her stepfather from captivity: "When my [step]father came home, I had to go. He did not like me."[66] From then on she had a foster mother, to whom she had to say "mother," and her biological mother, whom she for purposes of differentiation called "Rosl mother."[67]

Last but not least, economic problems played a role: the mothers were often single and had to pay for their own livelihood as well as that of their child. Neither the German nor the Austrian mothers could force the fathers who had returned to the Soviet Union—in the event that their address was even known—to make alimony payments.[68] Nevertheless, the majority of the mothers stood by their children: from 603 women across Austria whom welfare had requested to give up their children for adoption, only ninety-two were prepared to do so.[69]

Significantly, Renate M. grew up with foster parents after her mother had married an Austrian: "My childhood and my youth were more than difficult, as I was naturally discriminated against as the child of a foreign occupier in this small village. My mother married a man from the village in 1952 and I could not remain in the family as a result of my background, as I was an object of hatred for my stepfather. At the age of six I was taken in by foster parents."[70] The foster parents forbade all contact with her biological mother: "My daily route to school led me past the house of my mother, whom I often saw, and I was not allowed to say one word to her. My mother's attempts to make contact were also hesitant, as I was after all the troublemaker in the marriage between her and my stepfather."[71]

Other children of occupation were able to grow up in more loving surroundings in spite of a difficult general framework. After the death of her father, the adjutant of the Soviet High Commissioner in Baden, Monika G., who was one year old at the time, thus went to Vienna to an aunt from her mother's side of the family. Her mother had to earn money and take care of Monika's half-brother from an earlier marriage, who was six years older. Only five years later, when she once more married "for maintenance reasons," was Monika G. able to return to her mother. Her aunt, to whom she had developed a particularly close relationship, remained the main point of contact throughout her life. She was also lucky in other ways. Her stepfather treated her and her half-brother like his own children. She did not discern any discrimination toward her in comparison with her second half-brother, who was born later.[72]

Wall of Silence

"At the age of eleven, my father learnt—by chance, through a snide remark by one of the sisters of my grandmother—of his family background. Until very recently he was only able with great difficulty to discuss this subject with his mother. Only in recent times has she begun to remember details from this period."[73] This portrayal by the granddaughter of a Soviet occupation soldier in Austria points to two particularly significant characteristics in dealings with children of occupation: on the one hand, they were surrounded in many cases within their own nuclear family by a wall of silence. The physically absent father constituted a taboo, about which no-one spoke—often for years—out of shame, hurt or respect for the mother. On the other hand, many of those affected found out about their roots by chance and not very gently, for example through allusions made by relatives, schoolmates, teachers, or neighbors. This often caused a shock.

Karl K., who was born in 1947, remembers, for example, how a "country boy" said to him during a brawl: "You don't have a father anyway." At the age of about ten he began to suspect why he had a stepfather and—in contrast to his half-sister and his mother—why he had the maiden name of his mother. Questions as to his biological father went unanswered: "My grandmother and some of my aunts, who are younger than my mother, always comforted me, particularly in the early years of my youth, when I asked questions about my real father. It was said that no-one knew him and he was already dead. No picture of him existed and I should look in the mirror and then I would know what he looked like! [. . .] I always had the feeling that everyone knew everything but did not say anything about it."[74] Not until 2005 was Karl K. able to ask his mother who his father was.

In other families, the silence continues to this day. In particular those women themselves who had a relationship with an occupation soldier refuse to talk about this period. Eleonore H., for example, who gave birth in December 1946 to the son of a Soviet occupation soldier, still keeps this affair secret. Her son believes, therefore, that his father was a local. Eleonore H. would only tell him the truth if she could find his father.[75]

Some women take the truth to the grave. Scant clues can be found—if at all—in the legal estate or, as in the case of Rosa R., become known at the funeral feast: the mother promised to "tell it all" on her deathbed, but was then no longer able to. Only at the burial did the older relatives break their long-lasting silence.[76] Yet even those children of occupation who in principle know about their background are often confronted with an almost impenetrable wall of silence. This tabooing is most apparent when offspring in the search for their father or grandfather cling to the most meagre bit of information. The proverbial search for their roots constitutes for them an elementary and vital issue.

The Search for Roots

Whereas scores of mothers attempt to repress memories of this often painful experience in their past, most of the children affected occupy themselves—more or less intensively—with the absent father.[77] In the last few years they have started to form networks and help each other in the search for their roots. This is also a way to establish resilience.[78] Only very few of the Soviet children of occupation actually meet their father after the birth or are able to remember him. At the time of the withdrawal from Austria at the latest, any trace is mostly lost. Personal contact with the father or other relatives in the former Soviet Union is, therefore, the exception. Frequently, it is precisely in the most immediate surroundings where techniques of forgetting and repressing are practiced which could constitute an additional burden for the children affected. The silent memories have broken open all the more in the last few years, strengthened by the opening of the archives and by the end of the Cold War in their desire of finding a trace in the former Soviet Union.

In the foreground here are questions as to their own identity, as to the proverbial roots, only half of which are known. The uncertainty about who the father was, what kind of life he led, what kind of person he was, what he looked liked and whether he passed on certain talents, characteristics, or even illnesses, is for many a strain. Many of the children of occupation, who are now in retirement, were accompanied throughout their lives by identity crises, for which reason the search for their father played lifelong a key role.

Sometimes the children of those affected continue the search for the unknown grandfather. For example, the granddaughter of a Red Army soldier from Kyrgyzstan, who lives in Berlin, would now like to learn more about her central Asian origins: "In our family it is now the case that we are all blonde and blue-eyed with the exception of my father and me, who do indeed look 'somewhat' Asian. My grandmother loves me very much and always calls me insistently: 'my little black minx.' I know that I have inherited a lot from my grandfather and that my grandparents were connected by a heartfelt love. It is very important to me to find out more about my grandfather and maybe even to find him."[79]

From experience, the children of Soviet occupation soldiers do not know whether their father is still alive or already dead. The more time that elapses, however, the more unlikely it becomes that a successful search will lead to a living father. Yet this open question should also be clarified, says Angelika M., born in 1947 in Jessen/Elster: "If he is no longer alive, I would like to say goodbye to him and to our mutual history at his grave." In contrast to most of those affected, she possesses numerous souvenirs from her father, who gave her the nickname "little Sputnik" (*Sputnikchen*): "I think that I have a great treasure trove. I have letters from my father, I have pictures of my father and many people do not have that. I think that is really important. It is a piece of real life, which I have preserved in writing."[80] She would nevertheless like to know what happened to him after 1961, at which point the exchange of letters begun in 1958 abruptly broke off.

In this case, the long-term, intensive correspondence was only possible because her mother lived in the GDR and her father had good German language skills. At least during the occupation period itself and in the first two decades after it, however, written contact with women in Austria was barely possible. The fear on the part of the military personnel formerly deployed there that letters to foreign women would result in reprisals in their Soviet homeland may have been too big. Thus, many of the children of occupation have only inaccurate or fragmentary knowledge of the personal details of their fathers. Sometimes—regardless of the approximate place and time of deployment in Austria—merely a Russian first name has been passed down. In other cases, even this clue is absent.

The Search for "Fruits"

Sometimes, the former occupation soldiers also seize the initiative in the search for their former girlfriend and the—hitherto only presumed—mutual child. In this context, the question generally poses itself as to how the military personnel dealt with this issue following their return to their homeland. Did they conceal the sexual experiences which they had collected during their deployment in the West? Did they leave behind the children that they had fathered as a "blemish," to be forgotten about? How long did the fear of potential reprisals or discrimination in the Soviet Union, which could result from contact with foreign women, last? How did they react when the past also caught up with them?

Something characteristic for Soviet occupation soldiers is evident here: the political system would have made a long-term relationship with an Austrian or German woman practically impossible and more or less prevented all contact for decades on end. Many happy love attachments were broken up because of this strict regimentation. Against the backdrop of the Cold War, there was little hope of being able to resume the liaison ended under compulsion. Some, therefore, terminated this period of their past and attempted to forget it as best they could. Others initiated only intimates or disclosed the secret shortly before their death. Thanks to the altered political circumstances, several decided in the last few years to search more or less actively for their then girlfriend and their mutual child.

The number of those former Soviet occupation soldiers who were able to contact their child following their withdrawal should be of a manageable size. Some knew nothing of the existence of Austrian or German offspring and remembered merely a romantically idealized time in the West. Others initially had a great fear of potential reprisals (or also rejection within their family and surroundings) and then lost hope that a possible search would bear fruit. Others in turn failed in the enquiries which they had initiated via various channels.

The often-observed circumstance that (erstwhile) affairs were and still are kept secret of course in no way means that they did not exist. It was far easier for those men who had been stationed abroad to conceal such love attachments and resultant children following their return than it was for the women in question, who were subjected to social control in their surroundings to a much greater extent.[81] Even more than half a century after the end of the occupation, the traces of these—both voluntary and forced—associations stretch both over several generations as well as over geographical borders.

CONCLUSION

The majority of the children of occupation constitute a fatherless generation. The military personnel frequently did not know that they had conceived a child or were relocated before its birth. At the latest with the withdrawal of the troops, however, the Soviet fathers were no longer reachable. It was in accordance with both the politics of the Soviet government as well as the custom of many of the fathers not to acknowledge these children or to assume any responsibility for them.[82] In most cases, all contact—at least for many decades—was broken off as a result of the Cold War. The children thus grew up almost without exception without their biological father, about whom many know nothing more than a Russian first name and the region of the former Soviet Union as the place of origin. Some do not even know these details. This had not only economic—due to a lack of alimony payments, for example—but above all lifelong psychological consequences.[83]

The search for a father is for many children of the occupation—and their own children—an issue for the whole of their life. At the forefront is the discovery of their own identity, the question as to their personal roots. Even children who resulted from rapes devote themselves to this vital question. In some cases, former military personnel also attempt to find their Austrian or German child and its mother. Against this backdrop, there emerged in Russia the euphemistic expression "children of the liberation" (*deti osvobozhdenija*).[84] If a family reunion is achieved, the drama, emotion, and joy can in most cases hardly be exceeded. Yet some "fathers of the occupation" no longer want to be confronted with this aspect of their post-war biography and reject all forms of contact.[85]

In this context, scholarly research is very often accorded the role of breaking through the taboo within family and community and—in some cases—assisting in the search. Particularly the children of Western, though also of Soviet, occupation troops in Germany have been the subject of scholarly studies.[86] Concerning Austria as well, several works on the children of American,[87] British,[88] Soviet,[89] and French,[90] or Moroccan[91] occupation soldiers have been published.[92] This research could at the same time provide the initial impetus for the establishment of self-help groups, such as those already active in other countries. An embedment in the international, interdisciplinary, and trans-era field of research termed "children born of war" has been particularly useful.[93]

NOTES

1. Getrud Srncik, "Besatzungskinder—ein Weltproblem," *Arbeiter-Zeitung*, November 3, 1955, p. 5. This contribution is based on: Barbara Stelzl-Marx, "Die unsichtbare Generation. Kinder sowjetischer Besatzungssoldaten in Österreich und Deutschland," in Ingvill C. Mochmann, Sabine Lee, and Barbara Stelzl-Marx, eds., *Children Born of War: Second World War and Beyond. Focus. Kinder des Krieges: Zweiter Weltkrieg und danach, Historical Social Research/Historische Sozialfor-*

schung, Vol. 34 (2009), No. 3 (Cologne: Zentrum für Historische Sozialforschung, 2009), pp. 352–373; Barbara Stelzl-Marx, *Stalins Soldaten in Österreich. Die Innensicht der sowjetischen Besatzung 1945–1955*. (Vienna/Munich: Oldenborg/Böhlau, 2012), pp. 466–558. The last two works mentioned were primarily supported by the Austria Academy of Sciences and Zukunftsfonds der Republik Österreich.

2. Srncik, "Besatzungskinder—ein Weltproblem."

3. Marc Widmann and Mary Wiltenburg, "Kinder des Feindes," *Der Spiegel*, No. 52, 2006, pp. 39–41.

4. Franz Severin Berger and Christiane Holler, *Trümmerfrauen. Alltag zwischen Hamstern und Hoffen* (Vienna: Ueberreuter, 1994), p. 189; Barbara Stelzl-Marx, "Freier und Befreier. Zum Beziehungsgeflecht zwischen sowjetischen Besatzungssoldaten und österreichischen Frauen," in Stefan Karner and Barbara Stelzl-Marx, eds., *Die Rote Armee in Österreich. Sowjetische Besatzung 1945–1955. Beiträge* (Graz/Vienna/Munich: Oldenbourg, 2005), pp. 421–448, here p. 441. On this see also: Barbara Stelzl-Marx, "'Russenkinder' und 'Sowjetbräute.' Besatzungserfahrungen in Österreich 1945–1955," in Andreas Hilger, Mike Schmeitzner and Clemens Vollnhals, eds., *Sowjetisierung oder Neutralität? Optionen sowjetischer Besatzungspolitik in Deutschland und Österreich 1945–1955*, Vol. 32 of Schriften des Hannah-Arendt-Instituts für Totalitarismusforschung (Göttingen: Vandenhoeck & Ruprecht, 2006), pp. 479–508.

5. Ebba D. Drolshagen, "Wer die Mutter verachtet, schikaniert ihr Kind," in Wolfgang Remmers und Ludwig Norz, eds., *Né maudit—Verwünscht geboren—Kriegskinder* (Berlin: Verlag C & N, 2008), pp. 156–186, here p. 156.

6. Stelzl-Marx, "Freier und Befreier," pp. 422–423; Silke Satjukow, *Besatzer. "Die Russen" in Deutschland 1945–1994* (Göttingen: Vandenhoeck & Ruprecht, 2008), p. 296.

7. Ingrid Bauer and Renate Huber, "Sexual Encounters across (Former) Enemy Borderlines," in Günter Bischof, Anton Pelinka and Dagmar Herzog, eds., *Sexuality in Austria*, Vol. 15 of Contemporary Austrian Studies (New Brunswick/New Jersey: Transaction Publishers, 2007), pp. 65–101, here pp. 69–70.

8. Sabine Lee, "Kinder amerikanischer Besatzungssoldaten in Europa: ein Vergleich der Situation britischer und deutscher Kinder," in Mochmann, Lee and Stelzl-Marx, eds., *Children Born of War*, pp. 321–351.

9. Satjukow, *Besatzer*, p. 57; Silke Satjukow, "'Russenkinder.' Die Nachkommen von deutschen Frauen und Rotarmisten," in: Barbara Stelzl-Marx and Silke Satjukow, eds., *Besatzungskinder. Die Nachkommen alliierter Soldaten in Österreich und Deutschland* (Vienna/Cologne/Weimar: Böhlau Verlag 2015), pp. 136–165, here p. 143.

10. "Call from the Military Council to the troops of the 3rd Ukrainian Front," 4.4.1945. Reprinted in Stefan Karner, Barbara Stelzl-Marx and Alexander Tschubarjan, eds., *Die Rote Armee in Österreich. Sowjetische Besatzung 1945–1955. Dokumente. Krasnaya Armiya v Avstrii. Sovetskaya okkupaciya 1945–1955. Dokumenty* (Graz/Vienna/Munich: Oldenbourg, 2005), Doc. 9.

11. Stelzl-Marx, "Freier und Befreier," pp. 436–437.

12. Manfried Rauchensteiner, "Nachkriegsösterreich 1945," *Österreichische Militärische Zeitschrift*, Vol. 6 (1972), pp. 407–421, here p. 420.

13. Berger and Holler, *Trümmerfrauen*, p. 174.

14. Central Archives of the Ministry of Defence (hereafter TsAMO), f. 275, op. 140920s, d. 7, ll. 145–156, "Report of the High Command of the TsGV to the Chief of the General Staff, Sokolovskij, and the Chief of the Main Staff of the Land Forces, Malandin, regarding the withdrawal of Soviet troops from Austria," 24.9.1955. Reprinted in Karner, Stelzl-Marx, and Tschubarjan, eds., *Die Rote Armee in Österreich*, Doc. 188.

15. Berger and Holler, *Trümmerfrauen*, p. 174; Siegfried Mattl, "Frauen in Österreich nach 1945," in Rudolf G. Ardelt, Wolfgang J. A. Huber, and Anton Staudinger, eds., *Unterdrückung und Emanzipation. Festschrift für Erika Weinzierl. Zum 60. Geburtstag* (Vienna/Salzburg: Geyer, 1985), pp. 101–126, here p. 110.

16. On this see the coresponding contributions in: Hans-Erich Volkmann, ed., *Das Russlandbild im Dritten Reich* (Cologne/Weimar/Vienna: Böhlau, 1994).

17. Wolfram Wette, "Das Russlandbild in der NS-Propaganda. Ein Problemaufriß," in Volkmann, ed., *Das Russlandbild im Dritten Reich*, pp. 55–78, here p. 70.

18. Stelzl-Marx, "Freier und Befreier," pp. 424–425.

19. Günter Bischof, *Austria in the First Cold War, 1945–1955: The Leverage of the Weak*, Cold War History Series (London/New York: Macmillan, 1999), p. 33.

20. Marianne Baumgartner, "Vergewaltigungen zwischen Mythos und Realität. Wien und Niederösterreich im Jahr 1945," in *Frauenleben 1945. Kriegsende in Wien* (Vienna: Eigenverlag der Museen der Stadt Wien, 1995), pp. 59–73, here pp. 64–65; Wolfram Dornik, "Besatzungsalltag in Wien. Die Differenziertheit von Erlebniswelten: Vergewaltigungen—Plünderungen—Erbsen—Straßwalzer," in Stefan Karner and Barbara Stelzl-Marx, eds., *Die Rote Armee in Österreich. Sowjetische Besatzung 1945–1955. Beiträge* (Graz/Vienna/Munich: Oldenbourg, 2005), pp. 449–467, here p. 462.

21. Stefan Karner, *Die Steiermark im 20. Jahrhundert. Politik—Wirtschaft—Gesellschaft—Kultur* (Graz/Vienna/Cologne, Styria, 2000), p. 318.

22. Pia Bayer, "Die Rolle der Frau in der burgenländischen Besatzungszeit," in Michael Hess, ed., *befreien—besetzen—bestehen. Das Burgenland 1945–1955. Tagungsband des Symposions des Burgenländischen Landesarchivs vom 7./8. April 2005* (Eisenstadt: Amt der burgenländischen Landesregierung, 2005), pp. 139–160.

23. In 1945, Burgenland had approximately 200,000 inhabitants. (A few tens of thousands who fled westwards and approximately 38,000 Wehrmacht soldiers and prisoners of war are to be deducted from a total number of 280,000 inhabitants.) If one assumes—based on the estimated share of rape cases for Vienna and Lower Austria—a proportion of 10 percent, then one is left with a figure for Burgenland of at least 20,000 cases of rape. I am very grateful to Wolfram Dornik, Graz, for this information.

24. Gerald Hafner, "Das Mühlviertel unter sowjetischer Besatzung," in Karner and Stelzl-Marx, eds., *Die Rote Armee in Österreich*, pp. 503–522, here pp. 511–512.

25. Rauchensteiner, "Nachkriegsösterreich 1945," p. 420.

26. Satjukow, *Besatzer*, p. 57.

27. Berger and Holler, *Trümmerfrauen*, p. 178.
28. Stelzl-Marx, "Freier und Befreier," p. 431.
29. Bauer and Huber, "Sexual Encounters across (Former) Enemy Borderlines," pp. 77–78.
30. Stelzl-Marx, "Freier und Befreier," p. 436.
31. Jan Foitzik, "Russischer Soldatenalltag in Deutschland 1945–1994," in Margot Blank, ed., *Russischer Soldatenalltag in Deutschland. 1990–1994. Bilder des Militärfotografen Wladimir Borissow. Byt rossiiskikh soldat v Germanii. Snimki voennogo fotografa Vladimir Borisova* (Berlin: Druckverlag Kettler, 2008), pp. 14–31, here p. 9.
32. Ingrid Bauer, "'Besatzungsbräute.' Diskurse und Praxen einer Ausgrenzung in der österreichischen Nachkriegsgeschichte 1945–1955," in Irene Bandhauer-Schöffmann and Claire Duchen, eds., *Nach dem Krieg. Frauenleben und Geschlechterkonstruktionen in Europa nach dem Zweiten Weltkrieg* (Herbholzheim: Centaurus-Verlag, 2000), pp. 261–276, here p. 269.
33. Helke Sander, "Erinnern/Vergessen," in Helke Sander and Barbara Johr, eds., *Befreier und Befreite. Krieg, Vergewaltigung, Kinder* (Frankfurt am Main: Fischer Taschenbuch Verlag, 2005), pp. 9–20, here p. 14. The Wehrmacht soldiers in particular contributed—in the occupied territories of the Soviet Union as well—to this "interbreeding." Sander assumes that up to a million "German" children were born on the eastern front. See ibid., pp. 14–15.
34. Monika Diederichs, "Stigma and Silence: Dutch Women, German Soldiers and their Children," in Kjersti Ericsson and Eva Simonsen, eds., *Children of World War II: The Hidden Enemy Legacy* (Oxford/New York: Berg, 2005), pp. 151–164, here pp. 157–158.
35. Fabrice Virgili, "Enfants de Boches: The War Children of France," trans. Paula Schwartz, in Ericsson and Simonsen, eds., *Children of World War II*, pp. 138–150, here p. 145.
36. Bauer and Huber, "Sexual Encounters across (Former) Enemy Borderlines," p. 86.
37. Ingrid Bauer, "Die 'Ami-Braut'—Platzhalterin für das Abgespaltene? Zur (De-)Konstruktion eines Stereotyps der österreichischen Nachkriegsgeschichte 1945–1955," *L'Homme*, Vol. 1 (1996), pp. 107 121, here p. 113.
38. Bauer, "'Besatzungsbräute,'" p. 265.
39. Drolshagen, "Wer die Mutter verachtet," pp. 160–161.
40. Stelzl-Marx, "Freier und Befreier," p. 434.
41. Russian State Military Archives (hereafter RGVA), f. 32914, op. 1, d. 132, ll. 218–264, here l. 250, "Report of the commander of the 336th NKVD Border Regiment, Martynov, and the head of the Political Section of the Regiment, Churkin, to the head of the Political Section of the NKVD Troops for the Protection of the Rear of the 3rd Ukrainian Front, Colonel Nanejshvili, on the service, Party political work, the political-moral state and the discipline of the regiment in the 2nd Quarter of 1945," June 1945.
42. RGVA, f. 32914, op. 1, d. 132, ll. 329–339, here l. 336, "Report of the commander of the 336th NKVD Border Regiment, Lieutenant Colonel Martynov, and the head of the Political Section, Major Churkin, on the military deployment, the

political-moral state and the military discipline of the troops from November 1944 to August 1945," 23.8.1945.

43. TsAMO, f. 3415, op. 1, d. 102, l. 24, "Report of the head of the Political Section of the 6th Guards Army, Guards Lieutenant Filjashkin, to the head of the Political Sections on the ban on marriage with women of foreign states," 11.4.1945.

44. TsAMO, f. 3415, op. 1, d. 102, l. 35, "Report of the deputy head of the Political Section of the Front, Colonel Katugin, to the head of the Political Section of the 18th Tank Corps, Guards Colonel Sheleg, on the ban on attachments between military personnel and women of foreign states," 28.4.1945.

45. Satjukow, *Besatzer*, p. 296.

46. RGVA, f. 32914, op. 1, d. 13, ll. 1–2, "Operational daily report of the commandant of the 336th Border Regiment of the NKVD Troops, Lieutenant Colonel Martynov, and the Chief of Staff, Major Bushkov, to the Chief of the NKVD Troops for the Protection of the Rear of the TsGV, Major General Kuznecov," 25.7.1945.

47. RGVA, f. 38650, op. 1, d. 1222, ll. 173–178, here l. 176, "Report of the head of the MVD Troops for the Protection of the Rear of the TsGV, Colonel Zimin-Kovalev, and the deputy head of the Political Section, Lieutenant Colonel Goncharev, on the political-moral state of the troops," 26.7.1946.

48. Norman N. Naimark, *Die Russen in Deutschland. Die sowjetische Besatzungszone 1945 bis 1949* (Berlin: Propyläen, 1997), p. 164.

49. Srncik, "Besatzungskinder—ein Weltproblem," p. 5.

50. On this see the ongoing research by the author of this contribution.

51. "Die Kinder der Besatzer. Teil 2," an NDR production from Reinhard Joksch (2006).

52. Silke Satjukow and Barbara Stelzl-Marx, "Besatzungskinder in Vergangenheit und Gegenwart," in Barbara Stelzl-Marx and Silke Satjukow, *Besatzungskinder. Die Nachkommen alliierter Soldaten in Österreich und Deutschland* (Vienna/Cologne/Weimar: Böhlau Verlag 2015), pp. 11–14, here p. 11.

53. Naimark, *Die Russen in Deutschland*, p. 159.

54. Lee, "Kinder amerikanischer Soldaten in Europa."

55. Miriam Gebhardt, *Wir Kinder der Gewalt. Wie Frauen und Familien bis heute unter den Folgen der Massenvergewaltigungen bei Kriegsende leiden* (Munich: Deutsche Verlags-Anstalt 2019).

56. On this see the detailed: Naimark, *Die Russen in Deutschland*, p. 159.

57. Federal Archives of Styria (hereafter StLA), BH Bruck, Grp. 12, K 435, 1945, "Circular of the Provisional Styrian State Government to all health authorities regarding disruptions to pregnancies for medical or ethical reasons," 26.5.1945. Reprinted in: Karner, Stelzl-Marx and Tschubarjan, eds., *Die Rote Armee in Österreich*, Doc. 118.

58. Saskia Mitreuter, Marie Kaiser, Sophie Roupetz, Barbara Stelzl-Marx, Philipp Kuwert, Heide Glaesmer, "Questions of Identity in Children Born of War—Embarking on a Search for the Unknown Soldier Father," in *Journal of Child and Family Studies*, 2019, DOI 10.1007/s10826-019-01501.

59. Stelzl-Marx, "Freier und Befreier," p. 441.

60. Berger and Holler, *Trümmerfrauen*, p. 189.

61. Ferdinand Rieder, information kindly provided to Barbara Stelzl-Marx. Tulln, 17.6.2004. See Stelzl-Marx, "Freier und Befreier," p. 441.
62. Stelzl-Marx, "Freier und Befreier," pp. 441–442.
63. Rosa K., electronic message to Barbara Stelzl-Marx from 18.2.2008.
64. On this see Ingvill C. Mochmann and Stein Ugelvik Larsen, "The Forgotten Consequences of the War: The Life Course of Children Fathered by German Soldiers in Norway and Denmark during WWII—Some Empirical Results," *Historical Social Research*, Vol. 33 (2008), pp. 347-363; Ericsson and Simonsen, eds., *Children of World War II*.
65. Naimark, *Die Russen in Deutschland*, p. 159.
66. Oral History Interview (hereafter OHI), Anna E. Carried out by Barbara Stelzl-Marx (venue for interview anonymized) on 4.4.2007.
67. Ibid.
68. On the situation in the Soviet Occupation Zone of Germany see Naimark, *Die Russen in Deutschland*, p. 163.
69. Srncik, "Besatzungskinder—ein Weltproblem," p. 5; Stelzl-Marx, "Freier und Befreier," p. 441.
70. Renate M., electronic message to Barbara Stelzl-Marx from 26.1.2008.
71. Renate M., electronic message to Barbara Stelzl-Marx from 17.2.2008.
72. OHI, Monika G. Carried out by Barbara Stelzl-Marx in Graz on 23.7.2008.
73. Sabine D., electronic message to Barbara Stelzl-Marx from 6.10.2005.
74. Karl K., electronic message to Barbara Stelzl-Marx from 22.2.2006.
75. Eleonore H., information kindly provided to Barbara Stelzl-Marx. Vienna, 2.4.2007.
76. Rosa R., electronic message to Barbara Stelzl-Marx from 3.2.2006.
77. Bauer and Huber, "Sexual Encounters across (Former) Enemy Borderlines," p. 90; Stelzl-Marx, "Freier und Befreier," pp. 443–447; Regina Brunnhofer, "Liebesgeschichten und Heiratssachen. Das vielfältige Beziehungsgeflecht zwischen britischen Besatzungssoldaten und Frauen in der Steiermark zwischen 1945–1955," Ph.D. Diss., University of Graz, 2002.
78. Barbara Stelzl-Marx, "'Ich bin stolz, ein Besatzungskind zu sein.' Resilienzfaktoren von Nachkommen sowjetischer Soldaten in Österreich," in: Elke Kleinau and Ingvill C. Mochmann, eds., *Kinder des Zweiten Weltkrieges—Stigmatisierung, Ausgrenzung und Bewältigungsstrategien* (Frankfurt/New York: Campus, 2016), pp. 73–92, here pp. 85–90.
79. M. K., letter to Barbara Stelzl-Marx, Berlin, 6.5.2004. Quoted from: Stelzl-Marx, "Freier und Befreier," p. 444.
80. OHI, Angelika M., Berlin, 22.7.2008. The video was recorded as a request for information for the Russian television channel "Zhdi menja."
81. Bauer and Huber, "Sexual Encounters across (Former) Enemy Borderlines," p. 93.
82. On the comparable situation in the GDR see Satjukow, *Besatzer*, p. 297.
83. Stelzl-Marx, "Freier und Befreier," pp. 441–442.
84. See for example Eleonore Dupuis, *Befreiungskind* (Vienna: Edition Liaunigg 2015).

85. Stelzl-Marx, "Freier und Befreier," pp. 438 and 441–447.

86. See for example: Silke Satjukow and Rainer Gries, *"Bankerte!": Besatzungskinder in Deutschland nach 1945* (Frankfurt/New York: Campus, 2015); Barbara Stelzl-Marx and Silke Satjukow, *Besatzungskinder. Die Nachkommen alliierter Soldaten in Österreich und Deutschland* (Vienna/Cologne/Weimar: Böhlau Verlag, 2015); Ute Baur-Timmerbrink, *Wir Besatzungskinder. Töchter und Söhne alliierter Soldaten erzählen* (Berlin: Ch. Links Verlag, 2019).

87. See for example: Ingrid Bauer, *Welcome Ami Go Home. Die amerikanische Besatzung in Salzburg 1945–1955. Erinnerungslandschaften aus einem Oral-History-Projekt.* (Salzburg/Munich: Verlag Anton Pustet, 1998).

88. See for example: Karin M. Schmidlechner, *Frauenleben in Männerwelten: Kriegsende und Kriegszeit in der Steiermark*, Vol. 10 of Studien zur Gesellschafts- und Kulturgeschichte series (Vienna: Döcker Verlag, 1997); Brunnhofer, "Liebesgeschichten und Heiratssachen"; Lukas Schretter, *Die Nachkommen britischer Besatzungssoldaten und österreichischer Frauen*. Ph.D. Diss., University of Graz (in preparation).

89. See for example: Barbara Stelzl-Marx, "Soviet Children of Occupation in Austria: The historical, political and social background and its consequences," *in European Review of History. Revue européene d'histoire. Vol. 22. Nr. 2. April 2015, pp. 277–291*; Barbara Stelzl-Marx, "'Russenkinder.' Besatzung und ihre Kinder," in Stefan Karner and Gottfried Stangler, eds., *"Österreich ist frei!" Der Österreichische Staatsvertrag 1955. Beitragsband zur Ausstellung auf Schloss Schallaburg 2005* (Horn/Vienna: Verlag Berger 2005), pp. 163–168.

90. See for example: Renate Huber, "Regionale und nationale Identitäten in Vorarlberg (1945–1965). Geschlecht, Migration und Besatzung als Interaktionsfelder zwischen Zugehörigkeit und Differenz," Ph.D. Diss., University of Florence, 2002.

91. See for example: Clément Mutombo, *Les damnés innocents du Vorarlberg. Parianisme envers les enfants historiques (1946)* (Frankfurt am Main: Peter Lang, 2007).

92. Also see the volumes of essays, such as: Stelzl-Marx, Satjukow, eds., *Besatzungskinder*; Baur-Timmerbrink, eds., *Wir Besatzungskinder*; Kleinau and Mochmann, eds., *Kinder des Zweiten Weltkrieges—Stigmatisierung, Ausgrenzung und Bewältigungsstrategien.*

93. On this also see: CHIBOW (Children Born of War) is an H2020 Marie Curie Innovative Training Network (ITN), supporting a new generation of researchers to advance our knowledge and understanding of the lived experiences of children born of war in a variety of twentieth-century conflict and post-conflict situations. https://www.chibow.org/; Gisela Heidenreich, ed., *Born of War—Vom Krieg geboren. Europas verleugnete Kinder* (Ch. Links Verlag, Berlin: 2017).

Archival Sources

ARCHIV DES LUDWIG BOLTZMANN INSTITUTS FÜR KRIEGSFOLGENFORSCHUNG, GRAZ/VIENNA/RAABS (ADBIK)

Database of Austrian Civilian Convicts in the USSR

Correspondence

Anna-Maria Melichar, Vienna, information provided on 17.3.2008.
Ferdinand Rieder, Tulln, information provided on 17.6.2004.
Eleonore H., Vienna, information provided on 2.4.2007.
Sabine D., electronic message from 6.10.2005.
Karl K., electronic message from 22.2.2006.
Rosa K., electronic message from 18.2.2008.
Rosa R., electronic message from 3.2.2006.
Renate M., electronic messages from 26.1.2008 and 17.2.2008.
M. K., Berlin, letter from 6.5.2004.

Oral History Interviews (OHI)

Anna E. (venue of interview anonymized) on 4.4.2007. Interviewer: Barbara Stelzl-Marx.
Monika G. in Graz on 23.7.2008. Interviewer: Barbara Stelzl-Marx.
Angelika M. in Berlin on 22.7.2008. Video recorded as request for information for Russian television channel "Zhdi menja."
VD-0282b/0283a, Vasilii Tyukhtyaev in Moscow on 21.11.2003. Interviewer: Ol'ga Pavlenko.

ARKHIV PREZIDENTA ROSSIISKOI FEDERATSII, MOSCOW (AP RF)

F. 3   Decisions of the Politburo, the Central Committee, the Council of People's Commissars, the Ministerial Council, the Presidium of the Supreme Soviet

ARKHIV VNESHNEI POLITIKI ROSSIISKOI FEDERATSII, MOSCOW (AVP RF)

F. 06   V. Molotov
F. 07   A. Vyshinskii
F. 012   V. Dekanozov
F. 48z   Reference Library of the Archives
F. 059   (Edited) Ciphered Telegrams
F. (0)66   Austria
F. 0425   European Advisory Commission
F. 0431   Council of Foreign Ministers 1945-1949
F. 450   Allied Commission for Austria

BUNDESMINISTERIUM DES INNEREN DER REPUBLIK ÖSTERREICH, VIENNA (BMI)

Official Austrian Repatriation Transports from the Soviet Union

GOSUDARSTVENNYI ARKHIV ROSSIISKOI FEDERATSII, MOSCOW (GARF)

F. 7523   Supreme Soviet of the USSR

GLAVNAYA VOENNAYA PROKURATURA, MOSCOW (GVP)

Notification of Rehabilitation 41-N
Notification of Rehabilitation 5uv-835-97
Notification of Rehabilitation 5uv-6188-48

NATIONAL ARCHIVES AND RECORDS ADMINISTRATION (NARA)

Record Group 84

NIEDERÖSTERREICHISCHES LANDESARCHIV, ST. PÖLTEN (NÖLA)

L. A. III/3-a-29/8-1961

ÖSTERREICHISCHE BOTSCHAFT MOSKAU, MOSCOW (ÖBM)

Holding Personnel Files

ÖSTERREICHISCHES STAATSARCHIV/ARCHIV DER REPUBLIK, VIENNA (ÖSTA/ADR)

AA, II-pol. 1945
AA, II-pol 1947
BKA, Alliiertenverbindungsstelle 270/46
BMfF, Sekt. Vermögenssicherung: Staatsvertragsakten

ROSSIISKII GOSUDARSTVENNYI ARKHIV EKONOMIKI, MOSCOW (RGAE)

F. 1562

ROSSIISKII GOSUDARSTVENNYI ARKHIV NOVEISHEI ISTORII, MOSCOW (RGANI)

F. 2   Minutes of the Plenary Sessions of the Central Committee of the CPSU
F. 3   Resolutions of the Presidium of the Central Committee of the CPSU
F. 5   Apparatus of the Central Committee of the CPSU

ROSSIISKII GOSUDARSTVENNYI ARKHIV SOTSIAL'NO-POLITICHESKOI ISTORII, MOSCOW (RGASPI)

F. 17, op. 3	"Ordinary" Politburo Resolutions of the Central Committee of the VKP(b) until 14.10.1952
F. 17, op. 118	Papers on the Sessions of the Secretariat of the Central Committee of the VKP(b)
F. 17, op. 121	Technical Secretariat
F. 17, op. 125	Administration for Propaganda and Agitation of the Central Committee of the VKP(b)
F. 17, op. 128	Department for International Information of the Central Committee of the VKP(b)
F. 17, op. 132	Department for Propaganda and Agitation of the Central Committee of the VKP(b)
F. 17, op. 162	"Special Folder" of Politburo Resolutions of the Central Committee of the VKP(b) until 14.10.1952
F. 17, op. 163	Papers on the Politburo Resolutions of the Central Committee of the VKP(b) until 14.10.1952
F. 77, op. 3	Holding of the Secretary of the Central Committee of the VKP(b), A. A. Zhdanov
F. 82, op. 2	Holding of the Head of the Foreign Political Commission of the Central Committee of the VKP(b), Vyacheslav Molotov, 1949-1953
F. 495	Comintern

ROSSIISKII GOSUDARSTVENNYI VOENNYI ARKHIV, MOSCOW (RGVA)

F. 461	Civilians
F. 32900	Administration of the Troops of the NKVD for the Protection of the Rear Area of the Southern Group of Forces
F. 32902	17th Border Regiment
F. 32914	336th Border Regiment
F. 38650	Main Administration of the Internal Troops of the MVD
F. 38756	40th Border Regiment

STEIERMÄRKISCHES LANDESARCHIV, GRAZ (STLA)

BH Bruck, Grp. 12, K 435, 1945

TSENTRAL'NYI ARKHIV FEDERAL'NOI SLUZHBY BEZOPASNOSTI, MOSCOW (TSA FSB RF)

F. 4
F. 135

TSENTRAL'NYI ARKHIV MINISTERSTVA OBORONY ROSSIISKOI FEDERATSII, PODOL'SK (TSAMO)

F. 48
F. 148a   Directives of the Stavka
F. 243   3rd Ukrainian Front 1945 (High Commander and Military Council)
F. 254
F. 275   Political Section of the 3rd Ukrainian Front or the Central Group of Forces
F. 350   9th Guards Army of the 3rd Ukrainian Front
F. 3415

VERKHOVNYI SUD ROSSIISKOI FEDERATSII, MOSCOW (VSRF)

Notification 1n-01812/p-52
Notification 1n-02279/p-52
Notification 2-001/48

Bibliography

PRIMARY AND SECONDARY LITERATURE

Alfred Ableitinger, Siegfried Beer, and Eduard G. Staudinger, eds., *Österreich unter alliierter Besatzung 1945-1955*, Vol. 63 of Studien zu Politik und Verwaltung (Vienna: Böhlau, 1998).

Konrad Adenauer, *Vospominaniya (1953–1955)* (Moscow: Molodaya gvardiya, 1968).

Grant M. Adibekov, *Das Kominform und Stalins Neuordnung Europas: Zeitgeschichte—Kommunismus—Stalinismus. Materialien und Forschungen*, Vol. 1 (Frankfurt am Main: Peter Lang, 2002).

Grant M. Adibekov, K. M. Anderson, and L. A. Rogovaya, eds., *Politbyuro TsK RKP (b) – VKP (b). Povestki dnya zasedanii. Tom III: 1940–1952. Katalog* (Moscow: ROSSPEN, 2001).

Grant Adibekov, A. di B'yadzho [di Biagio], L. Ya. Gibianskii, F. Fori and S. Pons, eds., *Soveshchaniya Kominforma, 1947, 1948, 1949. Dokumenty i materialy* (Moscow: ROSSPEN, 1998).

Wilfried Aichinger, *Sowjetische Österreichpolitik 1943–1945: Materialien zur Zeitgeschichte*, Vol. 1 (Vienna: Eigenverlag der ÖGZ, 1977).

Richard J. Aldrich, *The Hidden Hand: Britain, America and Cold War Secret Intelligence* (Woodstock/New York: Overlook Press, 2002).

Christopher Andrew – Oleg Gordiewsky, *KGB. Die Geschichte seiner Auslandsoperationen von Lenin bis Gorbatschow* (Munich: Bertelsmann, 1990).

Christopher Andrew and Wassil Mitrochin, *Das Schwarzbuch des KGB. Moskaus Kampf gegen den Westen* (Munich: Ullstein, 2001).

Thomas Angerer, "Französische Freundschaftspolitik in Österreich nach 1945. Gründe, Grenzen und Gemeinsamkeiten mit Frankreichs Deutschlandpolitik," in Manfried Rauchensteiner and Robert Kriechbaumer, eds., *Die Gunst des Augenblicks. Neuere Forschungen zu Staatsvertrag und Neutralität*, Schriftenreihe des

Forschungsinstitutes für politisch-historische Studien der Dr.-Wilfried-Haslauer-Bibliothek (Vienna/Cologne/Weimar: Böhlau, 2005), pp. 113–138.

Thomas St. John Arnold, *Austria and the United States Forces* (Manhattan, KS: Sunflower University Press, 2001).

Dieter Bacher, "Austrian 'Spies' in the Early Cold War: The Recruitment of Austrian Citizens by Foreign Intelligence Services in Austria from 1945 to 1953," in Wladyslaw Bulhak and Thomas Wegener Friis, eds., *Need to Know: Eastern and Western Perspectives* (Odense: University Press of Southern Denmark, 2014), pp. 229–244.

Dieter Bacher, "Der Freund meines Feindes ist mein Feind. Die Kommunistische Partei Österreichs im Visier amerikanischer und britischer Nachrichtendienste 1945–1955," in *Jahrbuch für Historische Kommunismusforschung* 2016. (Berlin: Metropol, 2016).

Dieter Bacher, "Die KPÖ und die sowjetischen Nachrichtendienste. Zweiseitige Kontakte im frühen Kalten Krieg," in Stefan Karner and Barbara Stelzl-Marx, eds., *Stalins letzte Opfer. Verschleppte und erschossene Österreicher in Moskau 1950–1953*. Kriegsfolgen-Forschung. Wissenschaftliche Veröffentlichungen des Ludwig Boltzmann-Instituts für Kriegsfolgen-Forschung. Vol. 5 (Vienna/Munich: Böhlau, 2009), pp. 189–203.

Dieter Bacher, "Sowjetische Ermittlungen und Prozesse gegen österreichische "Spione" (1950–1953)," in Csaba Szabó, eds., *Sowjetische Schauprozesse*. Publikationen der ungarischen Geschichtsforschung in Wien. Vol. 13. (Vienna: Institut für ungarische Geschichtsforschung, 2015), pp. 299–316.

Dieter Bacher and Harald Knoll, "Spione und Stalinopfer. Die Rolle österreichischer Zivilisten in den Aktivitäten ausländischer Nachrichtendienste in Österreich 1950–1953," in ACIPSS, ed., *JIPSS (Journal for Intelligence, Propaganda and Security Studies)*, Vol. 2 (2008), No. 2 (Graz: ACIPSS, 2008), pp. 99–108.

Dieter Bacher and Peter Ruggenthaler, "Als GRU-Offizier in Österreich. Die Erinnerungen Vitaliy Nikolskiys. 1947–1955," in *JIPSS*, vol. 5, Nr. 1/2011, pp. 139–155.

William B. Bader, "Austria between East and West, 1945–1955," Ph.D. Diss., University of Stanford, 1966.

William B. Bader, *Österreich im Spannungsfeld zwischen Ost und West 1945 bis 1955* (Vienna: Braumüller, 2002).

William B. Bader, "Österreich in Potsdam," Österreichische Zeitschrift für Außenpolitik, Vol. 2 (1962), pp. 206–223.

Geoffrey Bailey, Sergei Kondrashov, and David Murphy, *Pole bitvy—Berlin* (Moscow: Little Brown, 2002).

Ivo Banac, ed., *The Diary of Georgi Dimitrov 1933–1949* (New Haven/London: Yale University Press, 2003).

Ingrid Bauer, "'Besatzungsbräute.' Diskurse und Praxen einer Ausgrenzung in der österreichischen Nachkriegsgeschichte 1945–1955," in Irene Bandhauer-Schöffmann and Claire Duchen, eds., *Nach dem Krieg. Frauenleben und Geschlechterkonstruktionen in Europa nach dem Zweiten Weltkrieg* (Herbholzheim: Centaurus-Verlag, 2000), pp. 261–276.

Ingrid Bauer, "Die 'Ami-Braut' – Platzhalterin für das Abgespaltene? Zur (De-)Konstruktion eines Stereotyps der österreichischen Nachkriegsgeschichte 1945–1955," *L'Homme*, Vol. 1 (1996), pp. 107–121.

Ingrid Bauer, *Welcome Ami Go Home: Die amerikanische Besatzung in Salzburg 1945–1955. Erinnerungslandschaften aus einem Oral-History-Projekt.* (Salzburg/Munich: Verlag Anton Pustet, 1998).

Ingrid Bauer and Renate Huber, "Sexual Encounters across (Former) Enemy Borderlines," in Günter Bischof, Anton Pelinka and Dagmar Herzog, eds., *Sexuality in Austria*, Vol. 15 of Contemporary Austrian Studies series (New Brunswick/New Jersey: Transaction Publishers, 2007), pp. 65–101.

Robert A. Bauer, ed., *The Austrian Solution: International Conflict and Cooperation* (Charlottesville: University Press of Virginia, 1982).

Marianne Baumgartner, "Vergewaltigungen zwischen Mythos und Realität. Wien und Niederösterreich im Jahr 1945," in *Frauenleben 1945. Kriegsende in Wien* (Vienna: Eigenverlag der Museen der Stadt Wien, 1995), pp. 59–73.

Ute Baur-Timmerbrink, *Wir Besatzungskinder. Töchter und Söhne alliierter Soldaten erzählen* (Berlin: Ch. Links Verlag, 2019).

Pia Bayer, "Die Rolle der Frau in der burgenländischen Besatzungszeit," in Michael Hess, ed., *befreien—besetzen—bestehen. Das Burgenland 1945–1955. Tagungsband des Symposions des Burgenländischen Landesarchivs vom 7./8. April 2005* (Eisenstadt: Amt der burgenländischen Landesregierung, 2005), pp. 139–160.

Siegfried Beer, "Die 'Befreiungs- und Besatzungsmacht' Großbritannien in Österreich, 1945–1955," in Manfried Rauchensteiner and Robert Kriechbaumer, eds., *Die Gunst des Augenblicks. Neuere Forschungen zu Staatsvertrag und Neutralität* (Vienna/Cologne/Weimar: Böhlau, 2005), pp. 23–74.

Siegfried Beer, "Das sowjetische 'Intermezzo.' Die Russenzeit in der Steiermark 8. Mai bis 23. Juli 1945," in Joseph F. Desput, ed., *Vom Bundesland zur Europäischen Region. Die Steiermark von 1945 bis heute* (Graz: Historische Landeskommission, 2004), pp. 35–59.

Siegried Beer, "Die US-Besatzungspolitik in Österreich bis Herbst 1945," in Manfried Rauchensteiner and Wolfgang Etschmann, eds., *Österreich 1945. Ein Ende und viele Anfänge*, Vol. 4 of Forschungen zur Militärgeschichte (Graz/Vienna/Cologne: Styria, 1997), pp. 207–228.

Siegfried Beer, "Wien in der frühen Besatzungszeit: Erkundungen des US-Geheimdienstes OSS/SSU im Jahre 1945. Eine exemplarische Dokumentation," in Ferdinand Opll and Karl Fischer, eds., *Studien zur Wiener Geschichte: Jahrbuch des Vereins für Geschichte der Stadt Wien*, Vol. 51 (Vienna: Selbstverlag des Vereins für Geschichte der Stadt Wien, 1995), pp. 35–92.

Czaba Békés, Malcolm Byrne and János M. Rainer, eds. *The 1956 Hungarian Revolution: A History in Documents*, National Security Archives Cold War Readers (Budapest: Central European University Press, 2002).

V. N. Beletskii, *Sovetskii Soyuz i Avstriya. Bor'ba Sovetskogo Soyuza za vozrozhdenie nezavisimoi demokraticheskoi Avstrii i ustanovlenie s nei druzhestvennykh otnoshenii (1938–1960gg.)* (Moscow: Izdatel'stvo Instituta Mezhdunarodnykh Otnoshenii, 1962).

Franz Severin Berger and Christiane Holler, *Trümmerfrauen. Alltag zwischen Hamstern und Hoffen* (Vienna: Ueberreuter, 1994).

Ernst Bezemek, "Dokumentation der Betriebe des USIA-Konzernes," in idem. and Otto Klambauer, *Die USIA-Betriebe in Niederösterreich: Geschichte—Organisation—Dokumentation* (Vienna: Selbstverlag d. NÖ Inst. für Landeskunde, 1983), pp. 80–340.

Perry Biddiscombe, *The Last Nazis: SS Werewolf Guerilla Resistance in Europe 1944–1947* (Stroud: Tempus, 2004).

Dieter A. Binder and Karl Maria Stepan, *Josef Dobretsberger: Verlorene Positionen des christlichen Lagers* (Vienna: Karl-von-Vogelsang-Institut, 1992).

Vadim J. Birstein, *Smersh. Stalin's Secret Weapon. Soviet Military Counterintelligence in WWII* (London: Biteback Publishing, 2011).

Günter Bischof, "Anglo-amerikanische Planungen und Überlegungen der österreichischen Emigration während des Zweiten Weltkrieges für Nachkriegs-Österreich," in Manfred Rauchensteiner and Wolfgang Etschmann, eds., Österreich 1945: Ein Ende und viele Anfänge (Graz/Vienna/Cologne: Styria, 1997), pp. 15–29.

Günter Bischof, *Austria in the First Cold War, 1945–1955: The Leverage of the Weak*, Cold War History Series (London/New York: Macmillan Press & St. Martin's Press, 1999).

Günter Bischof, "Austria looks to the West. Kommunistische Putschgefahr, geheime Wiederbewaffnung und Westorientierung am Anfang der fünfziger Jahre" in Thomas Albrich, Klaus Eisterer, Michael Gehler and Rolf Steininger eds., Österreich in den Fünfzigern. Vol. 11 of Innsbrucker Forschungen zur Zeitgeschichte (Innsbruck: Studienverlag 1995), pp. 183–196.

Günter Bischof, "Between Responsibility and Rehabilitation Austria in International Politics 1940–1950," Ph.D. Diss., Harvard University, 1989.

Günter Bischof, "Eindämmung und Koexistenz oder "Rollback" und Befreiung? Die Vereinigten Staaten, das Sowjetimperium und die Ungarnkrise im Kalten Krieg, 1948–1956," in Erwin A. Schmidl, ed., *Die Ungarnkrise 1956 und Österreich* (Vienna/Cologne/Weimar: Böhlau, 2003), pp. 101–146.

Günter Bischof, "Eisenhower, the Summit, and the Austrian Treaty, 1953–1955," in Günter Bischof and Stephen E. Ambrose, eds., *Eisenhower. A Centenary Assessment* (Baton Rouge: Louisiana State University Press, 1995), pp. 131–161.

Günter Bischof, "Karl Gruber und die Anfänge des 'Neuen Kurses' in der österreichischen Außenpolitik 1952/53," in Lothar Höbelt and Othmar Huber, eds., *Für Österreichs Freiheit. Karl Gruber—Landeshauptmann und Außenminister 1945–1953*, Vol. 7 of Innsbrucker Forschungen zur Zeitgeschichte series (Innsbruck: Haymon Verlag, 1991), pp. 143–183.

Günter Bischof, "Die Instrumentalisierung der Moskauer Deklaration nach dem Zweiten Weltkrieg," in *Zeitgeschichte*, Vol. 20 (1993), pp. 345–366.

Günter Bischof, "The Making of the Austrian Treaty and the Road to Geneva," in idem. and Saki Dockrill, *Cold War Respite: The Geneva Summit of 195?* (Baton Rouge, LA: Louisiana State University Press, 2000).

Günter Bischof, "Der Nationale Sicherheitsrat und die amerikanische Österreichpolitik im frühen Kalten Krieg," in Alfred Ableitinger, Siegfried Beer, and Eduard G. Staudinger, eds., *Österreich unter alliierter Besatzung 1945–1955*, Vol. 63 of Studien zu Politik und Verwaltung (Vienna: Böhlau, 1998), pp. 106–111.

Günter Bischof, "'Opfer' Österreich?: Zur moralischen Ökonomie des österreichischen historischen Gedächtnisses," in Dieter Stiefel, ed., *Die Politische Ökonomie des Holocaust: Zur wirtschaftlichen Logik von Verfolgung und 'Wiedergutmachung'* (Vienna: Verlag für Geschichte und Politik, 2001), pp. 305–335.

Günter Bischof, "Österreich—ein 'geheimer Verbündeter' des Westens?," in Michael Gehler and Rolf Steininger eds., Österreich und die europäische Integration 1945–1993 (Vienna: Böhlau, 1993), pp. 425–450.

Günter Bischof, "Österreichische Neutralität, die deutsche Frage und europäische Sicherheit 1953–1955," in Günter Bischof, Rolf Steininger et al., eds., *Die doppelte Eindämmung. Europäische Sicherheit und Deutsche Frage in den Fünfzigern* (Munich: v. Hase & Koehler, 1993), pp. 133–176.

Günter Bischof, "Die Planung und Politik der Alliierten 1940-1954," in Rolf Steininger and Michael Gehler, eds., Österreich im 20. Jahrhundert: Ein Studienbuch in zwei Bänden. Vom Weltkrieg bis zur Gegenwart, Vol. 2 (Vienna/Cologne/Weimar: Böhlau, 1997), pp. 107–146.

Günter Bischof, "The Politics of AntiCommunism in the Executive Branch during the Early Cold War: Truman, Eisenhower and McCarthy(ism)," in André Kaenel, ed., *AntiCommunism and McCarthyism in the United States, 1945–1954: Essays in the Culture and Politics of the Cold War* (Paris: Editions Messene, 1995).

Günter Bischof, "'Prag liegt westlich von Wien,'" in Günter Bischof and Josef Leidenfrost, eds., *Die bevormundete Nation. Österreich und die Alliierten 1945–1949* (Innsbruck: Haymon, 1988), pp. 315–345.

Günter Bischof, "'Recapturing the Initiative' and 'Negotiating from Strength.' The Hidden Agenda of the 'Short Treaty' Episode – The Militarization of American Foreign Policy and the Un/Making of the Austrian Treaty," in Arnold Suppan, Gerald Stourzh, and Wolfgang Mueller, eds., *Der österreichische Staatsvertrag 1955. Internationale Strategie, rechtliche Relevanz, nationale Identität/The Austrian State Treaty 1955. International Strategy, Legal Relevance, National Identity*, Vol. 140 of Archiv für österreichische Geschichte series (Vienna: Böhlau, 2005), pp. 217–247.

Günter Bischoff, "The Robust Assertion of Austrianism: Peaceful Coexistence in Austria after Stalin's Death," in Klaus Larres and Kenneth Osgood, eds., *The Cold War after Stalin's Death: A Missed Opportunity for Peace?*, The Harvard Cold War Studies Book Series, ed. Mark Kramer (Lanham: Harvard University Press, 2006), pp. 233–256.

Günter Bischof, "A Soviet 'New Look' on the Danube and the Emacipation of Austrian Foreign Policy in 1953: Peaceful Coexistence in Austria after Stalin's Death," in Siegfried Beer et al., eds., *Focus Austria. Vom Vielvölkerreich zum EU-Staat. Festschrift für Alfred Ableitinger* (Graz: Selbstverlag des Instituts für Geschichte der Karl-Franzens-Universität Graz, 2003), pp. 441–466.

Günter Bischof, Stefan Karner, and Barbara Stelzl-Marx, eds., *The Vienna Summit and Its Importance in International History*. Harvard Cold War Studies Book Series. (Lanham et al.: Lexington 2014).

Günter Bischof and Josef Leidenfrost, eds., *Die Bevormundete Nation. Österreich und die Alliierten*, Vol. 4 of Innsbrucker Forschungen zur Zeitgeschichte (Innsbruck: Haymon-Verlag, 1988).

Günter Bischof and Hans Jürgen Schröder, "'Nation Building' in vergleichender Perspektive: Die USA als Besatzungsmacht in Österreich und Westdeutschland 1945–1955," in Michael Gehler and Ingrid Böhler, eds., *Verschiedene europäische Wege im Vergleich. Österreich und die Bundesrepublik Deutschland 1945/49 bis zur Gegenwart. Festschrift für Rolf Steininger zum 65. Geburtstag* (Innsbruck: Studienverlag, 2007), pp. 155–176.

Günter Bischof and Dieter Stiefel, eds. & Hannes Richter, digital ed., *Images of the Marshall Plan: Film, Photographs, Exhibits, Posters* (Innsbruck: Studienverlag, 2009).

Günter Bischof, Anton Pelinka, and Dieter Stiefel, eds., *The Marshall Plan in Austria* (New Brunswick/London: Transaction Publishers, 2000).

Ladislav Bittman, *The KGB and Soviet Disinformation. An Insider's View* (Washington, DC, et al.: Pergamon-Brassey's, 1985).

Walter Blasi, *Die B-Gendarmerie 1952–1955* (Vienna: Bundesministerium für Landesverteidigung: Landesverteidigungsakademie Wien, 2002).

Reinhard Bollmus, "Ein kalkuliertes Risiko? Großbritannien, die USA und das 'Deutsche Eigentum' auf der Konferenz von Potsdam," in Günter Bischof and Josef Leidenfrost, eds., *Die bevormundete Nation: Österreich und die Alliierten 1945–1949* (Innsbruck: Haymon, 1988), pp. 107–126.

László Borhi, *Hungary in the Cold War 1945–1956: Between the United States and the Soviet Union* (Budapest/New York: Central European University Press, 2004).

László Borhi, "Containment, Rollback, Liberation or Inaction? The United States and Hungary in the 1950s," *Journal of Cold War Studies*, Vol. 1 (1999), No. 3, pp. 67–108.

László Borhi, "The Merchants of the Kremlin: The Economic Roots of Soviet Expansion in Hungary," CWIHP Working Paper No. 28, Cold War International History Project, Washington, DC, 2000.

Robert Bowie and Richard Immerman, *Waging Peace: How Eisenhower Shaped an Enduring Cold War Strategy* (New York: Oxford University Press, 1998).

Hermann Brändle and Kurt Greussing, "Fremdarbeiter und Kriegsgefangene," in Johann-August-Malin-Gesellschaft, ed., *Von Herren und Menschen: Verfolgung und Widerstand in Vorarlberg 1933–1945*, Vol. 5 of Beiträge zu Geschichte und Gesellschaft Vorarlbergs series (Bregenz: Fink's Verlag, 1985), pp. 172–175.

Julius Braunthal, *The Tragedy of Austria* (London: Victor Gollancz, 1948).

Ralph W. Brown, III, "A Cold War Army of Occupation? The U.S. Army in Vienna, 1945–1948," Ph.D. Diss., University of Tennessee, 1995.

Waltraud Brunner, "Das Deutsche Eigentum und das Ringen um den österreichischen Staatsvertrag 1945–1955," Ph.D. Diss., University of Vienna, 1976.

Regina Brunnhofer, "Liebesgeschichten und Heiratssachen. Das vielfältige Beziehungsgeflecht zwischen britischen Besatzungssoldaten und Frauen in der Steiermark zwischen 1945–1955," Ph.D. Diss., University of Graz, 2002.
Wladyslaw Bulhak and Thomas Wegener Friis, eds., *Need to Know. Eastern and Western Perspectives* (Odense: University Press of Southern Denmark, 2014).
"Bundesgesetz vom 7. Juli 1948 über die Fürsorge für Kriegsgräber aus dem ersten und zweiten Weltkrieg," *Bundesgesetzblatt für die Republik Österreich*, 1948, 175, 7 September 1948, pp. 669–670.
"Bundesgesetz vom 7. Juli 1948 über die Fürsorge und den Schutz der Kriegsgräber und Kriegsdenkmäler aus dem zweiten Weltkrieg für Angehörige der Alliierten, Vereinten Nationen und für Opfer des Kampfes um ein freies, demokratisches Österreich und Opfer politischer Verfolgung," *Bundesgesetzblatt für die Republik Österreich*, 1948, 176, 7 September 1948, p. 670.
Felix Butschek, *Die österreichische Wirtschaft im 20. Jahrhundert* (Stuttgart: Fischer, 1985).
Ruth Büttner, *Sowjetisierung oder Selbständigkeit? Die sowjetische Finnlandpolitik 1943–1948* (Hamburg: Verlag Dr. Kovac, 2001).
James Jay Carafano, *Waltzing into the Cold War: The Struggle for Occupied Austria* (College Station: Texas A & M University Press, 2002).
Feliks Chuev, *Molotov: Poluderzhavnyi Vlastelin* (Moscow: OLMA-Press, 1999).
Winston Churchill, *The Second World War*, Vol. IV (London: Cassell, 1951).
Stefan Creuzberger and Manfred Görtemaker, eds., *Gleichschaltung unter Stalin? Die Entwicklung der Parteien im östlichen Europa 1944-1949* (Paderborn: Schöningh, 2002).
Audrey Kurth Cronin, *Great Power Politics and the Struggle over Austria 1945–1955* (Ithaca/New York: Cornell University Press, 1986).
Audrey Kurth Cronin, "Eine verpasste Chance? Die Großmächte und die Verhandlungen über den Staatsvertrag im Jahre 1949," in Günter Bischof and Josef Leidenfrost, eds., *Die bevormundete Nation: Österreich und die Alliierten 1945–1949*, Vol. 4 of Innsbrucker Forschungen zur Zeitgeschichte series (Innsbruck: Haymon, 1988), pp. 347–370.
Eva-Marie Csáky, Franz Matscher and Gerald Stourzh, eds., *Josef Schöner: Wiener Tagebuch 1944/1945* (Vienna/Cologne/Weimar: Böhlau, 1992).
David J. Dallin, "Stalin, Renner und Tito: Österreich zwischen drohender Sowjetisierung und den jugoslawischen Gebietsansprüchen im Frühjahr 1945," *Europa-Archiv*, Vols. 13–17 (1958), pp. 11030–11034.
I. C. B. Dear, ed., *The Oxford Companion to World War II* (Oxford: Oxford University Press, 1995).
Peter Deriabin and T. H. Bagley, *KGB. Masters of the Soviet Union* (London: Robson, 1990).
Peter S. Deriabin and Joseph C. Evans, *Inside Stalin's Kremlin: An Eyewitness Account of Brutality, Duplicity, and Intrigue* (Washington/London: Brassey's, 1998).
Isaac Deutscher, *Stalin: Eine politische Biographie* (Berlin: Dietz, 1990).

Monika Diederichs, "Stigma and Silence: Dutch Women, German Soldiers and Their Children," in Kjersti Ericsson and Eva Simonsen, eds., *Children of World War II: The Hidden Enemy Legacy* (Oxford/New York: Berg, 2005), pp. 151–164.
Diplomaticheskii slovar'. V 3-kh tomakh (Moscow: Nauka, 1985).
Saki Dockrill, *Eisenhower's New Look National Security Policy, 1953-61* (Basingstoke: Macmillan, 1996).
Dokumentationsarchiv des österreichischen Widerstandes, ed., *Gedenken und Mahnen in Wien 1934-1945: Gedenkstätten zu Widerstand und Verfolgung, Exil, Befreiung. Eine Dokumentation* (Vienna: Deuticke, 1998).
Dokumentationsarchiv des österreichischen Widerstandes, ed., *"Anschluß" 1938* (Vienna: Bundesverlag, 1988).
Wolfram Dornik, "Besatzungsalltag in Wien. Die Differenziertheit von Erlebniswelten: Vergewaltigungen—Plünderungen—Erbsen—Straßwalzer," in Stefan Karner and Barbara Stelzl-Marx, eds., *Die Rote Armee in Österreich. Sowjetische Besatzung 1945–1955. Beiträge* (Graz/Vienna/Munich: Oldenbourg, 2005), pp. 449–467.
Wolfram Dornik, "ZwangsarbeiterInnen im Kollektiven Gedächtnis der II. Republik," unpublished Diploma thesis, University of Graz, 2001.
Ebba D. Drolshagen, "Wer die Mutter verachtet, schikaniert ihr Kind," in Wolfgang Remmers und Ludwig Norz, eds., *Né maudit—Verwünscht geboren—Kriegskinder* (Berlin: Verlag C & N, 2008), pp. 156–186.
Jost Dülffer, *Jalta, 4. Februar 1945: Der Zweite Weltkrieg und die Entstehung der bipolaren Welt* (Munich: dtv, 1998).
Eleonore Dupuis, *Befreiungskind* (Vienna: Edition Liaunigg 2015).
A. Efremov, *Sovetsko-avstriiskie otnosheniya posle vtoroi mirovoi voiny* (Moscow: Gospolitizdat, 1958).
Klaus Eisterer, "Die französischen Archivalien zur Nachkriegsgeschichte Österreichs (1945–1955)," in Günter Bischof and Josef Leidenfrost, eds., *Die bevormundete Nation: Österreich und die Alliierten 1945–1949*, Vol. 4 of Innsbrucker Forschungen zur Zeitgeschichte series (Innsbruck: Haymon, 1988), pp. 433–445.
Natal'ja Eliseeva, "Zum Schutz des Hinterlandes der Roten Armee. Der Einsatz der NKVD-Truppen in Österreich von April bis Juli 1945," in Stefan Karner and Barbara Stelzl-Marx, eds., *Die Rote Armee in Österreich: Sowjetische Besatzung 1945–1955* (Graz/Vienna/Munich: Oldenbourg, 2005), pp. 91–104.
Gertrude Enderle-Burcel, Rudolf Jeřábek, and Leopold Kammerhofer, eds., *Protokolle des Kabinettsrates 29. April 1945 bis 10. Juli 1945: Protokolle des Kabinettsrates der Provisorischen Regierung Karl Renner 1945*, Vol. 1 (Horn/Vienna: Berger, 1995).
Gertrude Enderle-Burcel and Rudolf Jeřábek, eds., *Kabinettsratsprotokoll Nr. 30 bis Kabinettsratsprotokoll Nr. 43. 12. September 1945 bis 17. Dezember 1945: Protokolle des Kabinettsrates der Provisorischen Regierung Karl Renner 1945*, Vol. 3 (Vienna: Verlag Österreich, 2003).
Edda Engelke, "Zum Thema Spionage gegen die Sowjetunion," in Erwin A. Schmidl, ed., *Österreich im frühen Kalten Krieg 1945–1958: Spione, Partisanen, Kriegspläne* (Vienna/Cologne/Weimar: Böhlau, 2000), pp. 119–136.

V. M. Falin, *Vtoroi front. Antigitlerovskaya koalitsiya. Konflikt interesov* (Moscow: Tsentrpoligraf, 2000).
Friedrich Feichtinger and Hermann Spörker, *ÖMV–OMV: Die Geschichte eines österreichischen Unternehmens* (Horn: Berger, 2005).
Helmut Fiereder, "Zur Geschichte der KZ-Gedenkstätte Mauthausen," in Fritz Mayrhofer and Walter Schuster, eds., *Nationalsozialismus in Linz*, Vol. 2 (Linz: Archiv der Stadt Linz, 2001), pp. 1565–1583.
Alexei [Aleksei] M. Filitov, "Österreich, die Deutsche Frage und die sowjetische Diplomatie (40-50er Jahre des 20. Jh.s)," in *200 Jahre Russisches Außenministerium: Mitteilungen des Österreichischen Staatsarchivs*, Vol. 50 (Vienna: Studienverlag 2003), pp. 123–132 and 261–270.
Aleksej Filitov, "Sowjetische Planungen zur Wiedererrichtung Österreichs 1941–1945," in Stefan Karner and Barbara Stelzl-Marx, eds., *Die Rote Armee in Österreich: Sowjetische Besatzung 1945–1955* (Graz/Vienna/Munich: Oldenbourg, 2005), pp. 27–37.
Aleksei M. Filitov, "SSSR i germanskii vopros. Povorotnye punkty (1941–1946)," in N. I. Egorova and A. O. Chubar'yan, ed., *Kholodnaya voina. 1945–1963 gg. Istoricheskaya retrospektiva* (Moscow: Olma Press, 2003), pp. 223–256.
Jörg Fisch, *Reparationen nach dem Zweiten Weltkrieg* (Munich: Beck, 1992).
Ernst Fischer, *Das Ende einer Illusion: Erinnerungen 1945–1955* (Vienna: Molden, 1973).
Jan Foitzik, "Aus der Buchhaltung der Weltrevolution. Finanzhilfen der 'regierenden kommunistischen Parteien' für den internationalen Kommunismus 1950–1958," *Jahrbuch für Historische Kommunismusforschung*, 1994, pp. 140–147.
Jan Foitzik, "Russischer Soldatenalltag in Deutschland 1945–1994," in Margot Blank, ed., *Russischer Soldatenalltag in Deutschland. 1990–1994. Bilder des Militärfotografen Wladimir Borissow. Byt rossiiskikh soldat v Germanii. Snimki voennogo fotografa Vladimir Borisova* (Berlin: Druckverlag Kettler, 2008), pp. 14–31.
Jan Foitzik, *Sowjetische Militäradministration (SMAD) in Deutschland 1945–1949* (Berlin: Akademie Verlag, 1999).
Florian Freund and Bertrand Perz, *Die Zahlenentwicklung der ausländischen Zwangsarbeiter und Zwangsarbeiterinnen auf dem Gebiet der Republik Österreich 1939–1945. Gutachten im Auftrag der Historikerkommission der Republik Österreich* (Vienna: Oldenbourg, 2000).
Manfred Fuchs, *Der österreichische Geheimdienst. Das zweitälteste Gewerbe der Welt* (Vienna: Ueberreiter, 1994).
John Lewis Gaddis, *Der Kalte Krieg. Eine neue Geschichte*, trans. Klaus-Dieter Schmidt (Munich: Siedler, 2007).
John Lewis Gaddis, *Strategies of Containment: A Critical Appraisal of American National Security Policy* (New York: Oxford University Press, 1982).
John Lewis Gaddis, *We Now Know: Rethinking Cold War History* (Oxford/New York: Oxford University Press, 1998).
Heinz Gärtner, *Zwischen Moskau und Österreich. Die KPÖ—Analyse einer sowjetabhängigen Partei* (Vienna: Braumüller, 1979).

Miriam Gebhardt, *Wir Kinder der Gewalt. Wie Frauen und Familien bis heute unter den Folgen der Massenvergewaltigungen bei Kriegsende leiden* (Munich: Deutsche Verlags-Anstalt 2019).

Michael Gehler, "Kurzvertrag für Österreich? Die westliche Staatsvertrags-Diplomatie und die Stalin-Noten von 1952," *Vierteljahrshefte für Zeitgeschichte*, Vol. 42 (1994), No. 2, pp. 243–278.

Michael Gehler, "Der Staatsvertrag, die Bundesrepublik Deutschland und die Deutsche Frage 1937/49–1955," in Manfried Rauchensteiner and Robert Kriechbaumer, eds., *Die Gunst des Augenblicks. Neuere Forschungen zu Staatsvertrag und Neutralität* (Vienna/Cologne/Weimar: Böhlau, 2005), pp. 379–431.

Michael Gehler, "'. . . this nine days wonder'? Die 'Figl-Fischerei' von 1947 eine politische Affäre mit Nachspiel," in Michael Gehler and Hubert Sickinger, eds., *Politische Affären und Skandale* (Thaur/Vienna/Munich: Studienverlag, 1995), pp. 346–381.

Leonid Gibianskii, "Kominform v deystvii. 1947–1948gg. Po arkhivnym dokumentam," *Novaya i noveyshaya istoriya*, 1996, No. 1, pp. 149–170.

Leonid Gibianskii, "Kominform v deystvii. 1947–1948gg. Po arkhivnym dokumentam," *Novaya i noveyshaya istoriya*, 1996, No. 2, pp. 157–172.

Leonid Gibianskij, "Osteuropa: Sicherheitszone der UdSSR, sowjetisiertes Protektorat des Kreml oder Sozialismus 'ohne Diktatur des Proletariats'? Zu den Diskussionen über Stalins Osteuropa-Politik am Ende des Zweiten Weltkrieges und am Anfang des Kalten Krieges," *Forum für osteuropäische Ideen- und Zeitgeschichte*, Vol. 8 (2004), No. 2, pp. 113–138.

L. Ya. Gibianskii, "Problemy Vostochnoi Evropy i nachalo formirovaniya sovetskogo bloka," in N. I. Egorova and A. O. Chubar′yan, eds., *Kholodnaya Voina 1945–1963 gg. Istoricheskaya retrospektiva* (Moscow: Olma Press, 2003), pp. 105–136.

L. Ya. Gibianskii, ed., *U istokov "sotsialisticheskogo sodruzhestva"." SSSR i vostochnoevropeiskie strany v 1944–1949 gg.* (Moscow: Nauka, 1995).

Maximilian Graf, *Österreich und die DDR 1949–1990. Politik und Wirtschaft im Schatten der deutschen Teilung* (Vienna: Verlag der Österreichischen Akademie der Wissenschaften, 2016).

A. A. Gromyko, ed., *Perepiska predsedatelya Soveta ministrov SSSR s prezidentami SShA i prem′er-ministrami Velikobritanii vo vremya Velikoi Otechestvennoi voiny*, Vol. 2 (Moscow: Politizdat, 1986).

Herbert Grubmayr, "60 Jahre mit den 'Russen': Erinnerungen an meine Zeit als Legationssekretär an der Österreichischen Botschaft in Moskau," in Stefan Karner and Barbara Stelzl-Marx, eds., *Die Rote Armee in Österreich: Sowjetische Besatzung 1945–1955* (Graz/Vienna/Munich: Oldenbourg, 2005), pp. 785–813.

Gerald Hafner, "Das Mühlviertel unter sowjetischer Besatzung," Stefan Karner and Barbara Stelzl-Marx, eds., *Die Rote Armee in Österreich: Sowjetische Besatzung 1945–1955* (Graz/Vienna/Munich: Oldenbourg, 2005), pp. 503–522.

Jussi Hanhimäki and Odd Arne Westad, eds., *The Cold War: A History in Documents and Eyewitness Accounts* (New York: Oxford University Press, 2004).

Jacques Hannak, *Karl Renner und seine Zeit: Versuch einer Biographie* (Vienna: Europa Verlag, 1965).

Jamil Hasanli, *At the Dawn of the Cold War: The Soviet-American Crisis over Iranian Azerbaijan, 1941–1946* (Lanham: Rowman & Littlefield, 2006).

Patrick J. Hearden, *Architects of Globalism: Building a New World Order during World War II* (Fayetteville, AR: University of Arkansas Press, 2002).

Gisela Heidenreich, ed., *Born of War—Vom Krieg geboren. Europas verleugnete Kinder* (Berlin: Ch. Links Verlag, 2017).

Ulrich Herbert, *Fremdarbeiter. Politik und Praxis des "Ausländer-Einsatzes" in der Kriegswirtschaft des Dritten Reiches* (Bonn: Verlag J.H.W. Dietz Nachf., 1999).

Andreas Hilger, "Sowjetunion (1945–1991)," in Łukasz Kamiński, Krysztof Persak and Jens Gieseke, eds., *Handbuch der kommunistischen Geheimdienste in Osteuropa 1944–1991*. (Göttingen: Vandenhoeck&Ruprecht, 2009), pp. 43–141.

Andreas Hilger, "Strafjustiz im Verfolgungswahn. Todesurteile sowjetischer Gerichte in Deutschland," in Andreas Hilger, ed., *"Tod den Spionen!" Todesurteile sowjetischer Gerichte in der SBZ/DDR und in der Sowjetunion bis 1953* (Göttingen: V&R unipress, 2006), pp. 95–156.

Andreas Hilger and Mike Schmeitzner, "Einleitung: Deutschlandpolitik und Strafjustiz: Zur Tätigkeit sowjetischer Militärtribunale in Deutschland 1945–1955," in Andreas Hilger, Mike Schmeitzner and Ute Schmidt, eds., *Die Verurteilung deutscher Zivilisten 1945-1955. Sowjetische Militärtribunale*, Vol. 2 (Cologne/Weimar/Vienna: Böhlau, 2003), pp. 7–34.

Andreas Hilger, Nikita Petrov, and Günther Wagenlehner, "Der 'Ukas 43': Entstehung und Problematik des Dekrets des Präsidiums des Obersten Sowjets vom 19. April 1943," in Andreas Hilger, Ute Schmidt and Günther Wagenlehner, eds., *Sowjetische Militärtribunale. Band 1: Die Verurteilung deutscher Kriegsgefangener 1941–1953* (Cologne/Weimar/Vienna: Böhlau, 2001), pp. 177–209.

"Historiography Roundtable," in Günter Bischof, Anton Pelinka and Ruth Wodak, eds., *Neutrality in Austria*, Vol. 9 of Contemporary Austrian Studies (New Brunswick/ London: Transaction Publications, 2001), pp. 236–292.

Renate Huber, "Regionale und nationale Identitäten in Vorarlberg (1945–1965). Geschlecht, Migration und Besatzung als Interaktionsfelder zwischen Zugehörigkeit und Differenz," Ph.D. Diss., University of Florence, 2002.

Clemens M. Hutter, *Kaprun: Geschichte eines Erfolgs* (Salzburg/Vienna: Residenz-Verlag, 1994).

Walter Martin Iber, "Die Sowjetische Mineralölverwaltung in Österreich, 1945–1955: Sowjetische Besatzungswirtschaft und der Kampf ums Öl als Vorgeschichte der OMV," Ph.D. Diss, University of Graz, 2008.

Walter M. Iber, "Erdöl statt Reparationen. Die sowjetische Mineralölverwaltung in Österreich 1945–1955," in *Vierteljahrshefte für Zeitgeschichte* Vol. 57 (2009), No. 4, pp. 571–605.

Walter Iber, *Die Sowjetische Mineralölverwaltung in Österreich. Zur Vorgeschichte der OMV 1945–1955* (Innsbruck/Vienna/Bozen: Studienverlag, 2011).

Walter M. Iber, "Sowjetische Wirtschaftsenklaven in Österreich: USIA, SMV und die Handelsbeziehungen zur Tschechoslowakei, 1945–1955," in Stefan Karner and Michal Stehlík, eds., *Österreich. Tschechien. geteilt—getrennt—vereint.*

Beitragsband und Katalog zur Niederösterreichischen Landesausstellung 2009 (Schallaburg: Schallaburg Kulturbetriebsges.m.b.H., 2009), pp. 192–195.

Walter M. Iber, "Wirtschaftsspionage für den Westen. Erdölarbeiter im Spannungsfeld des Kalten Krieges," in Stefan Karner and Barbara Stelzl-Marx, eds., *Stalins letzte Opfer. Verschleppte und erschossene Österreicher in Moskau 1950–1953*, Vol. 5 of Kriegsfolgen-Forschung series (Vienna/Munich: Böhlau, 2008), pp. 169–188.

Walter M. Iber and Peter Ruggenthaler, eds., *Stalins Wirtschaftspolitik an der sowjetischen Peripherie. Ein Überblick auf der Basis sowjetischer und osteuropäischer Quellen*. Veröffentlichungen des Ludwig Boltzmann-Instituts für Kriegsfolgen-Forschung, Vol. 19 (Innsbruck et al.: Studienverlag, 2012).

Institut Voennoi Istorii, ed., *Krasnaya Armiya v stranakh Tsentral'noi Evropy i na Balkanakh: Dokumenty i materialy 1944-1945. Russkii Arkhiv. Velikaya Otechestvennaya Voina*, Vol. 3(2) (Moscow: Terra, 2000).

Harald Irnberger, *Nelkenstrauß ruft Praterstern. Am Beispiel Österreich: Funktion und Arbeitsweise geheimer Nachrichtendienste in einem neutralen Staat* (Vienna: promedia, 1983).

Istoriya diplomatii, Vol. 5 (Moscow: 1974).

Peter Jahn, ed., *Triumph und Trauma: Sowjetische und postsowjetische Erinnerung an den Krieg 1941–1945* (Berlin: Ch. Links Verlag, 2005).

Lewis Jill, "Auf einem Seil tanzen: Die Anfänge des Marshall-Planes und des Kalten Krieges in Österreich," in Günter Bischof and Dieter Stiefel, eds., *'80 Dollar.' 50 Jahre ERP-Fonds und Marshall-Plan in Österreich 1948–1998* (Vienna/Frankfurt am Main: Ueberreuter, 1999), pp. 297–314.

Łukasz Kamiński, Krysztof Persak and Jens Gieseke, eds., *Handbuch der kommunistischen Geheimdienste in Osteuropa 1944–1991*. (Göttingen: Vandenhoeck & Ruprecht, 2009).

Frank Kämpfer, "Vom Massengrab zum Heroen-Hügel. Akkulturationsfunktionen sowjetischer Kriegsgräber," in Reinhard Koselleck and Michael Jeismann, eds., *Der politische Totenkult: Kriegerdenkmäler in der Moderne* (Munich: Wilhelm Fink Verlag, 1994), pp. 327–349.

Rainer Karlsch, *Uran für Moskau: Die Wismut—Eine populäre Geschichte*, 3rd rev. ed. (Berlin: Ch. Links Verlag, 2008).

Rainer Karlsch and Raymond G. Stokes, *Faktor Öl: Die Mineralölwirtschaft in Deutschland 1859–1974* (Munich: Beck, 2003).

Stefan Karner, *Die Steiermark im 20. Jahrhundert. Politik—Wirtschaft—Gesellschaft—Kultur* (Graz/Vienna/Cologne, Styria, 2000).

Stefan Karner, "Die sowjetische Gewahrsamsmacht und ihre Justiz nach 1945 gegenüber Österreichern," in Claudia Kuretsidis-Haider and Winfried R. Garscha, eds., *Keine "Abrechnung." " NS-Verbrechen, Justiz und Gesellschaft in Europa nach 1945* (Leipzig/Vienna: Akademische Verlagsanstalt, 1998), pp. 102–129.

Stefan Karner, ed., *Geheime Akten des KGB: "Margarita Ottilinger"* (Graz: Leykam, 1992).

Stefan Karner, *HALT! Tragödien am Eisernen Vorhang. Die Verschlussakten* (Salzburg: Ecowin, 2013).

Stefan Karner, "'Ich bekam zehn Jahre Zwangsarbeit.' Zu den Verschleppungen aus der Steiermark durch sowjetische Organe im Jahr 1945," in Siegfried Beer, ed., *Die "britische Steiermark."" Forschungen zur geschichtlichen Landeskunde der Steiermark*, Vol. 38 (Graz: Historische Landeskommission, 1995), pp. 249–259.

Stefan Karner, *Im Archipel GUPVI. Kriegsgefangenschaft und Internierung in der Sowjetunion 1941–1956* (Vienna/Munich: Oldenbourg, 1995).

Stefan Karner, *Im Kalten Krieg der Spionage. Margarethe Ottillinger in sowjetischer Haft 1948–1955* (Innsbruck/Vienna/Bolzano: StudienVerlag 2016).

Stefan Karner, *Kärntens Wirtschaft 1938–1945. Unter besonderer Berücksichtigung der Rüstungsindustrie*, Vol. 2 of Wissenschaftliche Veröffentlichungen der Landeshauptstadt Klagenfurt series (Klagenfurt: Magistrat d. Stadt Klagenfurt, 1976).

Stefan Karner, "Schuld und Sühne? Der Prozess gegen den Chef der Gendarmerie von Černigov von 1941–1943: Karl Ortner," in Stefan Karner, ed., *Graz in der NS-Zeit 1938–1945*, Special Vol. 1 of Veröffentlichungen des Ludwig Boltzmann-Instituts für Kriegsfolgen-Forschung series (Graz: Selbstverlag, 1999), pp. 159–178.

Stefan Karner, "Zu den sowjetischen Demontagen in Österreich 1945/46: Ein erster Aufriss auf russischer Quellenbasis," in Michael Pammer, Herta Neiß and Michael John, eds., *Erfahrung der Moderne: Festschrift für Roman Sandgruber zum 60. Geburtstag* (Stuttgart: Steiner, 2007), pp. 301–312.

Stefan Karner, "Zum Umfang der sowjetischen Demontagen in Österreich 1945/46. Eine erste Aufstellung aus russischen Quellen," *Mitteilungsblatt der Korrespondenten der Historischen Landeskommission für Steiermark*, Vol. 9 (2007), pp. 117–168.

Stefan Karner, "Zur Politik der sowjetischen Besatzungs- und Gewahrsamsmacht: Das Fallbeispiel Margarethe Ottillinger," in Alfred Ableitinger, Siegfried Beer and Eduard G. Staudinger, Österreich unter alliierter Besatzung 1945–1955 (Vienna/Cologne/Graz: Böhlau, 1998), pp. 401–431.

Stefan Karner and Karl Duffek, eds., *Widerstand in Österreich 1938–1945. Die Beiträge der Parlaments-Enquete 2005* (Graz/Vienna: Verein zur Förderung der Forschung von Folgen nach Konflikten und. Kriegen, 2007).

Stefan Karner and Peter Ruggenthaler, "'Eine weitere Unterstützung der jugoslawischen Gebietsforderungen bringt uns in eine unvorteilhafte Lage.' Der Artikel 7 des Österreichischen Staatsvertrags als diplomatischer Kompromiss mit Österreich und den Westmächten," in Stefan Karner and Andreas Moritsch, eds., *Aussiedlung—Verschleppung—nationaler Kampf. Kärnten und die nationale Frage*, Vol. 1 (Klagenfurt: Hermagoras—Heyn, 2005), pp. 99–118.

Stefan Karner and Peter Ruggenthaler, "Stalin und Österreich. Sowjetische Österreich-Politik 1938 bis 1953," *Jahrbuch für Historische Kommunismusforschung*, 2005, pp. 102–140.

Stefan Karner and Peter Ruggenthaler, "Stalin, Tito und die Österreich-Frage," in Günter Bischof and Josef Leidenfrost, eds., *Die bevormundete Nation: Österreich und die Alliierten 1945–1949*, Vol. 4 of Innsbrucker Forschungen zur Zeitgeschichte series (Innsbruck: Haymon, 1988), pp. 81–105.

Stefan Karner and Peter Ruggenthaler, "Unter sowjetischer Kontrolle: Zur Regierungsbildung in Österreich 1945," in Stefan Karner and Barbara Stelzl-Marx, eds., *Die Rote Armee in Österreich: Sowjetische Besatzung 1945–1955. Beiträge* (Graz/Vienna/Munich: Oldenbourg, 2005), pp. 97–140.

Stefan Karner and Peter Ruggenthaler, *Zwangsarbeit in der Land- und Forstwirtschaft auf dem Gebiet der Republik Österreich 1939–1945*. Veröffentlichungen der Österreichischen Historikerkommission. Vermögensentzug während der NS-Zeit sowie Rückstellungen und Entschädigungen seit 1945 in Österreich). Vol. 26/2. (Vienna/Munich: Oldenbourg, 2004).

Stefan Karner and Barbara Stelzl, "Strafrechtssystem und Gerichtspraxis in der Sowjetunion 1941–1956. Teilstudie des Projektes 'Die Nachkriegsgerichtsbarkeit als nicht-bürokratische Form der Entnazifizierung: Österreichische Justizakten im europäischen Vergleich,'" unpublished manuscript, Graz, 1998.

Stefan Karner, Peter Ruggenthaler and Barbara Stelzl-Marx, "Die sowjetische Besatzung der Steiermark 1945," in Stefan Karner and Othmar Pickl, eds., *Die Rote Armee in der Steiermark: Sowjetische Besatzung 1945* (Graz: Leykam, 2008), pp. 9–42.

Stefan Karner and Othmar Pickl, eds., *Die Rote Armee in der Steiermark: Sowjetische Besatzung 1945*, in cooperation with Walter M. Iber, Harald Knoll, Hermine Prügger, Peter Ruggenthaler, Arno Wonisch and Silke Stern (Graz: Leykam, 2008).

Stefan Karner and Barbara Stelzl-Marx, eds., *Stalins letzte Opfer. Verschleppte und erschossene Österreicher in Moskau 1950–1953*, Vol. 5 of Kriegsfolgen-Forschung series (Vienna/Munich: Böhlau, 2008).

Stefan Karner and Barbara Stelzl-Marx, eds., *Die Rote Armee in Österreich. Sowjetische Besatzung 1945–1955. Beiträge* (Graz/Vienna/Munich: Oldenbourg, 2005).

Stefan Karner, Erich Reiter, and Gerald Schöpfer, eds., *Kalter Krieg. Beiträge zur Ost-West-Konfrontation 1945 bis 1990* (Graz: Leykam, 2002).

Stefan Karner, Barbara Stelzl-Marx, and Alexander Tschubarjan, eds., *Die Rote Armee in Österreich: Sowjetische Besatzung 1945–1955. Dokumente. Krasnaya Armiya v Avstrii: Sovetskaya okkupatsiya 1945–1955. Dokumenty* (Graz/Vienna/Munich: Oldenbourg, 2005).

Stefan Karner and Alexander Tschubarjan, eds., *Die Moskauer Deklaration 1943. "Österreich wieder herstellen"* (Vienna/Munich: Böhlau, 2015).

Robert H. Keyserlingk, *Austria in World War II. An Anglo-American Dilemma* (Kingston/Montreal: McGill Queens University Press, 1988).

Herbert Killian, *Geraubte Freiheit. Ein Österreicher verschollen in Nordostsibirien* (Berndorf: Kral, 2008).

Herbert Killian, *Geraubte Jahre. Ein Österreicher verschleppt in den GULAG* (Vienna: Amalthea, 2005).

Herbert Killian, *Geraubte Jugend. Ein Österreicher kehrt zurück aus Sibirien* (Berndorf: Kral, 2010).

Herbert Killian, "Im GULAG von Kolyma. Betroffene erzählen," in Harald Knoll, Peter Ruggenthaler and Barbara Stelzl-Marx, eds., *Konflikte und Kriege im 20. Jahrhundert. Aspekte ihrer Folgen* (Graz: Eigenverlag, 2003), pp. 73–90.

Otto Klambauer, "Die Frage des deutschen Eigentums in Potsdam," *Jahrbuch für Zeitgeschichte*, 1978, pp. 127–174.
Otto Klambauer, "Staat im Staate: Sowjetisches Vermögen in Österreich 1945–1955," in Stefan Karner and Gottfried Stangler, eds., *"Österreich ist frei!": Der österreichische Staatsvertrag 1955. Beitragband zur Ausstellung auf Schloss Schallaburg 2005* (Horn/Vienna: Berger, 2005), pp. 182–187.
Erich Klein, ed., *Die Russen in Wien: Die Befreiung Österreichs* (Vienna: Falter Verlag, 1995).
Robert Knight, "The Main Records of the Public Record Office for Post-War Austria," in Günter Bischof and Josef Leidenfrost, eds., *Die bevormundete Nation: Österreich und die Alliierten 1945–1949*, Vol. 4 of Innsbrucker Forschungen zur Zeitgeschichte series (Innsbruck: Haymon, 1988), pp. 427–432.
Harald Knoll and Dieter Bacher, "Nachrichtendienste und Spionage im Österreich der Besatzungszeit," in Stefan Karner and Barbara Stelzl-Marx, eds., *Stalins letzte Opfer. Verschleppte und erschossene Österreicher in Moskau 1950–1953*, Vol. 5 of Kriegsfolgen-Forschung series (Vienna/Munich: Böhlau, 2008), pp. 157–168.
Harald Knoll and Barbara Stelzl-Marx, "Die Fälle Marek und Kiridus. Zur sowjetischen Strafjustiz in Österreich," in Stefan Karner and Gottfried Stangler, eds., *"Österreich ist frei!" Der Österreichische Staatsvertrag* (Horn/Vienna: Berger, 2005), pp. 143–147.
Harald Knoll and Barbara Stelzl-Marx, "Sowjetische Strafjustiz in Österreich. Verhaftungen und Verurteilungen 1945–1955," in Stefan Karner and Barbara Stelzl-Marx, eds., *Die Rote Armee in Österreich. Sowjetische Besatzung 1945–1955. Beiträge* (Graz/Vienna/Munich: Oldenbourg, 2005), pp. 275–321.
Reinhold Knoll and Martin Haidinger, *Spione, Spitzel und Agenten. Analyse einer Schattenwelt* (St. Pölten/Vienna: NP Buchverlag, 2001).
A. I. Kokurin and N. V. Petrov, *Lubyanka. Organy VChK-OGPU-NKVD-NKGB-MGB-MVD-KGB 1917-1991. Spravochnik. Rossiya XX vek. Dokumenty* (Moscow: ROSSPEN, 2003).
Volker Koop, *Himmlers letztes Aufgebot. Die NS-Organisation "Werwolf"* (Vienna/Cologne/Weimar: Böhlau, 2008).
Bruno W. Koppensteiner, "Béthouarts Alpenfestung. Militärische Planungen und Verteidigungsvorbereitungen der französischen Besatzungsmacht in Tirol und Vorarlberg," in Erwin A. Schmidl, ed., *Österreich im frühen Kalten Krieg 1945–1958. Spione, Partisanen, Kriegspläne* (Vienna/Cologne/Weimar: Böhlau, 2000), pp. 193–238.
A. V. Korotkov, A. D. Chernov and A. A. Chernobaev, Posetiteli kremlevskogo kabineta I. V. Stalina, *Istoricheskii arkhiv*, 1996/4, pp. 66–131.
Wolfgang Kos and Georg Rigele, eds., *Inventur 45/55. Österreich im ersten Jahrzehnt der Zweiten Republik* (Vienna: Sonderzahl, 1996).
Hans-Günter Kowalski, "Die European Advisory Commission als Instrument alliierter Deutschland-Planungen 1943-1945," *Zeitschrift für Geschichtswissenschaft*, Vol. 19 (1971), pp. 261–293.
S. Kozlov, *Spetsnaz GRU. Ocherki istorii. Istoriya sozdaniya ot rot k brigadam 1950–1979 gg.* (Moscow: SPSL–Russkaya Panorama, 2009).

Mark Kramer, "Stalin, Soviet Policy, and the Consolidation of a Communist Bloc in Eastern Europe, 1944–1953," in Vladimir Tismaneanu, ed., *Stalinism Revisited: The Establishment of Communist Regimes in East-Central Europe* (Budapest/New York: Central European University Press, 2009) pp. 50–102.

Olga Kurilo, ed., *Der Zweite Weltkrieg im deutschen und russischen Gedächtnis* (Berlin: Avinus-Verlag, 2006).

G. P. Kynin and J. Laufer, *SSSR i germanskii vopros. 22 iyunya 1941g.-8 maya 1945. SSSR i germanskii vopros 1941–1949*, Vol. 1 (Moscow: Izdatel'stvo Instituta Mezhdunarodnykh Otnoshenii,1996).

Klaus Larres, *Churchill's Cold War. The Politics of Personal Diplomacy* (New Haven//London: Yale University Press, 2002).

Jochen Laufer, "Der Friedensvertrag mit Deutschland als Problem der sowjetischen Außenpolitik. Die Stalin-Note vom 10. März 1952 im Lichte neuer Quellen," *Vierteljahrshefte für Zeitgeschichte*, Vol. 52 (2004), pp. 99–118.

Jochen Laufer, "Die UdSSR und die Zoneneinteilung Deutschlands (1943/44)," *Zeitschrift für Geschichtswissenschaft*, Vol. 43 (1995), pp. 309–331.

Ol'ga Lavinskaja, "Das Militärtribunal der Zentralen Gruppe der Sowjetischen Streitkräfte und die Verurteilung von Personen nicht-österreichischer Staatsangehörigkeit," in Stefan Karner and Barbara Stelzl-Marx, eds., *Stalins letzte Opfer. Verschleppte und erschossene Österreicher in Moskau 1950–1953*, Vol. 5 of Kriegsfolgen-Forschung series (Vienna/Munich: Böhlau, 2008), pp. 205–224.

Ol'ga Lavinskaja, "Zum Tode verurteilt. Gnadengesuche österreichischer Zivilisten an den Obersten Sowjet der UdSSR," in Stefan Karner and Barbara Stelzl-Marx, eds., *Die Rote Armee in Österreich. Sowjetische Besatzung 1945–1955. Beiträge* (Graz/Vienna/Munich: Oldenbourg, 2005), pp. 323–338.

Natal'ja Lebedeva, "Österreichische Kommunisten im Moskauer Exil: Die Komintern, die Abteilung für internationale Information des ZK der VKP(b) und Österreich 1943–1945," in Stefan Karner and Barbara Stelzl-Marx, eds., *Die Rote Armee in Österreich: Sowjetische Besatzung 1945–1955. Beiträge* (Graz/Vienna/Munich: Oldenbourg, 2005), pp. 39–60.

Sabine Lee, *Children Born of War in the Twentieth Century* (Manchester: Manchester University Press 2017).

Sabine Lee, "Kinder amerikanischer Besatzungssoldaten in Europa: ein Vergleich der Situation britischer und deutscher Kinder," in Ingvill C. Mochmann, Sabine Lee and Barbara Stelzl-Marx, eds., *Children Born of War: Second World War and Beyond. Focus. Kinder des Krieges: Zweiter Weltkrieg und danach, Historical Social Research/Historische Sozialforschung*, Vol. 34 (2009), No. 3 (Cologne: Zentrum für Historische Sozialforschung, 2009), pp. 321–351.

Melvyn P. Leffler, *For the Soul of Mankind: The United States, the Soviet Union and the Cold War* (New York: Hill and Wang, 2007).

Melvyn P. Leffler, "Inside Enemy Archives: The Cold War Reopened," *Foreign Affairs*, Vol. 74 (1996), No. 4, pp. 122–125.

Josef Leidenfrost, "Die amerikanische Besatzungsmacht und der Wiederbeginn des Politischen Lebens in Österreich, 1944–1947," Ph.D. Diss., University of Vienna, 1984.

Hannes Leidinger and Verena Moritz, *Russisches Wien: Begegnungen aus vier Jahrhunderten* (Vienna/Cologne/Weimar: Böhlau, 2004).
Jill Lewis, *Workers and Politics in Occupied Austria, 1945–1955* (Manchester: Manchester University Press, 2007).
Michael Ludwig, Klaus Dieter Mulley and Robert Streibel, *Der Oktoberstreik 1950. Ein Wendepunkt der Zweiten Republik* (Vienna: Picus, 1991).
Nikolai M. Lun'kov, *Russkii diplomat v Evrope: Tridtsat' let v desyati evropeiskikh stolitsakh* (Moscow: Olma-Press, 1999).
Wilfried Mähr, *Der Marshallplan in Österreich* (Graz: Styria, 1989).
Charles S. Maier with Günter Bischof, eds., *The Marshall Plan and Germany: West German Development within the Framework of the European Recovery Program* (Oxford: Berg, 1991).
Eduard Mark, "Revolution by Degrees: Stalin's National-Front Strategy for Europe, 1941–1947," CWIHP Working Paper No. 31, Washington, DC, 2001.
Hans Maršálek, *Die Geschichte des Konzentrationslagers Mauthausen. Dokumentation* (Vienna/Linz: Österreichische Lagergemeinschaft, Mauthausen-Aktiv–Oberösterreich, 2006).
Karl Marschall, *Volksgerichtsbarkeit und Verfolgung von nationalsozialistischen Gewaltverbrechen in Österreich* (Vienna: Bundesministerium für Justiz, 1987).
Vojtech Mastny, *The Cold War and Soviet Insecurity: The Stalin Years* (New York/Oxford: Oxford University Press, 1996).
Vojtech Mastny, "Die NATO im sowjetischen Denken und Handeln," in Vojtech Mastny and Gustav Schmidt, *Konfrontationsmuster des Kalten Krieges, 1949–1956* (Munich: Oldenbourg, 2003), pp. 381–471.
Vojtech Mastny, *Russia's Road to the Cold War: Diplomacy, Warfare, and the Politics of Communism, 1941–1945* (New York: Columbia University Press, 1979).
Vojtech Mastny, "Stalin and the Militarization of the Cold War," in *International Security*, Vol. 9 (1984-85), pp. 109–129.
Siegfried Mattl, "Frauen in Österreich nach 1945," in Rudolf G. Ardelt, Wolfgang J. A. Huber and Anton Staudinger, eds., *Unterdrückung und Emanzipation. Festschrift für Erika Weinzierl. Zum 60. Geburtstag* (Vienna/Salzburg: Geyer, 1985), pp. 101–126.
Ernest R. May, ed., *American Cold War Strategy: Interpreting NSC 68* (Boston, MA: St. Martin's Press, 1993).
Thomas J. McCormick, *America's Half Century: United States Foreign Policy in the Cold War* (Baltimore: The Johns Hopkins University Press, 1989), pp. 92–108.
Barry McLoughlin, Hans Schafranek, and Walter Szevera, *Aufbruch. Hoffnung. Endstation. Österreicherinnen und Österreicher in der Sowjetunion 1925–1945* (Vienna: Deuticke, 1997).
Ministerstvo inostrannykh del SSSR, ed., *SSSR – Avstriya, 1938–1979. Dokumenty i materialy* (Moscow: Politizdat, 1980).
Wilson D. Miscamble, *From Roosevelt to Truman: Potsdam, Hiroshima, and the Cold War* (Cambridge: Cambridge University Press, 2002).
Saskia Mitreuter, Marie Kaiser, Sophie Roupetz, Barbara Stelzl-Marx, Philipp Kuwert, Heide Glaesmer, "Questions of Identity in Children Born of War—Embarking

on a Search for the Unknown Soldier Father," in *Journal of Child and Family Studies*, 2019, DOI 10.1007/s10826-019-01501.

Kid Möchel, *Der geheime Krieg der Agenten. Spionagedrehscheibe* (Vienna/Hamburg: Rasch und Röhring, 1997).

Ingvill C. Mochmann and Stein Ugelvik Larsen, "The Forgotten Consequences of the War: The Life Course of Children Fathered by German Soldiers in Norway and Denmark during WWII—Some Empirical Results," *Historical Social Research*, Vol. 33 (2008), pp. 347–363.

Fritz Molden, *Fepolinski & Waschlapski: Auf dem berstenden Stern* (Vienna/Munich/Zürich: Molden, 1976).

Martin Moll, ed., *"Führer-Erlasse" 1939–1945. Edition sämtlicher überlieferter, nicht im Reichsgesetzblatt abgedruckter, von Hitler während des Zweiten Weltkrieges schriftlich erteilter Direktiven aus den Bereichen Staat, Partei, Wirtschaft, Besatzungspolitik und Militärverwaltung* (Stuttgart: Franz Steiner, 1997).

Wolfgang Mueller, *A Good Example of a Peaceful Coexistence? The Soviet Union, Austria and Neutrality, 1955–1991* (Vienna: Verlag der Österreichischen Akademie der Wissenschaften, 2011).

Wolfgang Mueller, "Anstelle des Staatsvertrages: Die UdSSR und das Zweite Kontrollabkommen 1946," in Manfried Rauchensteiner and Robert Kriechbaumer, eds., *Die Gunst des Augenblicks. Neuere Forschungen zu Staatsvertrag und Neutralität* (Vienna/Cologne/Weimar: Böhlau, 2005), pp. 291–320.

Wolfgang Mueller, "'Die Kanonen schießen nicht . . . Aber der Kampf geht weiter.' Die Propaganda der sowjetischen Besatzungsmacht in Österreich im Kalten Krieg," in Stefan Karner and Barbara Stelzl-Marx, eds., *Die Rote Armee in Österreich: Sowjetische Besatzung 1945–1955. Beiträge* (Graz/Vienna/Munich: Oldenbourg, 2005), pp. 339–362.

Wolfgang Mueller, *Die sowjetische Besatzung in Österreich 1945–1955 und ihre politische Mission* (Vienna/Cologne/Weimar: Böhlau, 2005).

Wolfgang Mueller, "Kulturpolitik und Propaganda der sowjetischen Besatzungsmacht in Österreich," Stefan Karner and Gottfried Stangler, eds., *"Österreich ist frei!": Der österreichische Staatsvertrag 1955. Beitragband zur Ausstellung auf Schloss Schallaburg 2005* (Horn/Vienna: Berger, 2005), pp. 241–244.

Wolfgang Mueller, "Sowjetbesatzung, Nationale Front und der 'Friedliche Übergang zum Sozialismus': Fragmente sowjetischer Österreich-Planung 1945–1955," in *200 Jahre Russisches Außenministerium*, Vol. 50 of Mitteilungen des Österreichischen Staatsarchivs series (Vienna: Studienverlag 2003), pp. 143–145.

Wolfgang Mueller, "Die Teilung Österreichs als politische Option für KPÖ und UdSSR 1948," *Zeitgeschichte*, Vol. 32 (2005), No. 1, pp. 47–54.

Wolfgang Mueller, Arnold Suppan, Norman M. Naimark, and Gennadij Bordjugov, eds., *Sowjetische Politik in Österreich 1945-1955. Dokumente aus russischen Archiven*, Vol. 93 of Fontes Rerum Austriacarum. Zweite Abt. Diplomararia et Acta (Vienna: Verlag der Österreichischen Akademie der Wissenschaften, 2005).

Manfred Mugrauer, "'Teilungspläne' und 'Putschabsichten.' Die KPÖ im Gedenkenjahr 2005," in *Mitteilungen der Alfred Klahr Gesellschaft*, Vol. No. 4 (2005), pp. 8–15.

Jean-Paul Mulders, *Auf der Suche nach Hitlers Sohn. Eine Beweisaufnahme* (Munich: Herbig, 2009).
Stefan A. Müller, *Die versäumte Freundschaft. Österreich-Mexiko 1901–1956. Von der Aufnahme der Beziehungen bis zu Mexikos Beitritt zum Staatsvertrag*, Vol. 3 of Lateinamerikanistik series (Vienna: LIT-Verlag, 2006).
G. P. Murashko et al., *Vostochnaya Evropa v dokumentakh rossiiskikh arkhivov 1944–1953*, Vol. 1 (1944-1948) (Moscow/Novosibirsk: Sibirskii khronograf, 1997).
Bogdan Musial, *Stalins Beutezug. Die Plünderung Deutschlands und der Aufstieg der Sowjetunion zur Weltmacht* (Berlin: Propyläen, 2010).
Bogdan Musial, "Modernisierung durch Demontagen? Zur Wirtschaftspolitik Stalins nach dem Zweiten Weltkrieg," in Wolfram Dornik, Johannes Gießauf and Walter M. Iber, eds., *Krieg und Wirtschaft: Von der Antike bis ins 21. Jahrhundert* (Innsbruck: Studienverlag, 2010).
Clément Mutombo, *Les damnés innocents du Vorarlberg. Parianisme envers les enfants historiques (1946)* (Frankfurt am Main: Peter Lang, 2007).
D. G. Nadzhafov, "Antiamerikanskie propagandistskie pristrastiya Stalinskogo rukovodstva," Aleksandr Chubar'yan et al., eds., *Stalinskoe desyatiletie kholodnoi voiny. Fakty i gipotezy* (Moscow: Nauka, 1999), pp. 134–150.
D. G. Nadzhafov, "K voprosu o genezise kholodnoi voiny," in *Kholodnaya Voina 1945–1963* pp. 65–104.
Norman N. Naimark, *Die Russen in Deutschland. Die sowjetische Besatzungszone 1945 bis 1949* (Berlin: Propyläen, 1997).
Norman N. Naimark, "Stalin and Europe in the Postwar Period, 1945–53: Issues and Problems," *Journal of Modern European History*, Vol. 2 (2004), No. 1, pp. 28–57.
Norman Naimark and Leonid Gibianskii, *The Establishment of Communist Regimes in Eastern Europe, 1944–1949* (Boulder/Oxford: Westview Press, 1997).
Mikhail M. Narinskii, "Sovetskaya vneshnyaya politika i Komintern 1939–1941," in A. O. Chubaryan, ed., *Voina i Politika 1939–1941* (Moscow: Nauka, 1999), pp. 38–49.
Mikhail Narinsky, "The Soviet Union, Finland and the Marshall Plan," in Jukka Nevakivi, ed., *Finnish-Soviet Relations 1944–1948* (Helsinki: University of Helsinki, 1994), pp. 80–99.
Siegfried Nasko, ed., *Karl Renner—vom Bauernsohn zum Bundespräsidenten* (Vienna/Gloggnitz: Österreichisches Gesellschafts- und Wirtschaftsmuseum, 1979).
Siegfried Nasko, "Zur Rolle Dr. Renners im April 1945," in Siegfried Nasko, ed., *Gedenkraum 1945: Hier entstand Österreich wieder. Katalog zu "Gedenkraum 1945"* (Vienna/Wiener Neustadt/Hochwolkersdorf: Österreichisches Gesellschafts- und Wirtschaftsmuseum, 1981).
Franz Nemschak, *Zehn Jahre österreichische Wirtschaft 1945–1955* (Vienna: Österreichisches Institut für Wirtschaftsforschung, 1955).
Vitaliy Nikolskiy, *GRU v gody Velikoi otechestvennoi voiny* (Moscow: Yauza–Eksmo, 2005).

Arnold A. Offner, *Another Such Victory: President Truman and the Cold War 1945–1953* (Stanford, CA: Stanford University Press, 2002).
I. I. Orlik, "Vostochnaya Evropa v dokumentakh rossiiskikh arkhivov. 1944–1953," *Novaya i noveishaya istoriya*, 1999/5.
Christian Ostermann, "Das Ende der 'Rollback'-Politik: Eisenhower, die amerikanische Osteuropapolitik und der Ungarn-Aufstand von 1956," in Winfried Heinemann and Norbert Wiggershaus, eds., *Das Internationale Krisenjahr 1956: Polen, Ungarn, Suez*, Vol. 48 of Beiträge zur Militärgeschichte (Munich: Oldenbourg, 1999), pp. 515–532.
"Österreichs Wirtschaftsverkehr mit der Sowjetunion," *WIFO-Monatsberichte*, Supplement 33 to No. 11, 1955, p. 6.
Donal O'Sullivan, *Stalins "Cordon sanitaire": Die sowjetische Osteuropapolitik und die Reaktionen des Westens 1939–1949* (Paderborn: Schöningh, 2003).
Donal O'Sullivan, "'Wer immer ein Gebiet besetzt . . .' Sowjetische Osteuropapolitik 1943–1947/48," in Stefan Creuzberger and Manfred Görtemaker, eds., *Gleichschaltung unter Stalin? Die Entwicklung der Parteien im östlichen Europa 1944–1949* (Paderborn: Schöningh, 2002), pp. 45–84.
Ol'ga Pavlenko, "Österreich im Kraftfeld der sowjetischen Diplomatie 1945," in Stefan Karner and Barbara Stelzl-Marx, eds., *Die Rote Armee in Österreich: Sowjetische Besatzung 1945–1955. Beiträge* (Graz/Vienna/Munich: Oldenbourg, 2005), pp. 566–601.
Kurt Peball, "Die Benützungsbestimmungen des Österreichischen Staatsarchivs," in Günter Bischof and Josef Leidenfrost, eds., *Die bevormundete Nation: Österreich und die Alliierten 1945–1949*, Vol. 4 of Innsbrucker Forschungen zur Zeitgeschichte series (Innsbruck: Haymon, 1988), pp. 409–413.
V. Pechatnov, "The Big Three After World War II: New Documents on Soviet Thinking about Post-War Relations with USA and Great Britain," CWIHP Working Paper No. 13, Cold War International History Project, Washington, DC, 1995.
V. O. Pechatnov, *Ot soyuza k kholodnoi voine. Sovetsko-amerikanskie otnosheniya v 1945–1947gg.* (Moscow: MGIMO, 2006).
V. O. Pechatnov, "Ot soyuza—k vrazhde (sovetsko-amerikanskie otnosheniya v 1945–1946 gg.)," in *Kholodnaya Voina 1945–1963*, pp. 21–65.
Nikita Petrov, "Die militärische Spionageabwehr in Österreich und die Todesstrafe. Struktur, Funktionen, Praxis," in Karner and Stelzl-Marx, eds., *Stalins letzte Opfer. Verschleppte und erschossene Österreicher in Moskau 1950–1953*, Vol. 5 of Kriegsfolgen-Forschung series (Vienna/Munich: Böhlau, 2008), pp. 79–96.
Nikita Petrov, *Die sowjetischen Geheimdienstmitarbeiter in Deutschland. Der leitende Personalbestand der Staatssicherheitsorgane der UdSSR in der Sowjetischen Besatzungszone Deutschlands und der DDR von 1945–1954. Biografisches Nachschlagewerk* (Berlin: Metropol, 2010).
Anton Pelinka, *Karl Renner zur Einführung* (Hamburg: Junius, 1989).
Peter Pelinka, *Erbe und Neubeginn: Die Revolutionären Sozialisten in Österreich 1934–38* (Vienna: Europaverlag, 1981).
Anton Pelinka and Rolf Steininger, eds., *Österreich und die Sieger* (Vienna: Braumüller, 1986).

Perepiska predsedatelya Soveta ministrov SSSR s prezidentami SShA i prem'er-ministrami Velikobritanii vo vremya Velikoi Otechestvennoi voiny 1941–1945 gg., Vol. 1 (Moscow: Izdatel'stvo politicheskoi literatury, 1957).

Jiří Pernes, "The Establishment and First Crisis of the Communist Regime in Czechoslovakia (1948–1958)," in Jaroslav Pánek and Oldřich Tůma et alii, *A History of the Czech Lands* (Prague: Karolinum Press, 2009), pp. 493–520.

Edith Petschnigg, "Stimmen aus der Todeszelle. Kurzbiographien der Opfer," in Stefan Karner and Barbara Stelzl-Marx, eds., *Stalins letzte Opfer. Verschleppte und erschossene Österreicher in Moskau 1950–1953*, Vol. 5 of Kriegsfolgen-Forschung series (Vienna/Munich: Böhlau, 2008), pp. 301–588.

Nikita Petrov, "Die Inneren Truppen des NKVD/MVD im System der sowjetischen Repressionsorgane in Österreich 1945–1946," in Stefan Karner and Barbara Stelzl-Marx, eds., *Die Rote Armee in Österreich. Sowjetische Besatzung 1945–1955. Beiträge* (Graz/Vienna/Munich: Oldenbourg, 2005), pp. 219–242.

Harry Piotrowski, "The Soviet Union and the Renner Government of Austria, April-November 1945," *Central European History*, Vol. 20 (1987), pp. 246–279.

Dieter Pohl, *Nationalsozialistische Judenverfolgung in Ostgalizien 1941–1944. Organisation und Durchführung eines staatlichen Massenverbrechens* (München: Oldenbourg, 1996).

M. A. Poltavskii, *Diplomatiya imperializma i malye strany Evropy (1938–1945 gg.)* (Moscow: 1973).

Pavel Polyan, *Zhertvy dvukh diktatur. Zhizn', trud, unizhenie i smert' sovetskikh voennoplennykh i ostarbaiterov na chuzhbine i na rodine* (Moscow: Rosspen, 2002).

Silvio Pons, "Sumerki Kominforma," in Grant Adibekov, A. di B´yadzho [di Biagio], L. Ya. Gibianskii, F. Fori and S. Pons, eds., *Soveshchaniya Kominforma, 1947, 1948, 1949. Dokumenty i materialy* (Moscow: ROSSPEN, 1998), pp. 374–398.

Silvio Pons, "The Twilight of the Cominform," in Giulano Procacci, Grant Adibekov, Anna Di Biagio, Leonid Gibianskii, Francesca Gori and Silvio Pons, eds., *The Cominform. Minutes of the Three Conferences 1947/1948/1949* (Milan: Feltrinelli Ed.,1994), pp. 483–503.

Hugo Portisch, *Am Anfang war das Ende: Österreich II. Die Geschichte Österreichs vom 2. Weltkrieg bis zum Staatsvertrag*, Vol. 1 (Munich: Wilhelm Heyne Verlag, 1993).

Hugo Portisch, *Der lange Weg zur Freiheit*, Vol. 4 of Österreich II. *Die Geschichte Österreichs vom 2. Weltkrieg bis zum Staatsvertrag* (Munich: Wilhelm Heyne Verlag, 1993).

Nina Prelec, "Das Russendenkmal in Bad Radkersburg: Ende des Krieges in Radkersburg 1945. Aufbau und Abbau des Russendenkmals," unpublished paper, Bad Radkersburg, 1996.

Michail Prozumenščikov, "Nach Stalins Tod. Sowjetische Österreich-Politik 1953–1955," in Stefan Karner and Barbara Stelzl-Marx, eds., *Die Rote Armee in Österreich: Sowjetische Besatzung 1945–1955. Beiträge* (Graz/Vienna/Munich: Oldenbourg, 2005), pp. 729–753.

János M. Rainer, "Der Weg der ungarischen Volksdemokratie: Das Mehrparteiensystem und seine Beseitigung 1944–1949," in Stefan Creuzberger and Manfred Görtemaker, eds., *Gleichschaltung unter Stalin? Die Entwicklung der Parteien im östlichen Europa 1944–1949* (Paderborn: Schöningh, 2002), pp. 319–352.

Christoph Ransmayr, "Kaprun: Oder die Errichtung einer Mauer," in Christoph Ransmayr, *Der Weg nach Surabaya: Reportagen und kleine Prosa* (Frankfurt am Main: Fischer Taschenbuch-Verlag, 1997).

Oliver Rathkolb, "Politische Propaganda der amerikanischen Besatzungsmacht in Österreich 1945 bis 1950. Ein Beitrag zur Geschichte des Kalten Krieges in der Presse-, Kultur- und Rundfunkpolitik," Ph.D. Diss., University of Vienna, 1981.

Oliver Rathkolb, *Washington ruft Wien. US-Großmachtpolitik und Österreich 1953–1963* (Vienna/Cologne/Weimar: Böhlau, 1997).

Manfried Rauchensteiner, "Nachkriegsösterreich 1945," Österreichische Militärische Zeitschrift, Vol. 6 (1972), pp. 407–421.

Manfried Rauchensteiner, *Der Sonderfall: Die Besatzungszeit in Österreich 1945 bis 1955*, new ed. (Graz/Vienna/Cologne: Böhlau, 1995).

Manfried Rauchensteiner, *Stalinplatz 4. Österreich unter alliierter Besatzung* (Vienna: Edition Steinbauer, 2005).

Manfried Rauchensteiner, *Die Zwei. Die Große Koalition in Österreich 1945–1966* (Vienna: Österreichischer Bundesverlag, 1987).

Manfried Rauchensteiner, ed., *Zwischen den Blöcken: NATO und Warschauer Pakt und Österreich* (Vienna: Böhlau, 2010).

Manfried Rauchensteiner and Wolfgang Etschmann, eds., Österreich 1945: Ein Ende und viele Anfänge (Graz/Vienna/Cologne: Styria, 1997).

Manfried Rauchensteiner and Robert Kriechbaumer, eds., *Die Gunst des Augenblicks. Neuere Forschungen zu Staatsvertrag und Neutralität*, Schriftenreihe des Forschungsinstitutes für politisch-historische Studien der Dr.-Wilfried-Haslauer-Bibliothek (Vienna/Cologne/Weimar: Böhlau, 2005).

Hans Raupach, *Geschichte der Sowjetwirtschaft* (Hamburg: Rowohlt, 1964).

Kimmo Rentola, "Vesna 1948 goda: kakoy put' vyberet Finlyandiya?," in O. V. Chernysheva, *Severnaya Evropa. Problemy istorii. Vypusk 4* (Moscow: Nauka, 2003), pp. 61–89.

Albert Resis, ed., *Molotov Remembers: Inside Kremlin Politics. Conservations with Felix Chuev* (Chicago: Ivan R. Dee, 1993).

Helmut Roewer, Stefan Schäfer, and Matthias Uhl, *Lexikon der Geheimdienste im 20. Jahrhundert* (Munich: Herbig, 2003).

A. I. Romanov, *Nights Are Longest There: Smersh from the Inside* (London: Hutchinson, 1972).

Wilhelm Romeder, *Das Jahr 1945 in Weitra und Umgebung. Ereignisse. Erlebnisse. Schicksale. Mit einem ausführlichen Beitrag über die Hitler-Verwandten* (Horn: Berger, 2003).

A. A. Roshchin, *Poslevoennoe uregulirovanie v Evrope* (Moscow: Mysl', 1984).

Peter Ruggenthaler, "Die Kärntner Grenze als Verhandlungspoker im frühen Kalten Krieg," *Kärntner Jahrbuch für Politik* (2007), pp. 188–207.

Peter Ruggenthaler, "On the Significance of Austrian Neutrality for Soviet Foreign Policy under Nikita S. Khrushchev," in Günter Bischof, Stefan Karner and Barbara Stelzl-Marx, eds., *The Vienna Summit and Its Importance in International History*. Harvard Cold War Studies Book Series. (Lanham et al.: Lexington 2014), pp. 329–348.

Peter Ruggenthaler, *The Concept of Neutrality in Stalin's Foreign Policy 1945–1953*. Harvard Cold War Studies Book Series (Lanham et al.: Lexington, 2015).

Peter Ruggenthaler, "The 1952 Stalin Note on German Unification. The Ongoing Debate," in *Journal of Cold War Studies*, Vol. 13 (2011), No. 4, pp. 172–212.

Peter Ruggenthaler, "Warum Österreich nicht sowjetisiert werden sollte," in Stefan Karner and Barbara Stelzl-Marx, eds., *Die Rote Armee in Österreich: Sowjetische Besatzung 1945–1955. Beiträge* (Graz/Vienna/Munich: Oldenbourg, 2005), pp. 61–87.

Peter Ruggenthaler, "Warum Österreich nicht sowjetisiert wurde: Sowjetische Österreich-Politik 1945–1953/55," in Stefan Karner and Barbara Stelzl-Marx, eds., *Die Rote Armee in Österreich: Sowjetische Besatzung 1945–1955. Beiträge* (Graz/ Vienna/Munich: Oldenbourg, 2005), pp. 649–726.

Peter Ruggenthaler, ed., *Stalins großer Bluff. Die Geschichte der Stalin-Note in Dokumenten der sowjetischen Führung*, Vol. 95 of Schriftenreihe der Vierteljahrshefte für Zeitgeschichte (Munich: Oldenbourg, 2007).

Peter Ruggenthaler and Walter M. Iber, eds., *Hitlers Sklaven—Stalins "Verräter." Aspekte der Repression an Zwangsarbeitern und Kriegsgefangenen. Eine Zwischenbilanz.* (Innsbruck/Vienna/Bozen: Studienverlag 2010).

O. A. Rzheshevskii, "Sekretnye voennye plany U. Cherchillya protiv Rossii v mae 1945 goda," *Novaya i noveishaya istoriya*, 1999/3, pp. 98–123.

O. A. Rzheshevskii, *Stalin i Cherchill'. Vstrechi. Besedy. Diskussii. Dokumenty, kommentarii 1941–1945* (Moscow: Nauka, 2004).

O. A. Rzheshevskii, N. B. Borisov, and E. K. Zhigunov, eds., *Kto byl kto v Velikoi Otechestvennoi Voine, 1941–1945: Lyudi. Sobytiya. Fakty. Spravochnik* (Moscow: Respublika, 2000).

Helke Sander, "Erinnern/Vergessen," in Helke Sander and Barbara Johr, eds., *Befreier und Befreite. Krieg, Vergewaltigung, Kinder* (Frankfurt am Main: Fischer Taschenbuch Verlag, 2005), pp. 9–20.

Roman Sandgruber, "Das wirtschaftliche Umfeld des Staatsvertrages," in Manfried Rauchensteiner and Robert Kriechbaumer, eds., *Die Gunst des Augenblicks. Neuere Forschungen zu Staatsvertrag und Neutralität* (Vienna/Cologne/Weimar: Böhlau, 2005), pp. 359–377.

Thomas Sandkühler, *"Endlösung" in Galizien. Der Judenmord in Ostpolen und die Rettungsinitiativen von Berthold Beitz 1941–1944* (Bonn: Dietz, 1996).

Silke Satjukow, *Besatzer. "Die Russen" in Deutschland 1945–1994* (Göttingen: Vandenhoeck & Ruprecht, 2008).

Silke Satjukow, "'Russenkinder.' Die Nachkommen von deutschen Frauen und Rotarmisten," in Barbara Stelzl-Marx and Silke Satjukow, eds., *Besatzungskinder. Die Nachkommen alliierter Soldaten in Österreich und Deutschland* (Vienna/ Cologne/Weimar: Böhlau Verlag, 2015), pp. 136–165.

Silke Satjukow and Rainer Gries, *"'Bankerte!'"*: *Besatzungskinder in Deutschland nach 1945* (Frankfurt/New York: Campus, 2015).

Silke Satjukow and Barbara Stelzl-Marx, "Besatzungskinder in Vergangenheit und Gegenwart," in Barbara Stelzl-Marx and Silke Satjukow, *Besatzungskinder. Die Nachkommen alliierter Soldaten in Österreich und Deutschland* (Vienna/Cologne/Weimar: Böhlau Verlag 2015), pp. 11–14.

Sbornik osnovnykh dokumentov SSSR, SShA, Anglii, Frantsii ob Avstrii, Vol. 1 (Moscow: 1953).

Adolf Schärf, *Österreichs Erneuerung 1945–1955: Das erste Jahrzehnt der Zweiten Republik* (Vienna: Verlag der Wiener Volksbuchhandlung, 1955).

Adolf Schärf, *Österreichs Wiederaufrichtung im Jahre 1945* (Vienna: Verlag der Wiener Volksbuchhandlung, 1960).

Norbert Schausberger, *Rüstung in Österreich 1938–1945* (Vienna: Hollinek, 1970).

Alfons Schilcher, "Die Politik der Provisorischen Regierung und der Alliierten Großmächte bei der Wiedererrichtung der Republik Österreich," Ph.D. Diss., University of Vienna, 1985.

Erwin A. Schmidl, ed., *Österreich im frühen Kalten Krieg 1945–1958. Spione, Partisanen, Kriegspläne* (Vienna/Cologne/Weimar: Böhlau, 2000).

Karin M. Schmidlechner, *Frauenleben in Männerwelten: Kriegsende und Kriegszeit in der Steiermark*, Vol. 10 of Studien zur Gesellschafts- und Kulturgeschichte series (Vienna: Döcker Verlag, 1997).

Lukas Schretter, *Die Nachkommen britischer Besatzungssoldaten und österreichischer Frauen.* Ph.D. Diss., University of Graz (in preparation).

Sergej Matwejewitsch Schtemenko, *Im Generalstab*, Vol. 1 ([East] Berlin: Militärverlag der Deutschen Demokratischen Republik, 1985).

Klaus Segbers, *Die Sowjetunion im Zweiten Weltkrieg: Die Mobilisierung von Verwaltung, Wirtschaft und Gesellschaft im "Großen Vaterländischen Krieg" 1941–1943* (Munich: Oldenbourg, 1987).

Hans Seidel, *Österreichs Wirtschaft und Wirtschaftspolitik nach dem Zweiten Weltkrieg* (Vienna: MANZ'sche Verlag- und Universitätsbuchhandlung, 2005).

V. A. Sekistov, "Kto nagnetal voennuyu opasnos,'" *Voenno-istoricheskii zhurnal*, 1989/7-10, pp. 20–26.

S. M. Shtemenko, *General'nyi shtab v gody voiny. Kniga vtoraya* (Moscow: Voenizdat, 1974).

S. M. Shtemenko, *General'nyi shtab v gody voiny. Kniga vtoraya* (Moscow: Voennoe izdatel'stvo, 1973).

Peter Sixl, *Sowjetische Kriegsgräber in Österreich*, Special Edition No. 6 of the Veröffentlichungen des Ludwig Boltzmann-Instituts für Kriegsfolgen-Forschung Graz-Wien-Klagenfurt (Graz: Verein zur Förderung der Forschung von Folgen nach Konflikten und Kriegen, 2005).

Peter Sixl, ed., *Sowjetische Tote des Zweiten Weltkrieges in Österreich. Namens- und Grablagenverzeichnis. Ein Gedenkbuch.* Veröffentlichungen des Ludwig

Boltzmann-Instituts für Kriegsfolgen-Forschung, Sonderband 11 (Graz et al.: Verein zur Förderung der Forschung, 2010).
Soveshchaniya Kominforma 1947, 1948, 1949: Dokumenty i Materialy (Moscow: ROSSPEN, 1998).

Sovetskii Soyuz na mezhdunarodnykh konferentsiyakh perioda Velikoi Otechestvennoi voiny 1941–1945 gg. Moskovskaya konferentsiya ministrov inostrannykh del SSSR, SShA i Velikobritanii (19–30 oktyabrya 1943 g.). Sbornik dokumentov, Vol. 1 (Moscow: Politizdatel´stvo, 1978).
Sovetsko-angliiskie otnosheniya vo vremya Velikoi Otechestvennoi voiny, 1941–1945. Dokumenty i materialy, Vol. 1 (Moscow: Izdatel'stvo politicheskoi literatury, 1983).
"'Soyuzniki nazhimayut na tebya dlya togo, chtoby slomit' u tebya volyu . . .': Perepiska Stalina s Molotovym i drugimi chlenami Politibyuro po vneshnepoliticheskim voprosam v sentyabre-dekabre 1945 goda," *Istochnik*, 1999/2, pp. 70–85.
Hubert Speckner, *In der Gewalt des Feindes: Kriegsgefangenenlager in der "Ostmark" 1939 bis 1945*, Vol. 3 of Kriegsfolgen-Forschung series (Vienna/Munich: Oldenbourg, 2003).
Nicolas Spulber, "Soviet Undertakings and Soviet Mixed Companies in Eastern Europe," *Journal of Central European Affairs*, Vol. 14 (1954/55), pp. 154–173.
SSSR v bor'be za nezavisimost' Avstrii (Moscow: Politizdat, 1965).
"Staatssozialistische Zentralplanwirtschaft," in *Gabler Wirtschaftslexikon, Sp–Z*, rev. ed. (Wiesbaden: Gabler, 1992), pp. 3075–3077.
"Staatsvertrag, betreffend die Wiederherstellung eines unabhängigen und demokratischen Österreichs," *Bundesgesetzblatt für die Republik Österreich*, 1955, 30 July 1955, 152, p. 730.
"Staatsvertrag von Saint-Germain-en-Laye vom 10. September 1919," *Staatsgesetzblatt für die Republik Österreich*, 1920, 21 July 1920, 303, pp. 995–1245.
William L. Stearman, *The Soviet Union and the Occupation of Austria: An Analysis of Soviet Policy in Austria, 1945–1955* (Geneva: Siegler, 1961).
Marcel Stein, *Österreichs Generäle 1938–1945 im Deutschen Heer. Schwarz/Gelb—Rot/Weiß/Rot—Hakenkreuz* (Bissendorf: Biblio, 2002).
Hubert Steiner, "Die USIA-Betriebe: Ihre Gründung, Organisation und Rückgabe in die Österreichische Hoheitsverwaltung," *Mitteilungen des Österreichischen Staatsarchivs*, Vol. 43 (1993), pp. 206–220.
Rolf Steininger, "1955. The Austrian Treaty and the German Question," in *Diplomacy & Statecraft*, Vol. 3 (1992), pp. 211–225.
Rolf Steininger, *Austria, Germany, and the Cold War. From the Anschluss to the State Treaty 1938–1955* (New York/Oxford: Berghahn Books, 2008).
Barbara Stelzl-Marx, "Carl Szokoll und die Operation 'Radetzky.' Militärischer Widerstand in Wien 1945 im Spiegel sowjetischer Dokumente," in Dokumentationsarchiv des österreichischen Widerstandes, (ed.), Jahrbuch 2009. Schwerpunkt: Bewaffneter Widerstand – Widerstand im Militär. (Vienna/Berlin: Lit 2009), pp. 95–113.

Barbara Stelzl-Marx, "Death to Spies: Austrian Informants for Western Intelligence Services and Soviet Capital Punishment during the Occupation of Austria," in *Journal of Cold War Studies*, Vol. 14, No. 4, Fall 2012, pp. 167–196.

Barbara Stelzl-Marx, "Die Innensicht der sowjetischen Besatzung in Österreich 1945–1955. Erfahrung, Wahrnehmung, Erinnerung," post-doctoral (*Habilitation*) thesis, University of Graz, 2009.

Barbara Stelzl-Marx, "Die unsichtbare Generation. Kinder sowjetischer Besatzungssoldaten in Österreich und Deutschland," in Ingvill C. Mochmann, Sabine Lee and Barbara Stelzl-Marx, eds., *Children Born of War: Second World War and Beyond. Focus. Kinder des Krieges: Zweiter Weltkrieg und danach, Historical Social Research/Historische Sozialforschung*, Vol. 34 (2009), No. 3 (Cologne: Zentrum für Historische Sozialforschung, 2009), pp. 352–373.

Barbara Stelzl-Marx, "Ein ganz normaler Kriegsverbrecher? Der Prozesse gegen den ehemaligen Lagerkassier des Stalag XVII B Krems-Gneixendorf," in Stefan Karner and Vjačeslav Selemenev, eds., *Österreicher und Sudetendeutsche vor sowjetischen Militär- und Strafgerichten in Weißrussland 1945–1950. Avstriiskie i sudetskie nemtsy pered sovetskimi voennymi tribunalami v Belarusi 1945–1950 gg.* (Graz/Minsk: Selbstverlag, 2007), pp. 368–406.

Barbara Stelzl-Marx, "Entnazifizierung in Österreich: Die Rolle der sowjetischen Besatzungsmacht," in Wolfgang Schuster and Wolfgang Weber, eds., *Entnazifizierung im regionalen Bereich* (Linz: Archiv der Stadt Linz, 2004), pp. 431–454.

Barbara Stelzl-Marx, "Erbsen für Wien: Zur sowjetischen Lebensmittelhilfe 1945," in Stefan Karner and Gottfried Stangler, eds., *"Österreich ist frei!": Der österreichische Staatsvertrag 1955. Beitragsband zur Ausstellung auf Schloss Schallaburg 2005* (Horn/Vienna: Berger, 2005), pp. 54–57.

Barbara Stelzl-Marx, "Freier und Befreier. Zum Beziehungsgeflecht zwischen sowjetischen Besatzungssoldaten und österreichischen Frauen," in Stefan Karner and Barbara Stelzl-Marx, eds., *Die Rote Armee in Österreich. Sowjetische Besatzung 1945–1955. Beiträge* (Graz/Vienna/Munich: Oldenbourg, 2005), pp. 421–448.

Barbara Stelzl-Marx, "'Ich bin stolz, ein Besatzungskind zu sein.' Resilienzfaktoren von Nachkommen sowjetischer Soldaten in Österreich," in Elke Kleinau and Ingvill C. Mochmann, eds., *Kinder des Zweiten Weltkrieges—Stigmatisierung, Ausgrenzung und Bewältigungsstrategien* (Frankfurt/New York: Campus, 2016), pp. 73–92.

Barbara Stelzl-Marx, "Kolyma – Jahre in Stalins Besserungsarbeitslagern," in Norbert Weigl, ed., *Faszinationen der Forstgeschichte. Festschrift für Herbert Killian*, Vol. 42 of Schriftenreihe des Instituts für Sozioökonomik der Forst- und Holzwirtschaft (Vienna: Eigenverlag, 2001), pp. 147–160.

Barbara Stelzl-Marx, "Marshall Plan Dead Ends and Anti-USIA Campaigns: The Soviet Economic Propaganda Campaign in Austria," in Günter Bischof and Dieter Stiefel, eds., *Images of the Marshall Plan in Europe. Films, Photographs, Exhibits, Posters* (Innsbruck/Vienna/Bozen: Studienverlag, 2009), pp. 117–128.

Barbara Stelzl-Marx, "'Russenkinder.' Besatzung und ihre Kinder," in Stefan Karner and Gottfried Stangler, eds., *"Österreich ist frei!" Der Österreichische Staatsver-*

trag 1955. Beitragsband zur Ausstellung auf Schloss Schallaburg 2005 (Horn/ Vienna: Verlag Berger 2005), pp. 163–168.

Barbara Stelzl-Marx, "'Russenkinder' und 'Sowjetbräute.' Besatzungserfahrungen in Österreich 1945–1955," in Andreas Hilger, Mike Schmeitzner and Clemens Vollnhals, eds., *Sowjetisierung oder Neutralität? Optionen sowjetischer Besatzungspolitik in Deutschland und Österreich 1945–1955*, Vol. 32 of Schriften des Hannah-Arendt-Instituts für Totalitarismusforschung (Göttingen: Vandenhoeck & Ruprecht, 2006), pp. 479–508.

Barbara Stelzl-Marx, "Soviet Children of Occupation in Austria: The Historical, Political and Social Background and Its Consequences," in *European Review of History. Revue européene d'histoire*. Vol. 22. Nr. 2. April 2015, pp. 277–291.

Barbara Stelzl-Marx, *Stalins Soldaten in Österreich. Die Innensicht der sowjetischen Besatzung 1945–1955*. (Vienna/Munich: Oldenborg/Böhlau, 2012).

Barbara Stelzl-Marx, ed., *Unter den Verschollenen. Erinnerungen von Dmitrij Čirov an das Kriegsgefangenenlager Krems-Gneixendorf 1941 bis 1945*, Vol. 43 of Schriftenreihe des Waldviertler Heimatbundes (Horn/Waidhofen/Thaya: Waldviertler Heimatbund, 2003).

Barbara Stelzl-Marx, "Verschleppt und erschossen. Eine Einführung," in Stefan Karner and Barbara Stelzl-Marx, eds., *Stalins letzte Opfer. Verschleppte und erschossene Österreicher in Moskau 1950–1953*, Vol. 5 of Kriegsfolgen-Forschung series (Vienna/Munich: Böhlau, 2008), pp. 21–78.

Barbara Stelzl-Marx, *Zwischen Fiktion und Zeitzeugenschaft: Amerikanische und sowjetische Kriegsgefangene im Stalag XVII B Krems-Gneixendorf* (Tübingen: Narr Verlag, 2000).

Barbara Stelzl-Marx and Silke Satjukow, eds., *Besatzungskinder. Die Nachkommen alliierter Soldaten in Österreich und Deutschland* (Vienna/Cologne/Weimar: Böhlau Verlag, 2015).

Christian Stifter, *Die Wiederaufrüstung Österreichs. Die geheime Remilitarisierung der westlichen Besatzugnszonen 1945–1955* (Innsbruck/Vienna: Studienverlag, 1997).

K. A. Stolyarov, *Golgofa, Diplomaticheskaya povest'* (Moscow: Fizkul'tura i Sport, 1991).

Gerald Stourzh, "The Origins of Austrian Neutrality," in Alan T. Leonhard, ed., *Neutrality. Changing Concepts and Practises* (Lanham: University Press of America, 1988), pp. 35–57.

Gerald Stourzh, "Der österreichische Staatsvertrag in den weltpolitischen Entscheidungsprozessen," in Arnold Suppan, Gerald Stourzh and Wolfgang Mueller, eds., *Der österreichische Staatsvertrag 1955. Internationale Strategie, rechtliche Relevanz, nationale Identität/The Austrian State Treaty 1955. International Strategy, Legal Relevance, National Identity*, Vol. 140 of Archiv für österreichische Geschichte series (Vienna: Böhlau, 2005), pp. 965–995.

Gerald Stourzh, *Um Einheit und Freiheit: Staatsvertrag, Neutralität und das Ende der Ost-West-Besetzung Österreichs 1945–1955*, Vol. 62 of Studien zu Politik und Verwaltung series, 4th rev. and exp. ed. (Graz/Vienna/Cologne: Böhlau, 1998).

Gerald Stourzh, *Um Einheit und Freiheit: Staatsvertrag, Neutralität und das Ende der Ost-West-Besetzung Österreichs 1945–1955*, 5th ed. (Vienna/Cologne/Graz: Böhlau, 2005).

Bernd Stöver, *Die Befreiung vom Kommunismus. Amerikanische Liberation Policy im Kalten Kriegs 1947–1991* (Cologne/Weimar/Vienna: Böhlau, 2002).

Karl Stuhlpfarrer, "Österreich – Mittäterschaft und Opferstatus," in Ulrich Herbert and Axel Schildt, eds., *Kriegsende in Europa: Vom Beginn des deutschen Machtzerfalls bis zur Stabilisierung der Nachkriegsordnung 1944–1948* (Essen: Klartext-Verlag, 1998), pp. 301–317.

S. Stykalin, "Propaganda SSSR na zarubezhnuyu auditoriyu i obshchestvennoe mnenie stran Zapada v pervye poslevoennye gody (po dokumentam rossiiskikh arkhivov)," in *Vestnik Moskovskogo universiteta*, 1997/1 [Zhurnalistika], pp. 57–70, No. 2, pp. 35–46.

Wladislaw Subok and Konstantin Pleschakow, *Der Kreml im Kalten Krieg. Von 1945 bis zur Kubakrise*, trans. Ulrich Schweizer (Hildesheim: Claassen, 1997).

Pavel Sudoplatov and Anatolii Sudoplatov, *Special Tasks. The Memoirs of an Unwanted Witness: A Soviet Spymaster* (London: Little Brown, 1994).

Arnold Suppan, Gerald Stourzh, and Wolfgang Mueller, eds., *Der Österreichische Staatsvertrag. Internationale Strategie, rechtliche Relevanz, nationale Identität*, Vol. 140 of Archiv für österreichische Geschichte (Vienna: Böhlau, 2005).

Viktor Suvorov, *GRU. Die Speerspitze. Was der KGB für die Polit-Führung, ist die GRU für die Rote Armee. Spionage-Organisation und Sicherheitsapparat der sowjetischen Militärs—Aufbau, Ziele, Strategie, Arbeitsweise und Führungskader*. 3. ed. (Solingen: Barett, 1995).

Tessa Szyszkowitz, *Stalins letzte Opfer*, in: *Profil*, 12 February 2007, pp. 34–41.

László von Taubinger, "Die sowjetisch-rumänischen Gesellschaften," *Osteuropa*, Vol. 2 (1956), pp. 145–149.

Bruno Thoss, "Österreich in der Entstehungs- und Konsolidierungsphase des westlichen Bündnissystems (1947–1967)," in Manfred Rauchensteiner, ed., *Zwischen den Blöcken: NATO und Warschauer Pakt und Österreich* (Vienna: Böhlau, 2010), pp. 19–88.

Prokop Tomek, "Die Struktur der Staatssicherheit in der ČSSR," in Pavel Žáček, Bernd Faulenbach and Ulrich Mählert, eds., *Die Tschechoslowakei 1945/48 bis 1989. Studien zu kommunistischer Herrschaft und Repression* (Leipzig: Leipziger Universitätsverlag, 2008), pp. 99–128.

V. A. Torchinov and A. M. Leontyuk, *Vokrug Stalina: Istoriko-biograficheskii spravochnik* (St. Petersburg: FilFak SPbGU 2000).

Stefan Troebst, "Warum wurde Finnland nicht sowjetisiert?," *Osteuropa*, 48/2, 1998, pp. 178–191.

Chris Tudda, *The Truth Is Our Weapon: The Rhetorical Diplomacy of Dwight D. Eisenhower and John Foster Dulles* (Baton Rouge: Louisiana State University Press, 2006).

Kurt Tweraser, *US-Militärregierung Oberösterreich, Vol. 1: Sicherheitspolitische Aspekte der amerikanischen Besatzung in Oberösterreich-Süd 1945–1950* (Linz: Oberösterreichisches Landesarchiv, 1995).

Kurt Tweraser, *US-Militärregierung Oberösterreich 1945–1950, Vol. 2: Amerikanische Industriepolitik in Oberösterreich am Beispiel VOEST und Steyr-Daimler-Puch* (Linz: Oberösterreichisches Landesarchiv, 2008).
US Department of State, *Foreign Relations of the United States, 1945*, Vol. II: *Conference of Berlin (Potsdam Conference)* (Washington, DC: US Government Printing Office, 1960).
US Department of State, *Foreign Relations of the United States* (FRUS), *Diplomatic Papers: The Conferences at Cairo and Tehran, 1943* (Washington, DC: US Government Printing Office, 1961).
US Department of State, *Foreign Relations of the United States* (FRUS). *Diplomatic Papers: General: Political and Economic Matters, 1945* (Washington, DC: US Government Printing Office, 1967).
US Department of State, *Foreign Relations of the United States, Diplomatic Papers: 1945*, Vol. III: *European Advisory Commission–Austria–Germany* (Washington, DC: US Government Printing Office, 1968).
US Department of State, *Foreign Relations of the United States, 1952–1954*, Vol. II/1 (Washington, DC: US Government Printing Office, 1984).
US Department of State, *Foreign Relations of the United States, 1952–1954*, Vol. II/2 (Washington, DC: US Government Printing Office, 1986).
Fabrice Virgili, "Enfants de Boches: The War Children of France," trans. Paula Schwartz, in Kjersti Ericsson and Eva Simonsen, eds., *Children of World War II: The Hidden Enemy Legacy* (Oxford/New York: Berg, 2005), pp. 138–150.
Vneshnyaya politika Sovetskogo Soyuza v period Otechestvennoi voiny. Dokumenty i materialy, Vol. 1 (Moscow: Ob"edinenie gosudarstvennykh izdatel'stv, 1946).
Voenno-istoricheskii zhurnal, 1989/2, pp. 16–31.
Hans-Erich Volkmann, ed., *Das Russlandbild im Dritten Reich* (Cologne/Weimar/Vienna: Böhlau, 1994).
V. K. Volkov, *Uzlovye problemy v noveishei istorii stran Tsentral'noi i Yugo-Vostochnoi Evropy* (Moscow: Indrik 2000).
T. V. Volokitina, "Stalin i smena strategicheskogo kursa Kremlya v kontse 40-kh godov. Ot kompromissov k konfrontatsii," in Aleksandr Chubar'yan et al., eds., *Stalinskoe desyatiletie kholodnoi voiny. Fakty i gipotezy* (Moscow: Nauka, 1999), pp. 10–22.
T. V. Volokitina, eds., *Sovetskii faktor v Vostochnoi Evrope 1944–1953, Vol. 1: 1944–1948. Dokumenty* (Moscow: ROSSPEN, 1999).
Vooruzhenie Avstrii. Dokumenty i fakty (Moscow: Izd. IL, 1952).
S. I. Voroshilov, *Rozhdenie vtoroi respubliki v Avstrii* (Leningrad: Izdatel'stvo LGU, 1968).
Rolf Wagenführ, *Die deutsche Industrie im Kriege: 1939–1945* (Berlin: Duncker & Humblot, 2006 [1954]).
Wolfgang Wagner, "Die Besatzungszeit aus sowjetischer Sicht: Die Errichtung der sowjetischen Besatzungsmacht in Österreich von 1945 bis 1946 im Spiegel ihrer Lageberichte," Master Thesis, University of Vienna, 1998.
Reinhold Wagnleitner, *Coca-Colonisation und Kalter Krieg. Die Kulturmission der USA in Österreich nach dem Zweiten Weltkrieg* (Vienna: Verlag für Gesellschaftskritik, 1991).

Reinhold Wagnleitner, "Großbritannien und die Wiedererrichtung der Republik Österreich," Ph.D. Diss., University of Salzburg, 1975.
Katharina Wegan, "Monument—Macht—Mythos: 'Resistance-' und 'Opfermythos' als hegemoniale Vergangenheitserzählungen und ihre Denkmäler nach 1945 im austro-französischen Vergleich," Ph.D. Diss., University of Graz, 2003.
Gerhard L. Weinberg, "Franklin D. Roosevelt," in: idem, *Visions of Victory: The Hopes of Eight World War II Leaders* (Cambridge: Cambridge University Press, 2005), pp. 175–210.
Nicolas Werth, "Sowjetunion (1917–1945)," in: Kamiński, Persak and Gieseke, eds., *Handbuch der kommunistischen Geheimdienste in Osteuropa 1944–1991*, pp. 15–41.
Wolfram Wette, "Das Russlandbild in der NS-Propaganda. Ein Problemaufriß," in Hans-Erich Volkmann, ed., *Das Russlandbild im Dritten Reich* (Cologne/Weimar/Vienna: Böhlau, 1994), pp. 55–78.
Gerhard Wettig, *Stalin and the Cold War in Europe. The Emergence and Development of East-West Conflict, 1939–1953* (Lanham: Rowman & Littlefield Publishers, 2008).
Gerhard Wettig, "Stalins Aufrüstungsbeschluss. Die Moskauer Beratungen mit den Parteichefs und Verteidigungsministern der 'Volksdemokratien' vom 9. bis 12. Januar 1951," *Vierteljahrshefte für Zeitgeschichte*, Vol. 53 (2005) No. 4, pp. 635–650.
Gerhard Wettig, "Stalins Deutschland-Politik 1945–1949 vor dem Hintergrund seines Vorgehens im Osten Europas," in Stefan Creuzberger and Manfred Görtemaker, eds., *Gleichschaltung unter Stalin? Die Entwicklung der Parteien im östlichen Europa 1944–1949* (Paderborn: Schöningh, 2002), pp. 15–44.
"Die wirtschaftliche Lage Österreichs am Ende des ersten Nachkriegsjahrzehntes," in *Monatsberichte des österreichischen Institutes für Wirtschaftsforschung*, Vol. XIX, No. 1–6, issued on July 31, 1946, pp. 5 and 50.
Robert Wolfe, "Records of U.S. Occupation Forces in Austria, 1945–55," in Günter Bischof and Josef Leidenfrost, eds., *Die bevormundete Nation: Österreich und die Alliierten 1945–1949*, Vol. 4 of Innsbrucker Forschungen zur Zeitgeschichte series (Innsbruck: Haymon, 1988), pp. 415–426.
Pavel Žáček, Bernd Faulenbach and Ulrich Mählert, eds., *Die Tschechoslowakei 1945/48 bis 1989. Studien zu kommunistischer Herrschaft und Repression* (Leipzig: Leipziger Universitätsverlag, 2008), pp. 99–128.
Jürgen Zarusky, *Die Stalin-Note vom 10. März 1952. Neue Quellen und Analysen*, with contributions by Wilfried Loth, Hermann Graml and Gerhard Wettig (Munich: Oldenbourg, 2002).
Wolfgang Zdral, *Die Hitlers. Die unbekannte Familie des Führers* (Frankfurt am Main: Campus, 2005).
I. G. Zhiryakov, *SSSR i Avstriya v 1945–1975 gody* (Moscow: Molodaya gvardiya, 1982).
I. G. Zhiryakov, *SSSR–Avstriya. Itogi i perspektivy sotrudnichestva: K 30-letiyu podpisaniya Gosudarstvennogo dogovora.* (Moscow: Mezhdunarodnye otnosheniya, 1985).

Vladislav M. Zubok, *A Failed Empire: The Soviet Union in the Cold War from Stalin to Gorbachev* (Chapel Hill, NC/London: University of North Carolina Press, 2007).
Wladislaw Zubok and Constantine Pleschakow, *Der Kreml im Kalten Krieg: Von 1945 bis zur Kubakrise*, trans. by Ulrich Schweitzer [original title: *Inside the Kremlin's Cold War: From Stalin to Khrushchev*] (Hildesheim: Claassen, 1996).

NEWSPAPER ARTICLES

"73 kehrten aus Schweigelagern heim," in *Kleine Zeitung*, August 7, 1955
"Den Helden der Roten Armee, die für Wiens Befreiung fielen," *Österreichische Zeitung*, August 19, 1945, p. 2
"Doppelter Menschenraub in Wien," *Arbeiter Zeitung*, April 8, 1951, p. 3.
"Ehrung der gefallenen Sowjetsoldaten durch die Stadt Wien," *Österreichische Zeitung*, November 7, 1947, p. 4
"Enthüllung des Denkmals für General Karbyschew in Mauthausen," *Österreichische Zeitung*, March 2, 1948, pp. 1 and 3
Der Erdölarbeiter, No. 17, September 30, 1948
"Ewiger Ruhm den gefallenen Helden der Befreiung Wiens," *Österreichische Zeitung*, August 21, 1945, p. 3
"Generaloberst Kurassow zum Jahrestag der Befreiung: Unabhängigkeit Österreichs – Ziel der Sowjetregierung," *Österreichische Zeitung*, April 13, 1948, pp. 1–2
"Hitlers letzte Verwandte," *News*, 08/2010, pp. 34–39
Izvestiya, February 19, 1954
Izvestiya, February 9, 1955
Literaturnaya Gazeta, October 29, 1947
"Machtvolle Großkundgebung: Das Heldendenkmal für die gefallenen Rotarmisten enthüllt," *Österreichische Zeitung*, August 1945 21, pp. 1–2
Neues Österreich, February 11, 1955
New York Herald Tribune, April 18, 1955
Newsweek, May 16, 1955
Österreichische Volksstimme, May 6, 1952
Österreichische Zeitung, October 23, 1945, p. 1
Getrud Srncik, "Besatzungskinder—ein Weltproblem," *Arbeiter-Zeitung*, November 3, 1955, p. 5
"Stalinplatz, Tolbuchinstraße und Malinowskibrücke in Wien," *Österreichische Zeitung*, April 12, 1946, p. 1
"Unsterbliche Helden," *Österreichische Zeitung*, August 21, 1945, p. 1
"Die Verhaftung des Abgeordneten Gruber," *Arbeiter-Zeitung*, July 17, 1946, p. 2
Washington Post, May 19, 1955
Marc Widmann and Mary Wiltenburg, "Kinder des Feindes," *Der Spiegel*, No. 52, 2006, pp. 39–41
Wiener Zeitung, June 19, 1954
"Zum Tag der Befreiung: Straßenbenennungen zu Ehren der Roten Armee," *Arbeiter-Zeitung*, April 12, 1946, p. 1
"Zwei Jahre befreites Wien," *Österreichische Zeitung*, April 13, 1947, pp. 1–2

WEBSITES

Control Council Law No. 5 (in German), 30.10.1945: http://www.verfassungen.de/de/de45-49/kr-gesetz5.htm, accessed on 25.6.2009

Wolfram Dornik, "'Sie wurden durchwegs gut behandelt'? NS-SklavenarbeiterInnen im Kollektiven Gedächtnis der II. Republik," *eForum zeitGeschichte*, 3/4 (2001): http://www.eforum-zeitgeschichte.at/

"Exhumierung von Kriegstoten in Mönichwald": http://steiermark.orf.at/stories/372514/, accessed on 10.7.2009

Werner Fenz, "Die Steiermark im 20. Jahrhundert: Kunst zwischen 1938 und 1999": http://www.uni-graz.at/werner.fenz/texte/stmk_kunstvolltext.html, accessed on 23.6.2009

"Sieben sowjetische Kriegstote in der Steiermark gefunden," http://www.bik.ac.at/pdf-dateien/Presse_Aussendung_Exhumierung_01072009.pdf, accessed on 10.7.2009

STATISTIK AUSTRIA: http://www.statistik.at/web_de/statistiken/preise/verbraucherpreisindex_vpi_hvpi/zeitreihen_und_verkettungen/index.html, accessed on 17.6.2009

FILMS

"Die Kinder der Besatzer. Teil 2," an NDR production from Reinhard Joksch (2006)

Index

Adenauer, Konrad, 13, 82
Aderklaa (region), 132
Administration for Soviet Property in Austria (Upravlenie sovetskim imushchestvom v Avstrii, USIA), 79, 102–108, 114, 117, 124, 131–135, 137, 146n76, 170; Soviet assets, 79, 124
Admont, 171
alcoholism, 200, 202
Allied Commission for Austria, 5, 49, 53, 59, 142n32, 151–152, 178; British Element of the Allied Commission for Austria (ACA/BE), 142n32; Soviet Element of the Allied Commission for Austria (SChSK), 59, 153, 158, 178; section for propaganda of SChSK, 59
Allied Control Council in Germany, 129
Allied Council in Austria, 5
Allied occupation powers, 5, 7, 15, 119
Altmark, 29
Anhalt, 29
Anschluss, 4, 25, 41, 45, 84–87
anti-Soviet agitators, 156
Antonov, Aleksei I., 40
Aryanization, 129, 142n34
Attlee, Clement, 59

Austria:
Army, 7, 16; as "first victim," 4, 76. *See also* Moscow Declaration; B-Gendarmerie, 7; cabinet council, 51; Communist Party of (Kommunistische Partei Österreichs, KPÖ), 40, 41, 44, 46–47, 53–55, 57–59, 62, 66n25, 67n32, 80, 103, 108, 115, 119n35, 131, 137, 140n11, 154, 162n31, 170; *cordon sanitaire*, 43, 125; Federal Council of, 46; Liberation Front, 39; Mineral Oil Administration (OMV), 131, 136, 147n91; "Moscow Declaration" on Austria. *See* Moscow Declaration; National Council of, 46, 49, 54; People's Party (Österreichische Volkspartei, ÖVP), 5, 44–45, 53–54, 57–59, 60, 62, 70n75, 84, 99, 116n7; question ("Austrian question"), 4, 8, 11, 13–14, 27, 31, 39, 76–77, 81–83, 87, 96, 98–102, 109–110, 116n5; resistance (O5), 4, 38–57, 61; Socialist Party of (Sozialistische Partei Österreichs, SPÖ), 44, 53, 58–59, 62, 99, 172; State Treaty, 3, 5–8, 13, 15–16, 75, 77–82, 84–86, 95–96, 98–102, 104–109, 112–115,

116n5, 118n30, 119n35, 131–132, 134–135, 137, 142n37, 158–159, 165, 185; state police, 54, 159; Union Commission for, 99–100
Austrian-Hungarian federation, 27

B., Herbert, 189n29
B., Johann, 174
Bad Vöslau, 178, 186
Baden bei Wien, 132, 151–155, 158–160, 167–168, 170–171, 189n29, 197, 204
Baklanov, Boris, 153–155, 158–159
Balkan, 28
Batumi, 106
Baumgartner, Marianne, 196
Bavaria, 27, 29–30;
    Austrian-Bavarian border, 29–30
Bazarov, 31
Belgrade, 79
Beriia, Lavrentii P., 14, 53, 67n42, 69n60, 70n68, 97, 109–111, 117n22
Berlin, 12–13, 29–30, 98, 206;
    crisis, 7; Conference of Foreign Ministers 98–100, 104, 110, 116n5, 116n7; East Berlin, 82
Berlin-Wilmersdorf, 203
Bermuda, 12
Béthouart plan, 118n31
Bevin, Ernest 59
Bischof, Günter, 92n50, 135, 196
Bischoff, Norbert, 59, 97, 111
Bitumen Law, 128–129, 131, 136
Black Sea, 29
Blum, Léon, 59
Bohlen, Charles, 9
Boryslav, 176, 179
Bratislava, 29
Braunthal, Julius, 101
British:
    Communist Party, 26; Foreign Office, 9, 14; government, 5; Prime Minister, 9, 27
Brno, 69n59
Bruck an der Mur, 30

Brünn. *See* Brno
Brussels Pact, 7
Brussels, 64n8, 100
Buchinger, 71n91
Buger, Stefan, 170–171
Bulganin, Nikolai, 67n42, 69n60, 108
Bulgaria, 5, 37, 124, 128, 130;
    Bulgarian-Romanian border, 29; reparations, 134, 145n70
Byrnes plan, 77

Calloway, Major, 150
camps:
    Corrective Labor (Ispravitelno-trudovoy lager, ITL), 171, 173–175; for DPs, 157; forced labor, 155; provisional, 155; for repatriates, 158; concentration, 195; Soviet, 116, 154, 176–177, 179
Canada, 7
Carinthia, 6, 31–32, 61
censorship, 97, 104, 170
Central Group of Forces (Tsentralnaya Gruppa Voysk, TsGV), 132, 152, 153, 155, 158, 197; Commando in Baden, 151; Soviet Military Tribunal 28990, 167, 168, 174; internal prison, 158; Political Administration, 172
Chief of Staff, 65n19, 68n55
children:
    Austrian, 171; born of war, 214n93; illegitimate, 193, 201; of occupation, 193, 201, 202, 203, 204, 205, 207, 208; of rape, 201; of the enemy, 193; soldiers', 201, 208
Churchill, Winston, 4, 5, 9, 12, 27, 32, 76, 159
Central Intelligence Agency (CIA), 7, 9, 10, 14, 64n8, 134, 145n67
Clark, Mark, 5
Council for Mutual Economic Assistance (Sovet Ekonomicheskoy Vzaimopomoshchi, Comecon), 134, 138

Index

Information Bureau of the Communist and Workers' Parties (Cominform), 53, 59
Communist International (Comintern), 38
Commission for Ceasefire matters, 28
Committee:
for Information (Komitet Informatsii, KI), 157; of state security (Komitet gosudarstvennoy bezopasnosti, KGB), 158; Notter, 4; Senate Foreign Relations, 9; State Defence (Gosudarstvennyy komitet oborony, GOKO), 40
Communist Party:
of Austria (Kommunistische Partei Österreichs, KPÖ). *See* Austria, Communist Party of; Central Committee of the CPSU, 28, 40, 66n31, 73n114, 97, 98, 100, 105, 112, 116n3, 116n9, 117n14, 117n16, 117n22, 118n24, 168, 178; of Germany (Kommunistische Partei Deutschlands, KPD). *See* Germany, Communist Party of
Conant, James B., 10
Control Agreement:
First, 5; Second, 78
Council of Ministers of the USSR, 97, 102, 105, 108, 117n14, 132, 157, 158
Counter Intelligence Corps (CIC), 150, 159, 169, 189n29. *See also* intelligence
Cronin, Audrey Kurth, 19n27, 33, 34
Czechoslovakia, 27, 29–30, 52, 79, 86, 127, *127*, 150; Czechoslovakian–Austrian border, 29

Dallapozza, Emil, 167
Danube Steam Navigation Company (Erste Donaudampfschiffahrtsgesellschaft, DDSG), 106, 113, 114, 143n46. *See also* economy

Dekanozov, Vladimir, 31, 41, 66n32, 69n58, 69n60, 70n68
demarcation line, 28, 30–33, 97
demilitarization, 13, 77
demobilization, 155
denazification, 6, 80, 166, 169
Denmark, 203
denunciation, 198
Department for International Information of the Central Committee of the CPSU, 40
desertion, 153, 158, 170, 200
Didenko, Andrei I., 159
Dimitrov, Georgi, 38, 40, 41, 66n24, 66n29
Soviet Diplomatic Corps, 157
discrimination, 114, 193, 198, 199, 201, 204, 207
dismantling operations, 50, 51, 124, 126, 127, 128, 135, 146n78
displaced persons (DPs), 78, 155, 156, 158, 163n37, 169
Dobretsberger, Josef, 39, 64n12
Dollfuß, Engelbert, 42
Donskoe Cemetery, 166, 168
Dornik, Wolfram, 210n23
Drohobych, 176
Dubrovitskii, Colonel, 59
Dulles, Allen, 14, 64n8
Dulles, Joan, 64n8
Dulles, John Foster, 8, 9, 10, 12, 13, 14, 15, 118n29

E., Johann, 175
Eastern bloc, 113, 116n5, 138; consolidation of the, 62, 80, 87, 88; "satellite states," 75, 77, 124, 150
economy:
amalgamations, 133, 137; Austrian, 3, 50, 96, 130, 136, 138; bilateral companies, 124; compensation, 129, 138, 179; confiscations, 34, 51, 129, 130, 142n32; economic aid, 5, 6, 16; economic exploitation, 87, 123, 124,

125, 130, 136; economic losses, 123, 127; "economic miracle," 16; economic problems, 79, 101, 103, 203; economic recovery, 6, 16; enterprises, 50, 87, 107, 130; industrial plants, 30, 31, 34, 125, 126, 127, 128, 131, 133, 142n34; nationalized industry, 136; occupation, 124, 131, 133, 136; oil and gas industry, 126, *127*, 136; production goods, 127; production installations, 127; Sanafta, 125, 129, 140n10, 142n32; socialist, 102; Soviet industry, 127; war, 125, 128
Eden, Anthony, 13, 14, 27, 28
Egypt, 39
Eisenerz, 30
Eisenhower, Dwight D., 3, 8 –12, 13, 16, 33, 113
Elbe, 29
England, 8
Enns, 30
Entente, 25
Erhardt, John G., 133
European Advisory Commission (EAC), 4, 5, 28, 29, 31–32, 37, 38, 61, 63n5,
European Defence Community (EDC), 99–100
3rd European Department, Foreign Department USSR, 48–49, 55, 73n116, 178
European Recovery Programme (ERP), 6, 16, 137; Marshall Plan, 6–7, 16, 96, 133–137, 159

Falin, Valentin, 32, 33
fascism, 42, 44, 51, 100
Federation of Independents (Verband der Unabhängigen, VdU), 101
Figl, Leopold, 5, 13, 15, 51, 58–60, 62, 72n95
Finland, 15, 124, 128, *130*, 144n61
Fisch, Jörg, 134, 152n30
Fischer, Ernst, 40–41, 53–54, 66n24, 66n25, 68n47, 70n72

food donation, 6, 34, 50, 125, 133
forced laborers, 155, 174, 191n55, 198
Foreign Minister Conference Moscow, 115n1
foster parents, 201, 203
France, 4, 32, 64n8, 98, 111, 115n1, 116n5, 119n36, 136, 151, 169, 194, 198, 202–203
fraternization, 194–195
Fürnberg, Friedl, 40–41, 44, 57

G., Monika, 204
Gabriel, Josef, 176, 179
Galicia, 174–176, *182–183, 185*
Garin, Captain, 67n36
General Staff of the Red Army, 40, 45, 65n19, 67n42, 151
Geneva, Convention, 15, 78
German:
  assets, 5–6, 8, 14, 16, 79, 98, 104, 107, 114, 128–129, 132, 142n37;
  Democratic Republic (GDR), 8–9, 79, 82, 84–86, 96, 109–110, 124, 134, 194, 200, 206, 213n82;
  question ("German question"), 12–14, 20n33, 75–81, 84–86, 96, 98–99, 109–110; Reich, 4, 25, 41, 75–77, 125, 130, 198–199; Wehrmacht, 116n3, 153, 156, 175, 196–197, 199, 203, 210n23, 211n33
Germany:
  Communist Party of (Kommunistische Partei Deutschlands, KPD), 46, 81; division of, 15, 80, 82, 84; reunification of, 109;
  Social Democratic Party of (Sozialdemokratische Partei Deutschlands, SPD), 65n17, 117n18
Glagolov, 42
Gloggnitz, 41–42, 45–46, 66n20
gonorrhea. *See* sexually transmitted diseases
Göring, Hermann, 28
Government of Austria:

Austrian Union, 39; Provisional
Austrian National Committee
(Provisorisches Österreichisches
Nationalkomitee, POEN), 38, 61;
Provisional Government, 4–5, 39–40,
42, 44–46, 48–53, 55–58, 61–62,
70n75, 72n101, 77; Republic of
German-Austria (Republik Deutsch-
Österreich), 41
Grachegg, Gustav, 175
Graz, 44, 170, 173
Great Britain, 4, 32, 47–48, 52, 98, 101,
115n1, 116n3, 119, 126, 128, 136,
138, 169, 194
Greece, 6
Greene, Graham, 150
Gromov, 42
Gruber, Franz, 172–173, 190n44
Gruber, Karl, 11, 52, 64n8
Guatemala, 10
Gusev, Fedor T., 29, 37

H., Otto, 176
Habsburg monarchy, 27
Habsburg, Otto, 27, 39
Hainfeld, 30
Harrison, Geoffrey, 14
Hearst, William Randolph Jr., 117
Heiligenhafen, 28
Hejl, Wilfried, 189n30
Hitler, Adolf, 171, 176, 190n42
Hitler, Paula, 176
Hochwolkersdorf, 42
Hof, 29
Honner, Franz, 40, 52–54
Horn, 30
Hungary, 6–7, 29, 31, 37, 62, 70n76,
73n116, 77–79, 85–86, 124, *127,
130,* 134, 150, 170

Iber, Walter M., 87
identity checks, 97
imperialism, 100, 124
India, 11, 82
Indochina, 12

intelligence, 57, 66n25, 78, 82, 126, 129,
133, 149–160, 162n31, 169–170;
blackmailing, 154; counterespionage,
149, 152, 157; counterintelligence,
149–154, 156–159, 161–169,
173; counterpropaganda, 153;
counterrevolutionary sabotage,
172–173; dissidents, 153, 156;
diversionary tactics, 169, 171–172
179; informants, 73n118, 142n32,
151–152, 158, 160, 169; sabotage,
51, 106, 156, 159, 171–172;
subversion, 7, 159; surveillance, 45,
68n55, 153–154, 158, 170; "tipper,"
155
International Atomic Energy Agency
(IAEA), 149
inter-war period, 41, 136
Iran, 10, 126, 141n19
Iron Curtain, 85, 137, 149
Isakov, Ivan, 30
Italy, 7, 27–28, 84, 98, 149, 151
Ivano-Frankivs'k/Stanyslaviv, 176

Jessen/Elster, 206
Jews, 174–176, 179, *182–183,* 192n69,
196
judiciary (measures):
 amnesty, 159, 177–178; arrest, 11,
 57, 77, 153–154, 156–160, 165–168,
 171–179, *180–181,* 189n29, 190n44;
 Butyrka Prison, 168; civilian
 convicts, 166, 174, 177, 178, 179,
 186, 186n1crime, 165–166, 168,
 173–179, *183;* conviction, 97,
 153–154, 160, 165–179, *181–183;*
 Criminal Code of the RSFSR, 153,
 169, 173, 174, 201; death penalty,
 57, 166–168, 170, 175, 181;
 interrogation, 158–159, 168, 172;
 imprisonment, 97, 154–156,
 158–159, 172, 175-177, 179, *181,
 184–185,* 192n71; prison, 57, 116n3,
 157, 165, 167, 172, 174, 175–176,
 179, 195; prosecution, 166–167;

punitive measures, 198; war crimes, 4, 75, 78, 165, 168, 174–175, 178–179; "werewolves," 156–157, 165–166, 171–172, *182–183*, 189n41

K., Rosa, 202
Kay, Alex J., 63n1
Käs, Ferdinand, 39
Kautsky, Karl, 40, 65n17
Kekkonen, Urho, 84
Kennan, George, 52, 61
Keyes, Geoffrey, 7
Khrushchev, Nikita S., 14, 67n38, 84–86, 92n56, 98, 108–111, 113, 115, 117n16, 145n73
Killian, Herbert, 177
Kiridus, Franz, 159, 165
Kiselev, Evgenii, 57–58, 67n39, 73n114
Knoll, Harald, 162n26
Kolomyia, 176
Konev, Ivan, 51, 56, 72n95, 73n116, 132
Koplenig, Johann, 40–41, 46, 51, 53, 66n24, 66
Koppensteiner, Adolf, 177
Koppensteiner, Ignaz, 176
Koppensteiner, Maria, 177
Koptelov, Mikhail, 47, 52, 56–57, 72n106
Korea, 7, 9; Korean War, 7–9
Korneuburg, 114
Köttlach, 42
Krakow, 65n20
Kramer, Mark, 92n54
Krauland, Peter, 159, 165
Kreisky, Bruno, 39
Kremlin, 9–15, 39, 58 60–62, 83–87, 97, 99, 101, 104, 106, 108, 111, 123–125, 133, 134, 137–138, 195, 200
Krems, 30, 175
Kurasov, Vladimir, 177
Kyrgyzstan, 206

L'viv, 106
"Länderkonferenz," 52
Langfeld, 176
Lavant, 30
Lavrov, Ivan, 48
Lederer, Isabella, 170
Lemberger, Ernst, 38, 61–62
Lenin, 44, 65n20
Leoben, 30
Lime, Harry, 150
Linz, 193
Litvinov, Maksim, 27–28
London, 6, 11, 13–14, 25, 28, 37–38, 61, 81–82, 153; Agreements, 13
Lübeck, 28
Lun'kov, Nikolai, 58, 73n116

Maczejka, Michael, 170
Main Administration: for Camps (Glavnoe upravlenie lagerey, GULag), 156, 166, 171, 177, 179; for Counterespionage (SMERSH), 70n75; for prisoners of war and internees (GUPVI), 156; Main Intelligence Administration (Glavnoe razvedyvatelnoe upravlenie, GRU), 149–153, 157
Maiskii, Ivan, 25–27, 30, 64n6
Malenkov, Georgii, 9, 14, 53, 70n68, 105, 108–110, 117n16, 117n22, 118n24
Malinovskii, Marshal, 50
maneuvers, 34, 118n31
marauding. See plundering
Marek, Anton, 159, 165, 178
Marshall Funds. See Marshall Plan
Marshall, George C., 6
Mastny, Vojtech, 67n38, 86
Matzen, 79, 132
McCarthy, Joseph, 9–10
Mecklenburg, 28–29
Melichar, Anna-Maria, 167–168

Merkulov, Vsevolod, 53, 79
Middle East, 126
Miklas, Wilhelm, 46
Mikoyan, Anastas, 53, 67n38, 68n43, 105–107, 110
militarization, 7, 25, 20n29, 82
Military council (of 3rd Ukrainian front), 50, 53; of the Supreme Court of the USSR, 168
Military Intelligence, British:
Military Intelligence Section 1 (Cryptology, MI1) 160
Military Intelligence Section 5 (Counterintelligence, MI5) 149
military tribunals, 165, 167, 171, 178
Military Tribunal of the Central Group of Forces, 153, 167–168, 174, 189n29
Ministry:
  of state security (Ministerstvo gosudarstvennoy bezopasnosti, MGB), 83, 151, 155, 157–160, 167–168, *181*; for Internal Affairs (Ministerstvo vnutrennykh del, MVD), 156–157, 168, 177, *181*
Mittas, Leopold, 192n71
Mödling, 153
Molden, Fritz, 38, 61–62, 64n8
Molotov, Vyacheslav M., 11, 13–15, 25–27, 29, 31, 49, 52, 61–62, 66n32, 67n42, 68n43, 68n45, 69n60, 70n68, 70n76, 70n 78, 76, 77, 78n84, 79, 84–85, 92n56, 93n63, 98–99, 108–112, 117n22, 128, 132, 157
Moravia, 41
Moscow:
  conference, 27–28, 88n2;
  Declaration, 4, 28, 76, 83, 109, 194
Moscow Foreign Office, see People's Commissariat for Foreign Affairs
Mühlviertel, 126, 176, *180*, 196
Mukachevo, 106
Mürzsteg, 30

Naimark, Norman, 86
National People's Front, 38, 40, 44
National Security Council, 7, 10–12, 14
National security strategy (USA), 7, 10–11
National Socialist, 42, 46, 51, 57, 128, 153; German Workers Party (Nationalsozialistische Deutsche Arbeiterpartei, NSDAP), 26, 154, 156, 175, 190n42; former, 153; system, 26, 42, 57, 59, 75, 100, 126, 130, 132, 142n34, 153, 154, 156, 174, 175, 195–196, 199
Netherlands, 65n17, 198, 203
neutrality, 12–16, 80–81, 84–87, 112, 118n29, 149; declaration of, 115; German, 82, 96
"neutralization," 11–13, 15, 77, 83, 86, 92n51, 113; Swiss model, 12–16, 112
New York, 4, 14, 64n8, 126
Nikolskii, Vitalii N., 151–152
Nixon, Richard, 8
Nobel Peace Prize, 60
North Atlantic Treaty Organization (NATO), 8, 13, 15, 82, 84–87, 92n51, 112–113, 169; North Atlantic Treaty Pact, 7
Norway, 203
nuclearization, 7, 10;
  nuclear arsenal, 7, 10, 152; nuclear disarmament, 9, 12; nuclear missile units, 152; nuclear war, 8, 10

occupation zones, 4, 99, 128;
  negotiations during the war, 28–32, 37; Soviet, 51, 75, 78, 81, 85, 97, 103, 107, 114, 125, *127*, 132, 140n11, 151, 158–159, 168, *181*, 194, 197, 201; USA, 3; Yugoslavian, 61
October Revolution, 65n20
ordinary congress of the Supreme Soviet, 108

"Ostarbeiter," 174
Österreichische Zeitung, 60
Ottillinger Margarethe, 159, 165–166, 178

Paris, 15, 38–39, 61, 64n8, 77, 82–83; Agreement, 109–110; Conference, 77–78; Foreign Minister negotiations 1946, 6
parliamentary elections, 5, 46, 52, 54, 57–60, 62, 109, 125
partisans, 156
peace treaty, 4–6, 13–14, 75, 84, 98–99, 109
Pearl Harbor, 4
People's Commissar for Nationality Affairs, 66n20
People's Commissariat:
for Foreign Affairs (= Moscow Foreign Office) (Narodnyi Kommissariat Inostrannykh Del, NKID), 47–48, 52, 55, 73n116;
for Internal Affairs (Narodnyi Kommissariat Vnutrennykh Del, NKVD), 45, 53, 57, 69n63, 155–157, 159, 163n43, 170, 172–173, *181*, 200; of state security (Narodnyy Kommissariat Gosudarstvennoy Bezopasnosti, NKGB), 156–157
people's democracy, 84, 96
Piterskii, Georgii, 45, 48, 55, 70n72
Plenum of the Central Committee, 110
Pleshakov, Constantine, 85
plundering, 34, 50, 77, 200
Podol'sk military archives, 45
Poland, 5, 37, 52, 127, *127*, 176
Politburo of the Central Committee:
of the Communist Party of the Soviet Union (CPSU), 28, 73n114;
of the All-Union Communist Party (Bolsheviks) (Vsesoyuznaya Kommunisticheskaya Partiya (bolshevikov), VKP(b)), 66n31, 168, 178
Pöll, Josef, 192n71

Potsdam, 129, 131, 132, 142n37; conference, 6, 55, 128, 136; agreement, 125, 128–130, 155
Prague, 7, 51, 56
prejudices:
against children born of war (CHIBOW), 193, 194; anti-Communist, 196; anti-Slavic, 196
Presidium of the:
Central Committee of the Communist Party of the Soviet Union (CPSU), 97–98, 100; Supreme Soviet, 168, 178105–106, 108–110, 112, 116n3, 117n22, 118, 168
Primakov, Yevgenii, 179
prisoners of war, 54, 78, 97, 116, 158, 166, 170, 174–175, 177–179, *185*, 191n55, 192n83, 195, 198, 210n23
propaganda, 4, 9, 11, 80–82, 109, 115, 116n5, 153, 156, 159–160, 171, 178, 194–196, 202; image of "the Russians," 195, 197, 202
Prozumenshchikov, Michail, 87
Prussia, 26, 29
psychological warfare, 10–11

R., Karl, 173
R., Robert, 174
Raab, Julius, 11, 14–16, 62, 84, 87, 100, 104, 107, 112, 118n29, 118n34, 145n73
Radford, Arthur, 10–12
radio propaganda. *See* Signal Intelligence
Rákosi, Mátyás, 79
Ramadier, Paul, 59
Rattersdorf, *186*
reconstruction, 39, 51, 66n25, 123–124, 127
rehabilitation, 166, 173–175, 179, *186*
Renner, Karl, 4–5, 37–62, 65n20, 66n32, 67n38, 67n40, 68n55, 69n63, 69n64, 69n65, 69n67, 70n72, 71n84, 73n118, 77, 130

reparations, 6, 54, 125, 128–130, 132, 134–136, 138, 145n70
repatriation, 78, 97, 116n3, 155, 158, 163n37, 165, 175, 177–178, *184–186*, 192n83
resilience, 205;
 psychological consequences, 208
 repressing and forgetting, 205
 stigmatization, 193, 199, 201–203;
 taboo, 201–202, 204–205, 208;
 wall of silence, 201, 204–205
resistance, 11, 61, 64n8, 93n63, 117n9, 156
Retz, 30
revolutionary socialists, 46, 48, 69n59
Rhine, 8, 25
Rhineland, 25–26
Rieder, Ferdinand, 202
Roberts, Frank, 49
"rollback" of communism, 10–11
Romania, 5, 37, 52, 68n51, 77–79, 85, 124, 126, 128, *130*, 134, 145n70
Romanov, A. I. *See* Baklanov, Boris
Roosevelt, Franklin D., 5, 27, 62
Roshchin, Aleksei, 32
Ruggenthaler, Peter, 137
Rural federation, 48
Ryzewski, Roman, 189n30

saboteurs. *See* sabotage
Salzburg, 17n6, 31–32, 107, 118, 151, *186*, 202
Sander, Helke, 198, 211n33
Satjukow, Silke, 201
Saxony, 29
Soviet Occupation Zone/German Democratic Republic (Sowjetische Besatzungszone/Deutsche Demokratische Republik, SBZ/DDR), 81, 124, 145n70, 145n70
Schäfer, Hugo, 175
Schärf, Adolf, 59–60, 67n38, 68n43, 87
Scharf, Erwin, 93n62
Scharitzer, Karl, 178
Schumacher, Kurt, 59

Schuschnigg, Kurt, 39
"Schutzstaffel" (SS), 155, 176
Schüssel, Wolfgang, 179
Second Republic of Austria, 37, 45, 58, 60, 62
Secret Service, 64n12, 65n14, 150, 165–166, 171, 189n29, 200
Secretary of State (USA), 6, 8–9, 12, 27
Seidel, Hans, 3, 135, 146n79
Senate Foreign Relations Committee, 9
Senin, lieutenant, 57
sentences, 159, 165, 167–171, 173–179, *181, 184,* 189n29, 192n71
sexual relations, 193–195, 198–199, 207; illegal abortion, 201; illegitimate births, 201; liaison, 38, 207; marriage, 194, 200, 204; pregnancy, 195; prostitution, 194; rape, 50, 57, 77, 193, 195–197, 200–202, 208, 210n23; relationship, 195–200, 202, 204–205, 207; sexual assaults, 197; sexually transmitted diseases, 196, 200
Sforza, Carlo Graf, 27
Short Treaty, 8, 81–83, 87, 92n50, 101
"Short Treaty" draft, 8, 11–12
Shtemenko, Sergei, 40, 43, 45, 67n42
Signals Intelligence (SIGINT), 149, 153
Silistra, 29
Semenov, Vladimir, 33
Smirnov, Andrei, 32, 45, 66n31, 73n116, 178
Soviet Mineral Oil Administration (Sowjetische Mineralölverwaltung, SMV), 79, 124–125, 131–132, 134–137, *135*, 140n10, 142n32, 143n47, 146n76, 146n77, 147n91, 170; oil industry, 8, 126; crude oil, 79, 106–107, 113–114, 129, 134–135, 146n77; mineral oil, 79, 86–87, 132, 134, 136, 138, 142n 32; petroleum deposits, 125–126
Social Democrats, 39–40, 42–44, 46, 48, 53–54, 65n20, 69n59
socialism, 44, 53, 66n25, 85

"Solarium exercises," 10–11
Soviet:
   domestic policies, 15; foreign policy, 9, 14, 62, 85–87, 96, 115; global security policy, 38; High Commissioner in Austria, 67n39, 92n51, 108, 177, 204; industry, 101–103, 106–108, 127, 133–136, 145n69; Military Bank, 103, 131, 146n76; policy in Austria, 55–56; reconstruction, 124; repatriation organs, 155; State Bank, 131
Sovietization, 81, 124–125, 134, 138
Spital near Weitra, 176
St. Valentin, 159
Stalin, Iosif, 6, 8, 9, 14, 25–26, 29, 31–33, 37–47, 50–53, 57, 59–62, 63n3, 65n19, 65n20, 66n23, 66n24, 66n32, 67n38, 67n42, 68n45, 68n50, 68n53, 69n60, 69n65, 70n68, 70n72, 75–77, 79–84, 86–87, 95–97, 102, 108, 111, 113, 116n3, 118n23, 124–126, 140n11, 152, 165–167, 171, 177–179, 195;
Stalin Note, 8, 82–83, 87, 92n50
Stalingrad, 175
Standard Oil New York, 126
Starchevskii, Yakov, 46, 69n63
Stassen, Harold, 12
State Administration of Soviet Assets Abroad (Gosudarstvennoe upravlenie sovetskim imushchestvom za granitsei, GUSIMZ), 79, 131
State Opera House, reconstruction of the, 50, 58, 125
Steininger, Rolf, 3, 87
Stelzl-Marx, Barbara, 164n55, 164n59,
Stendebach, Max, 101
Stockholm, 39
Stourzh, Gerald, 3, 16n2, 86
Styria, 6, 31–32, 44, 61, 125–126, 166, 171, *180*, 196, 201
Summer, Josef, 52
Supreme Command (USSR), 51

Supreme Headquarters Allied Expeditionary Forces (SHAEF), 38
supreme military command staff (Stavka), 43
Süßenbrunn, 132
Sviridov, Vladimir, 92n51
Sweden, 39, 85
Switzerland, 13, 73n116, 84, 118n29, 151

T., Leopold, 173
Tatarescu, Gheorge, 68n51
technical espionage, 152
Ternopil, 176
terror, acts of, 169, 173, 179, 196
terrorism, 171–172
The Third Man (Movie), 150
Third World, 10;
   War, 96, 118
Thuringia, 29
Tito, 6, 15, 61, 79–80, 85–86
Tolbukhin, Fedor, 39–43, 45–51, 66n20, 66n32, 68n45, 68n53, 69n63
trade agreement, 137
traitors, 59, 153, 174–175
treason, 158, 195, 198–200
Trieste, 8, 81, 84, 98
Truman, Harry S., 5–6, 10, 16, 18n16, 159
Tulln, 30
Turkey, 39
Turnau, 30
Tweraser, Kurt, 3

US government, 5, 9;
US charge d'affaires in Moscow, 52
US High Commissioner, 7
US State Department, 8
Ukraine, 169
unauthorized weapons possession, 165, 167, 172, 178
United States of America (USA), 4–8, 10–16, 27–32, 47–49, 52, 61, 77, 98, 101, 111, 113, 115n1, 116n5,

119n36, 126, 128, 131, 134, 136, 138, 169, 194

Versailles treaty, 25
Vickery, Philip, 149
Vienna:
  Commission, 115n1; Memorandum, 15
"Volksdeutsche," *185*
"Volkssturm," 190n42
Voroshilov, Kliment Yefremovich, 28; commission, 28, 30–31, 34, 125–126
Vyshinskii, Andrei, 48

Waldviertel, 177
wall of silence, 201, 204–205. *See also* children
Warsaw Pact Treaty, 15, 113, 169
Washington, DC, 5, 11–12, 14, 49, 64n8, 71n84, 81, 113
Weimar Republic, 25

Welles, Orson, 150
"Werkschar," 190n42
West Germany, 13, 85–86, 96, 113–114, 201
White House, 8–10, 12, 27
Whitehall, 5
Wiener Neudorf, 174
Wiener Neustadt, 46, 69n64, 178, *186*
world revolution, 124
Wurttemberg, 27

Yalta, 37, 63n3
Ybbs-Persenbeug power station 107
Yugoslavia, 6, 15, 30–31, 40, 61, 80–81, 85–86, 90n29n, 113, 118n31, 128

Zedong, Mao, 118
Zheltov, Aleksei, 42–43, 45–46, 50, 53–55, 67n39, 68n53
Zhukov, Georgii, 108
Zistersdorf, 79, 132, 142n32
Zubok, Vladislav, 85–86, 139n8

About the Contributors

Stefan Karner, Ph.D., Professor at the University of Graz. Former Chair of the Institute for Economic, Social and Business History at the University of Graz and Founder and longstanding Director of the Ludwig Boltzmann Institute for Research on Consequences of War (BIK), Graz/Vienna/Raabs.

Barbara Stelzl-Marx, M.A., Ph.D., Director of the Ludwig Boltzmann Institute for Research on Consequences of War (BIK), Graz/Vienna/Raabs, and Professor for Contemporary History at the University of Graz.

Dieter Bacher, M.A., Research Associate at the Ludwig Boltzmann Institute for Research on Consequences of War (BIK), Graz.

Günter Bischof, Mag. Phil., M.A., Ph.D., Marshall Plan Professor of History and Director of Center Austria, University of New Orleans.

Aleksei Filitov, M.A., Ph.D., Professor and Chief Research Associate at the Institute for Global History at the Russian Academy of Sciences (RAN), Moscow.

Walter M. Iber, M.A., Ph.D., Research Associate at the Ludwig Boltzmann Institute for Research on Consequences of War (BIK), Graz, and Assistant Professor at the Institute for Economic, Social and Business History at the University of Graz.

Harald Knoll, M.A., Research Associate at the Ludwig Boltzmann Institute for Research on Consequences of War (BIK), Graz.

Mikhail Prozumenshchikov, M.A., Ph.D., Deputy Director of the Russian State Archives for Contemporary History (RGANI), Moscow.

Peter Ruggenthaler, M.A., Doz., Ph.D., Vice Director at the Ludwig Boltzmann Institute for Research on Consequences of War (BIK), Graz/Vienna/Raabs.

www.ingramcontent.com/pod-product-compliance
Lightning Source LLC
Chambersburg PA
CBHW020112010526
44115CB00008B/792